Restaging the Past

Restaging the Past

Historical Pageants, Culture and Society in Modern Britain

Edited by Angela Bartie, Linda Fleming, Mark Freeman, Alexander Hutton and Paul Readman

UCLPRESS

First published in 2020 by
UCL Press
University College London
Gower Street
London WC1E 6BT

Available to download free: www.uclpress.co.uk

A CIP catalogue record for this book is available from The British Library.

ISBN: 978-1-78735-407-4 (Hbk.)
ISBN: 978-1-78735-406-7 (Pbk.)
ISBN: 978-1-78735-405-0 (PDF)
ISBN: 978-1-78735-408-1 (epub)
ISBN: 978-1-78735-409-8 (mobi)
DOI: https://doi.org/10.14324/111.9781787354050

Index compiled by Regents Court Press Ltd.

Contents

List of figures and tables

List of contributors

Angela Bartie is Senior Lecturer in Scottish History at the University of Edinburgh. She was a Co-Investigator on the *Redress of the Past* historical pageants project.

Amy Binns is Senior Lecturer in Journalism at the School of Journalism, Media and Performance, University of Central Lancashire.

Arthur Burns is Professor of Modern British History at King's College London. He was a member of the *Redress of the Past* Advisory Board.

Linda Fleming is Research Associate on the *History of British Humanism* project at the University of Glasgow. She was also a Research Associate on the *Redress of the Past* historical pageants project.

Mark Freeman is Reader in Education and Social History at the UCL Institute of Education, University College London. He was a Co-Investigator on the *Redress of the Past* historical pageants project.

Tom Hulme is Lecturer in the School of History, Anthropology, Philosophy and Politics, Queen's University Belfast. He was a Research Associate on the *Redress of the Past* historical pageants project.

Alexander Hutton is a Leverhulme Early Career Research Fellow at King's College London. He was a Research Associate on the *Redress of the Past* historical pageants project.

Keith Johnston, an independent researcher, is Secretary of the Scarborough Archaeological and Historical Society and editor of its *Transactions*.

Daryl Leeworthy is the Rhys Davies Research Fellow at the South Wales Miners' Library, Swansea University. His recent books include *A Little Gay History of Wales* (Cardiff: University of Wales Press, 2019) and *Labour*

Country: Political Radicalism and Social Democracy in South Wales 1831–1985 (Cardigan: Parthian, 2018).

Paul Readman is Professor of Modern British History at King's College London. He was Principal Investigator on the *Redress of the Past* historical pageants project.

Ellie Reid is Local Studies Librarian at the Oxfordshire History Centre. She is also an independent researcher with a special interest in the material culture of historical pageants.

Michael Shallcross is an independent researcher. His book, *Rethinking G. K. Chesterton and Literary Modernism: Parody, Performance, and Popular Culture*, was published by Routledge in 2017.

Zoë Thomas is Lecturer in the History of Nineteenth-Century Britain and the Wider World at the University of Birmingham.

Acknowledgements

This book grew out of a major research project, *The Redress of the Past: Historical Pageants in Britain 1905–2016*, funded by the Arts and Humanities Research Council (award numbers AH/K003887/1 and AH/S011382/1). We are grateful to the AHRC for supporting the work, which has resulted in academic publications, public talks and workshops, exhibitions, film screenings and much more besides. Most notably, however, it has resulted in a free-to-use website where readers of this book may find, among other things, a database and interactive map containing detailed information on more than 650 historical pageants and over 1.5 million words of text, much of it in the form of essays on individual pageants. For access to this database, and other resources, go to http://www.historicalpageants.ac.uk.

The project has been a pleasure to work on from the beginning, and it remains so now. To invoke what has become a *Redress of the Past* catchphrase: 'pageants are the gift that keep on giving!' Working as a team has enabled us to survey the history of pageants in Britain in both breadth and depth – something that we could not otherwise have hoped to do. We are particularly grateful to Tom Hulme, one of the original research associates, who produced reams of interesting and illuminating research in the first two years of the project. Many others have made invaluable contributions to *The Redress of the Past*, not least our indefatigable collaborators at King's College London's Department of Digital Humanities – and later the King's Digital Lab – who did so much to make the *Redress of the Past* website and database such a success. Our thanks go to Paul Caton, David Little, Ginestra Ferraro, Luís Figueira, Geoffroy Noël, Miguel Vieira, Charlotte Tupman and Paul Vetch. Peter O'Neill's eagle eye and erudition (not least on matters musicological) saved us from many an embarrassing error in database entries; Arthur Burns offered much generous support to the project from a very early stage, helping to shape the original application to the AHRC (and graciously allowing us to go ahead without him on board); Michael Winstanley shared his experience researching pageants in and around Lancaster. We are also grateful to others who have been good friends of the project over the years, particularly Ellie Reid and Keith Johnston (both of whom have contributed chapters to this book), and also Juliet Renny, from whom we learned much about her late husband David Clarke – one of the leading pageant-masters of the post-war period. Juliet has recently deposited papers and other materials relating to David's life and work in local record offices (Cumbria, York, Surrey and Dorset), as well as King's College London, now home to the 'David Clarke Collection'. We are profoundly grateful to Juliet for her generosity.

Our Advisory Board has steered us in helpful directions, not least by encouraging us to simplify our data collecting practices. Peter Mandler's insistence that we should not allow 'the best to become the enemy of the good', to give just one example, made a real difference. Others have contributed at various points, and much evidence of this may be found on the website in the form of database entries or 'Featured Pageants': we are grateful to Laura Carter, Tosh Warwick, Ayako Yoshino and many others for their work, and for the opportunity to use it in our project. Mick Wallis gave us some of the fruits of his own research on historical pageants – a remarkable act of generosity, and one which has done much to enhance the database. We were also fortunate in having the services of undergraduate research fellows from King's College London and – thanks to the good offices of Martha Vandrei – the University of Exeter. Their contributions were much appreciated and made a real difference. We thank Tom Davis, Guy Gardener, Chandler Goddard, Chloe Ratcliffe and Kathryn Thompson for their assistance, enthusiasm and blog posts.

We are also grateful for the support of our project partners, who worked with us to co-create many of the most interesting and engaging outputs of the *Redress of the Past* project: our thanks to the Axbridge Pageant Association, Bury St Edmunds Magna Carta 800, Charles Kingsley 200, the English Folk Dance and Song Society, the Recorders of Uttlesford History, St Albans Museums, St Edmundsbury Heritage Service, Scarborough Archaeological & Historical Society, Scarborough Museums Trust, Tullie House Museum and Art Gallery Trust (Carlisle), Trestle Theatre Company and Windrose Rural Media Trust. We are also grateful for the support of the Gibson Library (Saffron Walden), North Yorkshire County Council, the Saffron Walden Town Library, the St Albans and Hertfordshire Architectural and Archaeological Society, the Sherborne Historical Society, Sherborne School Archives, and the Somerset and Dorset Family History Society. From these partners we particularly acknowledge the work of John Bailey, Trevor Bailey, Alan Baxter,

Julie Baxter, Helen Barnett, Barbara Elsmore, Martyn Everett, James Harrison, Rachel Hassall, Sarah Keeling, Keith Johnston (again), Harry Mottram, Catherine Newley, Peter Ormrod, Eleanor Payne, Matthew Reed, Edwin Rutherford, Nick Wall and Gillian Williamson, all of whom have played key roles in our many events, exhibitions and other activities. We also thank Amanda Boyd, Parker Gordon, Philip Sheail, Peter Swinson and Lucy Wright for their various and valued contributions to our work.

Two of the contributions to this volume have appeared in a different form elsewhere. We thank Oxford University Press and the editors of *Twentieth Century British History* for permission to reproduce a version of Zoë Thomas's article from volume 28, issue 3 (2017). This contribution was the winner of the Duncan Tanner Essay Prize for 2016, awarded by the journal to a postgraduate research student for work on twentieth-century Britain. We also acknowledge permission to publish Tom Hulme's chapter, an earlier variant of which originally appeared in a German journal, *Informationen zur Moderne Stadtgeschichte*, volume 2 (2016). Many organisations and individuals have also given permission for authors to reproduce images: they are thanked individually in the captions. Alexander Hutton would like to acknowledge the kind assistance of a grant from Isobel Thornley's bequest to the University of London for financing the images in his chapter and the Leverhulme Trust for the award of their Early Career Fellowship.

We are also immensely grateful to UCL Press for agreeing to publish this book, particularly as it will be available immediately in open access form, aligning with one of the key aims of our project. Through this book, as well as by means of our website and other activities, we have been committed to making our work as widely available as possible. Chris Penfold and colleagues at the Press have supported us in this endeavour. We hope that readers of the hard-copy version will also, with us, appreciate the high production values of UCL Press. Catherine Bradley, our copyeditor, has been supportive and thorough during the whole process, and we are immensely grateful to her.

Most of the chapters in this book began life as papers at a conference held under the auspices of *The Redress of the Past* at the UCL Institute of Education in September 2016. 'History in the Limelight' was a stimulating, supportive and – most importantly, perhaps – convivial occasion that showcased the range of research being carried out into aspects of the history of historical performance. It was a surprise and delight to see so many early-career and postgraduate researchers presenting papers on pageants and other manifestations of historical culture, ranging from

Scottish pantomime, to contemporary computer games, to radio drama in the 1930s and the BBC television series *Maid Marian and Her Merry Men*. The conference was also an opportunity to hear from some of those who are interested in individual pageants up and down the country. Among other things, *The Redress of the Past* has uncovered the depth of interest that exists among local historians in the pageants that were performed in their communities during the twentieth century. 'History in the Limelight' also featured a memorable account of the Exeter pageant of 1997 by Joy Thompson, one of those who organised the event in the historic garden of the Bishop's Palace.

Finally, the conference provided an opportunity for sociable interaction among a group of scholars interested in a common theme. We feel that such opportunities are invaluable, particularly in the current climate of higher education. It was a real pleasure to foster academic and social exchange among the early-career and postgraduate researchers – as well as those from beyond academia – who between them made up the bulk of the conference attenders and presenters. We particularly enjoyed the two evening receptions, which sparked various lively encounters and have provided us with some lasting memories. We thank the AHRC and UCL for supporting this important event, without which this book would not have appeared.

The Redress of the Past has been national in scale and sometimes international in its activities, but our project meetings have centred on two locations: Glasgow and London. Beyond our formal proceedings, we took the opportunity to partake in urban explorations of multifarious kinds. In Glasgow we benefited from the cultural amenities of the West End, making use of such locations as the Three Judges, Òran Mór and Ashoka Ashton Lane, all of which have played important parts in our ongoing academic and personal development. Meanwhile, in London we have found the Seven Stars on Carey Street to be an especially useful venue for intellectual (and less intellectual) exchange, followed closely by the Edgar Wallace on Essex Street and the Harp on Chandos Place. Needs of a perhaps more corporeally nourishing sort have been met by – inter alia – Ba Shan on Romilly Street and several branches of Franco Manca. Finally, some members of the project team are regular attenders at the annual 'Alethon', and we must express our gratitude here to key participants in that event, including Rona Cran, Stuart Drummings, Laura Forster, Hélène Maloigne, Christian Melby, David Monger, Tuva Skjelbred Nodeland, Tim Reinke-Williams, Martin Spychal, Ian Stewart, Martha Vandrei and Brian Wallace. Above all we must acknowledge the important role played by John Price, the founder of the Alethon in 2009.

A full history of this annual extravaganza of learning and wit (and occasional singing) would fill a small but significant gap in contemporary intellectual history.

Finally, we would also like to express our gratitude to our partners and families: Andrew, Orla and Cormac Perchard; Rod, Claire and Flora Fleming, Dave, Rebekah, James and Ruaridh Constable, and Roderick Fleming; Ijay Onyechi and Sofuchi Okpali; and Martha Vandrei. By convention, edited collections such as this do not carry a dedication – but were we able to supply one, it would be to them.

1
Introduction

Angela Bartie, Linda Fleming, Mark Freeman, Alexander Hutton and Paul Readman

This book examines one of the most significant aspects of popular engagement with the past in twentieth-century Britain. Historical pageants began as an Edwardian craze, but persisted as important events in communities and organisations across Britain for much of the next hundred years. Although popular interest in pageantry has undoubtedly declined, remnants of it survive and echoes still occur. A notable recent example is the Opening Ceremony of the London 2012 Olympic Games, created by Danny Boyle and Frank Cottrell Boyce; this dramatically portrayed the industrial revolution and its effects, inspired by the film-maker and anthologist Humphrey Jennings.[1] There is widespread enthusiasm for the dramatic representation of the past in films and television programmes, in period-costume theatres, such as Shakespeare's Globe in London, and in the myriad uses of 'living history' in museums, country houses and other tourist attractions in Britain and beyond.[2] Moreover, historical pageants themselves have enjoyed a small revival, in both fact and fiction. The next staging of the decennial pageant at Axbridge in Somerset is planned for August 2021; the long-running BBC Radio 4 series *The Archers* featured a village pageant in 2016; and – as the penultimate chapter in this book explains – a regular pageant now takes place each year, staged on weekends throughout the summer, at Bishop Auckland in County Durham.[3] The historical pageant craze – we might even call it a movement[4] – began with Louis Napoleon Parker's pageant at Sherborne, Dorset in 1905 (Fig. 1.1). This set the style, and in some cases the tone, for pageants of the Edwardian era and beyond. Although subsequent pageants varied in terms of length, style and content, the essential structure was largely unchanged: a series of dramatic representations of particular

Figure 1.1 Performers and audience at the Sherborne pageant, 1905. Reproduced with permission of the Dorset History Centre, ref. D2259/6.

episodes in the history of a community or organisation. At Sherborne there were 11 such episodes, beginning with the foundation of the town by St Aldhelm in 705 AD and ending with the visit of Sir Walter Raleigh in 1593: for reasons explored elsewhere, many early twentieth-century pageants featured an Elizabethan finale.[5] Later pageants often took the action forward to the nineteenth or even the twentieth century, but all shared the presentation of successive scenes from history (or sometimes prehistory and occasionally even the future). Pageants not infrequently blended fact and fiction, but they were always primarily concerned with the past and its representation in the present. Many pageants insisted on faithfulness to the historical record and strove for 'authenticity', as far as possible, in costume, dialogue and content.[6]

Pageants could involve hundreds of performers (there were 800 at Sherborne); quite often cast lists ran into the thousands. As many as 5,000 people participated in the 'Spirit of Warwickshire' pageant in 1930,[7] 8,000 members of the Boy Scout movement made up the cast for the 1938 Pageant of Scottish History at Glasgow, staged in Ibrox football stadium,[8] and there were approximately 15,000 performers at the Pageant of London in 1911.[9] Spectator numbers were even more impressive. More than 120,000 attended the pageant of Newcastle-upon-Tyne, across 12 performances, in 1931,[10] for example, while at least one million saw the Pageant of Empire staged at Wembley in 1924.[11] Special trains were often laid on for Edwardian pageants, while in the interwar and post-war periods large car parks – five acres at Wisbech, Cambridgeshire in 1929 – accommodated spectators from far and wide, not just the (mostly local) people who performed.[12] Although pageants largely involved amateur performers, professional historians such as Charles Oman, Arthur Bryant and G. M. Trevelyan were enthusiastic supporters, with Trevelyan playing the part of Geoffrey Chaucer in the Berkhamsted pageant of 1922, for example.[13]

Today pageants are certainly not forgotten, but they are rarely performed and do not attract the number of performers, organisers and spectators that they did in their heyday. It is easy, therefore, to overlook their importance in communities across the country during the twentieth century. Pageants generated considerable comment in the press, both local and national, and featured frequently in novels and plays. Moreover, they spawned a substantial culture of printed ephemera and souvenirs, including programmes and books of words, cutlery and crockery, commemorative medals and so on.[14] The verb 'to padge' or 'to paj', meaning to participate in a pageant, was in popular usage during the first third of the twentieth century.[15]

This book arises from a major research project funded by the UK Arts and Humanities Research Council, *The Redress of the Past: Historical Pageants in Britain 1905–2016*. One aspect of this project has been the creation of a database comprising information on more than 650 pageants; this is freely available on our website and we believe that it covers all major pageants and a sizeable sample of smaller ones.[16] Our research has shown that pageants were much more widespread than previously thought, and that practically every town and city – along with many villages and churches, stately homes and schools, social organisations and political parties – held one or more pageants at some point during the twentieth century. We now estimate that since 1905 there may have been up to 10,000 pageants in Britain involving several million performers, not to mention a huge volunteer army of organisers, costume- and prop-makers, stewards, programme and souvenir sellers, car parking attendants and so on. In terms of spectators, it seems reasonable to assume that at least ten million Britons saw at least one historical pageant during the twentieth century. The enthusiasm for pageants reached right across England, Scotland and Wales, and also – although beyond the scope of this book – into Ireland. As Joan FitzPatrick Dean's recent book *All Dressed Up* has shown, pageants formed a major part in key celebrations of Irish identity, reinforcing the island's unique and independent history after more than a century of British rule.[17]

Historical pageants spread well beyond the British Isles, too, not least across the empire. The noted pageant-master Frank Lascelles, for example, took his version of pageantry to several imperial cities, including Quebec, Cape Town and Kolkata, in the years before the First World War.[18] H. V. Nelles has shown how, in the Quebec tercentenary celebrations of 1908, Lascelles drew on his English experience to put together an episodic historical account of Canadian history with more than 3,000 performers. His aim was to bring together French- and English-speaking Canadians – as well as members of the Iroquois tribe, with whom Lascelles seems to have conceived a particular affinity – to forge a 'new consciousness of shared nationhood'.[19] Nelles suggests that, while the pageant itself was, on many measures, a great success, its failure to achieve this grand aim of transforming society was the main reason why it was subsequently 'forgotten' in historical accounts of Canadian national development.[20]

Elsewhere, pageants enlisted citizens in the performance of explicitly imperial identities. In Adelaide in 1936, for example, the centenary celebrations of the state of South Australia featured a pageant of empire performed by 13,000 schoolchildren; this was the culmination of a period in which school empire pageants were a feature of life in the state, often using scripts published in London. The huge spectacle promoted a largely unsustainable version of imperial citizenship to which the organisers hoped that the children and audiences would aspire.[21]

The United States also saw a substantial pageant movement in the early twentieth century. This was examined in a book by David Glassberg, published nearly one-third of a century ago.[22] Glassberg shows how Parker's model of pageantry crossed the Atlantic and was adapted to serve the promotion of civic identity in many locations across the country: here, as the pageant-master William Chauncy Langdon explained, 'the place is the hero and the development of the community is the plot'.[23] This emphasis on 'community development' was shared with the pageants of Parker and his successors in Britain, although the historical subject matter – not least, unsurprisingly, that of the centuries on which the scenes focused – was very different. The aim of pageants across the world, both in the stories they told and the ways in which they were organised, was to bring people together.[24] This did not always work. As Tom Hulme has shown in his work on pageants and other events in interwar Chicago, the aim of uniting divided civic and national communities through performed heritage was not entirely successful: the narrative of 'progressive evolution' was not always historically plausible or socially inclusive.[25]

Alternatives to the traditional pageant were thus created by the Irish, Jewish and African-American communities. These presented a different version of the relationship between past and present – and, incidentally, illustrated the adaptability of the pageant form, a theme that will recur across the wide-ranging contributions to this book.[26] Although American historical pageantry declined earlier, and perhaps even more precipitately, than its British counterpart, it retains a tangible legacy in a few places. The annual *Viva! El Paso* pageant in El Paso, Texas, for example, is aimed mainly at a local audience that returns year on year. It presents an account of local history that aims – even as pageant pioneers such as Parker, Lascelles and Langdon did – to draw the different groups that constitute the population of the city together in a shared historical understanding.[27] This pageant emerged in the early 1970s, taking its present title in 1978, and has run ever since. This American pageant tradition, however – as well as others beyond British shores – is beyond the scope of the present book.

We should explain at the outset that our definition of an historical pageant is quite narrow; if it were broadened, the scope of the project would be even wider. We include only pageants that had theatrical elements. Processional pageants, even where they included representations of identifiable historical figures, are not covered, nor are other civic rituals seen as important aspects of wider notions of urban 'governance' in the nineteenth and twentieth centuries, ranging from parades to carnivals to oyster feasts.[28] So defined, historical pageants had a number of distinctive features. Perhaps most notably, it was rare for them to be staged in the same place more than once in a generation: some towns had several large pageants during the twentieth century, but nowhere, or almost nowhere, did they become an annual event. The nearest exception is Arbroath in Scotland, which has staged 18 pageants since the Second World War, but this is exceptional. (The Arbroath pageants are examined in chapter 10.)

Because pageants were themselves significant moments in the histories of the communities that staged them, as well as capturing certain elements of the national mood, they are useful lenses through which to examine various aspects of social, cultural and political history. In the remainder of the introduction we will consider a number of these, which recur throughout the book. Pageants can offer insights into urban and rural history; intellectual history; women's and gender history (see in particular chapters 5 and 6); the history of political parties and movements;[29] the history of education;[30] the history of art and music; the history of theatre; the history of consumption, marketing and tourism; labour history (see chapter 8); costume history and the history of material culture (see chapter 11); and many more. They enable us to consider some of the key differences and similarities between the 'four nations' of the British Isles, although in this book we consider only England, Scotland and Wales.[31] We will discuss some of these themes in more depth. First, however, we outline the historiography of pageants and the key periods of the twentieth century on which it has focused.

Historians and pageants: periods and types

There is an emerging literature on historical pageants. The most significant contribution to this is Ayako Yoshino's 2011 study of the Edwardian period, *Pageant Fever*, which focuses on the early pageant craze and the productions of the most important pageant-masters: Parker, Lascelles and Frank Benson. Yoshino considers the consumerist appeal of pageantry and its relationship with a growing domestic and international tourist industry: small towns sought to attract the increasing number of middle- and upper working-class holidaymakers and day-trippers, and Yoshino argues that Edwardian pageants were as much a form of spectacle that appealed to the growing ranks of consumer society as they were the solemn acts of historical representation that some purported to be.[32]

Others have emphasised the community context of pageants, notably Paul Readman. He considers the Winchester 'national pageant' of 1908 and its forerunner, the Alfred millenary celebrations of 1901,[33] and argues for a reappraisal of Edwardian engagement with the past, suggesting that the period saw a growing interest in history, heralded by the rise of mass education and fears of social change.[34] For David Glassberg the Parker pageants were determinedly anti-modern, refusing to include any scenes set later than the Elizabethan period in order to avoid dealing with controversial subject matter: they were conservative spectacles that sought to promote and celebrate social harmony.[35] Readman, however, argues that Edwardian pageants, while attempting to project an image of continuity between past and present, took place within a set of social and cultural conditions that were distinctively modern – one aspect of which, as Yoshino suggests, was the boost they were often intended to supply to the tourist industry. While acknowledging the medieval tradition of community plays, and drawing heavily on local customs, legends and folklore, pageants did something which was concertedly new – though whether it is helpful to conceptualise what they did as amounting to the 'invention of tradition' remains a moot point.[36]

Other historians have shifted the focus on pageantry away from the Edwardian era to acknowledge the continuing importance of the phenomenon after 1914. Mark Freeman's *Social History* article on the pageants of St Albans, Hertfordshire, in 1907, 1948, 1953 and 1968 demonstrates some of the continuities and discontinuities of pageantry across the twentieth century. Freeman argues that pageants continued to play a role in reaffirming local identities in the context of rapid social and cultural change, alongside and in contrast to the growth of a 'national' culture epitomised by the BBC and showcased at the Festival of Britain and elsewhere.[37] Both Freeman and Readman downplay the importance of empire in historical pageantry – in contrast to Yoshino, who identifies imperial themes running through the content of Edwardian pageants.[38] Granted, there was a clear strand of imperial pageantry, epitomised by the spectacular showmanship of Lascelles. This has been explored by Deborah Sugg Ryan, who focuses on Lascelles' attempts to 'stage the empire' at the Festival of Empire in 1911; Lascelles indeed returned to this theme on many other occasions, both nationally and internationally, not least at the Wembley Empire Pageant in 1924.[39] Yet this was only one kind of pageant – and an atypical kind at that. Other scholars, such as Helen McCarthy and Mick Wallis, have shown that pageantry could be co-opted and adapted for use in other causes, specifically liberal internationalism and more radical left-wing politics.[40] It is true that empire could rear its head in civic pageantry, even in the interwar and post-Second World War periods,[41] but for the most part other themes were to the fore.

Historians have in fact identified at least six types of historical pageant during the interwar years. The first of these is the traditional Parker-type pageant, generally performed in a relatively small town and with a focus on the intersections of local and national history. There remains considerable debate on the characteristics of these pageants. Michael Woods, for example, considering Taunton in 1928, argues that the organisation and content of pageants both reflected and reinforced local power structures – in a period that saw the emergence of class politics and in the immediate context of the General Strike.[42]

A new kind of pageant, performed in the early post-war years, was the ironically named 'pageant of peace', which depicted scenes from the First World War, often involving veterans of the war itself. A spate of these pageants was performed in 1919, though they had little in common with the Parker pageants of the pre-1914 period beyond their episodic structure. They represented a disruption of the emerging tradition of historical pageantry, but the war did not kill off the tradition; indeed it was not long before pageants were able to incorporate the war into the longer history of the communities whose stories they told.[43] A third form of pageant was the empire pageant, mentioned above. This could range in scale from the huge extravaganzas of Lascelles to a tiny performance linked to a local Empire Day celebration.[44]

Alongside the military and imperial uses of pageantry, the form was also adapted by very different political traditions, forming a fourth strand of interwar historical pageants. All major parties staged pageants, with varying degrees of success. One of the largest such pageants was the Conservative-run 1934 Pageant of Parliament, the language of which Emily Robinson has linked to the emergence of a particular conception of 'progressive' political language based on efficiency and expertise rather than ideas of mass democracy.[45] While participatory democracy might not have been celebrated by all during this period, few pageants seemed to endorse the political structures of a pre-democratic age, or to set themselves in opposition to democracy itself. An *Evening Standard* cartoon by Low on the occasion of the Runnymede pageant of 1934, held around the same time as Oswald Mosley's fascist Olympia Rally, depicted a long line of figures including the barons and King John, Roundheads, the Tolpuddle Martyrs, Disraeli and Gladstone holding a copy of the 1867 Reform Act and, finally, contemporary voters, looking – with disdain – at Mosley recruiting to the British Fascist Party (Fig. 1.2).

Figure 1.2 'Pageant of Liberty at Runnymede', *Evening Standard*, 11 May 1934. Copyright David Low/Solo Syndication, British Cartoon Archive, University of Kent.

Beyond party politics, McCarthy has shown that pageants were very popular among groups such as the League of Nations Union (LNU) and the Women's Institute (WI), and were seen as instrumental in fostering political stability.[46] Pageants could be enlisted in the promotion of the liberal internationalist vision of the LNU or the pacifism supported by other groups. As well as real historical characters, personifications of figures such as Peace, War, Fear, Hatred, Jealousy and Suspicion were used in such performances, as well as Industry, Commerce, Science and Art.[47] Through such examples in particular – but also more generally – the study of pageants contributes to a growing body of work on the history of voluntarism and citizenship.[48]

Pageants could also have a more radical edge, as Wallis has shown in his work on the Popular Front pageants of the 1930s. Alongside developments in agitprop theatre that accelerated during and after the Second World War, these pageants presented a leftist interpretation of history to goad both performers and spectators into action against the twin evils of capitalism and fascism.[49] In this respect as in others, pageants were a significant way in which people, groups and communities made sense of the modern era in relation to the past.

A fifth strand of interwar pageantry was found in country houses and villages. It was widely depicted in imaginative literature, ranging from highbrow modernism to mass-market paperbacks and even children's books. Pageants featured in novels, the best-known being Virginia Woolf's *Between the Acts* (1941). Others included E. F. Benson's *Mapp and Lucia* books, Victor L. Whitechurch's *Murder at the Pageant* (1930) and Clifton Robbins's *The Man Without a Face* (1932), while Richmal Crompton's *More William* (1922) and *William the Outlaw* (1927) also featured pageants. The trend continued after the Second World War, for example in Noel Streatfeild's *Party Shoes* (1946), J. B. Priestley's *Festival at Farbridge* (1951) and Rosemary Manning's *Dragon in Danger* (1959).[50] Indeed, many authors, poets and playwrights wrote material for this kind of pageant. Jed Esty has argued that the interest in pageantry among interwar authors such as Woolf, E. M. Forster and T. S. Eliot reflected an inward-looking tendency of modern literature – one that sought solace from the disconcerting present in a vision of the past which presented a fixed and stable relationship to the land and to culture.[51] Wallis has examined the career of Mary Kelly, a major proponent of village drama who staged a number of interwar pageants, drawing close links between pageants and modern-day anxieties about rural life.[52] Pageants were also used by some voluntary organisations – in rural Scotland, for example – to address concerns about depopulation.[53]

Finally, many towns and cities staged pageants during the interwar period as a means of promoting the local economy in a period of protracted slump. In some places, particularly seaside towns such as Ramsgate, which held a pageant in 1934,[54] the aim was to give a boost to the tourist trade. This agenda was also evident in other places, one example being provided by the Ashdown Forest Pageant of 1929. Held near East Grinstead, Sussex, in a popular spot for London day-trippers, this pageant was a poignant evocation of the history of life in the forest, yet it was also fully attuned to the commercial realities of modern tourism. As the *East Grinstead Courier* remarked, 'Londoners who had often visited had never before realised how sacred and full of historical romance was the ground they had so often traversed on foot or in their motor cars'.[55] The pageant – which also featured a young Christopher Robin Milne and the animals of the Hundred Acre Wood created by his father and local resident A. A. Milne – represented a tangible link with the past and with nature which was easily accessible for Londoners. As with many other pageants, it provides further evidence of how – as David Matless and Jeremy Burchardt, among others, have suggested – appeals to lost rural idylls in the interwar period were more complex, and more modern, cultural phenomena than might be assumed. Designed to bolster a sense of identity in the here-and-now, and alive to the modern-day commercial potential of the tourist trade, such pageants were by no means simple laments for a past society.[56]

Pageantry as a means of boosting the local economy, as well as local identity and patriotism, was also a feature of larger towns and cities, as the work of Hulme in particular has shown.[57] The popularity of pageants in these places, during the interwar period especially, is difficult to exaggerate, although it has often been overlooked in previous scholarship. In the context of economic depression, concern about the fracturing effects of political extremism and high levels of unemployment, 'civic-booster' pageants were held in places such as Stoke-on-Trent (1930), Northampton (1930), Bradford (1931), Manchester (1932) and Wakefield (1933). Often connected to larger trade fairs and civic weeks, they were designed to draw visitors – and trade – to the town or city in question. These pageants presented a largely positive view of the growth of their towns or cities, and of their adaption to the industrial revolution. Held at a time of acute economic crisis, they demonstrated that such places were not merely resting on their laurels, dreaming of past glories, but rather remained dynamic and very much open for business. They do much to dispel claims that British culture was dominated by reactionary nostalgia or anti-industrial feeling during this period.[58] Hulme explores these themes further in chapter 7.

Historical pageants remained a significant aspect of popular engagement with the past in the early post-Second World War period. Yoshino notes a 'brief revival' of the form, mostly centred on the Festival of Britain (1951) and the coronation of Elizabeth II (1953), but there was in fact a high incidence of pageantry for at least a decade after the war. This even extended into the late 1950s and early 1960s, with notable productions at Bury St Edmunds in 1959 and Berkhamsted in 1966, among other places.[59] This period has been less widely explored in the historiography, though Freeman's work on the post-war St Albans pageants is one exception.[60] Freeman argues that many aspects of the Edwardian pageant craze persisted and even intensified in the post-war period. Notable among them was the emphasis on local pride and identity, seen as important in the context of economic, social and cultural developments which seemed to weaken local government, to undermine a sense of civic identity and, in some cases, to involve a significant alteration in the size and shape of towns.[61] Another example was at Nottingham in 1949, where a large pageant blended the traditional Parker form with influences from cinema and broadcasting. The event was explicitly presented as an inspiration to local people to take an active pride in their city and to perform all the duties of citizens in the post-war world.[62] Although the history of post-war pageants remains largely to be written, there is no doubt that themes of citizenship and civic identity will be important aspects of it.

Finally, it should be noted here that a number of works of local history have examined specific historical pageants, and that a wide interest in the phenomenon is apparent across much of the local history community.[63] Examples include Andrew Swift and Kirsten Elliott's *The Year of the Pageant* – which looks at 1909 in Bath through the lens of the large pageant in that year – and Philip Sheail's *Hertford's Grand Pageant 1914*, published to mark the centenary of the event and launched in 2014 with a concert featuring music from the pageant sung by a local choir.[64] These carefully researched studies provide a model for viewing pageants as a snapshot of a community at a particular point in time. Pageants feature regularly in the historical sections and letters pages of local newspapers,[65] and in a handful of cases are still performed from time to time, bringing together substantial sections of towns, cities and villages. One example is Axbridge in Somerset, where a pageant was first staged in 1967 to commemorate the opening of the town's bypass road; another was held in 1970, followed by one at ten-yearly intervals since.[66] Museums and local history societies have staged exhibitions and events examining pageants in specific areas: examples from the *Redress of the Past* project include Carlisle, Scarborough, St Albans and Bury St Edmunds, and others have taken place in Lancaster and Colchester.[67] As the contributions to our recently published *Local History Study Guide* show, there remains enormous scope and enthusiasm for local history research on pageants.[68]

Modernity, class and community

Historical pageants looked back to the past, and it is tempting to see them as reflective of a more generalised cultural disdain for modernity, as a reactionary or retrogressive phenomenon. As will already be apparent, this collection of essays suggests otherwise. It argues that far from being nostalgic evocations of an idealised history contrasted with a fallen present, pageants presented a complex means of negotiating the often bewildering times through which twentieth-century people and communities lived. Pageants were not so much an attempt at rejecting or withdrawing from contemporary modernity as a way of negotiating it. As Michael Saler has demonstrated, early to mid-twentieth-century British men and women were particularly struck by the often jarring interaction between the present and the past.[69]

Pageants can thus be seen as a part of what Saler has termed the 're-enchantment' of the modern world, where spectators could momentarily suspend disbelief to view historical characters appear in front of them.[70] Many commentators noted the strange, time-travelling effect at the end of a particularly engrossing pageant, in which the figures of the past melted away into the darkness to reveal the present. One such comment came from Basil Boothroyd, who described the finale of the East Grinstead pageant of 1951 in *Punch* magazine:

> It was eleven o'clock when the towered trumpeter reappeared, framed in a white, moth-flecked beam, to sound a long-drawn, lonely note; as it faded, the spotlight faded in sympathy, until there was nothing left of either, and the audience, long lost in the local repercussions of foreign invasion, religious intolerance, political corruption and industrial revolution, realized with a shock that they had been sitting in a Sussex meadow in the dark, with the dew stealthily creeping up their shins.[71]

Pageants' ability to re-enchant the modern was a function of their mobilisation of the technologies of mass spectacle, which itself was a demonstration of the modernity of the form. In this respect, pageants were part of the growth of twentieth-century spectator culture, and indeed competed with other forms of entertainment such as football matches and cinema.[72] From the beginning of the movement, many pageant-masters sought to integrate the newest technology and stage effects to make history come to life, from early public announcement systems – allowing audiences to hear the dialogue – to floodlighting, enabling performances to continue late into the night, to explosions, pyrotechnics and other effects that rivalled their counterparts in professional theatre.[73] In 1938 Gwen Lally's extraordinary Birmingham Centenary Pageant, which featured 8,000 performers, included a restaging of the Battle of Crécy, the siege of Aston Hall, the destruction of Joseph Priestley's house during the riots of 1791 and – most strikingly of all – a giant, fire-breathing dinosaur named Egbert, who fought with prehistoric cavemen on the pageant ground.[74] After 1945 Lawrence du Garde Peach, who had made his name as a broadcaster and film-writer, maintained that 'an audience remembers 90% of what it sees and 10% of what it hears' and thus insisted that a pageant must have 'entertainment value' – that is, 'it must compete with the cinema across the way, and the dance hall'.[75] His pageants at Sheffield (1944 and 1948), Wolverhampton (1948) and Nottingham (1949) were full of musical numbers, humour and – among other things – mechanised robots.

In form as well as content, then, the historical pageant movement was a fully integrated element of modern mass culture. Like the folk arts with which it was often linked – maypoles and morris dancing often featured in pageants – historical pageantry could never represent a polar opposite to modern life, emerging as it did directly from it.[76] As an important element of the British cultural experience of modernity, then, pageants illustrate how – as Martin Daunton and Bernhard Rieger have pointed out – nineteenth- and twentieth-century British responses to social, economic, technological and cultural change did not necessarily imply an acceptance of a sharp break between past and present. Indeed, as Daunton and Rieger note, 'casting the present as uniquely distinct from the past was by no means the only mode of interpreting temporal relations in debates about modernity'.[77] More often than not, in fact, the accent was less on fundamental transformation or rupture than on continuous development. Both in culture and politics, the idea of continuity between the past, present and future was a prominent element of the British experience of modernity.[78] Freeman has made this argument specifically in relation to the historical pageants of post-war Britain and, to emphasise the point, it was not unknown for pageants to include scenes depicting the future. One example was 'Pedlar's Ware', a pageant held in Preston, Lancashire, in 1935. In it a scene set in 2060 featured interplanetary travel and female worker-robots called 'autobetties'.[79] This was a comic and somewhat dystopian example, but a more serious and hopeful approach was present in many pageants, which ended with exhortations to members of the local community to work hard on its behalf in the future. Thus historical pageantry, rooted in modernity, was powerfully expressive of a desire to maintain a sense of continuity with the past.

This promotion of a sense of continuity was also one aspect of an educative agenda, which we have explored elsewhere.[80] In many cases the organisers of pageants saw themselves as instructing ordinary people both in the history of their communities and nation (and in some cases empire) and in the wider duties of morality and citizenship. This was reflected in the involvement of schools and adult educational institutions in the organisation of pageants and in the various activities and events that were staged alongside them, including historical lectures and exhibitions. Many schools staged pageants that told their own history, or the history of England, while some large civic pageants – such as those held in Preston in 1922 and 1928 – enlisted thousands of schoolchildren from across the locality.[81] The Workers' Educational Association was just one of many adult education organisations whose branches and individual members participated in historical pageantry, although not always without controversy.[82] Meanwhile, engaging in community drama was itself seen as an educational activity, regardless of the historical content of the performance. As one official report noted in 1935, involvement in drama 'carries with it those intellectual interests and moral qualities which are developed by the art of acting and all other arts incidental to the production of a play'.[83] In this respect pageants were remarkably successful, drawing in thousands of volunteers and mobilising whole communities. Parker congratulated himself on this, claiming that pageants were 'Festivals of Brotherhood' and were 'absolutely democratic' celebrations of history.[84] This was certainly an overstatement – as discussed below, there are many examples of disunity and disharmony relating to historical pageants. However, it is undoubtedly the case that pageantry enthused and inspired countless individuals both to take an interest in history and to serve their community.[85]

It is hard to determine quite what audiences, and indeed performers, made of pageants. Popular responses varied – and were sometimes markedly at variance with what organisers had intended. At the Runnymede pageant of 1934, whose narrative demonstrated the benign role of the aristocracy in the growth of British democracy, an over-exuberant crowd in the cheap seats enthusiastically cheered a scene in which the monks of Chertsey Abbey were slaughtered by marauding Vikings.[86] A rather different sort of misapprehension was noted by the Mass Observers sent to witness the St Paul's Steps Pageant, held in London at the height of the Second World War and sponsored by the Entertainments National Service Association. What was supposed to be a stirring rendition of martial poetry, recited by the great actors of the day – including Eric Portman, Sybil Thorndike, Edith Evans and Leslie Howard – was received with bemused incomprehension by a crowd who struggled to hear much of the performance and could not even recall the words of the National Anthem.[87] We certainly cannot assume that audiences simply internalised the content of pageants and accepted the political and cultural agendas of those who wrote and produced them.

Indeed, it was possible for pageants to be received very unenthusiastically among some sections of local communities, or even to prompt dissent. This could arise from the content or the social organisation of pageants, or indeed both. Sometimes political organisations took exception to the content. At Manchester in 1938, for example, the local branch of the Communist Party, along with some trade unions, objected to the initial plan not to depict the Peterloo Massacre of 1819, a key event in the social history of the city. Their campaign was eventually successful – the episode was presented as part of a processional tableau on the industrial history of Manchester – but the Communists went ahead with an alternative pageant, entitled *100 Years of Struggle: Manchester's Centenary, the Real Story*, staged in opposition to the main event.[88] Elsewhere there were elements of more aesthetic revolt: at St Albans in 1953, the organisers intended to use recorded music to save costs, but were forced to back down after a 'popular clamour' at a public meeting, and a small orchestra was used instead.[89]

At other pageants, local resentments had more serious consequences, most notably perhaps at Winchester in 1908. Here there was a riot, involving some 10,000 people, precipitated by the actions of the local authority, which had decided to remove the railings around a Russian gun captured during the Crimean War. During the course of the riot the pageant headquarters and venue were attacked and a replica Saxon chariot was thrown into the river.[90] Yoshino sees this episode as evidence of 'resentment of a pageant designed to raise money not for the poor but for the cathedral', in the context of deep social divisions within the city of Winchester.[91]

In the later twentieth century pageants could still bring out such divisions, albeit without the rioting. For example, when Bury St Edmunds attempted to follow its successful 1907 and 1959 pageants with a third, in 1970, focused on the life of the eleventh-century St Edmund, opposition was voiced both in the council chamber and the local press. There was criticism of the cost of the pageant, but also a wider sense that the performance of this medieval episode was unsuitable in what had become a modern town.[92] This was partly a generational conflict: the pageant organisers, headed by Lady Olga Ironside Wood, were opposed by the 'young set', some of whom staged an alternative puppet pageant entitled 'Was St Edmund a Toadstool?' in the abbey gardens. The 23-year-old ringleader, Julian Putkowski, had complained in the *Bury Free Press* in no uncertain terms:

> This town has never ceased to surprise me with the capacity to exhibit every sign of fossilization, and yet continue to exist. In your edition of July 3 the usual wealth of local news gems were augmented by an orgasm of worship praising the St Edmunds Pageant farce. In your supplement you ask the question, 'Who was St Edmund?' to which a not inconsiderable proportion of those freedom loving young people of Bury will reply 'who cares?' With the exception of a group of the frightfully frightfully 'county set', the town's businessmen and some egocentric senile delinquents, a large proportion of Bury's population do not know and do not care about St Edmund, or the pathetically embarrassing series of events intended to colour his 1100th anniversary ... The people on the estates around the old heart of the town are not involved in many of the so-called commemorative events, and see the whole affair as a waste of ratepayers [*sic*] money on what is proving to be an advertisement for the businesses of the town ... Rather than despair of any change occurring that might alter Bury and cause a radical shift in its conservative outlook, I continue to live in hope that this year's Pageant will serve to convince Burians of the monumental waste of their money.[93]

Oral history evidence also testifies to the relative failure of the 1970 pageant as a theatrical enterprise.[94] Yet pageants could still be produced and performed successfully in the last third of the twentieth century, as many examples attest. The Carlisle pageant of 1977, one of a number across the country staged to celebrate Elizabeth II's Silver Jubilee, involved up to 1,000 human cast-members and a variety of animals, had an audience capacity of 3,000, was performed seven times and made a profit of more than £2,000.[95] Oral history undertaken for the *Redress of the Past* project testifies to the widespread enthusiasm for this pageant in Carlisle and to the impact that it could have on individuals who took part.[96] This echoes many other personal reminiscences of pageants, across the twentieth century, as we have shown elsewhere.[97] At Axbridge and other places, pageants retain some of their former purchase today.

Chapters and key themes

The contributions to this book all focus on pageants as aspects of wider social and cultural history, and several key themes emerge from them. Perhaps the most significant of these – given its relative absence from studies of pageants thus far – is the role played by women. Chapters 5 and 6 both develop McCarthy's work on groups such as the LNU, which argues that it was through participation in societies and the events that they staged – not least pageants – that women were brought into a civic society from which they had previously been disenfranchised.[98] As fewer women, particularly middle-class women, were employed in the workforce, many pageants were female-dominated affairs, despite conforming to male-centred historical narratives in other respects: on occasion, in an ironic reversal of earlier theatrical conventions, key male parts would be taken by women.[99]

Moreover, many pageants took women's history as their subject matter. Chapter 5 demonstrates the importance that representations of history had for organisations such as the WI, which staged many county-level pageants during the interwar period. It shows how pageants provided an opportunity to celebrate women's histories, often taking great pains to ensure 'authenticity' – just as Parker and other pioneers had done at the outset of the Edwardian pageant craze. Again, the needs of the present were foremost in the minds of those who devised and staged these pageants, which were themselves viewed as significant historical events in their own right. Chapter 6 argues that many pageants by women's societies – such as the Women's Friendly Society, Girl Guides and the WI – which foregrounded women in history nevertheless sought to reinforce contemporaneous sexual morality, religious orthodoxy and social hierarchies at a time of their perceived erosion in the wider society. Gender relations and representations arise as themes in other chapters too. In describing pageants connected to the 1951 Festival of Britain, chapter 9 stresses the growing place of specifically women's history in pageants organised at this time by the WI and Townswomen's Guilds, and examines the sexual and cultural tensions surrounding the portrayal of a seemingly naked Lady Godiva in the Coventry pageant.

Local identity, as Freeman and Hulme have both emphasised,[100] held a lot of emotional appeal for much of the twentieth century; contributions to this volume confirm that it was a feature of many pageants. Chapter 4 shows how Parker's emphasis on locality and community resonated – both politically and aesthetically – with G. K. Chesterton, one of the most prominent literary supporters of pageantry. Chapter 2 demonstrates the popular appeal of pageants in Yorkshire before the First World War, arguing that these participated in a strikingly different tradition to other Edwardian pageants, dating back before Parker, to the Ripon pageants of the 1880s. The uniqueness of Yorkshire historical pageants, this chapter argues, both reflected and projected a fiercely independent county or regional identity: its own history was told in the pageants, sometimes in its own distinctive dialect.

Chapter 8 re-examines the tradition of pageants in South Wales, particularly the 1939 South Wales Miners' Pageant, staged simultaneously in three separate valleys. Rather than it being purely an expression of class politics, the pageant, organised by the South Wales Miners' Federation and the Labour Research Department, was a significant evocation of community spirit and the cultural traditions of the South Wales coalfield after a prolonged period of industrial depression. It therefore reflected an educational and cultural ethos that spanned the mining communities of the region.[101] Regional and local identities were also to the fore, perhaps surprisingly, in many Festival of Britain pageants. Chapter 9 shows how pageants simultaneously tried to channel the ethos of the Festival and made a point of distinguishing themselves from its centre on London's South Bank. The 'topophilia' which, as Harriet Atkinson has demonstrated, characterised the Festival more generally, was thus enacted in pageants which sought to bring communities together.[102] Chapter 7 emphasises the importance of pageants' representations of place and time in urban settings, showing how Romantic and conservative aspects of pageantry were adapted to promote social cohesion in modern industrial cities. Finally, chapter 11 discusses pageant souvenirs, revealing the extent to which these commemorative artefacts were a means of consuming both history *and* place. The theme of place and identity, heavily emphasised across this volume, builds on the work of many cultural geographers who have sought to understand the cultural meanings that people attach to the locales in which they live their daily lives.[103]

If regional identities were an important feature of many pageants, national identities were also showcased. Chapter 8 considers both region and nation – and, indeed, occupational communities – in its focus on South

Wales, while chapter 10, tracing the history of pageants at Arbroath Abbey from 1947 to 2005, shows how these events reflected a rising Scottish national consciousness and evolving political landscape. Here the pageant was held at the location associated with the 'Declaration of Scottish Independence' in 1320, and many of the organisers and writers were themselves activists in Scottish nationalist politics. Chapter 10 shows how a shift from cultural to political expressions of nationalism have reduced the importance of pageants and other forms of display in the twenty-first century.

Themes of national identity featured in English pageants too. Chapter 3 discusses the English Church Pageant of 1909, exploring how the Edwardian Church of England enlisted pageantry as part of its co-ordinated campaign to reaffirm the centrality of Anglicanism within English national life. This chapter explores the ways in which the pageant attempted, with mixed success, to steer a course between a variety of positions rooted in religious historical scholarship. In so doing it sought to present an unbroken account of Christianity in England as a way of easing disputes within the Church itself, as well as to cement the place of the national church within English history at a time in which society seemed to be fracturing along class and confessional lines.[104] This echoes a point that we have made elsewhere about the use of medieval history in other Edwardian pageants: many of them determinedly located the origins of English nationhood *and* religion in the Anglo-Saxon period, emphasising the long continuities of political and religious life, rooted in a common Christianity.[105] One participant in the English Church Pageant was G. K. Chesterton, and chapter 4 considers his distinctive approach to pageants, including this one.

Religion is also a major factor in chapter 6, which shows how Christianity provided an enduring and important basis for women's morality deep into the twentieth century, and how pageants emphasised the role that heroic women from recent history had played in spreading the gospel across the world. The later scenes in religious pageants transferred the action from the England of John Wesley to missionary work carried out throughout the empire in the Victorian era. Indeed, many religious pageants seemed unable or unwilling to engage with the paradox that, while missionary work had had remarkable success across the world, the place of Christianity at home appeared to be increasingly insecure.[106] Whereas the origins of English Christianity were a staple feature of Edwardian pageants, and still appeared on some occasions in the interwar period, it became easier with time to tell stories about English history without invoking religion at all, or at least reducing it to a less central role.[107] This was also true, as chapter 8 shows, in Wales: it illustrates how solidaristic notions of a cultural identity formed through class and work replaced a more traditional focus on Welsh Nonconformity within the space of a generation.

Class is a key issue in chapter 8 and also rears its head in chapter 9. It is, moreover, an implicit theme of the other contributions to this volume which show how the organisational structures of pageants mirrored – or, occasionally, subverted – the social structures of the communities that staged them. Chapter 7, for example, shows how pageants were used by industrial cities to help negotiate the economic turbulence of the interwar period and to diffuse class tensions. Meanwhile, chapter 8 argues that the South Wales Miners' Pageant should be viewed as much as an expression of local cultural identity as one of class consciousness, with the re-enactment of the Chartist rising of 1839 acting as a social form of remembering in the manner of the Yorkshire or Durham miners' galas. In this respect, the pageant differed from the agitprop of the Popular Front pageants of the time; it also stood in contrast to the various pageants staged by groups ranging from the Co-operative movement to the Communist Party – in which the historical scenes that were portrayed had little direct connection to the locations where they were performed, and often presented a highly stylised version of past events. Chapter 9 notes that many Festival of Britain pageants foregrounded the history of the 'common people', influenced by Cole and Postgate's popular book, *The Common People* (1938), among other developments in historiography.[108] Thus the 1951 pageants shared the Festival's vision of a more egalitarian and collective future, although they presented a localised version of the national past.

The last full chapter of the book – before the short afterword – considers a contemporary development: the new historical pageant called 'Kynren' at Bishop Auckland, which began in 2016 and which is envisaged as a permanent feature of the tourist landscape of the northeast of England. Although not named by its organisers as a pageant, Kynren has many features that would be recognised by Parker, Lascelles and the other pageant-masters of the early twentieth century. It blends accounts of the local and national past (while largely ignoring imperial histories); it has successfully mobilised a large group of volunteers who perform in, organise and steward the activities; it uses animals to good dramatic effect, as did many earlier pageants; it has a spectacular set, costumes and props; it is explicitly aimed at strengthening the local economy and encouraging tourism; and it advances a strong sense of place-based identity. There are of course some differences, reflecting the availability of technologies of amplification, lighting and recorded sound, while the show itself is shorter and has much less dialogue than the typical pageant of the early twentieth century.[109] It also features more recent history, taking the story down to the Second World War, and a fairly substantial amount of social and economic history, although – as with many Edwardian pageants – elements of social conflict and disharmony are downplayed. The appeal of Kynren demonstrates the continuing potential for theatrical performance, re-enactment and spectacle to engage audiences in stories about the past. Kynren is seen as one element of 'a bold, innovative and engaging arts, education and community development programme':[110] like pageants, it blends entertainment and education, in ways that can be both productive and problematic.

* * *

This volume is by no means exhaustive: it deals with some important themes arising from the study of historical pageants and relates them to wider debates within the historiography of modern Britain, but it leaves other areas largely untouched. Most notably, the depiction of race and ethnicities within pageants requires further exploration. It could be argued that, in most cases and for most of the twentieth century, there was an assumption of ethnic as well as cultural homogeneity in pageants' depictions of the communities in which they were staged. Perhaps unsurprisingly, most depictions of race in pageants were confined to scenes involving the empire, although pageants do provide some windows into different attitudes towards Jews in twentieth-century Britain, ranging from the moderately progressive to the downright anti-Semitic.[111] There is also more to be written about the gendered dimensions of historical pageants, although important steps in this direction have been made in this book. Other areas have been overlooked: we need more studies, for example, of the uses of music in pageants, as well as visual and material culture, although chapter 11 makes a useful contribution in the latter respect.[112] There is also room for a larger study of the decline of historical pageantry in the last third of the twentieth century: we make a start by considering the abatement of pageant fever in the afterword to this book.

What the contributions to this book clearly show is that the dramatic performance of the past was an important part of people's lives in Britain for much of the twentieth century – and that in some cases, as at Arbroath, this could still take the form of an historical pageant even into the twenty-first century. It is evident that, for several decades, pageants remained an especially important way in which large numbers of people negotiated their sense of belonging to a place and a community – and did so, moreover, in a period when long-term historical continuities seemed to be threatened by the pace of economic and social change.

Yet they also brought people together in a sense of shared purpose. This could take a wide range of forms: celebrating the work of pioneering women, strengthening social solidarities in the face of industrial dislocation, resisting challenges to the central place of the Church of England in national life, promoting the cause of Scottish independence, or reminding residents and visitors of the distinctiveness of regional and local history and identities. Pageants could, to many observers, seem rather ridiculous, but for many they also held poignant significance. Both these aspects were captured in a report in the *Yorkshire Post* on the Gildersome pageant of 1934:

> Pageants have become something of a fashion, and at times have been greeted with kindly smiles from outsiders. We have smiled at the earnest pride of the players, at togas worn over pin-stripe trousers and spectacles under Roundhead helmets ... But the players and their audience have the last smile. Fashions do not often come without a cause, and pageants are filling a need of the time in revealing past traditions and past achievements. We may read into them a hankering after unity of purpose, such as tradition gives; and a sense of fellowship, such as comes from the memory of deeds done together.[113]

In this case, it is worth noting that the pageant managed to raise more than £1,000 for the local hospital in a village with a population of only 3,000.[114] So while, on the one hand, pageants represented a yearning to anchor oneself in the fixed past, they could also serve a clear contemporary purpose. Pageants could themselves change – they depicted the past but took place in a rapidly changing present. This was reflected in the scenes and historical figures that they chose to depict, in the presentational technologies that they deployed and in the material culture with which they were surrounded.

Perhaps above all, pageants were – in most cases at least – *local* events that celebrated *local* history and identities. This was the aim of Parker when he set the craze going in 1905, and it remains the case at Axbridge and other places where historical pageantry survives today. The 'local roots of national identity' have been better recognised in the histories of other countries than in those of Britain, but pageants are powerfully indicative of the continuing importance of locality and place in the processes of identity formation here as elsewhere in the modern world (Germany is one obvious comparator).[115] Crucially, this remained important even after the supposedly socially unifying experience of two world wars and despite the promotion of a 'national' culture by institutions such as the BBC.[116] Even in the 1950s, civic pride and identity was presented in pageants as the foundation of wider allegiances. Thus in his comments in the souvenir programme for the Guildford pageant in 1957, the local mayor declared:

> The greater loyalties spring from the lesser, and if we are proud to be Her Majesty's subjects in a world-wide Commonwealth and Empire, we are proud, too, to be citizens of a town which has contributed its share to the founding of that Empire.[117]

Local loyalties, and even what K. D. M. Snell calls 'local xenophobia', could play an important role in mobilising support for pageants.[118] The sense of 'community' that they generated was powerful, even if not universally shared, and the 'community spirit' associated with a pageant was often remembered many years after the event had taken place.[119] These feelings of community should not simply be dismissed as illusory:[120] pageants both reflected and fostered a strong culture of participation and engagement in a shared social purpose. They were often successful in supporting a place-based identity, nurturing both topophilia and self-understanding. They channelled the focus of communities, usually for just a short period of time, but the versions of history that they presented helped many people to identify themselves as part of a wider collective group rooted in both time and place.

Notes

1. Frank Cottrell Boyce, 'London 2012: Opening Ceremony Saw All Our Dreams Come True', *Guardian*, 30 July 2012: https://www.theguardian.com/commentisfree/2012/jul/29/frank-cottrell-boyce-olympics-opening-ceremony?CMP=twt_gu (accessed 19 December 2018); Danny Boyle, *Creating Wonder: In Conversation with Amy Raphael* (London: Faber & Faber, 2013), 398; Ben Jones and Rebecca Searle, 'Humphrey Jennings, the Left & the Experience of Modernity in Mid-Twentieth-Century Britain', *History Workshop Journal* 75 (2013): 191.
2. See Raphael Samuel, *Theatres of Memory: Past and Present in Contemporary Culture* (London: Verso, 1996); Jerome de Groot, *Consuming History: Historians and Heritage in Contemporary Popular Culture* (Abingdon and New York: Routledge, 2008).
3. http://axbridgepageant.com/ (accessed 31 May 2020); the Axbridge pageant is discussed further below, and in the afterword to this book.
4. The term is used in David Glassberg, *American Historical Pageantry: The Uses of Tradition in the Early Twentieth Century* (Chapel Hill, NC: University of North Carolina Press, 1990).
5. Paul Readman, 'The Place of the Past in English Culture *c.*1890–1914', *Past and Present* 186 (2005): 177, 186–7; Mark Freeman, '"Splendid Display; Pompous Spectacle": Historical Pageants in Twentieth-Century Britain', *Social History* 38 (2013): 435.
6. Authenticity could take many forms. One observer expressed the rather extreme view that the best pageants involved cast members playing their own ancestors: Robert Barr, 'The Pageant Epidemic', *Idler* 31 (1907): 437. Even where this was not literally possible, social and political

hierarchies were replicated in casting: at Sherborne, residents of the town's almshouses played their own fifteenth-century predecessors in one episode.

7. Angela Bartie, Linda Fleming, Mark Freeman, Tom Hulme, Alex Hutton, Paul Readman, 'The Spirit of Warwickshire', *The Redress of the Past*, http://www.historicalpageants.ac.uk/pageants/1202/ (accessed 14 June 2017).
8. Angela Bartie, Linda Fleming, Mark Freeman, Tom Hulme, Alex Hutton, Paul Readman, 'Pageant of Scottish History; "The Roadmakers"', *The Redress of the Past*, http://www.historicalpageants.ac.uk/pageants/1442/ (accessed 14 June 2017).
9. Angela Bartie, Linda Fleming, Mark Freeman, Tom Hulme, Alex Hutton, Paul Readman, 'The Pageant of London', *The Redress of the Past*, http://www.historicalpageants.ac.uk/pageants/1305/ (accessed 10 January 2019).
10. 'The Pageant', *Hartlepool Northern Daily Mail*, 28 July 1931, 6. See Angela Bartie, Linda Fleming, Mark Freeman, Tom Hulme, Alex Hutton, Paul Readman, 'Historical Pageant of Newcastle and the North', *The Redress of the Past*, http://www.historicalpageants.ac.uk/pageants/1299/ (accessed 19 December 2018). There were eight scheduled performances and two extra ones.
11. According to General Sir William Rase, chief administrative officer of the pageant, 'nearly one million people had seen the pageant performances', with several performances still to go: 'The Pageant of Empire', *Observer*, 24 August 1924, 11.
12. On the first day of the Wisbech pageant 500 cars parked, and 600 on the second: 'Wisbech Pageant', *Stamford Mercury*, 13 September 1929, 4.
13. *Frank Lascelles: 'Our modern Orpheus'*, ed. Earl of Darnley [Esme Ivo Bligh] (Oxford: Oxford University Press, 1932), 4–5, 93–6; Charles Oman, In Praise of Pageantry', in *The Handbook of the Harrow Historical Pageant* (Harrow: pageant Offices, 1923), 7–9. Trevelyan wrote five scenes and an epilogue for the Berkhamsted pageant of 1922, held to commemorate the 700th anniversary of the Church of St Peter, Berkhamsted: see Mary Moorman, *George Macaulay Trevelyan: A Memoir* (London: Hamish Hamilton, 1980), 202. Arthur Bryant was responsible for the scripts of the Cambridgeshire (1924), Oxfordshire (1926) and Wisbech (1929) pageants, the manuscripts of which are held at the Liddell Hart Centre for Military Archives, King's College London (BRYANT J1, BRYANT J2, BRYANT C3).
14. For discussion of the rich material culture of historical pageantry, see chapter 11 in this volume.
15. J. C. Trewin, *Benson and the Bensonians* (London: Barrie and Rockcliffe, 1960), 160; *Observer*, 2 August 1931, 8.
16. See Angela Bartie, Paul Caton, Linda Fleming, Mark Freeman, Tom Hulme, Alex Hutton and Paul Readman, *The Redress of the Past*, http://www.historicalpageants.ac.uk/pageants/ (accessed 28 June 2019).
17. Joan FitzPatrick Dean, *All Dressed Up: Modern Irish Historical Pageantry* (Syracuse, NY: Syracuse University Press, 2014).
18. H. V. Nelles, *The Art of Nation-Building: Pageantry and Spectacle at Quebec's Tercentenary* (Toronto: University of Toronto Press, 1999); Loren Kruger, *The Drama of South Africa: Plays, Pageants and Publics since 1910* (New York: Routledge, 1999); Deborah Sugg Ryan, 'Staging the Imperial City: The Pageant of London, 1911', in *Imperial Cities: Landscape, Display and Identity*, ed. Felix Driver and David Gilbert (Manchester: Manchester University Press, 1999), 117–35. The title of 'pageant-master' was used by Louis Napoleon Parker in 1905 and was usually taken by other producers, both male and female, thereafter.
19. H. V. Nelles, *The Art of Nation-Building: Pageantry and Spectacle at Quebec's Tercentenary* (Toronto: University of Toronto Press, 1999), 154.
20. Nelles, *Art of Nation-Building*, esp. 314–19.
21. Jane Southcott, 'One Hundred Years of "Anglo-Saxondom" in the South: The Children's Demonstration Pageant of Empire, South Australia 1936', *Australian Journal of Music Education* 2 (2014): 159–83.
22. Glassberg, *American Historical Pageantry*.
23. Quoted in Glassberg, *American Historical Pageantry*, 69, 78.
24. Glassberg, *American Historical Pageantry*, 285 and *passim*.
25. Tom Hulme, *After the Shock City: Urban Culture and the Making of Modern Citizenship* (Woodbridge: Royal Historical Society/Boydell & Brewer, 2019), 117–24.
26. Hulme, *After the Shock City*, 124–30.
27. Carolyn D. Roark, '"Live! In the Canyon": Historical Pageantry as Community-Builder in the Paso del Norte', *Americana* 6 (2007): unpaginated; *Viva! El Paso*: https://vivaelpaso.org/

(accessed 4 July 2019). *Viva! El Paso* presents a selective account of the divisions that have beset local communities in the past. Roark points out that a particularly significant feature of this pageant – contrasting sharply with the belief of some early pageant-masters and enthusiasts that performers should play their own ancestors in pageants – is a 'colour-blind' casting policy, in which people from one ethnic group may be cast as characters from another. For a more critical recent reading of historical re-enactment on the US border with Mexico, see Valeria Luiselli, 'Staging the Frontier', *New Yorker*, 10 and 17 June: https://www.newyorker.com/magazine/2019/06/10/the-wild-west-meets-the-southern-border (accessed 5 July 2019). Whatever might be the practice in El Paso, in the historical re-enactments at Tombstone in southern Arizona whiteness seems to be an important determinant of the American community identity being celebrated: '[w]hen I went to Tombstone for the first time, with my family – all of us born in Mexico – we quickly noticed that there were no Mexicans being portrayed in the reënactments [*sic*]. No Native Americans, either. Non-whites seemed to have been completely erased from the popular narratives' (Luiselli, 'Staging the Frontier').

28. Simon Gunn, *The Public Culture of the Victorian Middle Class: Ritual and Authority in the English Industrial City 1840–1914* (Manchester: Manchester University Press, 2007); Dion Georgiou, 'Redefining the Carnivalesque: The Construction of Ritual, Revelry and Spectacle in British Leisure Practices through the Idea and Model of "Carnival", 1870–1939', *Sport in History* 35 (2015): 335–63; David Cannadine, 'The Transformation of Civic Ritual in Modern Britain: The Colchester Oyster Feast', *Past and Present* 94 (1982): 107–30; Richard H. Trainor, 'The "Decline" of British Urban Governance since 1850: A Reassessment', in *Urban Governance: Britain and Beyond since 1750*, ed. Robert J. Morris and Richard H. Trainor (Aldershot: Ashgate, 2000), 28–46.
29. Emily Robinson, *The Language of Progressive Politics in Modern Britain* (Basingstoke: Palgrave Macmillan, 2017), chapter 4, esp. 114–15; Helen McCarthy, 'The League of Nations, Public Ritual and National Identity in Britain, *c.*1919–56', *History Workshop Journal* 70 (2010): 108–32; *A Weapon in the Struggle. The Cultural History of the Communist Party in Britain*, ed. Andy Croft (London: Pluto Press 1998).
30. See Angela Bartie, Linda Fleming, Mark Freeman, Tom Hulme, Alexander Hutton and Paul Readman, '"History Taught in the Pageant Way": Education and Historical Performance in Twentieth-Century Britain', *History of Education* 48 (2019): 156–79.
31. On Ireland, see Dean, *All Dressed Up*.
32. Ayako Yoshino, *Pageant Fever: Local History and Consumerism in Edwardian England* (Tokyo: Waseda University Press, 2011), 57–98.
33. The anniversary date of 1901 is now known to be an error; in fact, Alfred died in 899.
34. Readman, 'Place of the Past'; Paul Readman, 'Commemorating the Past in Edwardian Hampshire: King Alfred, Pageantry, and Empire', in *Southampton: Gateway to the British Empire*, ed. Miles Taylor (London: I. B. Tauris, 2007), 95–113.
35. Glassberg, *American Historical Pageantry*, 149–50.
36. Readman, 'Place of the Past', 150, 198; *The Invention of Tradition*, ed. Eric Hobsbawm and Terence Ranger (Cambridge: Cambridge University Press, 1983); Cannadine, 'Transformation of Civic Ritual'. For a recent critique of the 'invention of tradition' model of explanation in relation to British historical culture, see Martha Vandrei, *Queen Boudica and Historical Culture in Britain: An Image of Truth* (Oxford: Oxford University Press, 2018), esp. introduction.
37. Freeman, '"Splendid Display"', 427, 440.
38. Freeman, '"Splendid Display"', 433–5, 441; Readman, 'Place of the Past', 185–9; Yoshino, *Pageant Fever*, esp. 124–5, 143–8, 179–80.
39. Ryan, 'Staging the Imperial City'; Deborah Sugg Ryan, '"Pageantitis": Frank Lascelles' 1907 Oxford Historical Pageant, Visual Spectacle and Popular Memory', *Visual Culture in Britain* 8 (2007): 63–82; Deborah Sugg Ryan, '"The Man Who Staged the Empire": Remembering Frank Lascelles in Sibford Gower 1875–2000', in *Material Memories : Design and Evocation*, ed. Marius Kwint, Christopher Breward and Jeremy Aynsley (Oxford: Berg, 1999), 159–79.
40. Mick Wallis, 'Pageantry and the Popular Front: Ideological Production in the "Thirties"', *New Theatre Quarterly* 10 (1994): 132–56; Mick Wallis, 'The Popular Front Pageant: Its Emergence and Decline', *New Theatre Quarterly* 11 (1996): 17–32.
41. Focused on Bristol's contribution to the expansion and development of the British Empire and Commonwealth, the Bristol Civic Pageant of 1946 was one notable example: Angela Bartie, Linda Fleming, Mark Freeman, Tom Hulme, Alex Hutton, Paul Readman, 'Bristol Civic Pageant', *The Redress of the Past*, http://www.historicalpageants.ac.uk/pageants/1012/ (accessed 14 June 2017).

42. Michael Woods, 'Performing Power: Local Politics and the Taunton Pageant of 1928', *Journal of Historical Geography* 25 (1999): 57–74.
43. Angela Bartie, Linda Fleming, Mark Freeman, Tom Hulme, Paul Readman and Charlotte Tupman, '"And Those Who Live, How Shall I Tell their Fame?" Historical Pageants, Collective Remembrance and the First World War, 1919–1939', *Historical Research* 90 (2017): 636–61.
44. Jim English, 'Empire Day in Britain, 1904–58', *Historical Journal* 49 (2006): 248; Andrew S. Thompson, *The Empire Strikes Back? The Impact of Imperialism on Britain from the Mid-Nineteenth Century* (Abingdon: Routledge, 2005), 118.
45. Robinson, *Language of Progressive Politics*, 107–55.
46. Helen McCarthy, 'Parties, Voluntary Associations, and Democratic Politics in Interwar Britain', *Historical Journal* 50 (2007): 891–912; Helen McCarthy, *The British People and the League of Nations: Democracy, Citizenship and Internationalism, c.1918–1945* (Manchester: Manchester University Press, 2011); Helen McCarthy, 'Service Clubs, Citizenship and Equality: Gender Relations and Middle-Class Associations in Britain between the wars', *Historical Research* 81 (2008): 531–52.
47. Bartie et al., '"And Those Who Live"', 652–3.
48. *The Ages of Voluntarism: How We Got to the Big Society*, ed. Matthew Hilton and James McKay (Oxford: Oxford University Press, 2011); *Understanding the Roots of Voluntary Action: Historical Perspectives on Current Social Policy*, ed. Colin Rochester, George Campbell Gosling, Alison Penn and Meta Zimmeck (Falmer: Sussex Academic Press, 2011).
49. Wallis, 'Pageantry and the Popular Front'; Wallis, 'Popular Front Pageant'; Mick Wallis, 'Heirs to the Pageant: Mass Spectacle and the Popular Front', in *Weapon in the Struggle*, ed. Croft, 48–67. See also Samuel, *Theatres of Memory*, 207–8.
50. Noel Streatfeild, *Party Frock* (London: Collins, 1946), published in the US in 1947 as *Party Shoes* and republished under this title by Oxford University Press in 2001; Noel Streatfeild, *Gemma* (London: May Fair Books, 1968); J. B. Priestley, *Festival at Farbridge* (London: William Heinemann, 1951); Rosemary Manning, *Dragon in Danger* (London: Constable, 1959).
51. Joshua D. Esty, 'Amnesia in the Fields: Late Modernism, Late Imperialism, and the English Pageant-Play', *ELH* 69 (2002): 245–76; Jed Esty, *A Shrinking Island: Modernism and National Culture in England* (Princeton, NJ: Princeton University Press, 2004). Esty may have pushed this argument too far, however. A rather different reading of interwar culture and its relationship to modernity is offered in Alexandra Harris, *Romantic Moderns: English Writers, Artists and the Imagination from Virginia Woolf to John Piper* (London: Thames & Hudson, 2010). For an important interpretation of interwar concern with land, landscape and the rural as by no means necessarily opposed to modernising trends, see David Matless, *Landscape and Englishness* (2nd ed., London: Reaktion Books, 2016 [1st ed. 1998]). See also Paul Readman, *Storied Ground: Landscape and the Shaping of English National Identity* (Cambridge: Cambridge University Press, 2018) for a similar perspective on pre-1914 English culture.
52. Mick Wallis, 'Unlocking the Secret Soul: Mary Kelly, Pioneer of Village Theatre', *New Theatre Quarterly* 16 (2000): 347–58.
53. As in the case of the historical pageant at Drum Castle at Banchory, Aberdeenshire, in 1951: see Angela Bartie, Linda Fleming, Mark Freeman, Tom Hulme, Alex Hutton, Paul Readman, 'Historical Pageant at Drum Castle', *The Redress of the Past*, http://www.historicalpageants.ac.uk/pageants/1052/ (accessed 14 June 2017).
54. Angela Bartie, Linda Fleming, Mark Freeman, Tom Hulme, Alex Hutton, Paul Readman, 'Ramsgate Historical Pageant and Charter Jubilee Celebrations', *The Redress of the Past*, http://www.historicalpageants.ac.uk/pageants/1309/ (accessed 14 June 2017).
55. *East Grinstead Courier*, 19 July 1929, 1.
56. Matless, *Landscape and Englishness*; Jeremy Burchardt, 'Rethinking the Rural Idyll', *Cultural and Social History* 8 (2011): 73–94; Jeremy Burchardt, *Paradise Lost: Rural Idyll and Social Change in England since 1800* (London: I. B. Tauris, 2002), chapters 8–12.
57. Tom Hulme, '"A Nation of Town Criers": Civic Publicity and Historical Pageantry in Inter-War Britain', *Urban History* 44 (2017): 270–92; Hulme, *After the Shock City*.
58. On this see Martin J. Wiener, *English Culture and the Decline of the Industrial Spirit 1850–1980* (2nd ed., Cambridge: Cambridge University Press, 2004 [1st ed. 1982]); W. D. Rubinstein, *Capitalism, Culture and Decline in Britain 1750–1990* (London: Routledge, 1993); Peter Mandler, 'Against "Englishness": English Culture and the Limits to Rural Nostalgia, 1850–1940', *Transactions of the Royal Historical Society*, 6th ser., 7 (1997), 155–75; Paul Readman, 'Preserving the English Landscape, *c.*1870–1914', *Cultural and Social History* 5 (2008): 197–218.

59. Yoshino, *Pageant Fever*, 247; Angela Bartie, Linda Fleming, Mark Freeman, Tom Hulme, Alex Hutton, Paul Readman, 'The Bury St Edmunds Pageant of Magna Carta', *The Redress of the Past*, http://www.historicalpageants.ac.uk/pageants/1018/ (accessed 14 June 2017). For the 1966 Berkhamsted pageant: 'Court Circular – Today's Engagements', *The Times*, 3 June 1966, 14 and 'Scrapbook of Pageant Held in Celebration of 900th Anniversary of Coronation of William I' [1966], Hertfordshire Archives and Local Studies Library, DEX235/Z1.
60. Freeman, '"Splendid Display"'.
61. Freeman, '"Splendid Display"', 453.
62. Angela Bartie, Linda Fleming, Mark Freeman, Tom Hulme, Paul Readman and Charlotte Tupman, 'The Redress of the Past: Historical Pageants in Twentieth-Century England', *International Journal of Research on History Didactics, History Education and History Culture: Yearbook/Jahrbuch/Annales* 37 (2016): 29–31.
63. For recent evidence of this interest see, for example, Ellie Read [Reid], 'Historical Pageants: A New Database for Local Historians', *Local History News* 123 (Spring 2017): 11–12; Jill Rolfe, 'The Pageant of Ashdown Forest', *Ashdown Forest News*, spring/summer 2019: 14–18; Sylvia Pitcher, 'The Siege of Corfe Castle' [on the 1929 Dorset pageant], *The Greenwood Tree* 42 (March 2017): 23.
64. Andrew Swift and Kirsten Elliott, *The Year of the Pageant* (Exeter: Akeman Press, 2009); Philip Sheail, *Hertford's Grand Pageant 1914* (Hertford: Molewood Hawthorn Publishing, 2014); Mark Freeman, 'A Pageant-Related Visit to Hertford', 9 June 2014: http://historicalpageants.ac.uk/publications/blog/pageant-related-visit-hertford/ (accessed 8 August 2018).
65. Memories of the St Albans pageant of 1907 appeared in the *Herts Advertiser*, 18 August 1967, 4; *St Albans Review*, 20 November 1975, 2; 21 April 1977, 10; 1 July 1977, 6. The 1948 pageant was covered in the *Herts Advertiser*, 18 June 1998, 6.
66. Angela Bartie, Linda Fleming, Mark Freeman, Tom Hulme and Paul Readman, 'Performing the Past: Identity, Civic Culture and Historical Pageants in Twentieth-Century Small Towns', in *Small Towns in Europe in the 20th and 21st Centuries: Heritage and Development Strategies*, ed. Luda Klusakova (Prague: Karolinum Press, Charles University, 2017), 43–8.
67. For details of exhibitions at Bury St Edmunds (May to August 2015), Carlisle (August to October 2015) and Scarborough (September to November 2016, two separate venues) see http://www.historicalpageants.ac.uk/events/ (accessed 2 July 2019). For details of the exhibition at Lancaster (July to October 2013) see *Lancaster Guardian*, 3 August 2013 and 'A Passion for Pageantry in Lancaster', http://www.lancashire.gov.uk/news/details.aspx?Id=PR13/0321 (accessed 2 July 2019). The Colchester exhibition, curated by Catherine Newley, took place at Hollytrees Museum in 2009, the centenary of the Colchester pageant of 1909: see 'Exhibition Recalls Town's Pageant', http://news.bbc.co.uk/local/essex/hi/people_and_places/arts_and_culture/newsid_8175000/8175998.stm (accessed 2 July 2019).
68. *Historical Pageants: Local History Study Guide*, ed. Angela Bartie, Linda Fleming, Mark Freeman, Tom Hulme, Alexander Hutton and Paul Readman (St Albans: Regents Court Press, 2020). As one local studies librarian recently wrote, '[p]ageants … make excellent subjects for family, community, and oral history projects' (Read [Reid], 'Historical Pageants', 12). For one example of such a project, focused on the participants of the 1905 Sherborne Pageant and run by the Somerset and Dorset Family History Society, see Barbara Elsmore and Rachel Hassall, 'Somerset & Dorset Family History Society: The Sherborne Pageant Participants', in Bartie et al., *Historical Pageants: Local History Study Guide*, 31–3, and 'Sherborne Pageant Participants', http://www.sdfhs.org/sdfhs-projects/introduction-to-sdfhs-projects/social-records/sherborne-pageant-participants/ (accessed 2 July 2019).
69. Michael T. Saler, *The Avant-Garde in Interwar England: Medieval Modernism and the London Underground* (Oxford: Oxford University Press, 1999); Michael Saler, 'Modernity and Enchantment: A Historiographic Review', *American Historical Review* 111 (2006): 692–716.
70. Michael Saler, '"Clap If You Believe in Sherlock Holmes": Mass Culture and the Re-Enchantment of Modernity c.1890–c.1940', *Historical Journal* 46 (2003): 599–622; Saler, 'Modernity and Enchantment'.
71. *Punch*, 18 July 1951, 62–3.
72. Stephen G. Jones, *Workers at Play: A Social and Economic History of Leisure 1918–1939* (London: Routledge, 1986); Brad Beaven, *Leisure, Citizenship and Working-Class Men in Britain 1850–1945* (Manchester: Manchester University Press, 2005).
73. See Ryan, '"Man Who Staged the Empire"'.

74. Angela Bartie, Linda Fleming, Mark Freeman, Tom Hulme, Alex Hutton, Paul Readman, 'Pageant of Birmingham', *The Redress of the Past*, http://www.historicalpageants.ac.uk/pageants/994/ (accessed 2 July 2019).
75. Memo from J. P. Lamb including foreword to Peach's script, 24 June 1948, Sheffield City Archives, CA990/31.
76. For this argument in relation to the folk movement see Frank Trentmann, 'Civilization and its Discontents: English Neo-Romanticism and the Transformation of Anti-Modernism in Twentieth-Century Western Culture', *Journal of Contemporary History* 29 (1994): 583–625. For the compatibility between the 'modern' and the past in mid-twentieth-century culture more generally see Harris, *Romantic Moderns*; and for earlier evidence of this compatibility, see Readman, *Storied Ground.*
77. Bernhard Rieger and Martin Daunton, 'Introduction', in *Meanings of Modernity: Britain from the Late-Victorian Era to World War II*, ed. Martin Daunton and Bernhard Rieger (Oxford: Berg, 2001), 5.
78. Rieger and Daunton, 'Introduction', esp. 8ff. On this theme see also *Singular Continuities: Tradition, Nostalgia, and Identity in Modern British Culture*, ed. George K. Behlmer and Fred M. Leventhal (Redwood, CA: Stanford University Press, 2000), esp. introduction; Readman, 'Place of the Past', 190–7; Freeman, '"Splendid Display"'.
79. Angela Bartie, Linda Fleming, Mark Freeman, Tom Hulme, Alex Hutton, Paul Readman, 'Pedlar's Ware', *The Redress of the Past*, http://www.historicalpageants.ac.uk/pageants/1241/ (accessed 19 December 2018).
80. Bartie et al., '"History Taught in the Pageant Way"'.
81. Angela Bartie, Linda Fleming, Mark Freeman, Tom Hulme, Alex Hutton, Paul Readman, 'Preston Historical Pageant', *The Redress of the Past*, http://www.historicalpageants.ac.uk/pageants/1308/ (accessed 14 June 2017); Angela Bartie, Linda Fleming, Mark Freeman, Tom Hulme, Alex Hutton, Paul Readman, 'Preston Children's Pageant', *The Redress of the Past*, http://www.historicalpageants.ac.uk/pageants/1433/ (accessed 14 June 2017).
82. Bartie et al., '"History Taught in the Pageant Way"', 164–5, 166.
83. *The Drama in Adult Education: A Report of the Adult Education Committee of the Board of Education* (London: HMSO, 1926), 25.
84. Louis N. Parker, *Several of My Lives* (London: Chapman & Hall, 1928), 279, 283–4.
85. Bartie et al., '"History Taught in the Pageant Way"', esp. 170–3.
86. *Manchester Guardian*, 11 June 1934, 8.
87. Angela Bartie, Linda Fleming, Mark Freeman, Tom Hulme, Alex Hutton, Paul Readman, 'St Paul's Steps', *The Redress of the Past*, http://www.historicalpageants.ac.uk/pageants/1318/ (accessed 2 July 2019). 'St Paul's Steps' – also known as 'Cathedral Steps' – was restaged the following week in front of the devastated Coventry Cathedral, but planned repeat performances at Exeter, Guildford and the Guildhall in London were cancelled: see Zoë Jane Varnals, 'The Entertainments National Service Association 1939–1946' (unpublished PhD diss., King's College London, 2009), 262.
88. *Manchester Guardian*, 8 January 1938, 14; 13 April 1938, 11; *Manchester Historical Pageant* (Manchester: Historical Pageant Committee, 1938); *100 Years of Struggle: Manchester's Centenary, the Real Story* (Manchester: Manchester and Salford District Communist Party, 1938).
89. Freeman, '"Splendid Display"', 446.
90. See especially Yoshino, *Pageant Fever*, 231–45.
91. Yoshino, *Pageant Fever*, 237.
92. Bartie et al., 'Performing the Past', 41–3.
93. 'Anyway, Who Cares about Edmund? Not Young Set', *Bury Free Press,* 10 July 1970, 12. See Angela Bartie, Linda Fleming, Mark Freeman, Tom Hulme, Alex Hutton, Paul Readman, 'Edmund of Anglia', *The Redress of the Past*, http://www.historicalpageants.ac.uk/pageants/1058/ (accessed 13 January 2019).
94. 'Tales from the Bury St Edmunds Pageant – (4) Liz Cole', *The Redress of the Past*, http://www.historicalpageants.ac.uk/publications/blog/tales-bury-st-edmunds-pageant-4-liz-cole/ (accessed 13 January 2019).
95. Angela Bartie, Linda Fleming, Mark Freeman, Tom Hulme, Alex Hutton, Paul Readman, 'Carlisle Historical Pageant', *The Redress of the Past*, http://www.historicalpageants.ac.uk/pageants/1025/ (accessed 14 June 2017).
96. 'Memories of Getting Involved in the 1977 Pageant', *The Redress of the Past*, http://www.historicalpageants.ac.uk/events/carlisle/memories-getting-involved-1977-pageant/ (accessed 2 July 2019).

97. Bartie et al., '"History Taught in the Pageant Way"', 175–8.
98. McCarthy, *British People and the League of Nations*; McCarthy, 'League of Nations'.
99. See, for example, the notes on episode III of the 1977 Carlisle pageant: Bartie et al., 'Carlisle Historical Pageant'.
100. Freeman, '"Splendid Display"'; Hulme, '"Nation of Town Criers"'.
101. See Dai Smith, *In the Frame: Memory and Society 1910–2010* (Cardigan: Parthian Books, 2010).
102. Becky Conekin, *'The Autobiography of a Nation': The 1951 Festival of Britain* (Manchester: Manchester University Press, 2003); Harriet Atkinson, *The Festival of Britain: A Land and Its People* (London: I. B. Tauris, 2012).
103. See, for example, *The Power of Place: Bringing Together Geographical and Sociological Imaginations*, ed. John A. Agnew and James S. Duncan (London: Routledge, 1989); Rob Shields, *Places on the Margin: Alternative Geographies of Modernity* (London: Routledge, 1992); Doreen Massey, *Space, Place and Gender* (Cambridge: Polity Press, 1994); Doreen Massey, *For Space* (London: Sage, 2005).
104. See James Kirby, *Historians and the Church of England: Religion and Historical Scholarship 1870–1920* (Oxford: Oxford University Press, 2016).
105. Angela Bartie, Linda Fleming, Mark Freeman, Tom Hulme, Alex Hutton and Paul Readman, 'Historical Pageants and the Medieval Past in Twentieth-Century England', *English Historical Review* 133 (2018): 866–902, esp. 880–2.
106. These anxieties are discussed in S. J. D. Green, *The Passing of Protestant England: Secularisation and Social Change c.1920–1960* (Cambridge: Cambridge University Press, 2011).
107. Bartie et al., 'Historical Pageants and the Medieval Past'.
108. G. D. H. Cole and Raymond Postgate, *The Common People 1746–1946* (London: Methuen, 1938).
109. Some pageants were performed entirely without dialogue, including a notable number in Scotland.
110. Eleven Arches, 'Our Vision', https://elevenarches.org/our-story/our-vision (accessed 2 July 2019).
111. For an example of anti-Semitism see Angela Bartie, Linda Fleming, Mark Freeman, Tom Hulme, Alex Hutton, Paul Readman, 'The Wisbech Pageant', *The Redress of the Past*, http://www.historicalpageants.ac.uk/pageants/1242/ (accessed 14 June 2017).
112. Parker Gordon, at the University of St Andrews, is currently working on music and pageants: 'E. M. Forster, Ralph Vaughan Williams, and William Blake's Pastoral Pageant: Literary and Musical Allusions to the Past' (unpublished paper: *E. M. Forster: Nature, Culture, Queer!* International E. M. Forster Society, University of Education, Ludwigsburg, Germany, 13 April 2018). Gordon has recently discovered the complete score of Martin Shaw's music for T. S. Eliot's pageant *The Rock* (1934): 'Echoes from the Vault', https://standrewsrarebooks.wordpress.com/2019/04/15/james-d-forbes-collecting-prize-2018-winner/ (accessed 2 July 2019).
113. *Yorkshire Post and Leeds Intelligencer*, 14 August 1934, 8.
114. *Yorkshire Post and Leeds Intelligencer*, 14 August 1934, 8; see Angela Bartie, Linda Fleming, Mark Freeman, Tom Hulme, Alex Hutton, Paul Readman, 'Gildersome Pageant', *The Redress of the Past*, http://www.historicalpageants.ac.uk/pageants/1070/ (accessed 14 June 2017).
115. See Readman, 'Place of the Past', 178; and for some discussion of regional as well as local variants of Englishness, see also Readman, *Storied Ground*. For the German case see, for example, Celia Applegate, *A Nation of Provincials: The German Idea of Heimat* (Berkeley, CA: University of California Press, 1990); Alon Confino, *The Nation as Local Metaphor: Württemberg, Imperial Germany and National Memory 1871–1918* (Chapel Hill, NC: University of North Carolina Press, 1997); Jan Palmowski, *Inventing a Socialist Nation: Heimat and the Politics of Everyday Life in the GDR, 1945–90* (Cambridge: Cambridge University Press, 2009).
116. See Thomas Hajkowski, *The BBC and National Identity in Britain 1922–53* (Manchester: Manchester University Press, 2010).
117. Quoted in Freeman, '"Splendid Display"', 444.
118. K. D. M. Snell, 'The Culture of Local Xenophobia', *Social History* 28 (2003): 1–30; Readman, 'Place of the Past', 177–8; Freeman, '"Splendid Display"', 432–3.
119. Bartie et al., '"History Taught in the Pageant Way"', 176–7.
120. Cf. Zygmunt Bauman, *Community: Seeking Safety in an Insecure World* (Cambridge: Polity, 2001).

Bibliography

Agnew, John A. and Duncan, James S., eds. 1989. *The Power of Place: Bringing Together Geographical and Sociological Imaginations*. London: Routledge.

Applegate, Celia. 1990. *A Nation of Provincials: The German Idea of Heimat*. Berkeley, CA: University of California Press.

Atkinson, Harriet. 2012. *The Festival of Britain: A Land and Its People*. London: I. B. Tauris.

Bartie, Angela, Caton, Paul, Fleming, Linda, Freeman, Mark, Hulme, Tom, Hutton, Alex and Readman, Paul. *The Redress of the Past*, http://www.historicalpageants.ac.uk/pageants/.

Bartie, Angela, Fleming, Linda, Freeman, Mark, Hulme, Tom, Hutton, Alexander and Readman, Paul. 2018. 'Historical Pageants and the Medieval Past in Twentieth-Century England', *English Historical Review* 133: 866–902.

Bartie, Angela, Fleming, Linda, Freeman, Mark, Hulme, Tom, Hutton, Alexander and Readman, Paul. 2019. '"History Taught in the Pageant Way": Education and Historical Performance in Twentieth-Century Britain', *History of Education* 48: 156–79.

Bartie, Angela, Fleming, Linda, Freeman, Mark, Hulme, Tom, Hutton, Alexander and Readman, Paul, eds. 2020. *Historical Pageants: Local History Study Guide*. St Albans: Regents Court Press.

Bartie, Angela, Fleming, Linda, Freeman, Mark, Hulme, Tom and Readman, Paul. 2017. 'Performing the Past: Identity, Civic Culture and Historical Pageants in Twentieth-Century Small Towns', in *Small Towns in Europe in the 20th and 21st Centuries: Heritage and Development Strategies*, edited by Luda Klusakova. Prague: Karolinum Press, Charles University, 24–51.

Bartie, Angela, Fleming, Linda, Freeman, Mark, Hulme, Tom, Readman, Paul and Tupman, Charlotte. 2016. 'The Redress of the Past: Historical Pageants in Twentieth-Century England', *International Journal of Research on History Didactics, History Education and History Culture: Yearbook/Jahrbuch/Annales* 37: 19–35.

Bartie, Angela, Fleming, Linda, Freeman, Mark, Hulme, Tom, Readman, Paul and Tupman, Charlotte. 2017. '"And Those Who Live, How Shall I Tell their Fame?" Historical Pageants, Collective Remembrance and the First World War, 1919–1939', *Historical Research* 90: 636–61.

Bauman, Zygmunt. 2001. *Community: Seeking Safety in an Insecure World*. Cambridge: Polity Press.

Beaven, Brad. 2005. *Leisure, Citizenship and Working-Class Men in Britain 1850–1945*. Manchester: Manchester University Press.

Behlmer, George K. and Leventhal, Fred M., eds. 2000. *Singular Continuities: Tradition, Nostalgia, and Identity in Modern British Culture*. Redwood, CA: Stanford University Press.

Burchardt, Jeremy. 2002. *Paradise Lost: Rural Idyll and Social Change in England since 1800*. London: I. B. Tauris.

Burchardt, Jeremy. 2011. 'Rethinking the Rural Idyll', *Cultural and Social History* 8: 73–94.

Cannadine, David. 1982. 'The Transformation of Civic Ritual in Modern Britain: The Colchester Oyster Feast', *Past and Present* 94: 107–30.

Conekin, Becky. 2003. *'The Autobiography of a Nation': The 1951 Festival of Britain*. Manchester: Manchester University Press.

Confino, Alon. 1997. *The Nation as Local Metaphor: Württemberg, Imperial Germany and National Memory 1871–1918*. Chapel Hill, NC: University of North Carolina Press.

Croft, Andy, ed. 1998. *A Weapon in the Struggle. The Cultural History of the Communist Party in Britain*. London: Pluto Press.

de Groot, Jerome. 2008. *Consuming History: Historians and Heritage in Contemporary Popular Culture*. Abingdon and New York: Routledge.

Dean, Joan FitzPatrick. 2014. *All Dressed Up: Modern Irish Historical Pageantry*. Syracuse, NY: Syracuse University Press.

English, Jim. 2006. 'Empire Day in Britain, 1904–58', *Historical Journal* 49: 247–76.

Esty, Josuha D. 2002. 'Amnesia in the Fields: Late Modernism, Late Imperialism, and the English Pageant-Play', *ELH* 69: 245–76.

Esty, Jed. 2004. *A Shrinking Island: Modernism and National Culture in England*. Princeton, NJ: Princeton University Press.

Freeman, Mark. 2013. '"Splendid Display; Pompous Spectacle": Historical Pageants in Twentieth-Century Britain', *Social History* 38: 423–55.

Georgiou, Dion. 2015. 'Redefining the Carnivalesque: The Construction of Ritual, Revelry and Spectacle in British Leisure Practices through the Idea and Model of "Carnival", 1870–1939', *Sport in History* 35: 335–63.

Glassberg, David. 1990. *American Historical Pageantry: The Uses of Tradition in the Early Twentieth Century*. Chapel Hill, NC: University of North Carolina Press.
Green, S. J. D. 2011. *The Passing of Protestant England: Secularisation and Social Change c.1920–1960*. Cambridge: Cambridge University Press.
Gunn, Simon. 2007. *The Public Culture of the Victorian Middle Class: Ritual and Authority in the English Industrial City 1840–1914*. Manchester: Manchester University Press.
Hajkowski, Thomas. 2010. *The BBC and National Identity in Britain 1922–53*. Manchester: Manchester University Press.
Harris, Alexandra. 2010. *Romantic Moderns: English Writers, Artists and the Imagination from Virginia Woolf to John Piper*. London: Thames & Hudson.
Hilton, Matthew and McKay, James, eds. 2011. *The Ages of Voluntarism: How We Got to the Big Society*. Oxford: Oxford University Press.
Hobsbawm, Eric and Ranger, Terence, eds. 1983. *The Invention of Tradition*. Cambridge: Cambridge University Press.
Hulme, Tom. 2017. '"A Nation of Town Criers": Civic Publicity and Historical Pageantry in Inter-War Britain', *Urban History* 44: 270–92.
Hulme, Tom. 2019. *After the Shock City: Urban Culture and the Making of Modern Citizenship*. Woodbridge: Royal Historical Society/Boydell & Brewer.
Jones, Ben and Searle, Rebecca. 2013. 'Humphrey Jennings, the Left and the Experience of Modernity in Mid-Twentieth-Century Britain', *History Workshop Journal* 75: 190–212.
Jones, Stephen G. 1986. *Workers at Play: A Social and Economic History of Leisure 1918–1939*. London: Routledge.
Kirby, James. 2016. *Historians and the Church of England: Religion and Historical Scholarship 1870–1920*. Oxford: Oxford University Press.
Kruger, Loren. 1999. *The Drama of South Africa: Plays, Pageants and Publics since 1910*. New York: Routledge.
McCarthy, Helen. 2007. 'Parties, Voluntary Associations, and Democratic Politics in Interwar Britain', *Historical Journal* 50: 891–912.
McCarthy, Helen. 2008. 'Service Clubs, Citizenship and Equality: Gender Relations and Middle-Class Associations in Britain between the Wars', *Historical Research* 81: 531–52.
McCarthy, Helen. 2010. 'The League of Nations, Public Ritual and National Identity in Britain, c.1919–56', *History Workshop Journal* 70: 108–32.
McCarthy, Helen. 2011. *The British People and the League of Nations: Democracy, Citizenship and Internationalism, c.1918–1945*. Manchester: Manchester University Press.
Mandler, Peter. 1997. 'Against "Englishness": English Culture and the Limits to Rural Nostalgia, 1850–1940', *Transactions of the Royal Historical Society*, 6th ser., 7: 155–75.
Massey, Doreen. 1994. *Space, Place and Gender*. Cambridge: Polity Press.
Massey, Doreen. 2005. *For Space*. London: Sage.
Matless, David. 2016 (2nd ed.); 1998 (1st ed.). *Landscape and Englishness*. London: Reaktion Books.
Moorman, Mary. 1980. *George Macaulay Trevelyan: A Memoir*. London: Hamish Hamilton.
Nelles, H. V. 1999. *The Art of Nation-Building: Pageantry and Spectacle at Quebec's Tercentenary*. Toronto: University of Toronto Press.
Palmowski, Jan. 2009. *Inventing a Socialist Nation: Heimat and the Politics of Everyday Life in the GDR, 1945–90*. Cambridge: Cambridge University Press.
Readman, Paul. 2005. 'The Place of the Past in English Culture, c.1890–1914', *Past and Present* 186: 147–99.
Readman, Paul. 2007. 'Commemorating the Past in Edwardian Hampshire: King Alfred, Pageantry, and Empire', in *Southampton: Gateway to the British Empire*, edited by Miles Taylor. London: I. B. Tauris, 95–113.
Readman, Paul. 2008. 'Preserving the English Landscape, c.1870–1914', *Cultural and Social History* 5: 197–218.
Readman, Paul. 2018. *Storied Ground: Landscape and the Shaping of English National Identity*. Cambridge: Cambridge University Press.
Rieger, Bernhard and Daunton, Martin. 2001. 'Introduction', in *Meanings of Modernity: Britain from the Late-Victorian Era to World War II*, edited by Martin Daunton and Bernhard Rieger. Oxford: Berg, 1–21.
Roark, Carolyn D. 2007. '"Live! In the Canyon": Historical Pageantry as Community-Builder in the Paso del Norte', *Americana* 6: unpaginated.
Robinson, Emily. 2017. *The Language of Progressive Politics in Modern Britain*. Basingstoke: Palgrave Macmillan.

Rochester, Colin, Gosling, George Campbell, Penn, Alison and Zimmeck, Meta, eds. 2011. *Understanding the Roots of Voluntary Action: Historical Perspectives on Current Social Policy*. Falmer: Sussex Academic Press.

Rubinstein, W. D. 1993. *Capitalism, Culture and Decline in Britain 1750–1990*. London: Routledge.

Ryan, Deborah Sugg. 1999. 'Staging the Imperial City: The Pageant of London, 1911', in *Imperial Cities: Landscape, Display and Identity*, edited by Felix Driver and David Gilbert. Manchester: Manchester University Press, 117–35.

Ryan, Deborah Sugg. 1999. '"The Man Who Staged the Empire": Remembering Frank Lascelles in Sibford Gower 1875–2000', in *Material Memories: Design and Evocation*, edited by Marius Kwint, Christopher Breward and Jeremy Aynsley. Oxford: Berg, 159–79.

Ryan, Deborah Sugg. 2007. '"Pageantitis": Frank Lascelles' 1907 Oxford Historical Pageant, Visual Spectacle and Popular Memory', *Visual Culture in Britain* 8: 63–82.

Saler, Michael T. 1999. *The Avant-Garde in Interwar England: Medieval Modernism and the London Underground*. Oxford: Oxford University Press.

Saler, Michael. 2003. '"Clap If You Believe in Sherlock Holmes": Mass Culture and the Re-Enchantment of Modernity c.1890–c.1940', *Historical Journal* 46: 599–622.

Saler, Michael. 2006. 'Modernity and Enchantment: A Historiographic Review', *American Historical Review* 111: 692–716.

Samuel, Raphael. 1996. *Theatres of Memory: Past and Present in Contemporary Culture*. London: Verso.

Sheail, Philip. 2014. *Hertford's Grand Pageant 1914*. Hertford: Molewood Hawthorn Publishing.

Shields, Rob. 1992. *Places on the Margin: Alternative Geographies of Modernity*. London: Routledge.

Smith, Dai. 2010. *In the Frame: Memory and Society 1910–2010*. Cardigan: Parthian Books.

Snell, K. D. M. 2003. 'The Culture of Local Xenophobia', *Social History* 28: 1–30.

Southcott, Jane. 2014. 'One Hundred Years of "Anglo-Saxondom" in the South: The Children's Demonstration Pageant of Empire, South Australia 1936', *Australian Journal of Music Education* 2: 159–83.

Swift, Andrew and Elliott, Kirsten. 2009. *The Year of the Pageant*. Exeter: Akeman Press.

Thompson, Andrew S. 2005. *The Empire Strikes Back? The Impact of Imperialism on Britain from the Mid-Nineteenth Century*. Abingdon: Routledge.

Trainor, Richard H. 2000. 'The "Decline" of British Urban Governance since 1850: A Reassessment', in *Urban Governance: Britain and Beyond since 1750*, edited by Robert J. Morris and Richard H. Trainor. Aldershot: Ashgate, 28–46.

Trentmann, Frank. 1994. 'Civilization and its Discontents: English Neo-Romanticism and the Transformation of Anti-Modernism in Twentieth-Century Western Culture', *Journal of Contemporary History* 29: 583–625.

Trewin, J. C. 1960. *Benson and the Bensonians*. London: Barrie and Rockliffe.

Vandrei, Martha. 2018. *Queen Boudica and Historical Culture in Britain: An Image of Truth*. Oxford: Oxford University Press.

Varnals, Zoë Jane. 2009. 'The Entertainments National Service Association 1939–1946.' Unpublished PhD diss., King's College London.

Wallis, Mick. 1994. 'Pageantry and the Popular Front: Ideological Production in the "Thirties"', *New Theatre Quarterly* 10: 132–56.

Wallis, Mick. 1996. 'The Popular Front Pageant: Its Emergence and Decline', *New Theatre Quarterly* 11: 17–32.

Wallis, Mick. 1998. 'Heirs to the Pageant: Mass Spectacle and the Popular Front', in *A Weapon in the Struggle. The Cultural History of the Communist Party in Britain*, edited by Andy Croft. London: Pluto Press, 48 – 67.

Wallis, Mick. 2000. 'Unlocking the Secret Soul: Mary Kelly, Pioneer of Village Theatre', *New Theatre Quarterly* 16: 347–58.

Wiener, Martin J. 2004 (2nd ed.); 1982 (1st ed.). *English Culture and the Decline of the Industrial Spirit 1850–1980*. Cambridge: Cambridge University Press.

Woods, Michael. 1999. 'Performing Power: Local Politics and the Taunton Pageant of 1928', *Journal of Historical Geography* 25: 57–74.

Yoshino, Ayako. 2011. *Pageant Fever: Local History and Consumerism in Edwardian England*. Tokyo: Waseda University Press.

2
Historical Pageants in Yorkshire before the First World War

Keith Johnston

Like much of the rest of Britain, Yorkshire displayed enthusiasm for pageants in the Edwardian period. In 1909 Alderman Border (chairman of the Executive Committee of the York pageant) said that the spirit of 'pageantitis' was abroad in York and they were all determined to make the show a gigantic success. Three years later a columnist in the *Scarborough Mercury* referred to 'pageantitis' having affected York, Pickering and Scarborough.[1] Notable pageants were held in these places – in 1909, 1910 and 1912 respectively – as well as at Thirsk in 1907; Whitby and Malton also contemplated staging similar events.[2] However, Yorkshire pageants have not until recently received much attention from scholars. For many years, historians of Edwardian pageants focused their attention mainly on events in the southern part of England. This was hardly surprising given, for example, that five of Louis Napoleon Parker's six productions were staged in the south, but it did mean that pageants elsewhere, including those in England's biggest county, were largely ignored. Ayako Yoshino's study, published as recently as 2011, only refers to one Yorkshire pageant of the pre-First World War period, Parker's at York.[3]

However, things have changed in the last few years, largely due to the work of those involved in the *Redress of the Past* project, and much more information about Yorkshire pageants is now available via the project's website.[4] The project database includes entries on the Thirsk, York, Pickering and Scarborough pageants, and there are articles on the first and last of these in the 'Featured Pageants' section of the website. Furthermore, much information about the Scarborough pageant was displayed at an exhibition staged in 2016 by the project in association with the Scarborough Museums Trust and the Scarborough Archaeological and Historical Society.[5] Given that there is so much information about the content of the pageants available on the *Redress of the Past* website, it is not necessary to describe them in detail here.

The aim of this chapter is to consider the Yorkshire historical pageants of the Edwardian period and to show, among other things, why they were held, what was involved in producing them and why they were regarded as successes – even in the case of Scarborough, which made a financial loss. In addition, what follows will elucidate the similarities between the pageants of this county and those staged elsewhere. It will also show how earlier Yorkshire historical pageants and plays in the 1880s and 1890s influenced those produced between 1907 and 1912. Such earlier productions were not in all ways identical to those produced by Parker and his imitators. Those at Grimston Park in 1885 and Ripon in 1886 and 1896, for example, took the form of a procession followed by a play, while at Helmsley in 1897 and 1898 the pageant plays covered only a part of the town's history.

However, these early productions – Ripon in 1886 is sometimes seen as the first modern historical pageant[6] – certainly influenced later Yorkshire pageants, especially through the influence of D'Arcy Ferrars, master of the revels at Grimston Park and Ripon, and subsequently pageant-master at Thirsk. In turn Ferrars undoubtedly influenced Gilbert Hudson, who also worked on the Thirsk pageant and later became pageant-master at Pickering and Scarborough: both Ferrars and Hudson put an emphasis on processions in their productions. It is also likely that the productions at Helmsley influenced the one at Thirsk. F. L. Perkins, who was responsible for the book of words, had discussed the Helmsley plays with the vicar of that nearby town.[7]

Why were Yorkshire pageants staged?

Various motives inspired those who staged historical pageants in Yorkshire in the years before the First World War. At Thirsk there was a desire to increase the amount insured by the fire policy of the parish church following the disastrous Selby Abbey fire of 19 October 1906, and to raise money for a new heating apparatus. But it was also hoped 'to widen the scope of attractions and to popularise the historic fame and charms of the town and vicinity'.[8] Such a mixture of motives was common among pageant organisers. At an early meeting of the General Committee of the Scarborough pageant Joshua Rowntree, a man long prominent in the town's affairs, gave the reasons why he believed a pageant should be produced in the town. He referred not only to making a profit, but also to what he described as 'higher objects', which included educational benefits, an increased pride in the town and the advantages derived from working together for a common purpose.[9]

Sometimes the impulse sprang, at least in part, from a wish to emulate a pageant or pageants held in a neighbouring town. In 1909 at Pickering a meeting decided to hold a pageant in the town in the following year, 'similar to that held at Thirsk in 1907'. In turn, according to 'Marie', who wrote a weekly column in the *Scarborough Mercury*, '[t]he wonderful success of the Pageant held at Pickering last year has no doubt been mainly responsible for the suggestion that one should be organised for Scarborough'. The Reverend F. G. Stapleton, the driving force behind the Scarborough 'Historical Pageant and Play' of 1912, was inspired by the 1909 York Pageant, as well as by the Pickering one. The latter pageant also led to the suggestion that Malton should follow its example, though nothing came of the idea.[10]

Financial considerations were often important, including the desire to raise money for good causes. At Grimston Park, near Tadcaster, the pageant held in 1885 was for the benefit of the York Association for the Care of Young Girls, while the Scarborough pageant raised money for the local hospital and dispensary by a collection taken when pageant performers paraded through the streets of the town.[11] But pageant organisers also had commercial motives. In her book, which has the revealing subtitle *Local History and Consumerism in Edwardian England*, Ayako Yoshino devotes a whole chapter to 'Tourism, Commercialism and Community'. Arguing that 'the focus on the political aspects of the pageant has risked distorting our understanding of the event', she suggests that

> In the case of the Edwardian period, the drives and motivations that made pageantry such a widespread movement were, in an important respect, commercial and touristic rather than narrowly political.[12]

Michael Dobson has shown that the 1910 Pickering pageant was intended to attract more visitors to the town, a motive that also applied in Thirsk, York and Scarborough.[13] At York in 1909 it was said that the pageant would 'attract visitors, not only from every part of the shire, but from all over England, and from across the Atlantic', and at Scarborough three years later Stapleton claimed that '[i]f the spectacle of the pageant were added to the attractions of the town it would succeed in advertising Scarborough more effectually than it had ever been done before'. This is in accord with Yoshino's idea that such events were often about advertising a town or city.[14] Special railway arrangements were sometimes made to help draw visitors – as at Thirsk, where there were reduced fares from any station in Yorkshire and special trains ran to fit the times of the performances.[15]

Sometimes pageants were produced to mark important anniversaries in the lives of communities and often also to inspire civic pride, as at Ripon when its millenary was celebrated in 1886.[16] But even when no particular anniversary was being marked, there was often a desire to involve members of a community in a joint effort. At York, Parker asserted that '[t]here is a great opportunity for sinking all petty distinctions and for bringing the population together in one great effort to show how fond they are of their city'.[17] It was sometimes simply suggested that a pageant could generate some excitement. In 1911 Gilbert Hudson, the Scarborough pageant-master (Fig. 2.1), claimed that 'a pageant banished the deadly plague of dullness'.[18]

Whatever other reasons there might have been for producing a pageant, however, it was usually about a specific place: pageants were generally to do with local history. According to Parker, '[t]he object of a Pageant ... is to represent the history of a great town, worthily and with dignity'.[19] Not all Yorkshire historical pageants were produced by 'great towns', perhaps, but all were concerned with portraying versions of a shared past. Of Pickering in 1910 it was said that

Figure 2.1 Gilbert Hudson, pageant-master of the Scarborough Historical Pageant and Play of 1912. Hudson also played key roles at the Thirsk (1907) and Pickering (1910) pageants. From 'A Pictorial Record of the Scarborough Historical Pageant 1912', album of photographs and memorabilia: Scarborough Museums Trust. Reproduced by kind permission of the Scarborough Museums Trust.

> Pickering is rich in historical lore and dates back to pre-Christian times. To reproduce in carefully chosen scenes the local story of bygone days in vivid colours and living pictures, is the purpose for which the Book has been written and the Play will be acted. The Pageant is a pictorial presentation in orderly array of important events that have marked the history and evolution of the town.[20]

This was often connected with a desire to educate people, particularly the young, about the past. Parker, never a man to understate things, said at York that

> You must look upon the Pageant from an educational point of view. You are going to show the children the entire history of their city, which is a great chapter, a large fragment of the history of England. … In three hours the children will learn more of history than they would be otherwise able to learn in their lives.[21]

At Scarborough in 1912 'the worth of the Pageant to the children from an educational standpoint' was pointed out in the local press, and it was claimed that '[n]othing was more educational than to acquire a knowledge of the history of the town in which they were located … The story is an interesting one, and should be educational in result'.[22]

From inception to staging: people, finances and publicity

Once the decision to stage a pageant was taken, it was important to have effective leadership if it were to succeed. In a small community this might mean one person taking charge. This was sometimes the local vicar, as at Helmsley in 1898, when the pageant-play was promoted by Rev. C. N. Gray.[23] In larger places it was more usual for a number of people to be the driving forces behind the pageant. At Scarborough the 1912 pageant was originally proposed by Rev. F. G. Stapleton, vicar of Seamer, who was supported by prominent local people, including some members of the town council. This was important because there was much work to be done.[24]

Getting other people involved was one of the first things that needed doing when it came to organising pageants. Public meetings were often used to do this, as at York, where such an event in April 1907 was attended by representatives of various public bodies. This was important as it was an advantage to make use of the experience of existing organisations, as York did with the York Amateur Operatic and Dramatic Society and the London Society of Yorkshiremen – the latter setting aside its own pageant plans to throw its full support behind the larger scheme.[25] At a meeting in Scarborough late in May 1911, the local mayor declared that anyone in the town who could help in any way would be welcomed. Such meetings were a way of gauging the amount of support for a proposed pageant, of recruiting people to assist with the effort and of advertising the scheme.[26] Some of the people whose support was gained were intended mainly as figureheads, acting as patrons – at York there were over 160 and at Scarborough more than 80 of these – and as subscribers or guarantors.[27] However, even some of the supposed figureheads might be encouraged to become more directly involved. A meeting in Scarborough early in May 1911 decided not only to appoint William Denison, the second Earl of Londesborough, to the office of president of the pageant, but also to ask both the Earl and Countess to lend their influence in making the pageant a success.[28] Other people were to be more actively involved and, if the scheme had sufficient support for it to go ahead, the formation of committees to do the work was important. Usually there was a general or executive committee and then a number of other committees, sometimes with sub-committees. At York in 1909 it was said that there was 'a committee for dealing with almost every imaginable contingency which may arise'.[29]

Another early and vital step was the appointment of a pageant-master. As Mary Kelly – founder of the Village Drama Society and author of *How to Make a Pageant* – later wrote, '[a] great deal hangs on the choice of a Pageant-Master'; he or she was a person with many different responsibilities when it came to producing a pageant, especially with regard to the larger schemes.[30] It was said of D'Arcy Ferrars at Grimston Park in 1885 that '[m]uch of his labour was hardly visible to the eye, nevertheless those who have been acting with him know how hard he has worked'.[31] In fact the pageant-master often had one or more deputies to help with the work. At York J. M. Gordon was responsible for rehearsals when Parker was absent from the city, while at Scarborough Gilbert Hudson had two assistants, J. W. Whitbread and Captain H. S. Riddell. At Thirsk in 1907 Ferrars was the pageant-master, but he was also involved in the larger pageant at Liverpool at the same time, so much of the work involved was done by Hudson. His efforts were much appreciated by the performers.[32]

The pageant-master often acted to inspire people to participate in the pageant, as with Parker at York and Hudson at Scarborough. Sometimes this involved direct liaison with outside organisations. Parker wrote to the Corporation of York to request that it would allow some of its employees to take part in the pageant. This direct appeal was successful, the Corporation deciding to allow between 50 and 100 men to participate.[33] Such efforts were necessary given the large casts of many pageants, serried masses of performers being seen as vital to the grandeur of the spectacle. But ensuring that pageants were spectacular events also meant close attention to the script and, where necessary, incorporating changes to add dramatic effect. Sometimes pageant-masters wrote episodes, as Hudson did at Pickering and Scarborough,[34] and they could also wield considerable influence over the choice of site.[35] In addition, they invested considerable time and effort in leading rehearsals – potentially a difficult job with a wholly amateur cast. At Pickering in 1910 Hudson 'took in hand the nervous actors, and rehearsed with them privately'.[36] At Scarborough one observer was very impressed by the qualities that Hudson displayed at a rehearsal: 'Mr. Hudson is an enthusiast, a clever actor, and the owner of that particular type of voice which seems to be specially necessary for Shakesperean [*sic*] plays and pageantic displays'.[37] Parker taught his York crowds to cheer, groan and laugh. During the performances he sat above the grandstand and signalled 'directions that are to make the living panorama move with the exactitude of clock-work'. This was done by means of electric bells, flags and a megaphone.[38]

So much was involved in the preparation of a pageant that a base was needed from which the logistical effort could be co-ordinated, and at which activities such as the making of costumes and props could be carried out. In 1908 the *Yorkshire Post* reported that at York 'the Pageant House is open morning, afternoon, and evening for the preparation of costumes, and the perfecting of the arrangements'. Early the following year the same newspaper indicated the growing scale of the organisational endeavour; it noted that two buildings were now in use, the Pageant House in Clifford Street being joined by a Property House in Petergate.[39] At Pickering a private residence was used as the pageant headquarters. At Scarborough, where, as at York, use was made of more than one building, Pageant House was used for the interviewing of would-be performers.[40]

Managing the money was a key part of the organisation. Often the final decision on whether or not to proceed with a pageant was not taken until it was clear that it could be financed. This was certainly the case at Scarborough, where it was reported at a meeting early in May 1911 that guarantees already promised amounted to the sum of £3,156; as a result 'the meeting sanctioned the Executive to proceed with the preparations for the pageant, which will be held in the early part of July next year'.[41] Pageant organisers were delighted if donations or subscriptions were given to help finance their schemes, but in practice guarantees were more important. York appealed for a subscription list of £1,000 and a guarantee fund of £4,000, while at Scarborough over 200 individuals and companies guaranteed amounts ranging from £1 to £100.[42]

Sales of tickets were very important, but various commercial activities also provided money to help finance pageants. At York in 1909 £2,568 was generated in this way.[43] For the July 1912 performances at Scarborough income was derived from various sources, including

> books of words £188, and advertisements in book of words, £73, making a total revenue from the book of words of £261; sale of music, £11; postcards, £8; advertisements in pamphlet, £53; souvenir rights, £52; catering rights, £10; photographic rights, £16; postcard rights, £14; profits on ball, £43.

The following month saw the pageant performed on a further four occasions, in an attempt to claw back some of the financial losses sustained on the first run: these repeat performances brought in 'books of words, £27; programmes, £14; profit on Pageant ball, £11'.[44] Selling the various items used in pageants was another way of bringing in money; in the case of Scarborough this included the sale of costumes and props. It was not uncommon for the wood used in the grandstand to be offered for sale, as happened at York in 1909. At Pickering the following year over £80 was made by selling wood and other materials used in the grandstand and other fittings of the pageant.[45]

Publicising a pageant was very important. Pageant-masters were often involved in this, for example by giving talks on a pageant or its historical background. Ferrars did this at Ripon in 1896, and Parker read part of the first episode of his Yorkshire pageant to the York Amateur Operatic and Dramatic Society.[46] In arranging such publicity, it helped to know what had happened at other places that had staged pageants; sometimes, as with Parker, the previous experience of the pageant-master was part of this. At an early meeting at York, correspondence from the promoters of pageants at Warwick, St Albans and elsewhere was read to those present, and Parker himself was also in communication with the organisers of the Scarborough pageant.[47] Later a public meeting in support of this pageant was addressed by a Mrs Gray of York and a Mr Whitehead of Pickering – individuals who had been involved with the successful pageants at those two places. They gave detailed advice.[48]

In addition to public meetings and events, posters were often used to publicise pageants, both locally and further afield. In connection with the Ripon festivities of 1896, the manager of the North-Eastern Railway agreed to display large posters at his stations.[49] At Scarborough, where it had been decided to spend £1,000 in advertising the pageant, it was reported that 'the N.E.R. Company, the Lancashire and Yorkshire

Railway, and Messrs. Thos. Cook had agreed to allow the committee to display free any show cards and posters in connection with the forthcoming Pageant'.[50] Press publicity was also important, and pageant organisers devoted much attention to it. The report of the Advertising Committee of the York Pageant made much of the importance of the press luncheon at which nearly 50 of the best-known London and provincial newspapers were represented: it had cost almost £40 but resulted in much valuable publicity.[51] Scarborough also held a press luncheon, to which representatives of newspapers from 'all parts of the country' were invited. Adverts for the repeat performances in August quoted favourable press reports.[52] The run-up to pageants was also covered in detail in the press. A full dress rehearsal of the Thirsk pageant of 1907 was attended by representatives and photographers of the London and Yorkshire press, and the resulting publicity was very positive.[53] In York a sort of pageant newspaper was produced. *Pageant Items*, as it was called, not only reported on the preparations but also acted as 'a means of intercommunication between pageanteers', as Parker put it.[54]

Local forms of publicity included historical lectures. This was the case at York in the spring of 1909, when Rev. C. C. Bell, vicar of St Olave's, gave a series of lectures on the events and people to be depicted in the forthcoming pageant.[55] Such activities were encouraged by pageant-masters and scriptwriters, the latter often being noted local historians or antiquaries. As others have shown, the emphasis on historical accuracy in pageants themselves, and on the educational value of participation in them and in associated events, remained an important feature of the movement well into the interwar period.[56] Perhaps exaggerating for a local audience, Parker claimed that 'in all his experience of pageants', he had 'never yet met a committee ... so insistent on the niceties of historical accuracy' as the one he encountered at York. Here, Parker emphasised, the pageant consisted of 'a series of scenes that were not only beautifully picturesque, but, as far as it could be secured by the most careful research, marked by historical accuracy'.[57] Of the Ripon production of 1896 it was said that 'the banners which have been got ready for the festival are models of skilful workmanship and historic accuracy' and, more generally, that 'from the point of view of historical accuracy', the whole thing 'was a decided and emphatic success'.[58]

The recruitment of performers was also important, especially as the numbers involved were often large. In York the cast totalled 2,500, while 1,300 took part at Scarborough. Pageant-masters were often involved in the selection of actors to play the principal characters. This could be a difficult task, as a writer in the *Yorkshire Post* explained:

> Not the least onerous of the tasks immediately confronting Mr. Parker is the casting of the principal parts – a matter which requires much nicety of judgment and discrimination. In this, as in other matters, Mr. Parker's long training and accumulated experience will prove equal to the occasion.[59]

In particular, it could be difficult to recruit sufficient male actors to participate. This was a problem at York and Pickering, and also at Scarborough where, even when men had agreed to take part, they did not always turn up to rehearsals.[60] Pageant-masters congratulated themselves on one feature of casting: actors playing their own ancestors. This was seen as a way of adding authenticity to a production: of the York pageant it was noted that 'an interesting feature will be that many of the nobility of the county will impersonate the characters of their own ancestors, who helped in olden days to make history in the city'.[61] In the Civil War episode Sir Thomas Fairfax was played by Mr Guy Fairfax, carrying – apparently – the very sword which his ancestor had used at Marston Moor.[62] Similarly, at Scarborough a number of participants played their own forebears.[63]

Costumes, props, music and setting

Given the size of pageants, a great many costumes were needed. These had to be made specifically for the event, or otherwise obtained. Often special committees were set up to deal with all matters relating to costumes, for example at York and Scarborough. As with the content of pageants, accuracy mattered: at York

> No labour or expense has been deemed too much to ascertain the correct habiliments for the three thousand performers. ... In fact, there is not a ribbon on any costume in use at the Pageant which is not sanctioned either by actual knowledge or by accepted tradition.[64]

Special attention was paid to military uniforms. At York, it was reported that 'uniforms of the Royalist and Parliamentary troops are being made in their true colours; and the same care is being bestowed on the accoutrements'.[65] At Scarborough, information on costume, armour and heraldry was obtained from books belonging to the London Library, as well as some loaned by individuals; advice was also obtained from the College of Heralds and other experts.[66] Expenses were kept down as far as possible, in the hope that nobody would be deterred from taking part.

Pageant-master Gilbert Hudson declared that 'the cost of the costumes need not be a stumbling block, as they can be bought from the committee at just the cost of the materials, because all the sewing will be done by voluntary workers'.[67]

Like costumes, many props – including armour, weapons, flags, banners and coaches – had to be made or obtained, often in very large numbers. This was one way in which the whole community could be involved. The manufacture of armour is mentioned in newspaper reports of many pageants. Again, considerable research was carried out to ensure that designs were accurate. A letter sent on behalf of the Library Committee of the York Pageant, for example, appealed for the loan of books on weapons, armour and costumes so that pageant workers could obtain designs and information.[68] The scale of the task was such that, according to one account, the prop-makers had 'no less than 72 suits of chain mail, 29 suits of complete armour, and 20 suits of mixed armour to construct'.[69] They seem to have done this successfully, for in 1910 it was reported that the organisers of the Army Pageant in London had placed an order in York for the production of plate-armour.[70] York's expertise also benefited Scarborough, where a meeting of the pageant's Properties and Armour Committee was addressed by Colonel Dittmas, who had played an important role at York. Scarborough also displayed some of its armour – and weapons and costumes too – at a public meeting intended to stimulate additional interest in the pageant.[71]

Music was also produced on a large scale, and dancing featured in numerous pageants. The music involved many local people, not only as performers – even the small pageant at Pickering had an orchestra, as did Scarborough, and choirs often performed – but also as composers, arrangers and musical directors. At Thirsk in 1907 the incidental music was composed and arranged by the organist of the parish church, A. J. Todd; two years later at York the Minster's organist, Tertius Noble, was 'master of the music' and also created some 'striking' compositions.[72] At Scarborough it was said that '[t]he music has received special attention, great pains having been taken to secure compositions synchronous with the varying times of the episodes. ... Altogether the music will hold a prominent place in the pageant.'[73] A competition was held to write the words for a special pageant song, 'The Song of Scarborough', to be sung during the epilogues; 30 entries were received.[74] Dances were of various types: at Scarborough, for example, a Flamborough sword dance and a morris dance were incorporated into one scene, while the hornpipe and 'Sir Roger de Coverley' were also performed. Sword dances were likewise a feature at Ripon in 1886, 1896 and 1906, with Ferrars making use of a team from Kirby Malzeard.[75] A lot of money and effort was spent on these aspects of pageants: more than £300 was spent on the music at Scarborough and almost £900 on music and dance at York.[76]

By contrast, pageants – at least in the period under consideration here – were often rather sparing when it came to artificial scenery, preferring to use existing outdoor settings. Parker insisted that '[w]ith the exception of a few stage trees, no scenery will be used in the York pageant'; the result, apparently, was that there was 'no incongruous sight to divert the play of the fancy'.[77] Hudson at Scarborough liked using the Castle headland for the pageant, not least because otherwise he would have had to erect 'a "property" castle, which would have been a most unsatisfactory and tawdry makeshift'.[78] Similarly, the existence of natural scenery in the grounds of Thirsk Hall added to the advantages of the pageant site.[79] It was felt that the authenticity of pageants was enhanced by their setting, and pageant-masters liked to depict events at or near the places where they had originally happened. This was the case at Helmsley in 1897 and 1898, where the pageant was staged at the castle.[80] Similarly, at York Parker believed that the Museum Gardens were the only suitable venue, as the pageant would depict the interdict laid by Archbishop Thurstan on St Mary's Abbey, the ruins of which lie in the gardens. The riot that ensued as a result of the interdict was thus to be theatrically re-enacted on the very site where it had originally occurred, nearly 800 years before.[81] Most pageants took place outdoors, and as a result much attention was devoted to the provision of covered seating in grandstands. The cost of this could in fact be one of the main expenses of a pageant. At Scarborough in 1912 the contract price was £2,799, but the actual cost eventually amounted to £3,163, the guarantors including this among their many criticisms of the financial management of the pageant.[82]

As should be clear from the foregoing, there were many different aspects to the organisation of a successful pageant. Probably the most important thing was having the right people in charge. The larger pageants needed both local people who knew the place, its population and its history, and an expert pageant-master whose role was multifaceted. Where the pageant-master was often absent, as happened with D'Arcy Ferrars at Thirsk in 1907, it was vital that a competent local deputy was available – in the case of Thirsk this was Gilbert Hudson, who later produced the Pickering and Scarborough pageants. The enthusiastic involvement of as many members of the local community as possible was also important if a scheme were to succeed. This was just as true in Yorkshire as in the pageants staged elsewhere in the early twentieth century, as Yoshino has emphasised.[83]

Judging success

Just as pageants were often inspired by a combination of motives, so too the success of a pageant was often judged in a number of ways. Specific facets were often highlighted, as in a report of the Ripon festivities of 1896, which offered the opinion that 'from the point of view of historical accuracy as well as in the splendour and magnificence of costumes it was a decided and emphatic success'.[84] It was a source of particular pleasure where a pageant met with both artistic and financial success, as at Thirsk in 1907 and York two years later.[85] Although the educational value of historical pageants was often advanced as a reason for staging them, success was much less often assessed in educational terms, perhaps because this was something that was very difficult to measure. However, the Scarborough pageant was claimed by the Secretary, F. P. Morgan, to have been a success in this respect – possibly because he was trying to detract attention from the criticisms of the financial loss.[86]

Indeed, as Morgan's choice of emphasis suggests, it is clear that financial performance was a key consideration in contemporaneous judgements of the success – or otherwise – of an historical pageant. Full financial records are not always available, but local newspapers provide useful information in many cases. Indeed, it seems from such sources that most historical pageants in Yorkshire made a profit, although two in the period 1885–1912 did make a loss. In one case (Ripon in 1896), the deficit was only a small one; Scarborough's loss in 1912 was rather larger, standing at £1,758 5s. 2d. The bottom line mattered: financial success was regarded so highly that it was often referred to even before all the performances of a pageant had been staged. Thus, in the words of a report carried in the *Manchester Courier*: 'York Pageant opened yesterday, and, it is stated, is already a guaranteed financial success'.[87] Where a loss was made, as at Scarborough, people such as Morgan might suggest that other measures of success were more important, but such claims carried little conviction – as was demonstrated by the feelings expressed at a meeting of the guarantors after the July performances.[88]

Artistic considerations were also important when it came to gauging success. Ripon in 1886 was praised by the London press for its attempts to produce 'an elaborate artistic display'.[89] At York the colours of the costumes in some of the early episodes were said to be 'artistic in the extreme', while the song 'When Hilda built her holy well' was similarly lauded for its 'artistic' merit.[90] Hudson was appointed pageant-master at Scarborough at least in part because the Thirsk and Pickering pageants had been successful artistically, as well as in other ways. The resulting production in the town was also judged to have succeeded in this respect, even if not in others.[91] Pageants were intended to be spectacles, and they were judged as such. The Grimston Park pageant in 1885 was reported to be 'a magnificent spectacular display'.[92] Reflecting in 1896 on the 'great festival in August held at Fountains Abbey', the Middlesbrough *North-Eastern Daily Gazette* felt that 'the citizens of Ripon have cause to congratulate themselves … as far as "spectacular display" was concerned'.[93] This was an evident ambition of pageant-masters themselves. Parker described his own pageant at York in immodestly fulsome terms: '[a] greater pageant, a finer spectacle, or a more inspiring sight neither they nor anybody else in England would ever see in their lives, let them live as long as they might'.[94]

Contemporaries believed that a range of things worked towards making a pageant scheme successful. A key one was enthusiasm. This could be the enthusiasm of individuals, as at Ripon in 1896 when Tom Williamson, who originated the idea of that year's festival and was greatly involved in both preparations for the event and the actual performance,[95] was singled out for special praise in this respect. But it could also be a more generalised, place-specific sense of enthusiasm, as in York and its environs:

> The pageant has been taken up by the citizens of York and their immediate neighbours with the utmost enthusiasm, rich and poor, high and low, vieing [*sic*] with one another in their desire to bring about success.[96]

It was hoped at Scarborough that the enthusiasm displayed at York might be emulated.[97]

Organisation was also important if a pageant was to be successful; a great deal of hard work for a common cause was needed. This was referred to in reports of the events at Grimston Park in 1885 and Ripon in 1896.[98] At Pickering in 1910, 'the whole of the characters, and those connected with the Pageant, are to be complimented upon the amount of earnest work which has been put into the effort, to ensure its success'.[99] Similarly, at Scarborough it was said that '[t]he main thing seems to be to get a band of willing workers who do not count anything as a trouble that will help to ensure the ultimate success of the pageant'. That certainly happened: a report commented that 'a large percentage of the townspeople of Scarborough have been wrestling with the work of resuscitating the ancient and picturesque history of the place'.[100]

In addition to enthusiasm and hard work, pageants could derive much benefit from the support of prominent local people. Major R. Bell was the president of the Thirsk pageant, and he and his wife allowed the grounds of Thirsk Hall to be used for performances.[101] Important local civic figures were involved at Scarborough, as were the town's Liberal MP and the Conservative party's prospective parliamentary candidate.[102] Those who produced the performances also had much to do with a pageant's success, with Ferrars at Ripon, Hudson at Thirsk and Parker at York all being among those given great credit in this respect. In turn, such people often gave praise to those who had assisted them. Parker publicly 'paid a tribute to the quiet and unremitting work done by the officials of the pageant' and Hudson lauded the efforts of the secretaries at Pickering in 1910.[103]

Finally, there was one thing that no one could control: the weather. Matters meteorological were always a worry for those staging pageants, who were all too conscious of 'the drawback of inauspicious elements'. This, felt the *Huddersfield Daily Chronicle*, was 'the one disadvantage of all out-door displays in this country. The weather simply cannot be depended on'.[104] Many newspaper articles expressed the view that the only thing needed for the success of pageants was good weather.[105] However, as the people of Scarborough were reassured, it was possible to succeed should this be lacking, as Mrs Edwin Gray of York knew from experience: she had been President of the Ladies' Committee at York in 1909.[106] On that occasion rain had marred some of the performances, but it had affected the cast more than the large audiences, most of whom were accommodated under cover.[107] The performance on 29 June took place during two hours of pelting rain,

> But the actors put a good heart into their work all the same. They tried to forget the weather, and through the succeeding episodes they played with a zest and vivacity that won the unstinted plaudits of the onlookers, who were moved as much by admiration for the performers in their trial as by the undoubted merit of the scenes which they portrayed.[108]

At Thirsk, however, the two extra performances to raise money for a new cricket pavilion had to be postponed because of heavy downpours.[109] Scarborough was more fortunate with regard to rain, but the wind for which the headland is renowned did make it difficult to hear the performers' voices at times.[110]

How did Yorkshire pageants compare to those held elsewhere?

In many ways, pageants staged in Yorkshire were similar to those held elsewhere in the country. Numerous features of their organisation and reception would have been familiar to those who staged pageants in the south of England, Wales and Scotland: the importance of the pageant-master, the effort involved in costume- and prop-making, the role of music and dance, the financial arrangements and publicity, the emphasis on authenticity in casting and setting. Despite their sometimes intense focus on the locality in which they were performed, pageants everywhere had some striking similarities.

Yorkshire, however, can stake a claim to pioneering the modern-day historical pageant form. The performances at Grimston Park in 1885, Ripon in 1886 and 1896 and Helmsley in 1897 and 1898 pre-dated Parker's 'invention' of 1905. Many features later associated with Parker and the twentieth-century pageant tradition were already present at Ripon in 1886. Here, for example, the local museum collection was augmented by specially loaned items at the time of the pageant, something also done at Ferrars's Liverpool pageant in 1907.[111] Ferrars himself produced his last pageant in 1914 (at Worsley in Lancashire, with 1,000 performers); though hitherto neglected, he should be seen as an important influence on the twentieth-century historical pageant tradition. His deputy at Thirsk, Gilbert Hudson, continued as a pageant-master after the First World War, putting on performances at Berkhamsted in 1922 and back at Pickering in 1930.[112]

It is not always clear which elements of the earlier pageants of the 1880s and 1890s survived into the twentieth century, nor what impact they had on pageantry in Yorkshire or beyond. However, it is likely that the processional elements of the early Ferrars pageants were particularly influential in Yorkshire. The York pageant, for example, contained a number of processions, including one that ended the pageant to good effect: '[t]hen all the characters march past the grand stand four abreast and off the arena, the procession taking nearly twenty minutes to pass'.[113] The Pickering pageant also ended with a procession of the actors out of the arena, and many of the Scarborough scenes incorporated processions, a particularly effective one being that in the episode depicting the visit of Edward I to the town (Fig. 2.2).[114] Outwith the performance proper, a procession before or during the run of a pageant was a good way of drawing more attention to it; at Scarborough some of the cast marched from the venue to the Pageant House after one of the showings.[115] Indeed, the lack of just such a procession at York caused some dissatisfaction: it was argued that local people who could not afford tickets for the actual performances were being denied an opportunity to witness the costumed spectacle. Here it was decided, however – perhaps at the insistence of Parker – that '[t]here would be no appearance in costume outside the ground, for they intended to retain their dignity and preserve the religious aspect of the festival'.[116]

Another notable aspect of the pageants was the use of Yorkshire dialect. Other pageants, including Parker's at Sherborne, had used dialect,[117] and the regional variations in spoken English provided ample opportunity to emphasise the distinctiveness of the region in which a pageant was being performed. At Pickering in 1910, for example, dialect played a significant role in Scene 9, which portrayed the 'Opening of Pickering Fair':

> *One of Crowd:* Ma wod! Thomas, but thou's gotten yon heeäd o' thine full of summat; thou owt to join Master Turcock in't King's Parliament.
>
> *Another of Crowd*: Aye, it's weel filled wi sike stuff as ah cahn't tak in.[118]

At Scarborough two years later, dialect was similarly 'employed on various occasions to good effect'.[119] One such was Episode VI, which depicted Edward I holding his court at Scarborough. In this scene the king and his wife processed through the arena without uttering a word, but their subjects were anything but silent, with much dialect featuring in the words spoken by 'a motley crowd of townsfolk, and people from neighbouring villages'.[120] To give one example:

Figure 2.2 Edward I in the Scarborough Historical Pageant and Play of 1912. From 'A Pictorial Record of the Scarborough Historical Pageant 1912', album of photographs and memorabilia: Scarborough Museums Trust. Reproduced by kind permission of the Scarborough Museums Trust.

1st woman. Noo, then, what's ta beealing oot lyke that for? Ho'd thi noise or Ah'll takt tha yam an' thoo weant see t'King.

1st boy. Yon lad bunched ma!

2nd boy. Ah didna bunch tha!

1st boy. Thoo's a leear, thoo is! Ah'll gie tha a cloot ower t'heead.

2nd boy. Happen thoo'll git yan thisen. Thoo blubbing babby, 'twas nobbut yon lahtle lass as bunched tha.

Children. Babby, babby buntin! (*Laughter.*)

2nd woman. Ah'll gie ya sike a lamming if ya deeant gi'e ower at yance, Ya shan't see t'King, noan o ya.[121]

Later, in the eighteenth-century miscellany that comprised Episode XIV, dialect was used again:

Mrs. Helperby. Well, ah niver! ti mak up all that grand poytry out of his awn 'eead. Eh! what it is to be a scholard!

Helperby. A scholar! Ger away with tha! Why e's 'ad it off these fower year an' all. What Ezzy Good-fer-nought, still 'inging about deein nowt? Gie us a 'and wi' t'stall and I'll gie yer tupence.

Ezekiel. Ah isn't goin' to tew mysen for tupence.[122]

As these examples show, the use of dialect was, at least in part, intended to add humour to pageants. More generally, however, it was a potent means of asserting the particularity of local identity while also adding to the sense of authenticity of the past that was being performed.

Of course, pageants' focus on local history was itself an opportunity to emphasise local and regional distinctiveness, although – as others have argued – a key aspect of this was a tendency to depict events in which the locality had played an important part in the national story. Yorkshire pageants were typical in this respect, portraying, for example, the capture of Piers de Gaveston in 1312 (Scarborough), the visit of Henry VIII in 1541 (York) and the Spanish Armada (Thirsk and Pickering). A pronounced local slant was sometimes given to the presentation of such events – and the larger history with which they were associated – in pageant performances. One Yorkshire example was the particularly negative portrayal of the state of northern England at the time of Domesday. At Thirsk a Saxon chorus bewailed the depredations of their Norman overlords, while at Pickering the same events were accompanied by the 'English Lament'.[123] Pageants everywhere offered the opportunity to merge major historical themes with local anecdote, myth and custom. For example, the episode at Scarborough illustrating religious differences in the reign of James II featured the tossing of the mayor of the time in a blanket – something which had actually happened, and which evoked hearty laughter when re-enacted in the pageant.[124] Yet the periods covered by the historical pageants of these years were much the same across England: in Yorkshire as elsewhere, they generally covered nothing later than the sixteenth century (Thirsk, Pickering) or the Civil War (York). Overall, the similarities between Yorkshire pageants and those staged in other places are much greater and more important than the differences. As such they are case studies in the wider development of historical pageantry in this period, albeit ones that have been hitherto overlooked in the historiography.

Conclusion

In the years before the First World War many thousands of people participated in historical pageants in Yorkshire, and many thousands more enjoyed watching them. These pageants provided an opportunity for people, women as well as men, to work together for the common good and promote their locality, as well as to derive enjoyment from the process and raise money for worthy causes. These early pageants were concentrated in the North Riding. There were pageants elsewhere in the county – such as the one at Woodsome, near Huddersfield, in 1906 – but these have left fewer records. It is therefore difficult to find out much about them, but they are likely to have been quite small-scale affairs.

After the First World War many more pageants were staged in Yorkshire and in the interwar period the geographical spread was much greater, although it seems that fewer were staged in the East Riding. Settlements of varying sizes had their pageants, varying from small villages such as Rillington (1927) and Ripley (1930), through towns like Pickering (1930) and Harrogate (1931), to larger urban centres such as Bradford (1931) and Wakefield (1933). The pre-war reasons for holding pageants still applied, but there were also new ones, such as the desire to boost local economies at a time of economic depression – something regarded as very important at both Bradford and Wakefield, to take two examples.[125] 'Pageantitis' clearly continued to affect Yorkshire during this period, just as it had done before 1914.

Notes

1. *Yorkshire Evening Post*, 21 July 1909, 5; *Scarborough Mercury*, 12 July 1912, 7.
2. *Whitby Gazette*, 19 July 1907, 7; *Yorkshire Gazette*, 20 August 1910, 6.
3. Ayako Yoshino, *Pageant Fever: Local History and Consumerism in Edwardian England* (Tokyo: Waseda University Press, 2011).
4. 'The Redress of the Past: Historical Pageants in Britain', http://www.historicalpageants.ac.uk/ (accessed 28 June 2019).
5. 'Scarborough Historical Pageant', http://www.historicalpageants.ac.uk/events/exhibition-scarborough-historical-pageant/ (accessed 28 June 2019).
6. *The Times*, 17 May 1930, 13.
7. This is clear from a newspaper report in a scrapbook in the possession of Thirsk Museum; unfortunately, it is not stated which newspaper it is from.
8. *Yorkshire Gazette*, 16 March 1907, 2
9. *Scarborough Mercury*, 5 May 1911, 9.
10. *Whitby Gazette*, 12 November 1909, 5; *Scarborough Mercury*, 3 March 1911, 7; *Scarborough Mercury*, 24 February 1911, 7; *Yorkshire Gazette*, 20 August 1910, 6.
11. *Yorkshire Post*, 3 August 1885, 5; *Daily Mail* (Hull), 29 August 1912, 4.
12. Yoshino, *Pageant Fever*, 59.
13. Michael Dobson, 'The Pageant of History: Staging the Local Past, 1905–39', in *Filming and Performing Renaissance History*, ed. Mark Thornton Burnett and Adrian Streete (Basingstoke: Palgrave Macmillan, 2011), 164.
14. *Daily Mail* (Hull), 6 April 1909, 3; *Scarborough Mercury*, 5 May 1911, 9; Yoshino, *Pageant Fever*, chapter 2.
15. *The Thirsk Historical Play* (Thirsk: Z. Wright, 1907), n.p.
16. For a more general discussion of pageants and anniversary celebrations, see Angela Bartie, Linda Fleming, Mark Freeman, Tom Hulme and Paul Readman, 'Commemoration through Dramatic Performance: Historical Pageants and the Age of Anniversaries, 1905–1920', in *The Age of Anniversaries: The Cult of Commemoration, 1895–1925*, ed. T. G. Otte (Abingdon and New York: Routledge, 2018), 195–218.
17. *Mr. Parker's Addresses* (York: The *Yorkshire Herald* Newspaper Co., Ltd., 1909), 5.
18. *Yorkshire Post*, 25 May 1911, 5.
19. *Mr. Parker's Addresses*, 5.
20. *The Book of the Pickering Pageant (Or Historical Play)* (Pickering: Boak & Sons, 1910), iii.
21. *Mr. Parker's Addresses*, 8.
22. *Scarborough Mercury*, 16 February 1912, 5, 10.
23. *Malton Gazette*, 16 July 1898, 5.
24. *Scarborough Mercury*, 24 February 1911, 7.
25. *Yorkshire Post*, 20 April 1907, 8; *Yorkshire Post*, 23 October 1908, 9; *Yorkshire Post*, 17 May 1907, 4.
26. *Scarborough Mercury*, 26 May 1911, 3.
27. *Mr. Parker's Addresses*; *Scarborough Historical Pageant & Play Souvenir* (York: Ben Johnson & Company, 1912), n.p.
28. *Yorkshire Evening Post*, 3 May 1911, 5.
29. *Yorkshire Evening Post*, 21 January 1909, 6.
30. Mary Kelly, *How to Make a Pageant* (London: Sir I. Pitman & Sons, 1936), 53.
31. 'Grand Pageant in Grimston Park', *York Herald*, 2 September 1885, 6. This individual's name appears in different versions – Ferrars, Ferrers, Ferris. I have used Ferrars, the version under which he appears in the *Oxford Dictionary of National Biography*: Roy Judge, 'Ferrars, Ernest Richard D'Arcy de (1855–1929)', *Oxford Dictionary of National Biography* (Oxford: Oxford University Press, 2004).
32. *Yorkshire Gazette*, 12 June 1909, 4; *Yorkshire Gazette*, 29 June 1912, 4; Mark Freeman, 'The Thirsk Historical Play of 1907', http://www.historicalpageants.ac.uk/featured-pageants/thirsk-historical-play-1907/ (accessed 28 June 2019); *Yorkshire Gazette*, 29 June,1907, 2.
33. *Yorkshire Post*, 7 February 1908, 7; *Yorkshire Post*, 25 May 1911, 5; *Yorkshire Gazette*, 1 May 1909, 8.
34. *Yorkshire Gazette*, 13 August 1910, 3; *Yorkshire Evening Post*, 28 October 1911, 5.

35. *Scarborough Mercury*, 10 November 1911, 8.
36. *Scarborough Mercury*, 26 May 1911, 3.
37. *Whitby Gazette*, 10 May 1912, 3.
38. *Yorkshire Evening Post*, 13 May 1909, 4; *Yorkshire Post*, 27 July 1909, 7; *Yorkshire Evening Post*, 28 July 1909, 4; *Yorkshire Evening Post*, 30 July 1909, 5.
39. *Yorkshire Post*, 23 October 1908, 9; *Yorkshire Evening Post*, 21 January 1909, 6.
40. *Yorkshire Gazette*, 13 August 1910, 3; *Scarborough Mercury*, 24 November 1911, 9; *Scarborough Mercury*, 8 December 1911, 9.
41. *Scarborough Mercury*, 5 May 1911, 9.
42. *Yorkshire Evening Post*, 24 February 1908, 6; *Scarborough Historical Pageant & Play*.
43. *Yorkshire Evening Post*, 30 October 1909, 5.
44. *Scarborough Mercury*, 4 October 1912, 6.
45. *Yorkshire Post*, 12 August 1913, 9; *Yorkshire Post*, 28 August 1909, 3; *Yorkshire Gazette*, 27 August 1910, 7.
46. *Yorkshire Herald and York Herald*, 19 June 1896, 3; *Yorkshire Herald and York Herald*, 19 June 1896, 3; *Yorkshire Post*, 23 October 1908, 9.
47. *Yorkshire Post*, 20 April 1907, 8; *Scarborough Mercury*, 19 May 1911, 7.
48. *Scarborough Mercury*, 26 May 1911, 3
49. *Leeds Mercury*, 2 June 1896, 3.
50. *Scarborough Mercury*, 6 October 1911, 3.
51. *Yorkshire Evening Post*, 14 August 1909, 4.
52. *Scarborough Mercury*, 21 June 1912, 10; *Whitby Gazette*, 3 August 1912, 8.
53. *Whitby Gazette*, 19 July 1907, 10.
54. *Yorkshire Gazette*, 13 February 1909, 5.
55. *Yorkshire Gazette*, 8 May 1909, 8.
56. Angela Bartie, Linda Fleming, Mark Freeman, Tom Hulme, Alexander Hutton and Paul Readman, '"History Taught in the Pageant Way": Education and Historical Performance in Twentieth-Century Britain', *History of Education* 48 (2019): 156–79.
57. *Yorkshire Evening Post*, 21 January 1909, 6; *Yorkshire Post*, 27 July 1909, 7.
58. *Leeds Mercury*, 5 August 1896, 3; *Yorkshire Evening Post*, 18 August 1896, 4.
59. *Yorkshire Post*, 10 February 1909, 8.
60. *Scarborough Mercury*, 26 May 1911, 7; *Scarborough Mercury*, 26 January 1912, 2; *Yorkshire Post*, 16 February 1912, 8; *Scarborough Mercury*, 26 April 1912, 5.
61. *Yorkshire Evening Post*, 14 May 1909, 4.
62. *Yorkshire Evening Post*, 27 July 1909, 4.
63. *Whitby Gazette*, 10 May 1912, 3.
64. *Yorkshire Evening Post*, 28 July 1909, 5.
65. *Yorkshire Gazette*, 8 May 1909, 4.
66. *Scarborough Historical Pageant & Play*.
67. *Scarborough Mercury*, 6 October 1911, 7.
68. *Yorkshire Post*, 20 August 1908, 4.
69. *Yorkshire Evening Post*, 17 December 1908, 5.
70. *Yorkshire Post*, 14 February 1910, 4.
71. *Scarborough Mercury*, 10 November 1911, 12; *Scarborough Mercury*, 26 January 1912, 2.
72. *Whitby Gazette*, 19 July 1907, 10; *Harrogate Advertiser*, 24 July 1909, 5.
73. *Yorkshire Gazette*, 29 June 1912, 4.
74. *Scarborough Mercury*, 24 November 1911, 7; *Scarborough Mercury*, 5 January 1912, 10. The text of 'The Song of Scarborough' can be seen in Angela Bartie, Linda Fleming, Mark Freeman, Tom Hulme, Alex Hutton, Paul Readman, 'Scarborough Historical Pageant and Play', *The Redress of the Past*, http://www.historicalpageants.ac.uk/pageants/1527/ (accessed 28 June 2019).
75. *Manchester Guardian*, 10 July 1912, 4; Judge, 'Ferrars'.
76. Bartie et al., 'Scarborough Historical Pageant and Play'; Angela Bartie, Linda Fleming, Mark Freeman, Tom Hulme, Alex Hutton, Paul Readman, 'The York Pageant', *The Redress of the Past*, http://www.historicalpageants.ac.uk/pageants/1354/ (accessed 28 June 2019).
77. *Yorkshire Evening Post*, 19 March 1909, 4; *Manchester Guardian*, 23 July 1909, 14.
78. *Scarborough Mercury*, 6 October 1911, 7.
79. *Yorkshire Gazette*, 29 June 1907, 2.

80. *Northern Echo*, 2 September 1897, 3; *Yorkshire Evening Post*, 25 June 1898, 3. For further commentary on the relationship between pageants' authenticity and their setting, see Bartie et al., '"History Taught in the Pageant Way"', 170.
81. *Yorkshire Post*, 30 November 1907, 13; *Yorkshire Gazette*, 8 May 1909, 4.
82. *Whitby Gazette*, 12 July 1912, 8; *Whitby Gazette*, 16 March 1912, 8; *Scarborough Mercury*, 4 October 1912, 6; *Whitby Gazette*, 9 August 1912, 4.
83. Yoshino, *Pageant Fever*, esp. chapter 5.
84. *Yorkshire Evening Post*, 18 August 1896, 4.
85. *Whitby Gazette*, 19 July 1907, 10; *Yorkshire Evening Post*, 28 July 1909, 5; *Yorkshire Post*, 19 August 1918, 4.
86. *Scarborough Mercury*, 2 August 1912, 7.
87. *Manchester Courier*, 27 July 1909, 6.
88. *Yorkshire Post*, 28 September 1912, 11; *Scarborough Mercury*, Friday 2 August 1912, 7.
89. *Standard* (London), 26 August 1886, 2.
90. *Yorkshire Evening Post*, 24 July 1909, 4; *Yorkshire Evening Post*, 7 August 1909, 3; *Yorkshire Evening Post*, 28 July 1909, 5.
91. *Scarborough Mercury*, 26 May 1911, 3; *Scarborough Mercury*, 2 August 1912, 7.
92. *York Herald*, 2 September 1885, 6.
93. *North-Eastern Daily Gazette* (Middlesbrough), 10 September 1896, 3.
94. *Yorkshire Post*, 9 December 1909, 8.
95. *Yorkshire Herald and York Herald*, 19 August 1896, 5; *Yorkshire Herald and York Herald*, 29 June 1896, 3; *Yorkshire Post*, 19 August 1896, 6.
96. *Harrogate Advertiser*, 24 July 1909, 5.
97. *Scarborough Mercury*, 24 February 1911, 7.
98. *York Herald*, 2 September 1885, 6; *Northern Echo* (Durham), 19 August 1896, 3.
99. *Whitby Gazette*, 12 August 1910, 3.
100. *Scarborough Mercury*, 6 October 1911, 7; *Yorkshire Evening Post*, 9 July 1912, 4.
101. *Yorkshire Gazette*, 1 January 1907, 2.
102. *Scarborough Mercury*, 16 February 1912, 5; *Mercury* (Lichfield), 12 July 1912, 2.
103. *Leeds Mercury*, 30 August 1886, 8; *Yorkshire Gazette*, 29 June 1907, 2; *Harrogate Advertiser*, 24 July 1909, 5; *Yorkshire Post*, 9 December 1909, 8; *Yorkshire Gazette*, 13 August 1910, 3.
104. *Huddersfield Daily Chronicle*, 24 August 1896, 3, referring to the Ripon festivities.
105. *York Herald*, 25 August 1886, 3; *Yorkshire Gazette*, 16 March 1907, 2.
106. *Scarborough Mercury*, 26 May 1911, 3.
107. *Yorkshire Post*, 23 July 1909, 7.
108. *Yorkshire Post*, 30 July 1909, 6.
109. *Yorkshire Gazette*, 6 July 1907, 3.
110. *Scarborough Mercury*, 12 July 1912, 10.
111. *Yorkshire Post*, 26 August 1886, 7; *Scotsman*, 13 July 1907, 10.
112. Laura Carter, 'Berkhamsted Pageant Play, 1922', *The Redress of the Past*, http://www.historicalpageants.ac.uk/pageants/991/ Angela Bartie, Linda Fleming, Mark Freeman, Tom Hulme, Alex Hutton, Paul Readman, 'Pickering Rural Deanery Church Pageant', *The Redress of the Past*, http://www.historicalpageants.ac.uk/pageants/1163/ (both accessed 28 June 2019).
113. *Yorkshire Post*, 22 July 1909, 7.
114. *Yorkshire Gazette*, 13 August 1910, 3; *Scarborough Mercury*, 12 July 1912, 10.
115. *Scarborough Mercury*, 19 July 1912, 3.
116. *Yorkshire Evening Post*, 16 April 1909, 8; *Yorkshire Post*, 7 February 1908, 7.
117. *The Times*, 13 June 1905, 4.
118. *Book of the Pickering Pageant*, 30.
119. *Scarborough Mercury*, 6 October 1911, 7.
120. *Scarborough Historical Pageant and Play ... Book of Words* (Scarborough, 1912), 31.
121. *Scarborough Historical Pageant and Play ... Book of Words*, 31–32.
122. *Scarborough Historical Pageant and Play ... Book of Words*, 70.
123. Angela Bartie, Linda Fleming, Mark Freeman, Tom Hulme, Alexander Hutton and Paul Readman, 'Historical Pageants and the Medieval Past in Twentieth-Century England', *English Historical Review* 563 (2018): 876–7.
124. *Scarborough Mercury*, 12 July 1912, 10.

125. Ayako Yoshino, 'The Bradford Pageant of 1931', http://www.historicalpageants.ac.uk/featured-pageants/bradford-pageant-1931/ Angela Bartie, Linda Fleming, Mark Freeman, Tom Hulme, Alex Hutton, Paul Readman, 'Historical Pageant of Bradford', The Redress of the Past, http://www.historicalpageants.ac.uk/pageants/1000/ Angela Bartie, Linda Fleming, Mark Freeman, Tom Hulme, Alex Hutton, Paul Readman, 'The Pageant of Wakefield and the West Riding', The Redress of the Past, http://www.historicalpageants.ac.uk/pageants/1227/ (all accessed 28 June 2019).

Bibliography

Bartie, Angela, Fleming, Linda, Freeman, Mark, Hulme, Tom, Hutton, Alexander and Readman, Paul. 2019. '"History Taught in the Pageant Way": Education and Historical Performance in Twentieth-Century Britain', *History of Education* 48: 156–79.

Bartie, Angela, Fleming, Linda, Freeman, Mark, Hulme, Tom and Readman, Paul. 2018. 'Commemoration through Dramatic Performance: Historical Pageants and the Age of Anniversaries, 1905–1920', in *The Age of Anniversaries: The Cult of Commemoration, 1895–1925*, edited by T. G. Otte. Abingdon and New York: Routledge, 195–218.

Dobson, Michael. 2011. 'The Pageant of History: Staging the Local Past, 1905–39', in *Filming and Performing Renaissance History*, edited by Mark Thornton Burnett and Adrian Streete. Basingstoke: Palgrave Macmillan, 163–77.

Yoshino, Ayako. 2011. *Pageant Fever: Local History and Consumerism in Edwardian England*. Tokyo: Waseda University Press.

3 A National Church Tells its Story: The English Church Pageant of 1909

Arthur Burns

The English Church Pageant of 1909 was nothing if not ambitious.[1] The opening night on 10 June commenced what was intended to be a run of six complete performances concluding on 16 June. This then was extended to nine, ending on 19 June, and by 12 June four additional evening shows had been arranged, each presenting half of the pageant and running from 21 to 24 June. There were thus in total 11 full performances.[2] Captain William Henry Waud, pageant steward-in-chief, estimated total attendance at 178,000, with a further 10,000 at least – another report claimed 70,000 – turned away disappointed.[3] Perhaps 11,000 musicians, performers and backstage hands participated and must be added to the audience numbers (though the two undoubtedly overlapped) in assessing the well-documented reach of the pageant.[4] What follows explores how this remarkable event reflected and engaged with a wider context beyond the pageantry movement. It also seeks to identify the nature of its intervention in contemporary debates more precisely than as an appeal to the past – and certainly not in a simplistic sense an 'invention of tradition' as a validating myth of origin.

We first need to understand the event's genesis and design. The English Church Pageant was the brainchild of Walter Marshall FSA (1859–1921), a Cambridge-educated antiquarian and archaeologist who was then (1907) vicar of St Patrick's, Hove, Sussex. He taught medieval church architecture in Oxford Extension lectures and was also a musician, with a particular interest in liturgical chant. In May 1908 Marshall proposed a pageant on a local Brighton football pitch to include scenes from the nation's ecclesiastical history, from the early British church up to the nineteenth century.[5] The scheme was developed under the guidance of Frank Lascelles – who had been responsible for the 1907 Oxford pageant and would become one of the most prolific pageant-masters of the age – although the pageant was eventually produced by Hugh Moss after Lascelles withdrew at the last minute. Its Executive Committee included M. R. James and Bishop George Forrest Browne of Bristol, but the most active members were William Henry St John Hope, Charles Reed Peers, Edward Earle Dorling, Clement Oswald Skilbeck and Percy Dearmer, with Arthur Croxton serving as literary secretary.[6] Both English Anglican archbishops, Randall Davidson and Cosmo Gordon Lang (like his predecessor, William Maclagan), served as patrons, and subcommittees were established to handle music, art, archaeology, history and costumes. In November 1908 Bishop Arthur Winnington-Ingram of London in effect took over the initiative, announcing that the pageant would now be staged in an elaborated version during the following June at his episcopal residence, Fulham Palace.[7] Modest sums might be raised for Church causes, but organisers insisted that the primary purpose was educational. This was just as well: after the pageant closed an embarrassed Winnington-Ingram publicly acknowledged that, though 'brilliantly successful as a spectacle', the event had been a financial failure. In consequence, the bishop negotiated a fee for the 1910 Army Pageant to reuse the pageant ground and its 6,500-capacity roofed grandstand (Fig. 3.1), built from more than 400 tons of wood and 45,000 ft^2 of corrugated iron. Costing £7,000 as it did, the grandstand partly explains the financial problems (it was optimistically advertised for sale in the pageant handbook).[8]

The grandstand reflected the pageant's scale. It was of such length that the main performances were staged in two parts. Members of the Executive Committee each 'devised'[9] scenes performed by different localities within the London diocese. Part One, starting at 3 p.m., covered the period up to the fourteenth century:

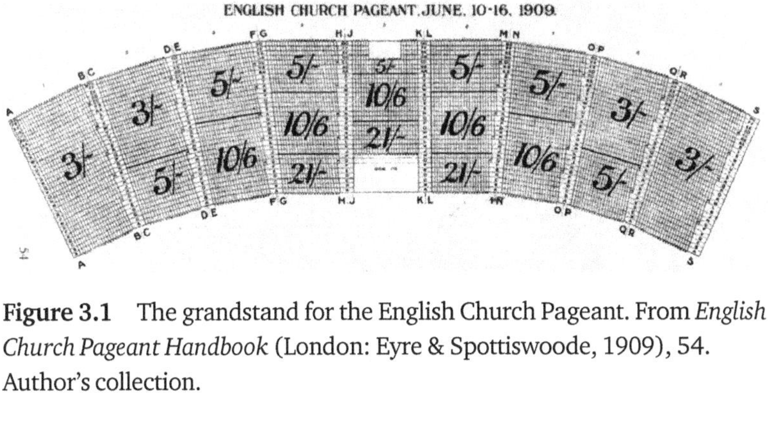

Figure 3.1 The grandstand for the English Church Pageant. From *English Church Pageant Handbook* (London: Eyre & Spottiswoode, 1909), 54. Author's collection.

The Prelude: The Founders of the Church (Saints George, Alban, Ninian, David, Patrick, Germans [*sic* Germanus], Ia) – written by Dearmer

1. *The Publication in Britain of the Edict of Constantine, 313* (at Silchester Church) – written by St John Hope; performers from the deanery of Westminster
2. *The Alleluya Victory, 430* – Dorling; the Welsh Church in London
3. *The Foundation of Iona by St Columba, 563* – Peers; deanery of Wimbledon
4. *The Coming of St Augustine, 597* – Dearmer; deanery of Hampstead
5. *Aidan and Oswald at Bamborough, c.635* – Skilbeck; parish of St Mary Abbot, Kensington
6. *Dunstan and the Monks, 964* – Peers; parish of Holy Trinity, Chelsea
7. *The Sacring of King William, 1066* – St John Hope; parish of St Peter, Eaton Square
8. *The Return and Murder of Thomas, Archbishop of Canterbury, 1170* – St John Hope; deanery of Willesden
9. *The Granting of the Great Charter, 1215* – Dorling; 'Blackheath'
10. *A Miracle Play and Pilgrimage Scene, c.1350* – Skilbeck; parish of All Saints, Margaret Street

Part Two, commencing at 8 p.m., took the story down to the eighteenth century:

1. *John Wycliffe at St Paul's, 1377* – Peers; deaneries of Hackney, Islington and Stoke Newington
2. *The Funeral Procession of King Henry V, 1422* – St John Hope and Dorling; the City of London
3. *The Refounding of King's College, Cambridge, 1446* – St John Hope; parish of St Mary Magdalen, Munster Square
4. *The Suppression of a Monastery and the Pilgrimage of Grace, 1536* – Peers; parish of St Stephen, Gloucester Road
5. *The Coronation Procession of Edward VI, 1547, and a Sermon by Latimer* – St John Hope; borough of Fulham
6. *The Consecration of Parker, 1559* – Dearmer; deanery of Lewisham
7. *Presentation of the Authorised Version of the Bible to James I, 1611* – Dearmer; deanery of Croydon
8. *The Execution of Archbishop Laud, 1645* – St John Hope and Dorling; parish of Clapham

9. *The Acquittal of the Seven Bishops, 1688* – Dorling; parishes of Putney and Wandsworth
10. *The Epilogue and Finale* (The Society for Promoting Christian Knowledge [1698], the Society for the Propagation of the Gospel [1701], the Methodist Revival, the Crusade against Slavery, the Evangelical Revival and Church Missionary Society [1799], 'Seven Immortal Churchmen of the Period' [Bishops Joseph Butler, Edmund Berkeley and Thomas Wilson; William Law, Samuel Johnson, Edmund Burke and William Cowper]) – Dearmer.

Marshall had originally envisaged 2,000 performers, but in the event 4,000 participated, all processing for a torchlit finale of Cecil B. DeMille proportions. *The Times* enthusiastically reported that 'the great host ... marched in a compact body stretching right across the ground, the glittering many-coloured mass brilliantly lit up by the tongues of fire which each of them carried'. The spectacle must have provided as enduring a memory for spectators as another gigantic vision in the Epilogue, that of a defiantly moustachioed G. K. Chesterton appearing as Dr Johnson. Less universally admired was the music, in which those on the pageant ground were assisted by a large choir and brass band. The impressive music advisory committee – Hugh Allen, Ralph Vaughan Williams and Barclay Squire[10] – opted for (dubiously) 'authentic' modal chants for the earlier scenes, which *The Times* judged 'apt to become tedious except to the ear of the purist', unlike the more palatable harmonies of later episodes. More popular was audience participation in communal hymn-singing, culminating in a rendition of the Nicene Creed to John Merbecke's then-familiar setting of 1550.[11]

Inclement weather throughout the run (1909 saw the wettest June for the best part of a century) caused problems, while insufficient rehearsal under Moss meant that the earlier scenes dragged at first (the first night did not end until 11.30 p.m.). One scene, the murder of Thomas Becket, proved so inadequate that it was cut.[12] Those who returned for later shows, however, saw a transformational improvement. Overall, press and spectators judged the pageant to be a success.

The English Church Pageant clearly reflects the contemporary fad for pageantry; indeed, it had close genealogical relationships both with earlier pageants such as the Chelsea Pageant of 1908, and those that followed, such as the Army Pageant. But the contemporary *ecclesiastical* context also matters. For the performances represented the leading part of a wider, co-ordinated intervention in discussion of the place of the Church of England in national life which had three other important components.

First there was the considerable press coverage, which owed much to the organisers' efforts to keep the pageant in the news from the outset. The original Brighton scheme received notice not only in the southeast and publications with a national reach, but across Britain in regional newspapers. Before the pageant was staged, interest focused on the practical preparations, the developing programme and casting calls. There was also, however, frequent discussion of the aims and argument of the pageant as articulated by its Executive Committee. Even the practical

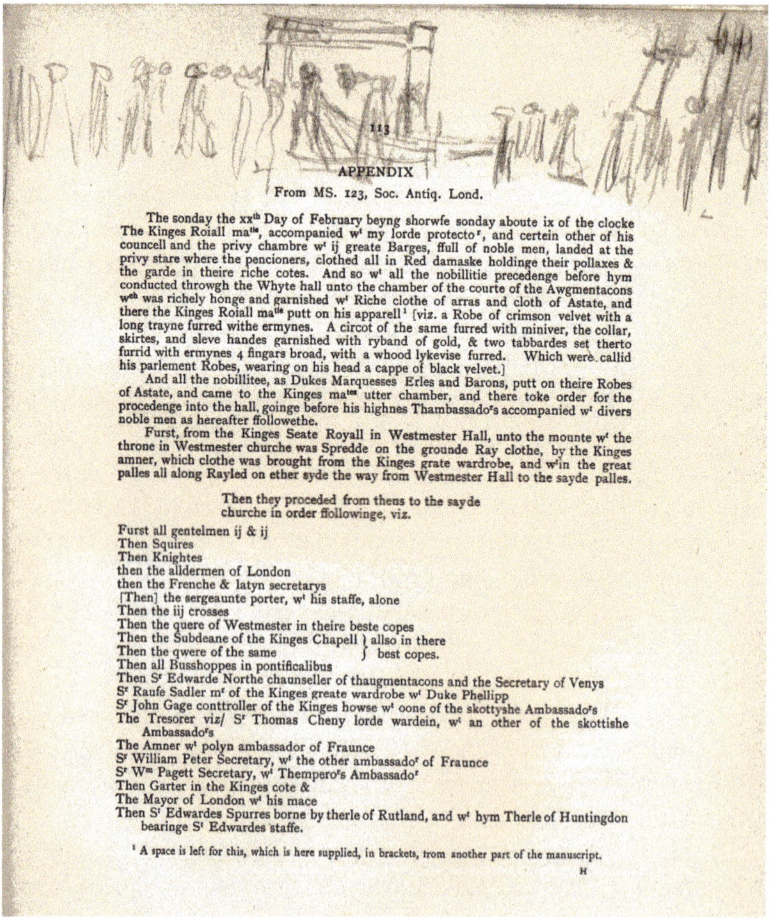

113

APPENDIX

From MS. 123, Soc. Antiq. Lond.

The sonday the xxth Day of February beyng shorwfe sonday aboute ix of the clocke The Kinges Roiall ma^{tie}, accompanied w^{t} my lorde protecto^{r}, and certein other of his councell and the privy chambre w^{t} ij greate Barges, ffull of noble men, landed at the privy stare where the pencioners, clothed all in Red damaske holdinge their pollaxes & the garde in theire riche cotes. And so w^{t} all the nobillitie precedenge before hym conducted throwgh the Whyte hall unto the chamber of the courte of the Awgmentacons wch was richely honge and garnished w^{t} Riche clothe of arras and cloth of Astate, and there the Kinges Roiall ma^{tie} putt on his apparell[1] [viz. a Robe of crimson velvet with a long trayne furred withe ermynes. A circot of the same furred with miniver, the collar, skirtes, and sleve handes garnished with ryband of gold, & two tabbardes set therto furrid with ermynes 4 fingars broad, with a whood lykevise furred. Which were callid his parlement Robes, wearing on his head a cappe of black velvet.]

And all the nobillitee, as Dukes Marquesses Erles and Barons, putt on theire Robes of Astate, and came to the Kinges ma^{tes} utter chamber, and there toke order for the procedenge into the hall, goinge before his highnes Thambassado^{r}s accompanied w^{t} divers noble men as hereafter ffollowethe.

Furst, from the Kinges Seate Royall in Westmester Hall, unto the mounte w^{t} the throne in Westmester churche was Spredde on the grounde Ray clothe, by the Kinges amner, which clothe was brought from the Kinges grate wardrobe, and w^{t}in the great palles all along Rayled on ether syde the way from Westmester Hall to the sayde palles.

Then they proceded from thens to the sayde churche in order ffollowinge, viz.

Furst all gentelmen ij & ij
Then Squires
Then Knightes
then the alldermen of London
then the Frenche & latyn secretarys
[Then] the sergeaunte porter, w^{t} his staffe, alone
Then the iij crosses
Then the quere of Westmester in theire beste copes
Then the Subdeane of the Kinges Chapell } allso in there
Then the qwere of the same } best copes.
Then all Busshoppes in pontificalibus
Then Sr Edwarde Northe chaunseller of thaugmentacons and the Secretary of Venys
Sr Raufe Sadler m^{r} of the Kinges greate wardrobe w^{t} Duke Phellipp
Sr John Gage conttroller of the Kinges howse w^{t} oone of the skottyshe Ambassado^{r}s
The Tresorer viz/ Sr Thomas Cheny lorde wardein, w^{t} an other of the skottishe Ambassado^{r}s
The Amner w^{t} polyn ambassador of Fraunce
Sr William Peter Secretary, w^{t} the other ambassado^{r} of Fraunce
Sr Wm Pagett Secretary, w^{t} Thempero^{r}s Ambassado^{r}
Then Garter in the Kinges cote &
The Mayor of London w^{t} his mace
Then St Edwardes Spurres borne by therle of Rutland, and w^{t} hym Therle of Huntingdon bearinge St Edwardes staffe.

[1] A space is left for this, which is here supplied, in brackets, from another part of the manuscript.

H

Figure 3.2 *English Church Pageant Handbook* (London: Eyre & Spottiswoode, 1909), showing a primary source included to accompany the staging of the coronation procession of Edward VI and a live sketch by the owner from 19 June 1909. Author's collection.

arrangements could make a point about the Church's relation to national life, as in discussion of the ethical sourcing of some 6,000 costumes from 'societies and other bodies whose object is the provision of work at fair wages to those who may otherwise be unemployed'.[13] Once the pageant opened, coverage of its content, audience reaction and associated comment and protest provided further opportunities to spread its message, with detailed accounts of the performances often being accompanied by illustrations, as in the *Illustrated London News* and the *Review of Reviews*, or the mass circulation *Daily Mirror* and *Daily Express*.[14]

Second, and most obvious, were satellite publications. Many pageants had related books, but the English Church Pageant came with an unusually large portfolio. First, there was a 60-page *English Church Pageant Handbook*, priced at 6d. and accommodating extensive advertising, both secular and ecclesiastical. This was in effect the programme, but was also issued weeks in advance as an advertisement and a recruiting tool for volunteers. It offered illustrated summaries of the scenes and the pageant's rationale, background articles on the preparations, endorsements from the Church authorities and suggestions for further reading. Those with deeper pockets, however, could splash out on a larger, 'sumptuous and admirably printed'[15] volume, confusingly bearing the same title but referred to as the *Book of the English Church Pageant*, priced at 2s. 6d. and running to 150 pages. Here the material from the *Handbook* was enhanced with more illustrations, cast lists and full texts of the scenes, along with the music used. In addition, key sources used in the preparation of the pageant were reproduced in full, such as the English Coronation Order employed in 1066 and William Laud's speech from the scaffold (Figs 3.2 and 3.4). This more elaborate volume could serve as both a *vade mecum* for the event and a lasting resource for the church-history enthusiast – a dual function apparent from a battered copy in the author's possession, in which 'on the spot' pencil sketches from the grandstand on the night of 19 June 1909 are accompanied by unrelated cuttings on church history, pasted in by an owner in the 1930s.

Another loose insert in this copy advertised a third publication: a flyer for Percy Dearmer's *Everyman's History of the English Church* (Fig. 3.3). Some 50,000 copies of Dearmer's book were printed to coincide with the pageant, being sold at Mowbray's pageant-ground stall. Lavishly illustrated (with some of its 100 pictures provided by the Pageant Committee), this 150-page volume priced at 1s. offered a 'clear, interesting and accurate' account of the history of English Christianity – backed up, as in the *Handbook*, by recommendations for further reading.[16] Finally, in 1910, there appeared the Rev. John Francis Kendall's

Short History of the Church of England, a 200-page work published by Adam & Charles Black at 7s. 6d. This was accurately summarised by the *Dublin Daily Express* as portraying '[t]he work of the Church of England in moulding and deepening the national character' through its 'influence ... upon the people of England' and 'only ... touch[ing] ... on the inner growth of its complicated organisation in so far as is necessary to explain changes in its outward influence'.[17] This volume also claimed to be the first book to publish colour photographs, those taken by Elliott and Fry at the pageant. Photography also served the pageant dissemination strategy through the extensive Rotary series of postcards of scenes and characters from the pageant. The steady stream of unused copies now available to purchase suggests that many of these found their way into collections rather than being used for communication.[18]

Finally, there were satellite events. Some were missionary or liturgical. Winnington-Ingram preached on the pageant to a packed opening communion service on 10 June at St Etheldreda's, Fulham.[19] On Sunday 13 June the Bishop of London's Evangelical Council organised a mission service on the pageant ground reportedly attended by 15,000–20,000 people; among them were territorial servicemen, the Boys' Brigade, the mayor and council of Fulham and, representing the royal family, Marie-Louise of Schleswig-Holstein.[20] A week later the Archbishop of Canterbury himself presided at a pageant-ground mass meeting organised by the Church of England Central Board of Missions. During this event some 8,000 attenders heard Archbishop Davidson describe the pageant as 'the best possible speech on the missionary cause', showing as it did how the nation had over time been fitted to witness God's cause, armed by 'the lessons of the past'.[21]

Other events were educational, directly supporting the didactic work of the pageant. Thus, in the weeks before the pageant Albert E. N. Simms, vicar of Grayshott in Surrey, delivered a series of five London University extension lectures on 'Turning Points in English History as Illustrated in the English Church Pageant' at Church House in Westminster;[22] in Croydon, that deanery's staging of the presentation of the Authorised Version to King James was re-enacted a few days after the pageant.[23] Later in the year the high-church historian and biographer Albert Clifton Kelway delivered an 'official' English Church Pageant lecture which his local newspaper reported as booked for 'various towns in Essex',[24] and late in 1910 magic lantern shows, featuring up to 70 slides depicting the pageant, were being staged at a variety of places and for various causes. A report of Mary Caroline Gorham's presentation of this material, as a prelude to slides of contemporary social church work in

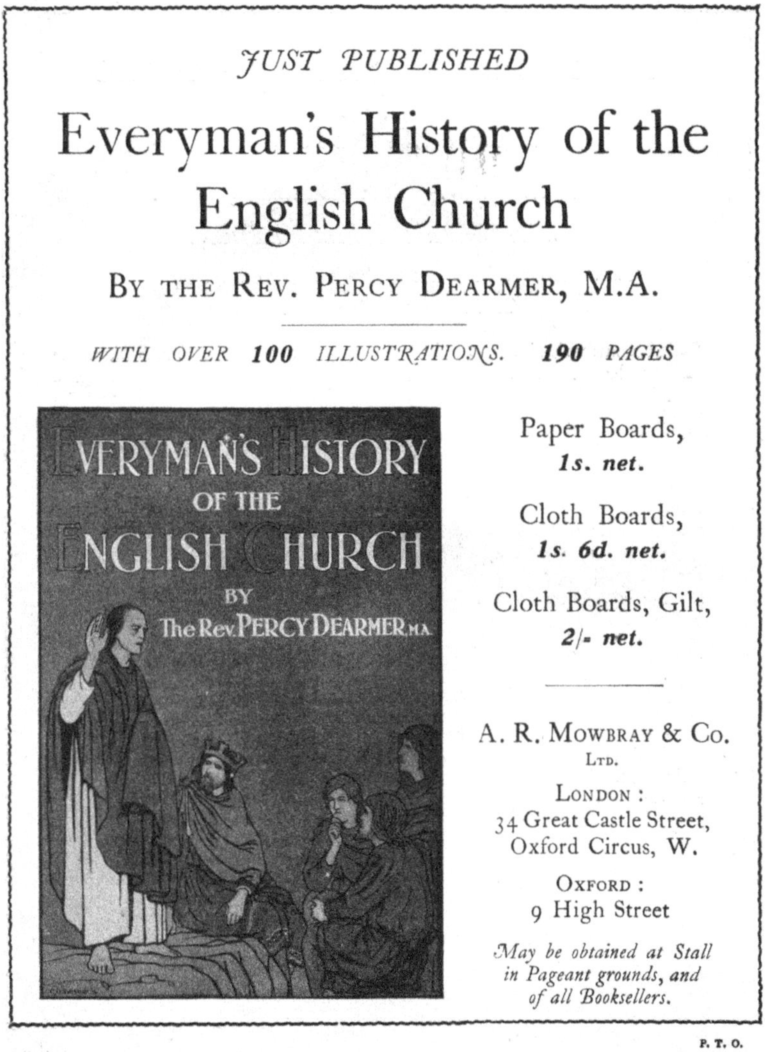

Figure 3.3 Flyer for Percy Dearmer, *Everyman's History of the English Church* (London: A. R. Mowbray, 1909), advertising its sale on the pageant ground. Author's collection.

November 1910 on behalf of Duxhurst Farm Colony for Inebriate Women in Surrey, described the evening as exciting great interest in its opportunity to view a 'vivid rendering of scenes of English Church history', especially as portrayed by 'so many well-known clergy and laymen from different parishes in London'.[25]

Although details of the contents and emphases varied, all these initiatives aligned with the aims and themes of the pageant – just as they did with its approach to spreading its message. It has already been suggested that these aims and themes were shaped by wider agendas than the requirements of pageantry, or of a general intention of promoting the Church. Rather, they addressed specifics of the situation of the Edwardian Church of England.

It is important to note that this situation was not one of crisis requiring urgent and unambiguous intervention on the Church's behalf. Indeed, a striking feature of the pageant, whose coverage of English Church history terminated at a safely pre-Tractarian moment in the eighteenth century, was that only one scene had immediate, pointed political relevance – and here it was as much a matter of casting as of content, and of its genesis. Initial plans included a scene of 'The foundation of the Cathedral Church of New Sarum' (1220). In February 1909, however, the Executive Committee claimed both to reflect its own instincts and a 'generally expressed desire', backed by Bishop John Owen of St David's, in substituting for the Salisbury scene a representation of the 'Alleluia' victory/battle of 429/30 AD. Germanus of Auxerre and Lupus of Troyes, in the wake of seeing off the Pelagian heresy, were shown leading unarmed Christian Celts to bloodless victory over a Pict and Saxon army through co-ordinated shouts of 'Alleluia'.[26]

It is hard to see the substitution of this scene, whose dubious historical credentials offered a painful contrast to the overall tenor of the pageant, as other than a pointed gesture towards the contemporary threat of Welsh disestablishment. Its significance was underlined by the choice of performers: members of the Welsh Church resident in London, who also furnished the choral forces for the closing 'Alleluias' and *Gloria Patri*. The scene was delivered in the Welsh language, with the pageant handbook providing a parallel translation for those defeated by this effort to achieve a 'real Kymric flavour'.[27] This feature, otherwise calculated to make the scene inaccessible to the bulk of the audience – '[i]n good modern Welsh, as I suppose, an ancient Briton spoke his fears of the savage Sassanach', recorded the *Church Times* reviewer – served to emphasise the authentic Welsh credentials of the established Church in Wales. No parallel effort was made to stage other medieval scenes in Latin, for example, though that language would at least have been familiar to a significant proportion of the audience.[28]

Pageant organisers desired the whole pageant to be genuinely educational. Along with commentators they repeatedly emphasised the potential of the pageant, and indeed pageantry more generally, as a pedagogic tool. Percy Dearmer wrote of the originator of the pageant, Walter Marshall, that '[i]n pageantry, reverently produced, he saw a vehicle of enormous power in educating through the eye and mind the people of the Country in the history of their Church'. Dearmer added that, in several respects, pageantry was more potent than print: '[w]e have lost the old quiet musing traditions; we live in an age of ignorant men who just can read that which had better not have been written'.[29] An editorial in *The Times* acknowledged that, although it was easy to poke fun, the pageant represented a resurrection of the medieval mode of combining amusement and instruction, and that, in contrast to most modern art forms, neither participation nor appreciation required specialised professional training, thus giving it an educational reach denied more sober productions.[30]

One person's education is another person's indoctrination. At first glance the Executive Committee's composition seems instructive here. Beyond Marshall, it was almost exclusively the preserve of lay and clerical high churchmen sharing an interest in liturgy and worship. Percy Dearmer, the maverick Primrose Hill parson responsible for *The English Hymnal* and *The Parson's Handbook*, wrote four scenes and an overall commentary for the *Pageant Handbook*. The other scenes were the work of the architect and archaeologist Charles Reed Peers, the heraldic writer E. E. Dorling, the artist Clement O. Skilbeck (who had published collections of continental altarpieces) and William St John Hope (1854–1919),[31] assistant secretary at the Society of Antiquaries from 1885 to 1910 and a powerful figure in antiquarian circles. Alongside Dearmer and Skilbeck, St John Hope was closely involved in the Alcuin Club founded in 1897 to promote the study of ceremonial – indeed his *English Altars* of 1899 was its first publication. Clerical costumes were supplied by a preferred high-church source of contemporary vestments, the St Dunstan's Society.

Lurking among the cast of thousands were also many well-known high-church figures, such as the Christian Socialist and member of Stewart Headlam's Church and Stage Guild J. G. Adderley. He had employed Dearmer as his assistant in Mayfair, and the pageant gave a perfect outlet to his theatrical inclinations (he appeared as St David in the Prelude, then again later as Bishop Luithard). There might thus appear grounds for characterising the pageant as a partisan, Ritualist attempt to 'invent' a 'tradition'[32] that would shift understandings of the Church of England in their direction – at a time when the legacy of the Oxford Movement was the subject of much debate within and outside the established church.[33]

This was certainly how some Protestant observers interpreted the pageant. John Alfred Kensit, who had succeeded his 'martyred' father as secretary of the Protestant Truth Society, was stirred into arranging a ‘Protestant Pageant Campaign’ during its first week. Four contingents of the anti-Catholic ‘Wickliffe preachers’ his father had established descended on Fulham for 100 open-air meetings. In these they protested that ‘some of the principal events of the Reformation’ had been omitted from the programme and that the whole enterprise amounted to a ‘glorification of vestments’. Winnington-Ingram was heckled on his arrival at the opening communion service, having earlier received a telegram from Kensit insisting that he distance himself from ‘popish idolatry’ and ‘the mass’. A ‘martyr commemoration’ demonstration on the middle Saturday on Eelbrook Common, about a mile from the pageant ground, was preceded by a Protestant procession from Hammersmith with ‘bands, banners, Orangemen, Boys Brigade and models of the rack, the iron maiden, the stake with chains and firewood and representations of other tortures’ – thereby giving the lie to Dearmer’s rather unconvincing excuse for the omission of scenes from Foxe’s *Book of Martyrs*, namely that burning at the stake could not easily be dramatically represented; he had, in any case, not shirked from including Laud’s beheading. Disorder ensued, and the police had to intervene.[34]

Related criticism could take less strident form. The *Review of Reviews*, edited by W. T. Stead, the scion of a Congregationalist manse, summarised the pageant as ‘a first-class funeral of Protestantism’, its contents a ‘travesty of history’. He argued that

> To make Wycliffe, the morning star of the Reformation, into a mere lay figure in a brawl in church was significant of a determination which found its ultimate expression in the scenes depicting the despoiling of the convents and the ‘martyrdom’ (Heaven save the mark!) of Archbishop Laud.[35]

A letter to the New York *Churchman* by the American Episcopalian minister Randolph Harrison McKim was later picked up by the British press. McKim suggested that any revival of the pageant should place more emphasis on the British church’s strength before Augustine imported Roman influences, and present more evidence – the Marian martyrs, Cranmer’s Bible, the Elizabethan settlement – ‘of the great religious revolution called the Reformation’. In the pageant McKim believed that ‘[t]he continuity of organization of the Church of England with the pre-Reformation Church was emphasized at the expense of that great breach of continuity in doctrine and ritual which took place in the sixteenth century’. The American quoted the evangelical dean of Canterbury, Henry Wace, who opined that

> The Pageant … at Fulham afforded lamentable illustration of the completely subordinate position which the Reformation now occupies in the minds of the Churchmen by whom it was organized.

He named the *Morning Post* and the *Graphic* as fellow critics.[36] Such issues may also have lain behind Lascelles' resignation from the project, as he explained it subsequently to the organisers of the Bath Pageant:

> They might be High Church or Low Church, but they were all members of the Church of England and it did not seem right to him … that different branches of the Church should not be represented on [the] Executive Committee. … That was the fundamental difference that existed.

However, his statement also hinted at issues of artistic control.[37]

Closer inspection nevertheless cautions against interpreting the pageant as a crude exercise in Anglo-Catholic propaganda. First, although cherishing ritual, the churchmen involved were generally concerned at the time to distance themselves from 'Ritualists' with a capital 'R' who sought to introduce Roman rites into the Church of England. Dearmer's aim was to recover a genuine English usage that was both superior to Roman forms and compatible with Anglican regulations; this was also the thrust of the Alcuin Club, formed 'to promote the study of the history and use of the Book of Common Prayer'.[38] Secondly, whatever their own allegiances, the organisers were determined that the pageant itself should be irenic and non-sectarian. It was this that secured them the backing not only of Winnington-Ingram (who could, depending on one's perspective, be regarded as either sufficiently Anglo-Catholic or sufficiently clueless[39] to have been immune to concern about Protestant reaction), but also of the Archbishop of Canterbury and a range of other bishops and dignitaries. And to counterbalance Protestant complaints about the programme, there were others, not necessarily high churchmen, who judged the pageant a judicious selection of historical events – even as some Anglo-Catholics found a number of scenes too 'Protestant', notably the expulsion of the secular canons from Winchester by Dunstan.[40]

Dearmer was precise about the educational effect that he personally sought from the pageant. So much is clear from his explanation of the pageant logo created for the *Book* and *Handbook* by the artist-designer George Edward Kruger (Fig. 3.4), which in 3D also appeared in the finale:

> [St George's] left hand is on the tiller, and he is looking backwards, for a sign that while the Church goes onwards ever she can look back across the centuries to a glorious past.

The rearward gaze mattered, because Dearmer believed that serious 'Church History … is hardly a factor in our present-day Civilization at all'. Instead, the public knew only 'false generalizations and crude prejudices'. The pageant was to be an 'ally to all who care to know and spread the truth about the historic Church of this country'; it would serve both to 'allay hatreds and prejudices, and [to] evoke loyalties'. Pageants, Dearmer felt, could

> only work in broad lines, but they can cut deep on those lines. They can stir the imagination. They can popularize the historic sense. They can point the way to future knowledge, and create the desire for it. … They can give proportion, balance, breadth. In a word they can educate.[41]

The English Church Pageant would seek to achieve its educational mission by correcting myth through scholarship. To a twenty-first-century eye, the role of antiquarians in the production can seem only too appropriate to the amateurish 'men-in-tights' aspects of pageantry. But this would be to ignore the intimate connections between late nineteenth-century

Figure 3.4 Front cover, *English Church Pageant Handbook* (London: Eyre & Spottiswoode, 1909), designed by George E. Kruger. Author's collection.

antiquarians and emergent academic history, especially in the Anglican context. Men such as Hope, Peers and Dorling were all stalwarts of the *Victoria County History*, for example. Dearmer indeed was quite clear that the emergence of the pageant as a viable didactic vehicle was dependent on the late nineteenth-century emergence of history as 'a genuine science'.[42] For him, in one sense, the presiding deities of the pageant were not theatrical men such as Lascelles and Moss. Rather they were writers such as John Richard Green and John Henry Overton, who were making serious history accessible to a wider public and whose works featured in the annotated reading lists provided in the *Book* and *Handbook*, alongside the scholars and editors publishing the original archival sources referenced or transcribed there. This was most apparent in the *Book of the English Church Pageant*, where the sources were reproduced to authenticate the action, not least its settings. Thus the opening scene featured a reconstruction of the Romano-British church recently excavated by St John Hope himself at Silchester, the conjectural plan of which was reproduced in the *Book* beneath a photograph of the excavation. Also featured was the Latin text of the edict of the emperors Constantine and Licinus, accompanied by a translation by the Camden professor of Ancient History at Oxford, Francis Haverfield (Figs. 3.2 and 3.5).[43]

How then best to characterise the pageant's historical argument? Initially, it is important to note that the spectacle was entitled not *The*

Figure 3.5 Rotary Photo postcard: Scene 1. The Publication of the Edict of Constantine, 313. The building recreates the Romano-British church excavated at Silchester in the 1890s by William St John Hope. Author's collection.

Church of England Pageant, but the English Church *Pageant*. The single most important message, reinforced through several devices, was of the inspiring and seamless continuity of Christian witness provided by the national Church, both pre- and post-Reformation. This was presented in a variety of ways. First, scenes did not, *pace* the title of Simms's associated lecture series, represent 'turning points' in English church history. The whole point was rather that they did not. Thus, as the critics noted, the Reformation was under-represented (no fires of Smithfield, for example); but then neither was the Synod of Whitby depicted, nor even the Restoration of Charles II – an unambiguously positive 'turning point' from the high-church perspective that some accused the pageant of adopting. Second, where scripts dramatised controversies, the text and commentaries went out of their way to avoid clear clashes between right and wrong. In the script for Part 1, Scene 6, for example, Dunstan was presented as facing an almost impossible choice between the English 'secular' model of monasticism and the Benedictine rule, rather than implementing what could be perceived as insensitive Romanising practices or purging corruption (although as actually staged a focus on abandoned families did shift the argument in a 'Protestant' direction).[44] Archbishop Laud was, as befitted one of Dearmer's heroes, presented as a martyr for decent worship in Part 2, Scene 8. However, he was also convicted of a temperament that destined him for the scaffold: according to the *Book*, 'he strode with a heavy foot over convictions that did not tally with his own', and was ultimately 'the victim, not less, perhaps, of his own austere and lofty character than of the triumphant malice of his enemies'.[45] Both Thomas Becket and Henry II had something to be said for them: 'there was right on both sides in that titanic struggle ... Henry ... was right in not letting the clergy slip outside the national system; on the other hand Thomas was right to resist the royal dictatorship in the name of the Church'.[46] The inclusive aim of seeking the best in different traditions was also apparent in the presentation of eighteenth-century Methodism in wholly positive terms, and the care taken to differentiate the seventeenth-century schismatic Puritans presented as harassing Laud from 'honest dissenters' seeking toleration outside the Church.

Third, the pageant stressed continuity above all in terms of the intricate and inextricable entanglement of the Church in the development of the wider English polity; indeed, several scenes had more claim to attention as part of national constitutional history than of that of the Church. There was little Christian militarism save for St George's clanking armour; in fact the military's main contribution was the striking fact that, until the scene was axed, three of the four actors responsible for portraying Becket's murderers were Major Christopher DSO, Major Finlayson and Lieutenant Bushell.[47] Instead, no fewer than three royal ceremonials were included with the sole purpose of demonstrating how the Church could appropriately handle such occasions.

At the same time this monarchical emphasis was counterbalanced by the finale of Act 1, the miracle play and pilgrimage for which the Christian Socialist Dearmer's commentary emphasised the guilds' status as medieval trade unions.[48] More generally, there was a Whiggish interpretation of the Church's role as godmother of English liberties, stressing its progressive tendency from Langton's role in Magna Carta to the abolition of slavery, a key emphasis in the finale. If these approaches to history might be expected, less so was the presentation of Becket, not as a 'high church' champion of clerical privilege, but as a man 'whose heroic … stand against the strong and terrible King laid the foundations for the free and united England that was to emerge'.[49]

This bigger national story was, of course, not new. This was rather the point. It is important for our broader understanding of the cultural work of pageants to recognise that this pageant at least was not an attempt to 'invent' a 'tradition' for the hegemonic purpose of manipulating the people with scant regard to historical accuracy.[50] Instead it was an attempt to employ historical scholarship to anchor the Church more firmly within an *existing*, widely diffused, indeed popular understanding of the national story, toning down its more dramatic polarisations and conflicts and nudging it in certain directions to enable the Church to take what the organisers believed to be its true place in an inclusive rather than divisive vision. The processes at work here, and the relations between 'popular(ising)' and professional/academic history that they imply, accord closely with those explored in Martha Vandrei's examination of Queen Boudica's place in British history-writing (though perhaps with an even more self-conscious dimension) rather than with the more simplistic suggestions of falsification, appropriation or distortion found in some earlier discussions of popular historical forms of the Romantic era and after.[51]

Why was this message seen as pertinent in 1909, and to whom did the pageant Executive Committee want to deliver it? One strength of the pageant, and of the variegated publishing programme that accompanied it, was that it offered a point of access to the arguments it sought to promote across a wide social spectrum. On the one hand, the pageant was a big enough event to attract 'movers and shakers' – bishops, royalty, Lloyd George, the London mayors and corporations. The professional middling classes also mattered: prices for the performances originally scheduled ran from 3s. to 21s. for one part and 5s. to 35s. for both. An indication of the organisers' rather elevated conception of the 'public' is given by plaintive demands that fashionable hats should not be allowed to spoil the view from the cheaper seats, and their declaration that the 'ignorance' of that public concerning Church history could be laid at the doors of the English public schools, whose alumni were probably one target of the university extension lectures.[52] Nevertheless it also mattered to both organisers and supporters that the pageant was accessible to a much wider constituency – hence the addition of the extra shows specifically targeted at poorer London parishioners, the conscious inclusion of the unemployed among the mass of performers and the delight of one observer in discovering slum children among the dancers.[53]

The target audience of the pageant project broadly considered was thus 'the people' as understood in terms of the 'nation', rather than a particular section of it. Why did 'the people' need this message? As I have argued elsewhere,[54] in the early nineteenth century the chief defence of the established position of the Church of England advanced by churchmen was the utilitarian/Burkean value of the Church as a guarantor of the social order and providential fortune of the state. This was a lesson that a reviving Toryism and a liberally-inflected Whiggism both took from the revolutionary ferment of the 1790s and the French Wars – one that was well-suited to the prevailing norms of reformist political argument in the early Victorian era.

As the political context changed, so did discursive practice. From the 1830s onwards, the legal and practical aspects of establishment came under sustained attack from a newly confident Dissenting community whose numerical strength came by mid-century to match that of Anglicanism. From this point on the Anglican leadership found itself required to abandon exposed political positions in what had become a denominationally pluralistic polity. In this context, to the state, establishment could seem a source of dissension and fragility rather than a source of stability and strength, making the old, state-focused utilitarianism harder to deploy in its defence.

Instead, the later nineteenth century saw Anglican apologists defend the established church as an emanation, guarantor and incarnation of national character and destiny, neatly encapsulated in Archdeacon William Emery's coinage in the Church Congress of 1885, 'the grand old national church of England'.[55] Rather than high theories of church and state (although it had important synergies with the Coleridgean and sub-Hegelian strands of Idealism associated with broad churchmen, and in particular T. H. Green), this language operated first and foremost in more everyday contexts. One key site was the antiquarian and guidebook literature which accompanied the rise of the parish church as heritage site. Its prevalence here was in part an inadvertent consequence of the much more polemical project of the Ecclesiologists – the Anglo-Catholic architectural movement promoting Gothic as the 'true' expression of Christian theology, which generated new knowledge and appreciation of the history of English church architecture.[56] This tradition, moreover, also lent itself to the theatrical: as the *Review of Reviews* noted in discussing the English Church Pageant, 'Protestantism … does not lend itself so well to pageantry as does Catholicism'.[57]

This approach was well adapted to the needs of the Church both externally and internally. Associating the Church with a patchily authoritarian state rather than the nation could no longer rally a politically variegated Anglican clergy, let alone the laity. In contrast, the rhetoric of national identity could accommodate not only liberal Anglicans who had pioneered it in the 1830s, but also low churchmen seeking to emphasise the Church's Protestantism, or high churchmen truffle-hunting increasingly improbably-named Cornish saints from the annals of the early English church.[58] It also sought to tie the Church into a popular understanding of English history from which it could be regarded as inseparable and which, at least in a party political sense, could be regarded as apolitical, or at least offering something to everyone. The various pageant projects – performance, commentary and offshoots – offer almost the definitive version of this narrative as it could be constructed from the Catholic wing of the Church. The latter's interest in history was here married to a more Protestant emphasis on liberty, and fused to a high Whiggish historical narrative refocused on the key conservative institution of the established church, which consequently sat easily with post-1867 Tory populism.[59]

Seeking alignment with the broad outlines of a national historical narrative might seem a failure of nerve for an institution such as the Church, which could be understood as being required to offer a witness against conventional wisdom. It should nevertheless be recognised that this was a bold move for an institution so imbricated with the state. Late Victorian Dissenters believed that it would not be long before the connection of church and state would be severed, and that a Free Church offered the ecclesiastical model best attuned to the Protestant liberty that defined the British polity. Their fears for that polity were only increased by the simultaneous revival in English Roman Catholic fortunes, as that Church claimed a new legitimacy for its adherents as citizens – most obviously asserted in the statement architecture of the new Westminster Cathedral (built 1895–1903). In this context, for Anglicanism to assert an organic relationship with the English nation made it easier for the voluntaryist Protestant and 'English' Catholic to justify intervention in the internal matters of the Church of England (as in anti-Ritualist agitation) in ways that otherwise seemed to contradict voluntaryist logic or the Catholic claim to be newly at ease in a pluralist nation. They could do so on the grounds that either the Protestant or the inclusive character of the national community which the Church of England now claimed to embody was in jeopardy through the Church's claim to an organic relation with the polity.

We earlier noted the interdenominational Kensitite Protestant protests against the pageant, and within a couple of years there was talk of a revisionist 'Free Church' pageant. But we should also note that the pageant provoked equally strong Roman Catholic reactions. Hostile reviews in the *Tablet* mocked the pageant's inadequacies of ritual, music and dress, and the 'Popeless continuity theory' it embodied. In April 1909 Monsignor Henry James Grosch (1860–1923), the Roman Catholic rector of St John's, Duncan Terrace, Islington, announced lectures on 'Pageants and their Purpose'; 'Half the truth worse than ______'; 'Collapse or Continuity'; 'England and the Popes'; 'Suggestions for another Scene'. A correspondent to the *Tablet* called for yet another ecclesiastical pageant, but this time a Catholic one,

> showing the true historical narrative of the Catholic Church from St. Augustine to the present day, showing the vicissitudes which the Church has gone through since the so-called 'Reformation' and then the gradual dawn of day culminating with the Catholic Emancipation Bill &c &c.[60]

Adopting a historicised rhetoric of the 'nation' thus created opportunities for opponents of both the Church of England and the pageant itself. Nonetheless it had important long-term and beneficial consequences for the future cultural authority of the institution in the new kind of national life made possible by democratisation, the rise of the mass media and the increasing speed of communications – and decisively accelerated in the early twentieth century by the psychological and social demands of total war. All these developments encouraged forms of cultural expression emphasising inclusiveness, collective national identity and a rootedness in national tradition. The fuzzy rhetoric of the 'grand old national church of England' would speak clearly to Baldwin's Britain and beyond. It would underpin a hegemonic place in the politico-religious culture for the Church of England until the end of the twentieth century, in which it could position itself as curating the religious expression of national identity even when that took a multidenominational, or even multireligious, form.[61]

In recent years, understandings of the timing and dynamics of British secularisation have changed dramatically. The focus of attention has shifted from the socio-economic developments of the nineteenth century to a range of social and cultural drivers operating in the twentieth, with many key developments occurring in the 1960s. In recent accounts of the institutional Church of England's contribution to English national life in the post-war era, written against the backdrop of this wider historiography, the role of the Church as 'curator' of major events in national life – not least of those with connections to the monarchy (for example, the death of Princess Diana) – has been a significant theme.[62] The Church's claim to this position in what was unquestionably in many other respects a secularising society still rested to a significant degree on assumptions derived from the argument for which, in an extended version, the English Church Pageant provided an early proving ground.

Notes

1. For other discussions, see Glyn Paflin, 'History for the People', *Church Times*, 8 May 2009, 19–21, which reproduces in colour the photographs by Elliott and Fry first published in J. F. Kendall, *A Short History of the Church* (London: A. & C. Black, 1910); Angela Bartie, Linda Fleming, Mark Freeman, Tom Hulme, Alex Hutton, Paul Readman, 'English Church Pageant', *Redress of the Past*, http://www.historicalpageants.ac.uk/pageants/1062/ (accessed 5 March 2018). The various newspapers cited in the notes were consulted using the following online digital resources: *The Times Digital Archive 1785–2012* (Gale); *The British Newspaper Archive* (Findmypast/British Library).
2. The total given on the pageants database omits the 17–19 June performances and assumes 21–4 June to be full performances.
3. *The Times*, 28 June 1909, 9; this surpassed Winnington-Ingram's pre-performance estimate of some 80,000 spectators (*The Times*, 9 June 1909, 12). Waud's total broke down into 20,000 visitors to dress rehearsals, 118,000 visitors to the first ten days and 40,000 to the last week. The Pageant Seating Committee reported that 10,000 more applications for the four extra performances had been received than the 24,000 that could be accommodated (*The Times*, 17 June 1909, 8). Another estimate for total attendance was 164,000 (14,000 at the dress rehearsals, 108,000 for the 18 full performances and 42,000 for the extra shows); this is from a report that claimed that 60,000–70,000 disappointed applicants for tickets could have sustained a month of performances (*Wells Journal*, 1 July 1909, 5). Such attendance encouraged plans for a revival in 1910, mixing existing and new scenes (see for example *Cambridge Independent Press*, 2 July 1909, 6). The financial woes which such a restaging in part intended to address, however, put paid to the idea.
4. Hugh Moss was presented with bound volumes containing some 11,000 names of 'participants': *Cambridge Independent Press*, 2 July 1909, 6; *Stage*, 1 July 1909, 15.
5. See report of Marshall's account in *The Times*, 13 May 1909, 4. See also *English Church Pageant Handbook*, ed. C. R. Peers (London: Eyre & Spottiswoode, 1909), ix. Peers's book shares both cover title and publication details with another, differently paginated, *English Church Pageant Handbook* (London: Eyre & Spottiswoode, 1909) containing overlapping but not identical contents. The former, however, carries the alternative title on its inner title page of *The Book of the*

English Church Pageant. Both are referenced below: to avoid confusion, the volume cited in this paragraph appears hereafter as *Book ECP*, with *Handbook ECP* referring to the second volume. Details of the initial membership of the Executive Committee are confused, with *The Times* list not matching that in the *Book ECP*.

6. James (1862–1936), author (especially of ghost stories), medievalist and provost of King's College, Cambridge; Browne (1833–1930), Disney professor of Archaeology at Cambridge (1887–92), suffragan bishop of Stepney (1895–7), alpinist and speleologist, historian of the early medieval church in England; Peers (1868–1952), architect and archaeologist, pupil of T. G. Jackson, architectural editor of the *Victoria County History* from 1903, inspector of historical monuments in the Ministry of Works from 1910; Dorling (1863–1943), FSA, curate of Ham, Surrey, former schoolmaster and vicar choral, author of *Heraldry of the Church*, served as chaplain in the First World War; Skilbeck (1865–1954), painter, designer, author and promotor of 'peasant crafts', associated with the pre-Raphaelites and friend of William Morris and Edward Burne Jones; Croxton (1866–1959), author and journalist, editor of *Tatler* (1906–8), and manager of the 11th edition of the *Encyclopaedia Britannica*, later manager of the London Coliseum. For Hope and Dearmer, see below.
7. *The Times*, 7 November 1908, 8.
8. For the grandstand, see *Handbook ECP*, 54–6; for the financial troubles, see *The Times*, 22 March 1910, 4. In addition, the bishop secured a commission on seats sold for the military show by churchmen seeking to bail out the ecclesiastical one. For the cost, see 'A Heavy Deficit', *Yorkshire Post and Intelligencer*, 1 October 1909, 7, which speculated that losses reflected the last-minute costs incurred once Moss had been brought in to direct.
9. Glossed in *Handbook ECP*, 27, as 'arranging' historical and archaeological details. Programme from *Book ECP*, xi–xiv.
10. Hugh Percy Allen (1869–1946), conductor of the Bach Choir, later professor of Music at Oxford and director of the Royal College of Music, described in his obituary in *The Times* as 'the acknowledged but unofficial head of the music profession in this country'; Ralph Vaughan Williams (1878–1952), then a rising composer, editor of *The English Hymnal*, 1904–6; W. Barclay Squire (1855–1927), musicologist and librarian at the British Museum.
11. For musical content, see *Book ECP*, xv–xvi; *The Times*, 11 June 1909, 9; *Church Times*¸ 18 June 1909, 841.
12. 'Pageants and Pageantry in Rainy Weather', *Review of Reviews* 40 (July 1909), 24: '[i]t was cruel – positively cruel – to see four thousand men, women and children splashing through the mud in Fulham Park while the rain rained ruthlessly hour after hour'. For useful full reviews, see *Church Times*, 18 June 1909, 841–2, and 25 June 1909, 858 ('Mr Dixon, who looks the part so well, cannot act a little bit, and the knights were terribly afraid of their own swords', 841); *Stage*, 17 June 1909, 17; *Athenaeum*, 19 June 1909, 729; *Saturday Review*, 12 June 1909, 745–7; *The Times*, 11 June 1909, 9 and 15 June 1909, 7; *Tablet*, 26 June 1909, 7.
13. See, for example, Walter Marshall to *The Times*, 14 January 1909, 7, and *Manchester Courier and Lancaster Advertiser*, 14 January 1909, 3. The vestments used in the production were the work of the St Dunstan's Society, recommended in Percy Dearmer's *The Parson's Handbook* (6th ed., London: Henry Frowde, 1907), 187, as making vestments 'under fair conditions'.
14. *llustrated London News*, 12 June 1909, 3; 'Pageants and Pageantry', 24–6; *Daily Mirror*, 11 and 12 June 1909; *Daily Express*, 3 June 1909.
15. *The Times*, 9 June 1909, 12.
16. Flier for Percy Dearmer, *Everyman's History of the English Church* (London: A. R. Mowbray, 1909), inserted in *Book ECP*, copy in author's possession. My copy of the book itself bears the dedication 'from Percy Dearmer, Vigil of the Church Pageant, 1909'.
17. *Dublin Daily Express*, 17 November 1910, 7. Kendall (1862–1931), incumbent of St Germain's chapel, Blackheath, Kent (1904–17); later principal and professor of History at Queen's College, London (1915–19).
18. Kendall, *Short History*. I have identified at least 15 different Rotary postcards and two others depicting the English Church Pageant. One, recently sold on e-Bay, sent by a spectator at a rehearsal, noted that those depicting general scenes were already sold out.
19. *Church Times*, 18 June 1909, 841.
20. See, for example, *Sheffield Evening Telegraph*, 14 June 1909, 4.
21. *Daily News*, 21 June 1909, 7.
22. *The Times*, 11 February 1909, 7; 2 March 1909, 10. Simms (1869–1952) campaigned for the Church League for Women's Suffrage.

23. *Croydon Advertiser and East Surrey Reporter*, 1 January 1910, 2, reporting on staging of 21 June 1909.
24. *Chelmsford Chronicle*, 26 November 1909, 5.
25. *South Bucks Standard*, 25 November 1910, 8 (High Wycombe). See also *Western Chronicle*, 11 November 1910, 6 (Duxhurst); *Dover Express*, 15 April 1910, 10 (Shepherdswell); *Western Chronicle*, 11 March 1910, 6 (Chard). For Gorham, see A. H. Neve, *The Tonbridge of Yesterday* (Tonbridge: Tonbridge Free Press, 1933), 168–9.
26. *The Times*, 1 February 1909, 19.
27. *The Times*, 1 February 1909, 19; *Book ECP*, Scene II; *Saturday Review*, 12 June 1909, 746.
28. *Church Times*, 18 June 1909, 841. In the *Book ECP* the contemporary resonance was emphasised by the insertion (facing p.28) of a colour plate of the coats of arms of the four modern Welsh Anglican sees (drawn by the scene's deviser, E. E. Dorling) in the middle of the script – inadvertently rendering the parallel translation unusable.
29. *Book ECP*, ix, 1.
30. *The Times*, 10 June 1909, 11.
31. See A. H. Thompson, rev. Bernard Nurse, 'Hope, Sir William Henry St John (1854–1919)', *Oxford Dictionary of National Biography* (Oxford: Oxford University Press, 2004).
32. In the classic sense defined by Eric Hobsbawm and Terence Ranger in *The Invention of Tradition*, ed. Hobsbawm and Ranger (Cambridge: Cambridge University Press, 1983).
33. From an extensive literature on Anglican Ritualism and the controversies around it, see for example John Shelton Reed, *Glorious Battle: The Cultural Politics of Victorian Anglo-Catholicism* (Nashville and London: Vanderbilt University Press, 1996); Nigel Yates, *Anglican Ritualism in Victorian Britain (1830–1910)* (Oxford: Oxford University Press, 1999); Martin Wellings, *Evangelicals Embattled: Responses of Evangelicals in the Church of England to Ritualism, Darwinism and Theological Liberalism (1890–1930)* (Carlisle: Paternoster Press, 1999): Paul Nicholls, *Khaki and the Confessional: A Study of a Religious Issue at the 1900 General Election in England* (Melbourne: Melbourne University Press, 2000); Bethany Kilcrease, *The Great Church Crisis and the End of English Erastianism, 1898–1906* (London and New York: Routledge, 2017).
34. *The Times*, 5 June 1909, 9; 9 June 1909, 2; 14 June 1909, 8; *Church Times*, 18 June 1909, 841; *Book ECP*, 16.
35. 'Pageants and Pageantry', 25. The scene was entitled the 'Execution' of Laud, and, according to the *Book ECP*, it was not described as a martyrdom in the performance. However, the introductory note to the scene in the same volume began 'William Laud, a martyr if ever there was one ... ': *Book ECP*¸ 135.
36. His letter reproduced in *Whitstable Times and Herne Bay Herald*, 21 August 1909, 3. Wace may have fed it to the Kent papers, since it also appeared in the *Canterbury Journal*.
37. See *Bath Chronicle and Weekly Gazette*, 10 June 1909, 5.
38. For the Alcuin Club, see Peter Jagger, *The Alcuin Club and its Publications: An Annotated Bibliography* (Norwich: Canterbury Press, rev. ed. 2012 [1987]).
39. Winnington-Ingram did not impress all his contemporaries as a deep thinker. For a balanced appraisal, see Jeremy Morris, 'Ingram, Arthur Foley Winnington- (1858–1946)', *Oxford Dictionary of National Biography*.
40. See *Church Times*, 18 June 1909, 841. This account indicates that Moss's staging departed from the scenario printed in the *Book ECP*. The setting of the frater at Winchester was replaced by an *al fresco* scene permitting more spectacle. The writer bemoaned what he regarded as a 'highly conjectural restoration of history' which was 'tawdry and theatrical in the worst sense'; it added an extended sequence at the end of the scene emphasising the disruption of families and Dunstan's authoritarianism, rather than a more nuanced resolution. There may have been some animus in his observation that the solemnity of the tableau was compromised by 'one little fellow squatting in an attitude which may be assumed in prayer at some Kensington churches – this was the work of the Kensington deanery – but which had other suggestions in the open'.
41. The *Book ECP*, vi, 2.
42. See James Kirby, *Historians and the Church of England: Religion and Historical Scholarship, 1870–1920* (Oxford: Oxford University Press, 2016); Dearmer in *Book ECP*, 1.
43. *Book ECP*, between 24–5, 152; *Handbook ECP*, 66–8.
44. See above, note 40.
45. *Book ECP*, 135, 136.
46. *Book ECP*, 8. Contrast the more one-sided treatment of the controversy in, for example, the near contemporaneous Conrad Noel, *Socialism in Church History* (London: Frank Palmer, 1910), 174–5.

47. *Book ECP*, xii. Only one other named part was taken by an individual identified as a serviceman, a Captain Garston who appeared as King Oswald. The only equivalent matching of player and part (save for the inevitable clerics playing clerics) came in the finale, when the founders of the Society for Promoting Christian Knowledge were portrayed by current staff: *Book ECP*, insert for corrections between 80 and 81.
48. *Book ECP*, 10.
49. *Book ECP*, 8.
50. For one example of such an interpretation of early twentieth-century pageantry, see Michael Woods, 'Performing Power: Local Politics and the Taunton Pageant of 1928', *Journal of Historical Geography* 25 (1999): 57–74.
51. See Martha Vandrei, *Queen Boudica and Historical Culture in Britain: An Image of Truth* (Oxford: Oxford University Press, 2018), esp. 5–7, 117–19.
52. Letters from William H. Waud, steward-in-chief to the pageant, in *The Times,* 11 February 1909, 7; 2 March 1909, 10.
53. *Church Times*, 25 June 1909, 858.
54. Arthur Burns, 'The Authority of the Church', in *Liberty and Authority in Victorian Britain*, ed. Peter Mandler (Oxford: Oxford University Press, 2006), 179–202.
55. *Church Congress Reports*, 1885, 479.
56. For the Ecclesiologists, see a classic treatment in James F. White, *The Cambridge Movement: The Ecclesiologists and the Gothic Revival* (Cambridge: Cambridge University Press, 1962).
57. 'Pageants and Pageantry', 25.
58. See, for example, Sabine Baring Gould and John Fisher, *The Lives of the British Saints: The Saints of Wales and Cornwall and such Irish Saints as have Dedications in Britain*, 4 vols (London: The Honourable Society of Cymmrodorion, 1913).
59. For an account noticing the (in that case abortive) potential conjunction of Church and populist Toryism, see Allen Warren, 'Disraeli, the Conservatives and the National Church, 1837–1881', *Parliamentary History* 19 (2000): 96–117.
60. *Tablet*, 29 May 1909, 10; 12 June 1909, 20; 19 June 1909, 7–8; 26 June 1909, 7–8. *The Times*, 27 April 1909, 12.
61. For an important treatment of Baldwinian versions of the trope, see Philip Williamson, 'The Doctrinal Politics of Stanley Baldwin', in *Public and Private Doctrine: Essays in British History Presented to Maurice Cowling*, ed. Michael Bentley (Cambridge: Cambridge University Press, 1993), 181–208.
62. For the classic statement of revised chronology for British secularisation, see Callum Brown, *The Death of Christian Britain: Understanding Secularization 1800–2000* (London and New York, Routledge, 2001). For examples of accounts of the institutional Church's role in twentieth-century British culture emphasising some of these themes, see especially the work of John Wolffe, *God and Greater Britain: Religion and National Life in Britain and Ireland 1843–1945* (London: Routledge, 1994); 'National Occasions at St Paul's since 1800', in *St Paul's: The Cathedral Church of London 604–2004*, ed. Derek Keene, Arthur Burns and Andrew Saint (London and New Haven: Yale University Press, 2004), 381–91; 'Royalty and Public Grieving in Britain: a Historical Perspective 1817–1997', in *Mourning for Diana*, ed. Tony Walter (Oxford and New York, Berg, 1999), 53–64.

Bibliography

Brown, Callum. 2001. *The Death of Christian Britain: Understanding Secularization 1800–2000*. London and New York: Routledge.

Burns, Arthur. 2006. 'The Authority of the Church', in *Liberty and Authority in Victorian Britain*, edited by Peter Mandler. Oxford: Oxford University Press, 179–202.

Hobsbawm, Eric and Ranger, Terence, eds. 1983. *The Invention of Tradition*. Cambridge: Cambridge University Press.

Jagger, Peter. 2012 (rev. ed.); 1987 (1st ed.). *The Alcuin Club and its Publications: An Annotated Bibliography*. Norwich: Canterbury Press.

Kilcrease, Bethany. 2017. *The Great Church Crisis and the End of English Erastianism, 1898–1906*. London and New York: Routledge.

Kirby, James. 2016. *Historians and the Church of England: Religion and Historical Scholarship 1870–1920*. Oxford, Oxford University Press.
Nicholls, Paul. 2000. *Khaki and the Confessional: A Study of a Religious Issue at the 1900 General Election in England*. Melbourne: Melbourne University Press.
Reed, John Shelton. 1996. *Glorious Battle: The Cultural Politics of Victorian Anglo-Catholicism*. Nashville and London: Vanderbilt University Press.
Vandrei, Martha. 2018. *Queen Boudica and Historical Culture in Britain: An Image of Truth*. Oxford: Oxford University Press.
Warren, Allen. 2000. 'Disraeli, the Conservatives and the National Church, 1837–1881', *Parliamentary History* 19: 96–117.
Wellings Martin. 1999. *Evangelicals Embattled: Responses of Evangelicals in the Church of England to Ritualism, Darwinism and Theological Liberalism (1890–1930)*. Carlisle: Paternoster Press.
White, James F. 1962. *The Cambridge Movement: The Ecclesiologists and the Gothic Revival*. Cambridge: Cambridge University Press.
Williamson, Philip. 1993. 'The Doctrinal Politics of Stanley Baldwin', in *Public and Private Doctrine: Essays in British History Presented to Maurice Cowling*, edited by Michael Bentley. Cambridge: Cambridge University Press, 181–208.
Wolffe, John. 1994. *God and Greater Britain: Religion and National Life in Britain and Ireland 1843–1945*. London: Routledge.
Wolffe, John. 1999. 'Royalty and Public Grieving in Britain: a Historical Perspective 1817–1997', in *Mourning for Diana*, edited by Tony Walter. Oxford and New York: Berg, 53–64.
Wolffe, John. 2004. 'National Occasions at St Paul's since 1800', in *St Paul's: The Cathedral Church of London 604–2004*, edited by Derek Keene, Arthur Burns and Andrew Saint. London and New Haven: Yale University Press, 381–91.
Woods, Michael. 1999. 'Performing Power: Local Politics and the Taunton Pageant of 1928', *Journal of Historical Geography* 25: 57–74.
Yates, Nigel. 1999. *Anglican Ritualism in Victorian Britain (1830–1910)*. Oxford: Oxford University Press.

4

The Pomp of Obliteration: G. K. Chesterton and the Edwardian Pageant Revival

Michael Shallcross

In 1904 the journalist, poet and critic G. K. Chesterton published his first novel, *The Napoleon of Notting Hill*, to immediate critical and commercial success. This satirical fantasia, set 80 years in the future, concerns an uprising of the citizens of the London borough of Notting Hill, led by Adam Wayne – the titular Napoleon figure – in protest against a plan to bulldoze a public square to make way for a major arterial road. Wayne's revolt is accompanied by an upsurge of pageantry, resulting from a prior decree by the king of England – a whimsical ironist named Auberon Quin – that all Londoners must adopt brightly coloured uniforms to advertise the borough to which they belong. Quin's absurdist plan to reinstate 'the full richness of … medieval garments', along with 'symbolic head-gears', banners and coats of arms, is inspired by a facetiously expressed wish to go down in 'history as the man who saved from extinction a few old English customs'.[1] As Chesterton's friend E. C. Bentley noted when reviewing the novel for the *Bystander*, Chesterton's own intent was entirely earnest: his construction of a dazzling fictional 'pageant of blue and green, of red, gold, and purple' in the streets of London was conceived to reawaken 'the sentiment of local patriotism' in the reader.[2]

In a curious case of life imitating art, a year after the novel's publication Chesterton's textual Napoleon accrued a real-life counterpart – in the form of the civic-minded impresario Louis Napoleon Parker, whose organisation of the Sherborne pageant, held from 12 to 15 June 1905, effectively inaugurated the Edwardian pageant revival. The philosophy underpinning Parker's movement, with its emphasis upon a spectacular resistance to the utilitarian demands of commercial modernity, closely mirrors that of Chesterton's novel. As Parker explained, the 'properly conducted pageant' should be 'designed to kill' the 'modernising spirit', which 'destroys all loveliness and has no loveliness of its own to put in its place'.[3] Equally Parker's mission to establish a new form of 'historical folk-play' grounded in populist aesthetics and designed to blur the boundaries between everyday life and dramatic spectacle might have been conceived expressly to command Chesterton's artistic sympathies.[4] Chesterton's earliest journalistic success had been founded upon articles in praise of popular culture, such as 'A Defence of Penny Dreadfuls'.[5] His subsequent rise to the status of literary celebrity had been substantially fostered by his habit of practising in real life what he preached in print, wandering the streets of London dressed as a brigand, flourishing a swordstick at astonished passers-by.

Accordingly Chesterton was among the first cultural critics to recognise the significance of Parker's movement; he engaged with the revival first as a commentator and spectator, and subsequently as a participant. In this chapter I explore the progress of Chesterton's engagement, focusing particularly upon the commercial and ideological tensions that increasingly infiltrated the movement in the period leading up to the English Church Pageant of 1909. Chesterton participated in this event, an experience he later documented in 'The Mystery of a Pageant', a semi-fictionalised account published in the *Daily News*.[6] I argue that the sense of psychological disquiet that suffuses 'The Mystery of a Pageant' is revelatory not only of the deeper emotional investments that had first drawn Chesterton to the concept of pageantry, but also the gradual erosion of Parker's idealistic precepts as the Edwardian era progressed. I end by discussing Chesterton's later embrace of a smaller-scale, do-it-yourself approach to the staging of pageantry in the interwar years, a development conceived to restore the ethos of principled amateurism that had first drawn him to the form.

Ceremonial rejoicing vs jerry-built jubilees

Jed Esty's influential account of early twentieth-century writers' engagements with pageantry turns upon an interpretation of Parker's movement as essentially jingoistic: the 'Parkerian pageant' was founded upon a 'hackneyed nationalism' and 'rote patriotism', which presupposed 'a particular relationship between regional myth and colonial ambition'.[7] In consequence, the 'riches of English tradition [became] both the motivation for and the exported good of imperialism', while English heritage was conceived 'to play an inspirational role for both centrifugal, colonial action and centripetal, nostalgic memory'.[8]

The contemporary reader, familiar with this critical narrative, might be surprised to discover that Chesterton's initial embrace of the pageant revival was inspired by his *anti*-imperialist politics. In addition to his paeans to popular culture, Chesterton's first journalistic renown had been built on opposition to the Second Boer War (1899–1902). This stance placed him at odds with a media consensus largely characterised by unreflective jingoism, but accorded with the position of his employer, the 'pro-Boer' Liberal periodical, the *Speaker*. He later described the war as '[p]erhaps the catastrophic event' of his life: '[t]here I saw something which seemed to me to be the meanest kind of financial grab'.[9] Thirty-four years after the conflict's end, the sense of outrage resounds with undiminished force in his *Autobiography* (1936): 'I hated the whole thing as I had never hated anything before'.[10]

As Anna Vaninskaya notes, the plot of *The Napoleon of Notting Hill* was designed to lead the reader to the conclusion that patriotism and imperialism were incompatible: 'patriotism is condemned' in the novel 'as soon as it turns aggressive and grasping, as soon as it turns into imperialism'.[11] Chesterton articulated his views on the matter in more direct terms at the height of the Boer conflict, distinguishing genuine patriotism from the 'rote' variety later discussed by Esty: 'this recent movement in England, which has honestly appeared to many a renascence of patriotism, seems to [me] to have none of the marks of patriotism'.[12] Instead, a strange 'decay of patriotism in England during the last year or two' has caused 'the current lust of territory' to become 'confounded with the ancient love of country'.[13] Chesterton goes on to posit the source of, and potential solution to, this malaise:

> What we really need for the frustration and overthrow of a deaf and raucous Jingoism is a renascence of the love of the native land … The peculiar lack of any generosity or delicacy in the current English nationalism [arises from] the condition of not knowing our own merits. We have played a great and splendid part in the history of universal thought and sentiment … in literature, science, philosophy, and political eloquence, if history be taken as a whole, we can hold our own with any [nation]. But all this vast heritage of intellectual glory is kept from our schoolboys like a heresy.[14]

A later article on 'Patriotism and Play-acting' develops the argument further.[15] Whereas militaristic competition is a trait universal to humanity, and therefore essentially 'anti-national', Chesterton argues that the 'things that are really patriotic' are only those 'which are really local and home grown', such as 'art and literature'.[16] Consequently, rather than celebrating imperial escapades, the English 'ought to have been jingo about the English drama … The evil of modern England is that she has historic flags but no historic theatre'.[17] Parker's inaugural Sherborne pageant took place just two months later.

Although Parker shared Chesterton's disdain for the sort of patriotism 'that got up and struck the stranger across the forehead', his view of the relationship between patriotism and empire was less strictly bifurcating than that of Chesterton. His Dover pageant, for example, concluded with a sentimental maternalisation of the imperial landing stage, surrounded by Dover's 'colonial "daughter-cities"'.[18] Nonetheless, Parker's prescription for the ideal pageant echoed Chesterton's emphasis upon 'the right kind of patriotism', the symbols of which are all domestically focused – 'love of hearth; love of town; love of country; love of England' – and he stressed that this philosophy must find pragmatic expression in the event's modes of production: 'every article of whatever kind used in the performance must be invented, designed, and made in the town; out of material purchased from local purveyors'.[19]

Parker's provincialist ethos can be interpreted partially as a critical response to other, transnational forms of patriotic celebration that had gained traction in recent years – forms against which Chesterton had also raised his voice. The year 1904 saw not only the publication of *The Napoleon of Notting Hill*, but also the importation of 'Empire Day' from Canada to the UK. Chesterton responded by decrying the 'movement in favour of Imperial pageantry' in a contemporaneous article in the *Daily News*.[20] He returned to the point four years later in 'Empire Day and England' in the *Illustrated London News*. In this article Chesterton argued that such events merely illustrated the emptiness of officially sanctioned festivity; he complained of 'jerry-built jubilees', established 'with entire solemnity' by the recently established League of the Empire and propped up by the propagandising of 'the Daily Jingo', as he contemptuously rebranded the *Daily Mail*.[21] For Chesterton, such events could never achieve true popular appeal because their ostentatious grandstanding contravened two crucial national characteristics, namely 'the English shyness and the English humour'.[22]

Chesterton was equally dismissive of more spontaneous expressions of nationalist enthusiasm. One example of these was Mafeking Night, which occurred on 18 May 1900 when press reports of a pyrrhic victory over the Boers inspired the public to take to the streets in celebration. Once again Chesterton punctured this mood of public and press consensus, later arguing that the event had left nothing but a cultural hangover in its wake: '[o]n Mafeking Night, celebrating a small but picturesque success against the Boers, nearly everybody in London came out waving little flags. Nearly everybody in London is now heartily ashamed of it'.[23] This sense of alienation from his fellow citizens placed Chesterton in a disconcerting position. A self-avowed populist who considered it 'painful to notice that at the present time mobs are not properly admired', he applauded the capacity of the collective public body to 'melt' the proud individual 'in a monstrous furnace' of festivity. Yet Chesterton was equally conscious of the power of the press to mould the mass mood for good or ill, and was anxious to establish an alternative, cogent, ethical standpoint to justify his own contribution to public discourse.[24] The true demagogue, he argued, is not 'one who pleases the populace, but one who leads it'. His later essay, 'An Apology for Buffoons', explains the methods through which he attempted to smuggle such demagoguery into the public consciousness:

> I myself, who am a very minor buffoon … do regularly and as a matter of business make a multitude of bad jokes. I do it for reasons connected with the duties of demagogy.[25]

Chesterton's use of buffoonery to convey ethical instruction is epitomised by his writing on imperialism, which consistently deploys bathetically materialistic analogies to expose rhetorical sophistry. An example arises in 'A Defence of Patriotism', in which the empire's geographic extremities are reconceived as 'its fists and its boots' – an image that associates brute oppression with the furthest reaches of an imperial body politic divested of an integral 'head and heart'.[26] A similarly corporeal image arises in his later polemical tract, *What's Wrong with the World* (1910), in which he observes: 'that an Empire whose heart is failing should be specially proud of the extremities, is to me no more sublime a fact than that an old dandy whose brain is gone should still be proud of his legs'.[27] In this way Chesterton manipulates what Alexander Pope termed 'the very bathos of the human Body' in order to parody the sentimental pseudo-sublimity of an empire upon which 'the sun never sets'.[28]

Chesterton's mastery of this form of comic counterargument was nurtured by his journalistic position at the *Speaker*. Following its takeover in 1899 by an insubordinate gang of Oxford graduates assembled by J. L. Hammond, the periodical's editorial tone continually 'parodied and ridiculed the language and demolished the moral and intellectual pretentions of empire'.[29] In his autobiography, Chesterton reports an incident at the height of the Boer War in which he and Hilaire Belloc – a fellow contributor to the *Speaker* and the dedicatee of *The Napoleon of Notting Hill* – put this spirit of pedagogic opposition into direct practice. Finding themselves in the midst of a 'Jingo mob', the pair initiated a game of 'patriotic parody', deliberately antagonising the crowd and effectively inciting a riot:

> I remember waiting with a Pro-Boer friend in the midst of a Jingo mob outside the celebrated Queens Hall Meeting which ended in a free fight. My friend and I adopted a method of patriotic parody or *reductio ad absurdum*. We first proposed three cheers for Chamberlain, then three cheers for Rhodes, and then by degrees for more and more dubious and demi-naturalised patriots. We actually did get an innocent cheer for Beit … But when it came to our impulsive appeal to the universal popularity of Albu, the irony of our intention was discovered; and the fight began.[30]

While Chesterton takes evident delight in reporting this incident, in which adversarial satire delivers an acerbic corrective to unreflective nationalism, he remained acutely conscious of the risk of the public body devolving into acrimonious division. Accordingly, he possessed a countervailing, reconciliatory urge to establish more constructive forms of 'patriotic parody'.

The pageant revival offered the perfect outlet for this urge. Rather than fostering a national sense of self through opposition to a foreign people, Parker sought to construct a shared sense of cultural identity via collective impersonation of local historical figures and re-enactment of local historical events. Esty reports that this emphasis upon communal endeavour came to be viewed as a potential handmaiden of 'interclass harmony', especially since Parker's emollient brand of 'English civic nationalism' seemed 'likely to promote and express just enough collective spirit to bind citizens together but not to trip over into the frightening power of fascist mob fever'.[31] Pageantry thus seemed to offer 'a quasi-mystical act of collective social healing … spectacle as communal ritual', as Ayako Yoshino puts it, and therefore suggested a means of bridging the 'chasm' that Chesterton considered to have lately 'opened in the community of beliefs and social traditions'.[32]

Parker's model also accords with Johan Huizinga's segregation of pageantry from sport, as distinct forms of game-playing: 'a pageant … [may] be altogether lacking in antithesis'.[33] This absence of competition is emphasised in Chesterton's view of the correct application of play, as articulated in implicitly anti-imperial terms in a two-part article on 'Some Urgent Reforms: Playgrounds for Adults', published in the *Speaker* on 16 and 30 November 1901: '[g]ames as ordinarily understood do not constitute play, they constitute sport. In a game, as the adult understands a game, the essential is competition, and the aim victory'.[34]

Conversely, Chesterton finds the communal ethos of children's play to resemble the origins of the dramatic spectacle:

> The theatre was originally what children's play is, a festival, a strictly ceremonial rejoicing. Children merely reproduce the theatre in a more human, direct, and powerful manner, by being themselves both the spectators and the actors.[35]

This last phrase finds an echo in Deborah Sugg Ryan's account of the Edwardian pageant. Here she acknowledges how an intensified sense of 'interaction between performers and audience' caused boundaries to become 'blurred between the spectators and the spectated', the audience's sense of quasi-participation engendering an atmosphere of heightened collective self-consciousness.[36] Ryan's terms correspond closely to Mikhail Bakhtin's famous exposition of the medieval carnival, in which 'the basic carnival nucleus of [medieval festive] culture' represents

> life itself, but shaped according to a certain pattern of play … Carnival does not know footlights, in the sense that it does not acknowledge any distinction between actors and spectators.[37]

Elsewhere Bakhtin explicitly links carnival to pageantry, describing the former as a 'ritualistic' mode of 'syncretic pageantry'.[38] The re-emergence of this ancient festive conflation of theatricality and 'real life' within Edwardian pageantry is illustrated both by the frequently 1:1 scale of the events – Parker's pageants incorporated a 'huge casts of actors, averaging five thousand people' – and the tendency for the performance to go on long after the official close of play: participants 'often wore their costumes in their everyday jobs and for weeks after the pageant ended'.[39]

This dissolution of conceptual boundaries was encouraged by the air of wider temporal disruption that these events engendered. Esty notes that the view of Edwardian pageantry as a form of 'modern folk ritual' arose partially from 'its technical demand for collective or choral voices, and its tight unity of place coupled with an almost magical dilation of historical time'.[40] A pageant organiser from Rochester described the temporal dilation that seemed to grip the town itself in 1931 during preparations for the event:

> We were discovering that it was an exciting thing to live in our city … Once again the city was becoming Saxon, medieval, Dickensian: there was only a thin veneer of modernism disguising it.[41]

This palimpsestic premise recalls Chesterton's exposition of the value of the pantomime 'transformation scene', in which 'the front scene is still there, but the back scene begins to glow through it'.[42] Pantomime is the subject of another of Chesterton's 'Defence' essays, 'A Defence of Farce'. This piece anticipates the report of the Rochester pageant organiser by espousing a juxtaposition of prosaic reality and fantastical art as a means of revealing the exciting possibilities of the city: 'it must be an actual modern door which opens and shuts, constantly disclosing different interiors; it must be a real baker whose loaves fly up into the air without his touching them' in order to produce the sense of an 'elvish invasion of civilization, [an] abrupt entrance of Puck into Pimlico'.[43]

As these imaginative correspondences suggest, the affinity of Parker's vision with that of Chesterton was not only social and cultural, but also aesthetic. Most significantly, the fabulous dimensions of Parker's version of pageantry appealed to Chesterton's love of what Bakhtin terms the 'folk grotesque' – an amalgamative, 'serio-comical' form, which functions as the aesthetic *métier* of carnival.[44] Parker decreed that the ideal pageant should include 'every form of drama: tragedy, comedy, even farce. It is based on authentic history, but it welcomes folk-lore', and consequently, '[t]here may also be grotesques, hobby-horses, etc.'.[45] In situating this cornucopia as the necessary backdrop for his 'great Festival of Brotherhood', Parker mirrored Chesterton's visionary celebration of carnival in *G. F. Watts* (1904) – another text that immediately predates the beginning of the pageant revival.[46] Here Chesterton invokes a carnivalesque nonsense-vision to illustrate his theological belief in what he terms elsewhere the 'vast metaphysical democracy of things':

> There is no fact of life, from the death of a donkey to the General Post Office, which has not its place to dance and sing in the glorious Carnival of theology.[47]

Four years later, this premise was given fictional life in the pageant of creation that concludes his novel, *The Man Who Was Thursday* (1908), in which

> [a] vast carnival of people were dancing in motley dress. Syme seemed to see every shape in Nature imitated in some crazy costume. There was a man dressed as a windmill with enormous sails, a man dressed as an elephant, a man dressed as a balloon.[48]

The surreal utopianism of the novel's conclusion has its origins in Chesterton's youthful embrace of a vision of comradeship influenced by Walt Whitman, whom he later described as 'the greatest man of the nineteenth century'.[49] It also closely anticipates Chesterton's later, more quotidian involvement in pageantry. In June 1908, just four months after the publication of *The Man Who Was Thursday*, Chesterton attended Harry Irvine's Chelsea Historical Pageant. While the typical Edwardian pageant may not have been quite as uproariously nonsensical as Chesterton's vision of metaphysical carnival, Paul Readman notes that 'May Day revels' were a frequent theme, and Irvine took up Parker's prescribed merger of 'authentic history [and] folk-lore' with gusto.[50] The photographs that have survived of the Chelsea pageant reveal a spectacle of decidedly carnivalesque dimensions, incorporating Mr Punch travelling in a carriage and a gargantuan effigy of Orgoglio from Edmund Spenser's *The Faerie Queene* (1590), paraded during a 'children's masque' section (Figs 4.1 and 4.2).[51]

Figure 4.1 Mr Punch and his retinue at the Chelsea Historical Pageant. Mr Punch is the small figure seated at the front of the carriage, whip in hand. Reproduced with permission of Royal Borough of Kensington and Chelsea Libraries.

Figure 4.2 Orgoglio at the Chelsea Historical Pageant. Reproduced with permission of Royal Borough of Kensington and Chelsea Libraries.

Such images hark back to the 'wicker-work carnival giants' that Peter L. Caracciolo identifies as a medieval 'feature of the north French fête des fols'. They also offer a striking counterpart to Chesterton's later account of the ancient tradition of mummery as a form of community 'ritual' in which the performers enact a 'pomp of obliteration and anonymity' within the collective historical body, 'making Man something other and more than himself when he stands at the limit of human things'.[52] For Chesterton, the costumery of the mummers' play produces 'a profound paradox: the concealment of the personality combined with the exaggeration of the person … [in] a rite [that] seeks to be at once invisible and conspicuous'.[53] It is little surprise that Chesterton was swept up by the Edwardian pageant's realisation of this premise via an audacious fusion of the amateur, the folkloric and the mass participatory, all wrapped up in a spectacle designed authentically to sublimate the patriotic impulse. As Chesterton later recalled, 'these shows and pageants meant immeasurably much to me, and profoundly affected my emotions'.[54]

Nonetheless, the gigantesque scale of Irvine's Chelsea pageant also hints at the commercial pressures that began to impinge upon the pageant phenomenon as its popularity grew, producing a dissonance with Parker's idealistic view that 'a pageant must never be undertaken with a view to making money'.[55] By 1907, talk of 'pageant mania' and 'pageantitis' permeated the media, with Chesterton himself describing the phenomenon as having become 'fashionable' around this time.[56] The emergence of the 'pageant as consumable product', as Yoshino puts it, is illustrated by the increasing ubiquity of commemorative souvenirs at such events – often taking the form of wares presented as authentic to the locality and sold to 'wealthy people with money to spend, many of whom had travelled from other areas'.[57] Accordingly, the tension between official and popular forms of festivity that Chesterton had identified as a design flaw of Empire Day began to exert a comparable stress upon Parker's model.

This change was reflected in the social organisation of both the performers and the spectators, which became increasingly segregated along class lines. Although Parker had declared 'that aristocrats should play serfs and vice versa', increasingly the 'most prominent parts were bagged by local elites' while the seating was segregated by cost.[58] Shortly after the Chelsea Historical Pageant, Chesterton alluded to this issue in an article on 'Local Pride and Pageants', positing two alterations that he felt would improve such events: 'first, cheaper prices; and second, a healthy atmosphere of popular derision'.[59]

Chesterton's article anticipates Yoshino's critique of the 'packaging of the locality for consumption by the visitor' by highlighting the increasingly tenuous connection between the popular history of the specific pageant location and the universally recognisable historical figures chosen to populate the show.[60] For Chesterton, rather than celebrating the fact that a famous person once passed through the area, 'a local pageant ought to be a festival of real local patriotism … concerned with the real pride of real people in their town'.[61] He alights upon the impoverished district of Pimlico – the same locale to which he had turned in his celebration of pantomime – to develop the point:

> Suppose they have a pageant in Pimlico – I hope they will. Then let Pimlico lift up in its pride anything that it is really proud of, if it be only the parish pump or the public-house sign … its best donkey, its blackest chimney-sweep, or even its member of Parliament.[62]

As the pageant revival came to be appropriated by the cultural mainstream, Parker's domestically oriented vision of patriotism also began to be adulterated, with events catering instead to more imperially propagandist impulses. This was especially true of the work of Frank Lascelles, who co-ordinated the celebration of the opening of the Union Parliament of South Africa in 1909, thus finding renown as the 'man who staged the empire'.[63] As Ryan notes, although Lascelles worked broadly within the same pageant framework, he was 'no imitator of Parker' – in addition to their ideological differences, Lascelles' aesthetic approach took Irvine's taste for spectacle a stage further, largely hollowing out narrative in favour of dramatic visual effects.[64] In the same year as the opening of the Union Parliament, Lascelles was invited to act as pageant-master at the English Church Pageant (see chapter 3), held at Fulham Palace on 10–24 June – an event that also saw Chesterton participating for the first time in a major pageant.

In view of Chesterton's conception of the Boer War as 'the meanest kind of financial grab', he would have found Lascelles' propagandising activities in South Africa especially uncongenial. It is perhaps not surprising, then, that the English Church Pageant should have crystallised the increasing tension between his idealistic hopes for the pageant revival and the corrupting influence of commercial modernity upon the movement. Moreover, in view of Chesterton's deeply held religious beliefs, the theological context of the event would have heightened his discomfort over the element of superficiality that he increasingly associated with his public celebrity. These stresses were also exacerbated by more intimate psychological anxieties. As he later explained of the effect produced by the pantomime 'transformation scene', although it engendered 'the delightful sensation of being in two places at once', a certain disquiet was instilled by 'the unreason and the vertigo of the vision'.[65] Thus, the pageants' magical dilation of time, along with the identity-confounding implications of melting into a costumed mob, merged with the heady 'emotions' that Chesterton had invested in the movement to produce a somewhat combustible mental state. Perhaps most strikingly, these manifold tensions came to be embodied literally in the form of the public figure whom Chesterton had been called upon to impersonate at the English Church Pageant: Samuel Johnson.

'The Mystery of a Pageant'

On 19 June 1909 Chesterton devoted his weekly column in the *Daily News* to an account of the English Church Pageant, entitled 'The Mystery of a Pageant'. This curious hybrid text negotiates a winding path between his preferred fictional and non-fictional forms – the mystery story and the journalistic essay – while combining burlesque buffoonery with more literal forms of travesty, the etymology of which is 'dressed in disguise'.[66] Most notably, the article juggles an audacious array of physical and textual parodies of Samuel Johnson.

As with Chesterton's burlesque methods of debunking imperialist rhetoric, Johnson often exploited the juxtaposition of 'official verbal machinery' and 'colloquial phrases' for the satirical purpose of 'confronting high ideas with "inelegant applications" to common life'.[67] Chesterton's narrative begins in a similar spirit of burlesque satire, inspired by his discovery that the man immediately preceding him in the pageant is impersonating Bishop George Berkeley, the Enlightenment philosopher who espoused an extreme form of immaterialism. Although Chesterton acknowledged Berkeley to have been a 'great' figure, he considered his philosophy to have been founded on the precept that 'everything is relative to a reality that is not there'.[68] For Chesterton, this was an example of the 'thought that stops thought' insofar as it encouraged solipsism, thus closing off the possibility of dialogue.[69] Accordingly, he proposes brutally to acquaint Berkeley with the objective existence of others. Taking inspiration from Johnson's famous dismissal of the Bishop's anti-materialism – in which he violently kicked a large stone, before responding to the credulous Boswell, 'I refute it thus!' – Chesterton goes one step further. Musing upon the burlesque possibilities of Berkeley's taste for 'bottomless fancies', he observes

> [h]ow picturesque and perfect it would be if I moved across the ground in the symbolic attitude of kicking Bishop Berkeley! How complete an allegorical group; the great transcendentalist walking with his head among the stars, but behind him the avenging realist *pede claudo*, with uplifted foot.[70]

In this way Johnson becomes the admired antecedent with whom Chesterton rides into battle against a philosophy with which he is unsympathetic and which he perceives to be paradigmatically modern; the intimacy of his identification with Johnson is heightened by the act of physical impersonation, which seems to meld the two personalities into one. The seasoned reader of Chesterton's pedagogic journalism therefore presumes that the ensuing article will be a playful satire, expanding upon the merits of Johnson's bluff, no-nonsense materialism and the contrary dangers of Berkeley's extreme Idealism. However, much as the conventional mystery story is built upon the confounding of expectation, 'The Mystery of a Pageant' soon pulls the rug from beneath the reader's feet, progressing by increments to a more ambiguous, disorientating mode of structural self-parody, while the confusion caused by the pageant's dressing-up game increasingly pollutes the satirical premise.

This air of disorientation first emerges when Chesterton becomes lost in the dark on the first night of the pageant. The experience causes his identification with Johnson to progress from a rational philosophical opposition to Berkeley to a more intimate, irrational affinity with Johnson's fears of personal isolation: 'I began almost to feel like my prototype, and to share his horror of solitude'.[71] This acknowledgement of psychological affinity is accompanied by bodily self-deprecation, via a vivid rendition of corporeal abjection:

> I was told that I was just like Dr. Johnson. Seeing that Dr. Johnson was heavily seamed with small-pox, had a waistcoat all over gravy, snorted and rolled as he walked, and was probably the ugliest man in London, I mention this *identification* as a fact and not as a vaunt (emphasis added).[72]

Later, Chesterton conceives his personality to be a presence quite as unwelcome as his physical form, when his pedantic insistence that the event should adhere literally to historical fact begins to grate on the nerves of the pageant's organisers. Soon after, he commits a burlesque pratfall in the dark, 'tumbl[ing] over tent ropes' – a mishap in which the inanimate world turns the practical joke of kicking the unwitting Berkeley back upon the complacent satirist.[73] This final indignity causes Chesterton to hypothesise the reader's thoroughgoing contempt: 'I am (you will say) naturally obtuse, cowardly, and mentally deficient'.[74]

At this moment of utmost authorial abjection an apparent knight in shining armour emerges in the shape of 'Paley' – a figure who 'used to guide men to the beginnings of Christianity', as Chesterton explains.[75] This is a reference to William Paley, the eighteenth-century theologian who sought to challenge the early stirrings of scepticism in the Enlightenment age by advancing the concept of intelligent design. A correspondence therefore emerges with the conclusion of *The Man Who Was Thursday*, in which the beneficent actions of the quasi-religious parental figure of Sunday direct the disorientated protagonist, Gabriel Syme, to the beginnings of Christianity – in the literal form of page one of the Bible – by engineering his participation in a pageant of creation. Similarly, the man playing Paley guides Chesterton away from confusion and isolation into an illuminated realm of companionship: 'we came out into the glare of gaslight and laughing men in masquerade'.[76] Once having returned to the revellers, who subsequently 'fooled as one does at a fancy-dress ball' throughout the night, Chesterton's re-attainment of mental balance is reflected in a renewed capacity for self-deprecating humour: 'I could easily laugh at myself'.[77]

A pedagogic account of the value of pageantry seems to emerge, as the temporal double vision that underpins this scene of costumed camaraderie causes the dogmatic barriers separating individuals to break down. Chesterton discovers that unlike his 'prototype' Johnson, he has more in common with the man playing Berkeley than the representative of Edmund Burke. Accordingly the tone of the piece progresses from the oppositional satire of his violent response to Berkeley towards a more balanced position encouraged by the identity confusion ingrained within the pageant format, which sets up a fugitive between-space of ideological amnesty.

However, when Chesterton's attention turns to the morning after the night before, the tone of the piece drifts away from this edifying spectacle into a more disturbingly nonsensical realm. Most curiously, the locus of disorientation turns out to be the figure of Paley. While the features of Chesterton's other 'old friends' remain 'fixed and familiar', Paley proceeds to 'swell and shrink' – a reversal of the progress of *The Man Who Was Thursday*, in which a gradual physical stabilisation takes hold of the previously protean supporting characters once the protagonist's mental equilibrium is re-established.[78] Indeed, despite the initial resemblance of Paley to Sunday, the article turns out to be structured upon a wholesale inversion of the novel's movement from chaos to order; it devolves instead from utopian carnival to ever-greater cognitive disarray, as the identity of the person playing Paley continues to alter inexplicably with each passing day:

> It certainly seemed odd that this one particular cleric should be so varying and elusive. It was singular that Paley, alone among men, should ... alter like a phantom, while all else remained solid.[79]

As with Syme's initial inability confidently to assess Sunday's true character in *Thursday*, this mutability eventually causes Chesterton's grasp of interpretive frameworks to collapse: '[d]id these perpetual changes prove the popularity or the unpopularity of Paley?'[80] Again the reader remains alert, since this kind of rhetorical play in Chesterton's journalism usually prefigures the arrival of a neat inversion through which reason will be conjured from disarray – a prospect apparently held out by the allegorical teaser that Chesterton's mental confusion was beginning to mirror that 'of the modern world ... in which all natural explanations have broken down and no supernatural explanation has been established' to replace them.[81] However, not only does such an explanation fail to materialise, but Paley is also made to dematerialise more radically:

> I cannot conjecture further about this true tale of mystery; and that for two reasons. First, the story is so true that I have had to put a lie into it. Every word of this narrative is veracious, except the one word Paley. And second, because I have got to go into the next room and dress up as Dr. Johnson.[82]

With that, the article abruptly concludes.

Whereas the mystery of *The Man Who Was Thursday* is dispersed by the consecutive erasure of a series of misapprehensions, here the central plank of the narrative is finally revealed to have been illusory, leaving us with an entirely unexplained mystery. This tale with 'the dark qualities of a detective story … that Sherlock Holmes himself could hardly unravel' ends on an aporetic note of non-resolution, 'which has never been explained and which still lays its finger on my nerve'.[83] While this premise establishes a superficial similarity to Sunday's propounding of unexplained textual riddles in *The Man Who Was Thursday*, once more the article establishes an effect contrary to that of the novel. Whereas Sunday's insoluble riddles operate as the paper trail that entices Syme onward towards his participation in the utopian pageant of creation, the riddle that Chesterton implants within this real-life Church Pageant renders the event dystopian and its chronicler untrustworthy. He confesses that he has been misleading the reader throughout as to the signifier of the individual who initially guided him to safety, whose identity has subsequently been subjected to various forms of erasure: 'I had been mystically moved by the man's presence; I was moved more by his absence'.[84]

Thus the 'pomp of obliteration' that Chesterton identified as a merit of mummery is rehearsed here in a rather more alarming sense. The verb *obliterare* derives from *littera* – a 'letter, something written' – so that its reverse connotes something 'struck out, erased'.[85] Paley, it seems, has been erased both from the narrative and from the event due to the contemporary unpopularity of his views. Earlier in the text Chesterton bumps into an old school friend, who confesses 'I don't know who [Paley] was' – to which Chesterton replies gloomily, 'nor does any one'.[86]

If Paley is a dead letter in the modern world, this is a category into which Malcolm Muggeridge also assigned Chesterton: 'a displaced person, a letter delivered at the wrong address'.[87] This element of dislocation helps to explain the uncanny quality of Chesterton's narrative. Freud's famous term, *unheimlich*, refers to 'what is not at home'.[88] Likewise, Chesterton's disorientated journey across the pageant ground radiates a sense of misplacement. This is compounded by the temporal double-exposure effect of the event itself, which threatens not to produce the reassuring sense of material superabundance that Chesterton associated with the folk grotesque, but instead to cast the time-traveller adrift, in a correspondence with the 'bottomless fancies' of Berkeley, or his account elsewhere of the modern 'sceptic' whose mind 'sinks through floor after floor of a bottomless universe'.[89]

The motif of physical dual identity that underpins pageant performance serves only to compound the disarray. In 'The Mummers', Chesterton alludes obliquely to the importance that physical disguise held for him as a psychologically stabilising conceit: 'merry-makers … adopt their costume to heighten and exaggerate their own bodily presence and identity; not to sink it, primarily speaking, in another identity'.[90] However, in this instance Chesterton's choice of disguise entails an imaginative conjunction with a figure possessed of a disruptive *internal* dual identity comparable to his own. While Chesterton considered Johnson to have been 'a splendidly sane man who knew he was a little mad', Jorge Luis Borges argued that Chesterton succeeded in maintaining his sanity only by forcibly 'restrain[ing] … something in the makeup of his personality [that] leaned toward the nightmarish'.[91] 'The Mystery of a Pageant' is a rare textual instance of Chesterton voluntarily slackening these restraints, and the pretext for doing so is the uncanny communion with Johnson that he experienced on the pageant ground.[92]

The grotesque underpinning of pageantry is a further contributing factor to the destabilising drive of Chesterton's narrative. As Philip Thomson notes, 'the satirist who uses the grotesque as a tool … must be careful', since the intended 'didactic point … may be obscured for the reader by the nonplussing, disorientating and generally overwhelming effect of the grotesque'.[93] As we have seen, if 'The Mystery of a Pageant' possesses a satirical message, it would seem to centre upon the organisers' failure to include Paley in a celebration of famous church figures. Such a lacuna illustrates the modern world's ignorance of his value(s) and results in the air of ontological chaos that suffuses the text. However, this moral is muddied by Chesterton's deliberate disorientation of the reader with the final twist in the tale. In this he confesses to implanting 'a lie' at the heart of the narrative, without going on to elaborate why he has done so. Despite his determined efforts to extricate himself from the disarray of his historical moment, this tension between the urge to offer satirical instruction and a contrary taste for grotesque complication situates Chesterton as a collaborator in, as much as a disperser of, the chaos of modernity.

This temperamental duality is played out in 'The Mystery of a Pageant' through a dextrous pastiche of Johnson's differing modes of literary expression. If Chesterton's conventional essay style is indebted to the witty moralising of Johnson's work in the *Idler* and the *Rambler*, his quasi-fictional approach in 'The Mystery of a Pageant' opens up a correspondence with the more equivocal traits of Johnson's creative work – most notably the famous ending of *The History of Rasselas, Prince of Abissinia* (1759), '[t]he conclusion, in which nothing is concluded'.[94] While attending lectures on modern literature at University College London in 1893, Chesterton had dwelt upon Johnson's phrase in his notes before adding, with implicit disapproval, 'very 19c n'est pas?' – by which he meant very much like the prevailing currents of modern philosophy.[95]

Despite Chesterton's implicit disapproval, 'The Mystery of a Pageant' concludes in precisely the same inconclusive manner. Towards the end of the narrative, he wonders why 'the giddy Paley [was] unfaithful among the faithful found' – a phrase that parodically inverts Milton's account of the seraph Abdiel in *Paradise Lost* (1667), who was 'faithful found / Among the faithless'. In this way the author gestures once more to *Rasselas*, which has been interpreted as a parody of *Paradise Lost*.[96] By embracing the inconclusive spirit of *Rasselas*, the author takes the opportunity to try on a rhetorical change of clothes, temporarily discarding the pedagogic guise in which he usually conducted his essays and thus establishing a means of avoiding unconscious self-parody.

As this sophisticated strategy suggests, a countervailing performance of self-possession offsets the article's experimentation with identity confusion – not only in the form of Chesterton's projection of awareness of the buffoonish figure he cuts, but also the playful deviation that he injects into the potentially mechanistic output of journalistic articles concerned with dispersing ontological and/or epistemological confusion. In this sense his final act of imitative repetition – 'I have got to go into the next room and dress up as Dr. Johnson' – could be interpreted in cyclical terms, as a return to the premise with which the essay began. Having enjoyed his interregnum of play, or the 'irresponsibility of a work of the imagination', as he would later describe *Rasselas* itself, Chesterton finally reclaims the reassuring status of Johnsonian moralist, returning to the fray to brutalise Berkeleyans once more.[97]

Indeed, as though anxious that his initial account of the event might have been too inscrutable, he followed up 'The Mystery of a Pageant' with a further journalistic dispatch, published in the *Illustrated London News* a fortnight later, in which the moral to be drawn from the English Church Pageant is set forth with scrupulous sobriety. If the first article highlights the psychological tensions that Chesterton experienced as an ontological feature of modernity, the follow-up article, 'Modern and Ancient

Pageants', concerns itself with the more prosaic stresses exerted upon the event by the commercial structures of modernity.[98]

In one sense, the event had realised the hopes that Chesterton had first entertained for the pageant movement, while also according with the precepts of his body double. Johnson's view that '[m]en may differ from each other in many religious opinions, and yet all may retain the essentials of Christianity' accords with the inclusive ethos of the pageant, as explained by Arthur Burns in chapter 3: 'the organisers were determined that the Pageant itself should be irenic and non-sectarian'.[99] Similarly, the 'power of the Pageant … as a pedagogic tool' was demonstrated by the series of university extension lectures given by Rev. Albert E. N. Simms to accompany the event. Burns reports the response of *The Times* to the pageant in terms reminiscent of Chesterton's practice of ethical buffoonery: it represented 'a resurrection of the medieval mode of combining amusement and instruction'.[100] Chesterton makes a similar point in 'Modern and Ancient Pageants':

> Things like the Church Pageant may do something towards snubbing this silly and derisive view of the past. Hitherto the young stockbroker, when he wanted to make a fool of himself, dressed up as Cardinal Wolsey. It may now begin to dawn on him that he ought rather to make a wise man of himself before attempting the impersonation.[101]

However, the English Church Pageant also encapsulated the increasingly elaborate and commercially demanding nature of such events as they became more popular: 11,000 performers were involved in the pageant, which ended by making a substantial financial loss. With the incremental commercialisation of the revival there had emerged an accompanying 'cult of celebrity and personality of the pageant master'; the organisers of the Church Pageant must consequently have been thrilled to secure the services of the celebrated Frank Lascelles, even if their most famous participant would have been rather more disquieted by the choice.[102] When Lascelles dropped out at the eleventh hour (due to a disagreement over creative control), the organisers could at least console themselves that their main celebrity performer – Chesterton – was still on hand to boost the ticket sales required to recoup expenses such as the extravagant £7,000 grandstand.

Other means of remuneration included a luxury version of the handbook, sold to the more well-heeled spectators for 2s. 6d.; even the standard 6d. edition offered up copious advertising space, resulting in

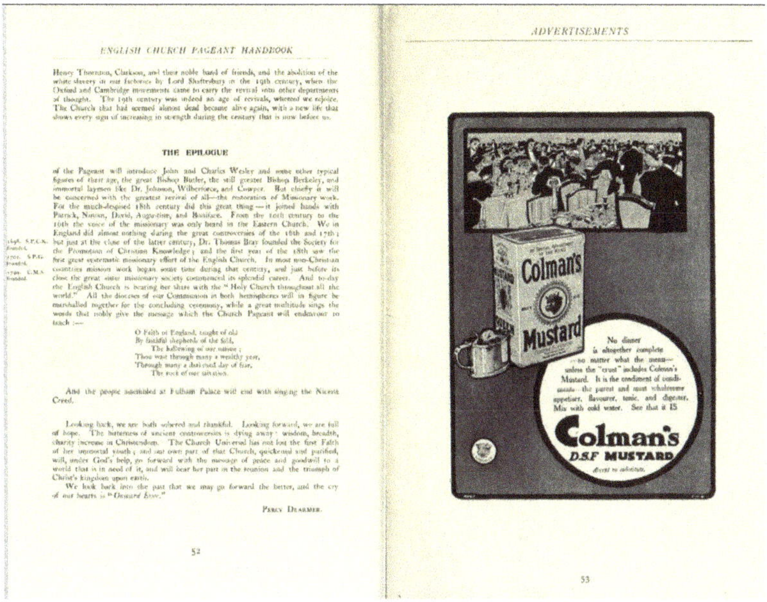

Figure 4.3 Advertisement for Colman's mustard in *English Church Pageant Handbook* (London: Eyre & Spottiswoode, 1909). Author's collection.

some rather absurdist non sequiturs. The précis of the episode in which Chesterton performed, for example, is juxtaposed with an instruction to the reader that '[n]o dinner is altogether complete no matter what the menu unless the "cruet" includes Colman's Mustard' (Fig. 4.3).

Five years earlier, in *The Napoleon of Notting Hill*, Chesterton had used an advertisement for Colman's Mustard for rather more subversive purposes. The visiting President of Nicaragua, whose culture is under imperial threat, demonstrates that he respects the principles of pageantry rather more than his British hosts: he slices a mustard yellow segment from a Colman's billboard in front of a crowd of spectators before pinning it to his chest to produce an improvised rendition of his national costume. Mustard also makes an appearance in Chesterton's article on 'Modern and Ancient Pageants' in a glancing reference that emerges within a discussion of the value of stately ceremonial garb: 'the yellow robes' of a Chinese emperor 'might remind [one] of Dash's Mustard'.[103] This free-associative cross-reference proceeds directly from Chesterton's observation that '[t]he only objection to the excellent series of Pageants that has adorned England of late is that they are too expensive' – a complaint that arises within a broader exposition of the 'baseness of modernity', as illustrated by the vacuity of advertising culture: 'the only real vulgarity of advertisements … [is] that [the colours] are much too good for the meaningless work they serve'.[104] The pageant handbook had perhaps hit a sore spot.

Accordingly 'Modern and Ancient Pageants' hinges upon an anxiety over meaning that again evokes existential unease:

> A thing is insignificant when we do not know what it signifies … modern life, with its vastness, its energy, its elaboration, its wealth, is, in the exact sense, insignificant. Nobody knows what we mean; we do not know ourselves.[105]

While this immersive 'we' might imply a fugitive self-criticism on the part of the celebrity pageant participant, the article quickly draws the spotlight away from any confusion infecting the arena of performance. It focuses instead upon the author's reciprocal spectatorship of the audience, whose literally irrelevant contemporary costumes are 'divorced from all reason'.[106] The collective pronoun thus shifts its orientation, now being used to reinstate Chesterton's detachment from the malaise: the article concludes, in lofty pedagogic fashion, that '[w]e have to teach' the public an alternative philosophy.[107]

In his earlier article on 'Local Pride and Pageants', Chesterton had developed a comparable argument about the dangers of insignificance, complaining that the absence of historical figures authentically connected to the locality resulted in pageants that ceased to be 'intelligible'.[108] To this end, he wonders why the resolutely modern figures of Thomas Carlyle, Dante Gabriel Rossetti and James Whistler are nowhere to be found in the Chelsea Historical Pageant, since pageants 'ought never to consist of mere dead history; but, as far as possible, of living traditions'.[109] He then cites Johnson as a figure who might be used to establish a genuine conjunction of celebrity to place: 'there was always something of Fleet Street about Dr. Johnson, there is still a great deal of Dr. Johnson about Fleet Street'.[110]

Chesterton's appearance in the English Church Pageant fulfils his prescription for an injection of relative modernity into the format. His performance formed part of a wider restaging of the 'much-despised' eighteenth century, as the pageant handbook has it – a step that contravened Parker's generic diktat that no scene should depict an historical era closer to the present day than the mid-seventeenth century.[111]

Likewise, a sense of living history was conveyed by the segment's anti-slavery theme (Wilberforce also makes an appearance in this section), which Chesterton might have appreciated as an implied sideways glance at the imperialist impulses of the now-departed Lascelles. However, in the broader context of the pageant's thematic purpose, if Chesterton the man had been delivered to the wrong time, Chesterton the actor has been sent to the wrong place. There may still have been a 'great deal of Dr. Johnson about Fleet Street' in the Edwardian era, but Johnson's relevance to a history of the English Church is far less intuitive. His inclusion among a series of 'immortal laymen', in the handbook's phrase, seems inspired more by the organisers' desire to guarantee Chesterton's participation by satisfying his sense of personal identification with Johnson than by a clear sense of meaningful connection to the purpose of the pageant itself.[112]

As this conceptual tension suggests, Chesterton's embrace of the pageant format as a means of propelling himself beyond the confines of a modernity from which he felt alienated foundered precisely because his presence was required while Paley's was not. The event's commercial basis caused it to have more use for a recognisable celebrity dressed as a famous layperson than an anonymous performer dressed as a relatively obscure clergyman.

Simultaneously, this dynamic propelled Chesterton beyond the reach of the populace with whom he insistently identified; although he boasts in 'Modern and Ancient Pageants' that 'I myself got in with the rabble [at] the Church Pageant', he remains cordoned off from the crowd by his celebrity status.[113] With these contexts in mind, an uneasy sense of implication in the degradation of once meaningful rituals can be read between the lines of both 'The Mystery of a Pageant' and 'Modern and Ancient Pageants'. The choice of *Rasselas* as a textual palimpsest for 'The Mystery of a Pageant' again proves more than adventitious: Chesterton later characterised the novel as 'an ironic tale of … disillusionments'.[114] He never participated in a pageant on this scale again.

Conclusion

Despite Chesterton's withdrawal from the mainstream of the pageant craze at the end of the Edwardian era, his experiences on the pageant ground continued to bear creative fruit. 'The Mystery of a Pageant' formed a decisive point of intersection between Chesterton's two most significant incursions into the mystery genre, emerging a year after *The Man Who Was Thursday* and a year before the first *Father Brown* stories. Whereas the journalistic article radically disrupts the utopian conceit of the conclusion to *Thursday*, Chesterton later re-inscribed a sense of order in the person of his priest-detective, whom Walter Raubicheck has discussed as a between-time figure who might have walked straight out of a pageant-play into modern society: he is 'an Aquinas transferred from thirteenth-century France and Italy to twentieth-century England, alienated from the spirit of his time'.[115]

Father Brown might equally be read as a fictional surrogate for Paley, the moral guide hitherto absent from the modern age. In 'The Mystery of a Pageant', the paranoid, irrational explanations that Chesterton claims to have entertained to account for Paley's evanescent persona – that 'no human being could support being Paley for one night and live till morning' or that there might exist 'some ancient vendetta against Paley [pursued by] some secret society of Deists' – are just the kind of fevered, conspiratorial interpretations of prosaic phenomena that Brown delights in debunking throughout the series.[116] Insofar as Chesterton's detective narratives depict this deductive process as a product of the grand lineage of Christian reason to which the English Church Pageant had also drawn attention, his fictional priest might be understood partially as a creative attempt to resolve his ambivalence over the event itself, by recovering its central pedagogic premise and articulating it to a mass readership.

Similarly, Chesterton's identification with Johnson was to find later creative expression in *The Judgement of Dr Johnson* (1927). This play for the professional stage draws upon the ethical lessons that Chesterton derived from the tenets of the pageant-play, while evincing a new degree of critical distance from his subject: the 'judgement' of the title remains equivocally poised between endorsement and evaluation. Meanwhile, the production proffers a remedy for Chesterton's complaint that Britain 'has historic flags but no historic theatre' by dedicating itself to an historical re-enactment of Johnson's time and by incorporating a critique of rote nationalism within the plot. In one scene we discover a flag placed derisively 'among the coloured handkerchiefs' of the female protagonist's household; a stage direction later requires a giant flag to be raised over the stage just as we are told that the boys around her 'never grow up'.[117]

While pursuing these fictional means of parsing the lessons of the pageant revival in the post-Edwardian period, Chesterton found a more prosaic method of extracting meaning from the phenomenon in later years by focusing his participatory efforts upon the small-scale, low-budget village pageants that increasingly sprang up in the interwar years, corroborating his dictum that 'England is most easily understood as the country of amateurs'.[118] Although Chesterton occasionally dusted down his impersonation of Johnson at such events, perhaps the exemplary instance of his involvement in this new mode of provincial pageantry was a 'pageant of Nursery Rhymes' that took place in his adopted home of Beaconsfield in 1920.[119] A far cry from the pomp of the English Church Pageant, the proceeds from this modest parade were donated to a charitable cause – the upkeep of a local convalescent home – rather than being redirected into attempts to recover the costs of a spectacular production.[120]

Chesterton's participation in the pageant took three forms. He manned the tobacco stall, paraded in the costume of Old King Cole and produced a makeshift handbook for the event in the form of a series of textual parodies of the Cole nursery rhyme, in the style of a range of modern poets including Robert Browning, Walt Whitman and W. B. Yeats. Of these the parody of Whitman, his youthful hero, is perhaps the most successful, its playful hints of exhaustion at the poet's prolixity finally inspiring a punning expression of departure:

> I salute your three violinists, endlessly making vibrations,
> Rigid, relentless, capable of going on for ever;
> They play my accompaniment; but I shall take no notice of any accompaniment;
> I myself am a complete orchestra.
> So long.[121]

Elsewhere the skit alludes to the accoutrements required by the spectator of commercial pageantry, for which the 'clairvoyant' poet of the common man has no purpose: '[n]eeding no telescope, lorgnette, field-glass, opera-glass, myopic pince-nez', the visionary versifier 'pierc[es] two thousand years with eye naked and not ashamed', before exclaiming 'I perceive that you drink. (I am drinking with you. I am as drunk as you are.)'[122] With this celebration of transtemporal, communal camaraderie, Chesterton captures the generous spirit of 'strictly ceremonial rejoicing' that had first drawn him to the pageant revival. While Lascelles went on to parade his grandiose vision of empire upon the world stage, presiding over the 15,000-strong Pageant of Empire at Wembley in 1924, Chesterton had recovered something of the original significance of pageantry in a quiet provincial backwater, in which 'the English shyness and the English humour' enjoyed a final, modest victory.

Notes

1. *The Collected Works of G. K. Chesterton* (San Francisco: Ignatius, 1986–) [hereafter *CW*], vol.6, 264–5, 256–7.
2. E. C. Bentley, 'A Novel of the Moment', *Bystander* (27 April 1904), in *G. K. Chesterton: The Critical Judgments 1900–1937*, ed. Denis J. Conlon (Antwerp: Antwerp University Press, 1976), 98.
3. Cited in Deborah Sugg Ryan, 'Spectacle, the Public and the Crowd: Exhibitions and Pageants in 1908', in *The Edwardian Sense: Art, Design, and Performance in Britain, 1901–1910*, ed. Morna O'Neill and Michael Hatt (New Haven and London: Yale University Press, 2010), 54.
4. Cited in Jed Esty, *A Shrinking Island: Modernism and National Culture in England* (Princeton, NJ: Princeton University Press, 2003), 57.
5. First published in *Speaker,* 16 March 1901, later collected in *The Defendant* (1901).
6. First published 19 June 1909, later collected in *Tremendous Trifles* (1909).
7. Esty, *Shrinking*, 57, 55, 57, 60.
8. Esty, *Shrinking*, 60, 59. Curiously Esty does not discuss Chesterton in his survey.
9. Interview from 1931: *The Man Who Was Orthodox: A Selection from the Uncollected Writings of G. K. Chesterton*, ed. A. L. Maycock (London: Dennis Dobson, 1963), 171.
10. G. K. Chesterton, *Autobiography* (London: Hutchinson, 1936), 113.
11. Anna Vaninskaya, '"My Mother, Drunk or Sober": G. K. Chesterton and Patriotic Anti-imperialism', *History of European Ideas* 34 (2008): 542.
12. 'A Defence of Patriotism' (*Speaker*, 4 May 1901), in G. K. Chesterton, *The Defendant* (London: J. M. Dent, 1932 [1901]), 167.
13. Chesterton, 'Defence of Patriotism', 165.
14. Chesterton, 'Defence of Patriotism', 167, 170, 169.
15. G. K. Chesterton, 'Patriotism and Play-Acting' (*Speaker*, 29 April 1905), 118–19. A copy of this article is held in the British Library, ref. BL MS 73381 ff.106. See *British Library Catalogue of Additions to the Manuscripts: The G. K. Chesterton Papers*, ed. R. A. Christophers (London: British Library, 2001).
16. Chesterton, 'Patriotism and Play-Acting'.
17. Chesterton, 'Patriotism and Play-Acting'.
18. Parker, cited in Paul Readman, 'The Place of the Past in English Culture *c.*1890–1914', *Past and Present* 186 (2005): 176; Esty, *Shrinking*, 60.
19. Louis Napoleon Parker, *Several of My Lives* (London: Chapman & Hall, 1928), 279, 285–6.
20. 'Mrs. Craigie and the Crowds' (19 November 1904), in *G. K. Chesterton at the Daily News: Literature, Liberalism and Revolution, 1901–1913*, ed. Julia Stapleton (8 vols., London: Pickering & Chatto, 2012), vol.2, 321.
21. 'Empire Day and England' (13 June 1908), in *CW*, vol.28, 120.
22. Chesterton, 'Empire Day and England', 122.
23. G. K. Chesterton, *The Appetite of Tyranny, Including Letters to an Old Garibaldian* (New York: Dodd, Mead, & Co., 1915), 112.
24. 'The Hysteria of Mobs', *Illustrated London News* (18 January 1908), in *CW*, vol.28, 26; 'The Unpopularity of the People' (18 December 1909), in *Chesterton at the Daily News,* vol.6, 164.
25. 'The Suffragist', in G. K. Chesterton, *A Miscellany of Men* (New York: Dodd, Mead, & Co., 1912), 7. 'An Apology for Buffoons' was first published in the *London Mercury* (June 1928) and later collected in *CW,* vol.3, 355.
26. Chesterton, *Defendant*, 167.
27. *CW,* vol.4, 90.
28. Pope cited in *On Bathos: Literature, Art, Music*, ed. Sara Crangle and Peter Nicholls (London: Bloomsbury, 2010), 4.
29. John Coates, *G. K. Chesterton as Controversialist, Essayist, Novelist, and Critic* (Lewiston, NY: Edwin Mellen Press, 2002), 68.
30. Chesterton, *Autobiography*, 110–11. The 'friend' is tentatively identified as Belloc by Julia Stapleton in Chesterton, *Chesterton at the Daily News,* vol.8, 6. Alfred Beit was a German financier with interests in South Africa. George Albu was a German-born magnate, whose fortune was made in the diamond and gold mines of South Africa.
31. Esty, *Shrinking*, 55.

32. Ayako Yoshino, 'The Modern Historical Pageant: Commodifying Locality', 5: https://case.edu/affil/sce/Texts_2005/Yoshino%20MLA%202005.pdf (accessed 26 May 2019); *CW*, vol.3, 356.
33. Johan Huizinga, *Homo Ludens: A Study of the Play Element in Culture* (London: Maurice Temple Smith, 1970), 67.
34. See BL MS Add.73381 ff.76.
35. See BL MS Add. 73381 ff.77.
36. Ryan, 'Spectacle', 44, 43.
37. Mikhail Bakhtin, *Rabelais and His World*, trans. Helene Iswolsky (Bloomington, IN: Indiana University Press, 1984), 7.
38. Mikhail Bakhtin, *Problems of Dostoevsky's Poetics*, ed. and trans. Caryl Emerson (Minneapolis, MN: Minnesota University Press, 2006), 122.
39. Ryan, 'Spectacle', 56.
40. Esty, *Shrinking*, 61.
41. Esty, *Shrinking*, 58.
42. 'The Peasant' (8 July 1911), in *Chesterton at the Daily News*, vol.7, 163.
43. 'Nonsense' (*Speaker*, 2 February 1901), in Chesterton, *Defendant*, 126.
44. Bakhtin, *Rabelais*, 39; Bakhtin, *Problems*, 106.
45. Parker, *Several*, 279, 282.
46. Parker, *Several*, 279.
47. 'A Good Miscellany' (10 October 1903), in *Chesterton at the Daily News*, vol.2, 137; G. K. Chesterton, *G. F. Watts* (Chicago, IL: Rand, McNally, and Co., 1904), 75.
48. *CW*, vol.6, 629.
49. 'Conventions and the Hero' (15 October 1904), in *Chesterton at the Daily News*, vol.2, 313.
50. Readman, 'Place of the Past', 187.
51. Ryan, 'Spectacle', 56.
52. Peter L. Caracciolo, '"Carnivals of Mass-Murder": The Frazerian Origins of Wyndham Lewis's *The Childermass*', in *Sir James Frazer and the Literary Imagination: Essays in Affinity and Influence*, ed. Robert G. Fraser and Carol Pert (Basingstoke: Macmillan, 1990), 211; 'The Mummers' (30 December 1911), in *Chesterton at the Daily News*, vol.7, 273–4.
53. *Chesterton at the Daily News*, vol.7, 273.
54. *CW*, vol.21, 451.
55. Parker, *Several*, 289.
56. Ryan, 'Spectacle', 52, 55; G. K. Chesterton, 'The Mystery of a Pageant', collected in *Tremendous Trifles* (London: Methuen, 1909), 257.
57. Ayako Yoshino, *Pageant Fever: Local History and Consumerism in Edwardian England* (Tokyo: Waseda University Press, 2011), 90, 79. On pageant souvenirs, see chapter 11 in this volume.
58. Ryan, 'Spectacle', 56–7.
59. *Illustrated London News*, 8 August 1908, in *CW*, vol.28, 155–6.
60. Yoshino, 'Modern', 12.
61. *CW*, vol.28, 155.
62. *CW*, vol.28, 155.
63. See Deborah Sugg Ryan, '"The Man Who Staged the Empire": Remembering Frank Lascelles in Sibford Gower, 1875–2000', in *Material Memories: Design and Evocation*, ed. Jeremy Aynsley, Christopher Breward and Marius Kwint (London: Berg, 1999), 159–79.
64. Ryan, 'Spectacle', 55.
65. Cited by Dora Marsden, in 'Views and Comments', *Egoist* (1 November 1915): 168.
66. Robert K. Barnhart, ed., *Chambers Dictionary of Etymology* (London: Chambers Harrap, 2011), 1162.
67. Johnson, cited in Freya Johnston, *Samuel Johnson and the Art of Sinking 1709–1791* (Oxford: Oxford University Press, 2005), 11.
68. Chesterton, *Tremendous*, 258; G. K. Chesterton, *St. Thomas Aquinas* (New York: Dover, 2009), 93.
69. G. K. Chesterton, *Orthodoxy* (London: John Lane, 1909), 56. This phrase arises in the course of a wider discussion of ontological scepticism.
70. Chesterton, *Tremendous*, 258. The term '*pede claudo*', meaning literally 'punishment comes limping', was coined by the Roman satirist Horace to convey the concept of retribution being meted out long after the original offence has been forgotten.
71. Chesterton, *Tremendous*, 259. In 'Dr Johnson' (1911), Chesterton notes that 'Johnson had a great dislike of being all alone … he knew [his] soul had its accidents and morbidities; and he liked to have it corrected by a varied companionship': G. K. Chesterton. *G.K.C. as M.C.* (London: Methuen, 1929), 66.

72. Chesterton, *Tremendous*, 257–8.
73. Chesterton, *Tremendous*, 259.
74. Chesterton, *Tremendous*, 260.
75. Chesterton, *Tremendous*, 259.
76. Chesterton, *Tremendous*, 260.
77. Chesterton, *Tremendous*, 260.
78. Chesterton, *Tremendous*, 262.
79. Chesterton, *Tremendous*, 261–2.
80. Chesterton, *Tremendous*, 263.
81. Chesterton, *Tremendous*, 262.
82. Chesterton, *Tremendous*, 263.
83. Chesterton, *Tremendous*, 257, 260.
84. Chesterton, *Tremendous*, 261.
85. *Oxford English Dictionary*: https://en.oxforddictionaries.com/definition/obliterate (accessed 26 May 2019).
86. Chesterton, *Tremendous*, 263.
87. Malcolm Muggeridge, 'GKC', *New Statesman* (23 August 1963), in *G. K. Chesterton: A Half-Century of Views*, ed. Denis Conlon (Oxford: Oxford University Press, 1987), 227.
88. The literal translation is 'unhomelike'. See Fredrik Svenaeus, 'Freud's Philosophy of the Uncanny', *Scandinavian Psychoanalytic Review* 22 (1999): 239.
89. 'The Orthodoxy of Hamlet' (18 May 1907), in *Chesterton at the Daily News*, vol.4, 224.
90. *Chesterton at the Daily News*, vol.7, 274.
91. Jorge Luis Borges, *Other Inquisitions: 1937–1952*, trans. Ruth L.C. Simms (London: Souvenir Press, 1973), 84; Chesterton, *G.K.C. as M.C.*, 69.
92. A measure of Chesterton's empathetic connection with Johnson is conveyed by Maisie Ward, who reports an incident in which he discussed Johnson's response to his wife's death. As Chesterton did so, 'the tears ran down his own face': Maisie Ward, *Return to Chesterton* (London: Sheed & Ward, 1952), 263.
93. Philip Thomson, *The Grotesque* (London: Methuen, 1972), 42.
94. Samuel Johnson, *The History of Rasselas, Prince of Abissinia* (Oxford: Oxford University Press, 1968), 122.
95. See BS MS 73328B. ff.18.
96. Chesterton, *Tremendous*, 263; John Milton, *Paradise Lost* (London: John Bumpus, 1821), 164. For this interpretation of *Rasselas*, see, for example, Christine Rees, *Johnson's Milton* (Cambridge: Cambridge University Press, 2010): 58–81.
97. Preface to 'Rasselas' (1926), in Chesterton, G.*K.C. as M.C.*, 198.
98. First published in *Illustrated London News*, 3 July 1909.
99. Cited in Jack Lynch, 'Johnson and Hooker on Ecclesiastical and Civil Polity', *Review of English Studies* 55 (2004): 53; see also chapter 3 in this volume.
100. See chapter 3.
101. *CW*, vol.28, 351.
102. Ryan, 'Spectacle', 63.
103. *CW*, vol.28, 353.
104. *CW*, vol.28, 352–3.
105. *CW*, vol.28, 352–3.
106. *CW*, vol.28, 352.
107. *CW*, vol.28, 353.
108. *CW*, vol.28, 157.
109. *CW*, vol.28, 155.
110. *CW*, vol.28, 156.
111. *English Church Pageant Handbook* (London: Eyre & Spottiswoode, 1909), 52.
112. *English Church Pageant Handbook*, 52. Perhaps conscious that others might arrive at this supposition, in 'The Mystery of a Pageant' Chesterton protests that 'I had nothing to do with the arrangement': Chesterton, *Tremendous*, 258.
113. *CW*, vol.28, 350.
114. Chesterton, *G.K.C. as M.C.*, 65.
115. Walter Raubicheck, 'Father Brown and the "Performance" Of Crime', *Chesterton Review* 19 (1993): 45.
116. Chesterton, *Tremendous*, 263.
117. *CW*, vol.11, 246, 249.

118. 'Shakspere and Zola', *Illustrated London News* (18 April 1908), in *CW*, vol.28, 85.
119. See Ward, *Return*, 148, for more details of Chesterton's continuing impersonations of Johnson.
120. See Ian Ker, *G. K. Chesterton: A Biography* (Oxford: Oxford University Press, 2011), 427.
121. G. K. Chesterton, *Collected Nonsense and Light Verse*, ed. Marie Smith (London: Methuen, 1989), 43.
122. Chesterton, *Collected Nonsense*, 43.

Bibliography

Bakhtin, Mikhail. 1984. *Rabelais and His World*, translated by Helene Iswolsky. Bloomington, IN: Indiana University Press.

Bakhtin, Mikhail. 2006. *Problems of Dostoevsky's Poetics*, edited and translated by Caryl Emerson. Minneapolis, MN: Minnesota University Press.

Barnhart, Robert K., ed. 2011. *Chambers Dictionary of Etymology*. London: Chambers Harrap.

Borges, Jorge Luis. 1973. *Other Inquisitions: 1937–1952*, translated by Ruth L. C. Simms. London: Souvenir Press.

Caracciolo, Peter L. 1990. '"Carnivals of Mass-Murder": The Frazerian Origins of Wyndham Lewis's *The Childermass*', in *Sir James Frazer and the Literary Imagination: Essays in Affinity and Influence*, edited by Robert G. Fraser and Carol Pert. Basingstoke: Macmillan, 207–31.

Coates, John. 2002. *G. K. Chesterton as Controversialist, Essayist, Novelist, and Critic*. Lewiston, NY: Edwin Mellen Press.

Crangle, Sara and Nicholls, Peter, eds. 2010. *On Bathos: Literature, Art, Music*. London: Bloomsbury.

Esty, Jed. 2004. *A Shrinking Island: Modernism and National Culture in England*. Princeton, NJ: Princeton University Press.

Huizinga, Johan. 1970. *Homo Ludens: A Study of the Play Element in Culture*. London: Maurice Temple Smith.

Johnston, Freya. 2005. *Samuel Johnson and the Art of Sinking 1709–1791*. Oxford: Oxford University Press.

Ker, Ian. 2011. *G. K. Chesterton: A Biography*. Oxford: Oxford University Press.

Lynch, Jack. 2004. 'Johnson and Hooker on Ecclesiastical and Civil Polity', *Review of English Studies* 55: 45–59.

Maycock, A. L., ed. 1963. *The Man Who Was Orthodox: A Selection from the Uncollected Writings of G. K. Chesterton*. London: Dennis Dobson.

Raubicheck, Walter. 1993. 'Father Brown and the "Performance" Of Crime', *Chesterton Review* 19: 39–45.

Readman, Paul. 2005. 'The Place of the Past in English Culture *c.*1890–1914', *Past and Present* 186: 147–99.

Rees, Christine. 2010. *Johnson's Milton*. Cambridge: Cambridge University Press.

Ryan, Deborah Sugg. 1999. '"The Man Who Staged the Empire": Remembering Frank Lascelles in Sibford Gower 1875–2000', in *Material Memories: Design and Evocation*, edited by Marius Kwint, Christopher Breward and Jeremy Aynsley. Oxford: Berg, 159–79.

Ryan, Deborah Sugg. 2010. 'Spectacle, the Public, and the Crowd: Exhibitions and Pageants in 1908', in *The Edwardian Sense: Art, Design, and Performance in Britain, 1901–1910*, edited by Morna O'Neill and Michael Hatt. New Haven and London: Yale University Press, 43–71.

Stapleton, Julia, ed. 2012. *G. K. Chesterton at the Daily News: Literature, Liberalism and Revolution, 1901–1913*. 8 vols, London: Pickering & Chatto.

Svenaeus, Fredrik. 1999. 'Freud's Philosophy of the Uncanny', *Scandinavian Psychoanalytic Review* 22: 239–54.

Thomson, Philip. 1972. *The Grotesque*. London: Methuen.

Vaninskaya, Anna. 2008. '"My Mother, Drunk or Sober": G. K. Chesterton and Patriotic Anti-imperialism', *History of European Ideas* 34: 535–47.

Yoshino, Ayako. 2011. *Pageant Fever: Local History and Consumerism in Edwardian England*. Tokyo: Waseda University Press.

5

Historical Pageants, Citizenship and the Performance of Women's History before Second-Wave Feminism

Zoë Thomas

The craze for historical pageants began after a 1905 pageant in the small town of Sherborne, Dorset, when pageant-master Louis Napoleon Parker recruited 800 local people for a performance watched by 30,000.[1] Before the First World War pageants regularly took place in small southern towns. They usually consisted of a chronological series of distinct episodes that began with the Roman occupation of Britain, depicted Queen Elizabeth I and a romanticised 'Merrie England', and ended before the eighteenth century. During the interwar period, however, historical pageants gained increasing popularity in industrial towns and cities and were used to commemorate industries, organisations and social movements; scenes from the nineteenth century now abounded.[2] Pageants had by this time become a distinct, popular way for people to research, perform and enjoy history (alongside an opportunity to socialise). The crowds these attracted – regularly in the thousands – provide convincing evidence of continued popular interest in history. In the face of such public enthusiasm for these spectacles, it is widely acknowledged that they cannot simply be seen as 'top-down' efforts by upper-middle-class instigators to impose culture on the uneducated masses.[3]

Yet scholarly assessments have not usually considered women's central involvement in historical pageantry in twentieth-century Britain (though see chapter 6 in this volume).[4] Mainstream pageants customarily had hundreds, sometimes thousands, of female participants, mostly taking non-speaking parts.[5] The interwar period saw a democratisation of their roles: before 1914 women rarely held committee roles and were often relegated to dress-making parties, but after the First World War many became more centrally involved. In 1934 a journalist in the *Observer* suggested women were particularly invested in the craze because they 'sewed, they secretaried, they embroidered, they rehearsed, they committeed, they carpentered, they made chariots out of boxes and swans out of motor-cars, they worked twenty hours a day'.[6] Small numbers of women even carved out prestigious roles as 'pageant-masters' [*sic*], for example Mary Kelly, Gwen Lally and Beatrice Maybury.[7] It is essential to draw attention to the gendered nature of historical pageantry, since it was clearly rooted in female participation and nourished by women's creativity and practical endeavours.

Female contributions came to the fore within a distinct subset of historical pageants organised by women's groups. There is evidence of at least 200 such pageants in the interwar years, with a particular surge in the 1930s by organisations including the Women's Institute, the Townswomen's Guilds, the National Spinsters' Association, women's church groups and a number of university colleges.[8] Mark Freeman has emphasised that when communities decided to stage historical pageants 'there needed to be some sense of a "usable" past, one which could be brought into the service of the present in some way'.[9] For women's associations this 'usable' past was often not a general history of the locality. Women instead used pageants to conjure up an inspirational imagined community of women banded together in common aim, united in a collective wish to educate the public – and one another – about the contributions women had made to local, national and international history. The women they chose to dress up as for these performances – from Florence Nightingale to Boudica, through to the 'ordinary' woman – provided people with female role models and inspirational figures who had been active in shaping public life through their bravery, creativity and intelligence. Many of these pageants took place in England, but there were also performances in Belfast and Aberdeen. Participants varied in age, class and marital status, although organisers tended to be middle-class. When compared with mainstream pageants, these female-dominated performances provided greater opportunity for women to articulate their understanding of history, heritage, 'progress' and the ways in which the past had shaped the modern world.[10] As such, these performances form the backbone of this research.

This chapter argues that historical pageants reveal the importance of women's groups – which often had no formal connections to each other – in creating, and sustaining, a national web of women's history-telling before second-wave feminism. Such a structure functioned as a powerful alternative to prevailing male-centred narratives. Prior to the professionalisation of women's history in the 1970s, when feminists advanced the study of women within the academy, thousands of people had already been invested in women's history since the interwar years. During this era women's history was regularly excluded from scholarly and popular discourse – including books, school textbooks, paintings and sculptures in national galleries and commissioned monuments – that claimed to tell the story of Britain's past.

Women employed numerous strategies to resist and revise such narratives. Historians such as Alice Clark and Ivy Pinchbeck documented the economic and social roles of women in past societies in their scholarly work.[11] Suffrage campaigners published autobiographies in an attempt to insert women's political contributions into historical narratives, and battled to get portraits of key figures onto the walls of national galleries.[12] But mainstream women's groups played arguably the most vital role in nurturing women's historical and visual imaginations. Historical pageants provided a particularly compelling way to construct popular 'usable' pasts which cemented group cohesion, and enabled these groups visually to depict the history and interests peculiar to each organisation – from institutional histories and women's historic religious, political and professional roles to the importance of international 'sisterhood'. These performances were part of an active roster of leisure activities – including amateur dramatics, music-making and handiwork exhibitions – arranged by women's groups. All were committed to the belief that a shared community culture was crucial for a democratic society and that female involvement should be central.

Crucially, historical pageants provided a non-controversial format through which women's groups could use visual spectacle to legitimate the pursuits of modern women in national life and to encourage a more expansive, feminised public sphere.[13] By stressing women's significance throughout history, such groups actively promoted the public role that women – both married and single – should play as newly enfranchised citizens. There has been much focus on female responses to suffrage in the national political arena. However, this chapter seeks to gain insight into how women – who probably did not consciously define themselves as feminists – engaged with debates about women's responsibilities in their local neighbourhoods.[14] This research captures the engagement of women who may have considered such ideas only momentarily, but who chose voluntarily, at least for one day, to participate in an exploration of women's history. Admittedly some of these historical pageants were undoubtedly conservative and overtly patriotic. Yet women's interwar culture cannot be properly understood, as Alison Light has suggested, 'unless we admit that feminist work must deal with the conservative as well as the radical imagination'.[15]

An exception to the historiographical neglect of women's pageantry concerns events staged earlier, at the height of the suffrage campaign. The most famous of these was 'A Pageant of Great Women', a 1909 play that toured across the country before the First World War. It featured approximately 50 suffrage supporters dressed up as 'great' historical women to showcase 'the physical, intellectual, creative and ethical strengths of women'.[16] Scholars have rightly seen in these openly polemical performances attempts to shape the political and social discourse around women in society.[17] However, interest has mirrored the traditional tactic taken by early feminist historians of twentieth-century Britain – interdisciplinary scholars have focused on suffrage pageants and then leap-frogged to evaluate drama performances during second-wave feminism in the 1970s – which consequentially perpetuates the idea that the interwar period was one of feminist retrenchment.[18] While recent scholarship has taken important steps to correct this misperception, historical pageants – and the continued use of visual spectacle for social and political needs – are only just beginning to form part of this critical recovery work.[19]

After partial emancipation for women due to the Representation of the People Act in 1918, a divergence in women's priorities did lead to a move away from openly radical feminism in favour of a variety of movements aimed at ameliorating social conditions and promoting new roles for women couched within the language of citizenship. The flourishing of women's associational historical pageants, however, reveals widespread interest in exploring the meaning of women's history in communities across the country. These performances functioned as a conduit of social change that facilitated a productive cross-pollination of ideas about the importance of female involvement in national life.

Women, politics and historical pageantry

After the initial burst of suffrage pageants, and a spate of female-led processions in London celebrating women's war work during the First World War, pageants organised by women's associations took place with regularity throughout the years between the wars.[20] These historical pageants were regularly praised in the press; they were also brought to life by Virginia Woolf in her 1941 novel *Between the Acts*.[21] The performances varied in size and use of space, taking place in less traditional venues such as church halls, girls' schools and forest glens. Local authorities usually had little formal involvement. Instead, events were set up by independent women's groups that sought to bring together a cross-section of society. In contrast to traditional civic pageants, explicit links to the local community were often tenuous or non-existent and female figures were summoned from across history. Women's groups were united, however, in their wish to educate and inspire the public about the contributions women had historically made. As Mary Kelly noted in her manual *How to Make a Pageant* in 1936, one of the main concepts of pageantry was 'to praise famous men'. Women's groups consciously sought to move away from this approach and to reclaim instead the histories of women.[22]

Unlike interwar organisations with roots in the militant suffrage movement (such as the Women's Freedom League), which required commitment to the cause and a clearly articulated feminist view about absolute equality, most women's associational pageants hoped to appeal to a broad spectrum and encouraged women from all classes and political beliefs to be involved. Although this would have been complicated by existing hierarchies of friendships and embedded class structures, it was an approach that evidently appealed to large numbers of women. Mrs Godwin King, of the Women's Institute, felt in 1931 that although many hobbies such as knitting, handicrafts and gardening gave local women 'relief without much thought', drama provided 'an entirely different kind of relief' because:

> Just for a time they were acting somebody else's life, and they had to get inside that somebody's mind. They were seeing life from somebody else's point of view. It had been said that man was the only being who knew how to laugh. They must not forget that. They must not be serious all the time … They might entirely disagree with some of the things in a play, but it made them think … The old-fashioned idea that acting was merely 'dressing up and showing off' was explored … They must all make their own properties and clothes … and to remember that there was no class distinction either in the Institutes or in the acting[.][23]

Historical pageants and drama were seen to provide numerous positive societal benefits: to disrupt class hierarchies and escape rigid gender roles, to provide opportunities for women to contribute imaginatively to community life and to explore more fully experiences and histories of others.

Nevertheless, anxieties about being designated as 'too political' were debated when staging historical pageants. Constance Smedley's hugely popular – but little studied – 'Pageant of Progress', produced in the Cotswolds with 1,300 performers in 1911, is emblematic of this. Smedley herself was comfortably middle-class. She greatly enjoyed the idyllic conditions of the countryside – which she described as providing an 'almost feudal peace' – but she was also deeply concerned about the realities of village life, with its poor housing conditions, sanitation and wages. Smedley decided to stage an historical pageant, among other local work, to engage members of her local community. In an attempt to make the performance more relevant to their interests she staged the scenes 'as they affected the people's progress', but such an approach was considered by the local elites to 'teem with political propaganda'. As Smedley recalled in her memoirs,

> in spite of the introduction of Kings, Bishops, and Lords and helpers and wise counsellors throughout and the restoration of the Monarchy as a commendable act, it was regarded as socialistic.[24]

Despite such hostility, Smedley persisted with her approach:

> At a time of great depression and unrest we felt some positive constructive note should be struck: such a lot of people were uncovering the hideous conditions round us. We did not want to cover them up: nor on the other hand did we wish to show the people in a sentimental light, and prejudices and narrowness were not glossed over, but we did feel a Pageant on which so much time would be spent and in which many hundreds would participate, should draw people together and unite them in hopeful and broad-minded views and deeds and aspirations.[25]

The ability of historical pageants to impact on local class relations and inspire the community is difficult to assess due to the lack of surviving evidence from working-class participants and observers. Nevertheless, the continued cross-class voluntary involvement of people throughout the interwar years shows that pageants were spaces where boundaries between women were explored. Clearly, for some, these spaces provided a productive venue at which to attempt to rework social hierarchies, alongside having feminist, creative, social and leisure values.[26]

The central role these events played in the community in the interwar era is suggested from their regular depiction, often on the front page, of local newspapers – and also through the efforts of different women to save programmes and ephemera and donate them to the Women's Library in London. Autobiographical writing complements this picture.

In a short autobiography Gladys K. Arnold explained that, as a young girl in 1909, she had seen an historical pageant in York and 'for the first time became aware that history was real and living'. After asking for money from her father to attend another pageant in Mancroft, Norwich, in 1912, Arnold found the evening such a 'revelation' that she went again the very next night. She derived particular enjoyment from seeing people she knew take part, such as 'Miss Offord, a well-known Norwich artist, and her sister Mrs George. They were always striking to look at, but in Elizabethan ruffs and farthingales they were quite beautiful'. Arnold's youthful interest in historical pageants led to her becoming immersed in the theatrical world over the next few decades.[27]

Women's organisations and interwar historical pageants

The pageants of the Women's Institute were the most frequent, large-scale events and most representative of this outpouring of community culture. Maggie Andrews has redefined the Women's Institute, which arrived in Britain in 1915 (having originated in Canada in the 1890s), from what had previously been perceived as a rather traditional, conservative institution into a quietly feminist organisation that provided an 'alternative cultural space, a form of female-run counter-culture' for women within local branches across the country.[28] Members showed great dedication to staging pageants and, as they were influenced by the wishes of those in the locality, events varied in their scope. Some had all-female pageant committees, others male pageant-masters and organisers; some told histories explicitly about women, while others depicted general histories of the area. Pageants provided opportunities for women of all ages to be involved, playing male and female roles (Fig. 5.1). Many of them encouraged participation on an impressive scale: one Women's Institute pageant at Worcester College, Oxford, in 1926 had over 1,000 actors, including fathers and children, while a Lincolnshire pageant at Bayons Manor in Tealby was said to have had over 3,500 spectators.[29]

The Girls' Friendly Society also staged many large-scale pageants, although these were far more moralistic in approach, with much emphasis on purity, caring, feminine roles, united sisterhood and religious role models. The society, which had begun in the 1870s, reached its peak by 1914 when it boasted 81,374 'candidates'. Central to its structure was the supposed maternalistic relationship between upper-class members, Anglican associates and working-girl members who were supposed to be unmarried and of 'virtuous character'.[30] From 1925 the society began to stage a

Figure 5.1 Women's Institute 'Outdoor Pageant', location unknown, 1927. Women's Library, LSE, 5FWI/I/1/3/4/1/023 Women's Institute Pageants.

pageant entitled 'The Quest', originally produced for a pageant on 4 July of that year at the Royal Albert Hall in London. The words were provided by the celebrated pageant-master Louis Napoleon Parker, and the event was devised and produced by Henry Millar. He subsequently also organised 'The Gift', a pageant performed by the Christian Mothers' Union in 1926.[31]

'The Quest' proved so popular that it went on to be staged in Sydney, Australia.[32] Its premise was a conversation between a young girl and an old woman about the 'crisis that comes in many women's lives when a choice arises between two ways – the easy and pleasant that leads to degradation, or the toilsome and dull that leads to true happiness'.[33] In 'The Quest', the girl was shown the bravery and hard work of famous pioneering women (see chapter 6), through scenes dedicated to prison reformer Elizabeth Fry (1780–1845) and 'Poor Women', St Elizabeth of Hungary (1207–31) and attendants, and St Hilda of Whitby (*c.*614–680) and nuns. After these women had paraded across the stage, the young girl declared that these women 'are dead! Their deeds are half forgotten' – to which the old woman replied, '[n]ot so! They sowed the seed: you reap the fruit'. At this point representatives of Scotland, Ireland, Wales and England arrived to tell the girl – and the audience – that one could not be 'Alone in England!' The hard work of these past female pioneers who had 'ploughed the wilderness and sowed the seed' had 'made the desert blossom like a garden … And ye armed us with self-confidence, And hope and faith and courage'.[34] The old woman pointed out the 'harvest' of this work as Girls' Friendly Society members marched confidently across the stage alongside female clerks, students, domestic servants, doctors, 'land girls', 'chauffeuses', 'factory girls', 'business girls' and more. Then the girl was 'awakened'; she realised the contribution that women had made – and could make – to national life. She also came to appreciate that she was part of an international sisterhood, a point reinforced by the arrival of female banner bearers representing countries ranging from New Zealand to Switzerland.

Admittedly, 'The Quest' was obvious propaganda, designed to showcase how this particular organisation envisioned that young women should conduct their lives. The pageant was infused with clear religious, moralistic and nationalistic elements, yet still possessed a progressive streak. It created a new space for young girls to discover that women had actively participated in past societies, as well as promoting the acceptability, for all classes of women, of pursuing work and relationships. Moreover, it is worth noting that the audiences of women's associations and magazines were not passive absorbers of culture.[35] Women could knit and chat their way through supposedly 'improving' sessions at the Women's Institute, but the protean nature of these spaces meant that they still provided opportunities for pleasure, learning and creativity.[36] Historical pageants did not just operate as cultural hegemony. Rather they provoked an assortment of interpretations and reactions from those who participated in and watched them.

Women's interwar organisations often staged pageants to draw attention to specific causes about which members felt strongly. Such performances enabled them to project their views onto a watchful audience; they were also likely to attract press interest. A useful illustrative example here is the International Council of Women, one of the best-known international female associations. The Council worked across national boundaries to advocate women's equality and staged an expertly marketed pageant in 1929 to remind members of its history since its formation in 1888.[37] The pageant, staged by William Henry, took place at the Wharncliffe Rooms in central London, as part of the Council's International Women's Festival, which celebrated the first Council meeting in London for 30 years. There were over 1,000 attendees, representatives from 40 countries and a speech from the newly-elected Labour prime minister Ramsay MacDonald.

The pageant itself comprised a series of chronological scenes, beginning with the depiction of the Council of 1888 as a child; it bore a star of hope on its forehead alongside representatives of the founders of the organisation. The second scene depicted the London conference of 1899. It included a succession of girls and women in the costumes of their respective nations bearing tributes of their work and national produce; they stood next to figures such as 'Public Opinion with her eyes bandaged' and a group of people 'representing the laws relating to women and an equal moral standard for men and women'. The next scene was titled 'The fight for the suffrage'; an Aberdeen newspaper told readers that it had included 'a jolly representative of the activities of the old-time suffragettes'.[38] After this there was a procession of the Red Cross Society, and representatives of 'Child Welfare, Education, Trades and the Arts'. Internationally recognised female figures who had worked across public life in the nineteenth century were portrayed, among them the queen consort of Romania, Carmen Sylva, French writer George Sand, British Quaker prison reformer and philanthropist Elizabeth Fry and prominent suffrage supporters such as the French feminist Isabelle Bogelot. The *Manchester Guardian* whimsically noted that representatives of women graduates in caps and gowns brought 'reminiscent smiles to the lips of some of the educational pioneers who looked on'.[39] The final scene was a triumphant portrayal of the Council in present day, now 'in full-grown power and dignity'. It was led by its president of 30 years, Lady Ishbel Hamilton-Gordon, alongside Council executives who all assembled on the stage. They included French writer Avril de Sainte-Croix, the Danish campaigner Fröken Forchhammer – who had fought against the sexual trafficking of women and children – and Maria Gordon, the Scottish geologist and palaeontologist. Reportedly, men and women stood up on their chairs as they were so eager to see this final scene.[40]

The pageant functioned as an influential visual reminder of the extensive activities of women in the fight for political and social equality. The *New York Times* heralded the pageant as having told the story 'of feminine progress' while the *Manchester Guardian* commented that it was 'a spectacle not to be lightly regarded either by those who know the past or by those who view with anxiety the effect of the preponderance of voting in women's hands'.[41] The newspaper praised the extensive use of symbolism – a decision felt to be very effective, as although it

> may be misinterpreted in detail … in broad principles it conveys the truth in a way far beyond the power of speech, which can be understood only by those who know the language of the speaker.[42]

An astute additional feature was that during the intervals, and at the end of the pageant, attendees could visit stalls set up by various branches of the Council, which included programmes and pamphlets detailing their aims.[43] The pageant provided an opportunity for the organisation to bolster interest in their activities and to conjure a supportive, emotional reaction from participants and audience alike.

Eight years later the Leeds branch of the National Spinsters' Pensions Association (NSPA) decided to stage an 'all-spinster' pageant, demonstrating how different groups used the established popularity of historical pageantry for specific political needs. This association contrasted with groups such as the Women's Institute in its rather more working-class roots; it had existed since 1935, when sisters Florence and Annie White, who ran a sweet shop in the suburbs of Bradford, had 'chatted with customers across the counter about the financial plight of elderly spinsters'. They felt it unfair that single women had to wait until the age of 65 for their pensions when widows received theirs at 50. Florence White decided to call a meeting for single women in Bradford about this matter; it was attended by 1,000 women, mainly factory workers.[44]

Over the next ten years the women staged a number of protest marches which received extensive press attention. The *New York Times*, for example, felt that '[i]n dogged determination, these individually demure women, rallied by their champion, give nothing to the suffragettes of 1918'.[45] The *Observer* similarly observed that the scenes were 'reminiscent of the days of the Suffragette movement' as members from across the country 'wearing little bows of white and violet ribbon on their plain and sensible cloth coats' gathered together at the House of Commons to demand pensions.[46] The NSPA gained an impressive membership of 150,000, and was said to have a petition signed by over one million women.[47]

The NSPA historical pageant, organised by members in Leeds, was meant to represent single women who had 'lit the Past's dim auras with their names'. The *Yorkshire Evening Post* reported the criteria for inclusion in this pageant: 'they must have done so in their maiden names and have retained those names, otherwise they can't be in it'.[48] The event echoed the Girls' Friendly Society's 'Quest' pageant in its attempt to awaken the audience's conscience. It began with a '20th century woman' who told the audience:

> Women today make great claims. They now vote on an equality with men and enjoy many privileges which used to be denied to them. The pages of history teem with stories of great men, but have women taken their part in the world's progress?

She then asked 'What have women done to earn the privileges they enjoy?'[49] The rest of the pageant forcefully answered this question with a long parade of women – all single – across the stage during a staggering

50 *tableaux vivants*. These included women dressed up as nineteenth-century figures such as lighthouse-keeper's daughter and heroine Grace Darling, social reformer Octavia Hill, illustrator of children's books Kate Greenaway and the ever-popular Florence Nightingale (Fig. 5.2). The pageant ended with the '20th century woman' thanking these figures:

> You have helped me to realise that women have indeed done a brave share of the world's work. I feel that now their work will broaden, because of the way in which the trail has already been blazed for them by the noble women pioneers of the past.

The organisers also sought to remind the audience of the continuing plight of women and of their individual responsibilities to help:

> We still have among us numberless women who are giving of themselves in service to mankind … We have with us tonight our own beloved leader who is devoting her life to the cause of obtaining for her needy fellow spinsters redress which is long overdue.[50]

Working- and middle-class women from church groups staged many small-scale historical pageants. These showcased the role of women they felt to have been important in history, from Boudica to suffrage

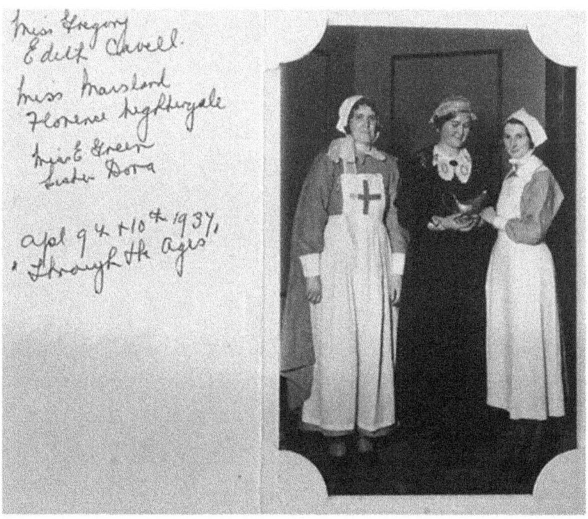

Figure 5.2 National Spinsters' Pensions Association, 'A Pageant Through the Ages', Leeds, 9–10 April 1937. Women's Library, LSE 7AA Acc No 2002/30, papers of Annie Marienne Marsland.

campaigners and prominent figures from the Bible. As usual the organisers chose to focus on specific women who captured their interests; one pageant in South Derby took the theme 'Motherhood Down the Ages', staged in 1938 at the Littleover Baptist Church.[51] Religious performances took place in local church halls in provincial industrial towns where nonconformity was prevalent, in counties such as Derbyshire, Yorkshire, Durham, Nottinghamshire and Lincolnshire. 'Women's Bright Hour' sessions, usually in the schoolrooms of churches, already female-dominated communal spaces, claimed to explore the role of women in history. Although with this grouping of women's pageants there are fewer detailed surviving records – presumably due to the social class of the participants – these performances provide useful evidence to confirm the existence of a widespread culture of pageants about women's history flourishing across the country, as well as of local, grassroots participation in 'feminist' activity.

Although many major pageants looked further into the past for role models, the most consistent feature of all women's associations' interwar pageants was that 'worthy' women were repeatedly cherry-picked from the nineteenth century for praise. Evidently women from recent history were particularly embedded within popular consciousness, and were even within the living memory of some older organisers. These pageants were labelled as 'women's progress', 'noble women' and 'pageant of women'. 'Great' women pageants were enacted in cities and villages across Britain. In 1938 the *Sheffield Independent* was emblazoned with the headline 'City to See Lives of Famous Women' when a branch of the Girls' Friendly Society staged a pageant. Produced by a Mrs Knyvet, daughter of the Bishop of Sheffield, it featured scenes from the lives 'of famous women' going back to the days of St Hilda of Whitby in AD 664.[52] Earlier, in 1934, in the wooded glades of Beachborough Park in Kent, spectators could see Florence Nightingale, Joan of Arc and 'other great figures from the pages of history whose brave deeds have echoed down the ages … brought to life for a brief space' by the Cherlton and Shorncliffe District Girl Guides Association, the pageant being performed under a canopy of overhanging trees.[53] This tactic of emphasising 'great women' was one adopted by many feminist scholars in the 1970s as they sought to reclaim a place for women within the historical canon, although it has subsequently been critiqued for providing inadequate insight into how different women actually lived.[54]

Telling histories of everyday life

Several attempts were also made by women's organisations to insert the lives and experiences of 'ordinary' women into pageants, in order to provide a more effective history of everyday life which included women from different backgrounds and nationalities. Laura Carter has recently shown how a new form of popular history, the 'history of everyday life', emerged in England after the First World War.[55] Within historical pageants we see a corresponding interest in telling an 'authentic' history through a focus on material culture, daily rituals and local lifestyles. In fact, 'H.K.C.', writing in the *Manchester Guardian* in 1934, felt it imperative that pageants should take care to use 'a thousand family records' to 'draw a picture of the Victorian woman' and bring 'into the present the memory of a thousand women unhonoured and unsung', rather than relying on Florence Nightingale as an inspirational figure.[56] As if in response to this, a Sheffield pageant of 'Noble women' in 1936 presented by the Everywoman Sisterhood at Wesley Hall, Crookes – which consisted of a series of tableaux of figures such as Joan of Arc, alongside nurse Edith Cavell and Salvation Army co-founder Catherine Booth – was one of a number of pageants that ended by depicting an 'ordinary mother' to inspire the audience about the important role of mothers in society.[57] The Mothers' Union, in a 1932 pageant entitled 'Gifts to Pandora', included cast members portraying the 'everyday woman', 'laundress', 'housemaid' and even a 'woman voter'.[58] The NSPA pageant went so far as to include living food writer Florence White 'in person' to show the range of ways in which women could contribute to society. The pageant also carefully pointed out the contributions of working-class women such as the nineteenth-century missionary Mary Slessor.[59]

These pageants often eschewed high political and economic histories dominated by elite men, instead incorporating a greater variety of historical figures. One Women's Institute 'miniature pageant', staged in a church hall in Sharnbrook, Bedford in 1937, was entitled 'The Domestic Life of England'; it portrayed scenes from seven periods, beginning in 100 BC with the depiction of the home of an 'Early Briton' and his family. Other scenes included a 'Norman Knight and his lady at the time the Domesday Book was Compiled' and 'Miss 1937 dressed as a flapper in beach pyjamas and big hat smoking a cigarette'.[60] Clearly pageants provided valuable opportunities to question and explore societal changes.

The following year, in 1938, over 1,000 members of the Sunderland Townswomen's Guild staged a 'Pageant of the Women's Movement' which depicted events and characters from the previous 150 years.

Townswomen's Guilds had been formed in 1929 after women had received full voting rights; their aim was to educate women about their new roles as citizens.[61] In the pageant of 1938, great efforts were taken to instruct the audience about the past suffering experienced by women due to their social, economic and legal subjection. Written by Miss W. J. E. Moul, Chair of the Townswomen's Guilds, it drew attention to Caroline Norton's 1836 fight for custody of her sons following her divorce from MP George Chapple Norton (see chapter 6), and to Lord Shaftesbury's 1842 commission to Parliament about women working in the mines; it also included a 'cinematographic presentation' of the women who had fought for the vote. The pageant ended with the firm declaration that 'women are not afraid of work of any sort, however difficult or exacting that is'.[62]

Authenticity and place

Although it has been established that the organisers of historical pageants carefully selected figures and scenes they felt to be most relevant – something professional historians also necessarily do – the surviving evidence suggests that those involved did take considerable interest in 'authenticity' and in providing accurately researched histories. Programmes were neatly compiled with mini-biographies of the historical women. Great interest was taken in educating audiences about the legitimacy of the locations and archival sources that were being used. In a 1926 article in the *Manchester Guardian* the reviewer of a Women's Institute pageant in Epping Forest happily felt that, '[f]rom the antiquarian point of view', it was full of scenes for which 'chapter and verse could be quoted from local archives'. Members of the Institute had carefully sought to provide intimate glimpses into the past, such as one 'very effective scene ... in which two widows described their forest rights'.[63] In the view of this reporter, the audience had

> remained conscious throughout of it being performed on the spot where it all happened, in a natural wild forest ... and whose deer are the actual descendants of those of the Forest Wardens.[64]

Reports and programmes were used to inform the audience about the authenticity of props such as 'a linen table cloth actually used in the civil wars' and '[a] Forester's horn of the date of George III'.[65] It was felt these objects held particular potential to evoke the past for an intrigued public. In the International Council of Women pageant, actual suffrage banners were repurposed: 'banners which had been carried in many more toilsome processions than this, and brought with them the memory of a hard fight now happily ended' were complemented by 'proper dresses of the period' for the 1888 and 1899 scenes. Women who had 'wherever possible ... actually been present, or their relatives' were invited to be involved for these scenes.[66] There was great encouragement to daughters to depict the roles that their mothers had once played – a clever ploy that forged new links between older and younger generations.[67] Similarly, in the 1938 Townswomen's Guild Pageant the dresses were designed by a Mrs J. T. Burnop and her daughter. The mother had been chosen as she was known to be 'an authority on styles as worn by members of women's movements years ago'.[68] Burnop sketched her own drawings for the period costumes after detailed 'research into reference books of the 19th century and the cooperation of the Sunderland's Director of Libraries'.[69]

Depicting womanhood: from the medieval to the 'modern'

Mirroring the approach of mainstream pageants – which sought to forge a tangible connection between past achievements and living, present-day communities – women's associations made sure that the historical figures and staged scenes were relevant to their community building aims in modern life. The final scene was routinely reserved to show the audience that they were all at that very moment in the process of making history. Although Colin M. Coates and Cecilia Morgan suggest that 'pageants were intended to reinforce and enliven material already taught in the classroom, not to introduce children to new historical knowledge', these events actually provided a rare opportunity to learn about women's history and to visualise one's own role within this narrative.[70]

A useful example here is a Women's Institute pageant at Windsor Park on 28 June 1928 which told the story of 'some of the chief events ... taking place on Berkshire soil'. As ever, it was an extensively planned and impressive sounding affair, led by pageant-master Mrs George Squire, musical conductor Ethel Nettleship and mistress of robes Mrs Dryland Haslam; the words were by George Kenneth Menzies, Vice-President of the Royal Society of Arts, and a host of other committee members contributed to the organisation. The pageant told a general history of Berkshire, with the usual care taken to sprinkle women's contributions throughout. It ended with an evocative scene showing 'a living map of Berkshire', in which Women's Institute banner-bearers stood in position representing their villages, surrounded by members from each local Institute. This spectacle was enhanced by a final speech blatantly designed to make attendees feel their personal responsibility towards both the local community and to national life:

> You have watched our story grow – it is your story also … May we remind you before we part that we are all still making history … Take with you, with the memory of our past, a desire to help in the present, that our land may never lack the loyal co-operation of its women, generation after generation, through the ages still to come.[71]

These final scenes were not overtly feminist manifestos, often taking the form of a tongue-in-cheek account of contemporary women's 'modern' lifestyles. At a Kent flower show in 1925 women presented a pageant of dress which finished with a future 'Miss 1930' wearing a man's costume and a horn-rimmed monocle, and carrying a cane and pipe. Female university students in Bangor, North Wales, used the 1932 Pageant of Bangor to celebrate women students; they also portrayed their future counterparts sporting monocles and cigarettes.[72] On one level this was a commentary on the rapid pace of social change, but pageant organisers also used humour to disarm an audience who might disapprove of women taking on 'male' roles.

Conversely, while the imagined future could be mocked for being too 'progressive', the past was sometimes derided for being too regressive. In 1930 Bedford College, a women's college of the University of London, staged a 20-scene pageant entitled 'Time's Daughters' in Regent's Park in aid of a college extension fund for new laboratories and lecture theatres. 'Time's Daughters' told the story of 'the evolution of the modern girl from the Middle Ages to the present day'. The pageant included a 'kaleidoscope' of huntresses of early England, Plantagenet queens and ladies weaving tapestry and Queen Elizabeth 'dancing before the Spanish Ambassador, but not, if you please, to his tune', before ending with 'the Woman of To-day', a scene that focused on students of the college.[73] The pageant, which proved so popular that spectators had to be turned away, provided a way for Bedford College students past and present, who were centrally involved in the planning, to define in their own terms the changes they felt had taken place for women across the centuries.[74] The *Yorkshire Post* told readers that the pageant was

> intended to provide an answer to two leading questions debated under various titles every morning with painstaking regularity in the columns of the popular Press: 'Who is responsible for making the modern girl what she is?' and 'What final picture will future generations have of her?'[75]

The *Observer* also picked out scenes to emphasise. It focused on the 'frumps' of the early days of the college, depicted through a much-ridiculed chaperone 'complete with knitting' who was said to have policed every lecture and boat race ever held at Bedford. Lady Rodd told the audience in the opening ceremony about her memories of student days, stating that Bedford College women had been 'rather old-fashioned girls, I'm afraid'.[76] By asserting – and exaggerating – the archaic nature of nineteenth-century practices of female respectability, these women placed themselves at the forefront of modern citizenship and sought to promote this perspective of women now living modern, public lives across mainstream culture.

Women's associational historical pageants diminished during the Second World War, partly as a result of women's organisations instead focusing their energies on supporting the war effort. Still, although staged less regularly, some women's groups did put on performances, and they continued to provide a popular way for people to find out about women's history after the war. The Leeds Townswomen's Guild performed an historical pageant titled 'Mrs Leeds, 1850 to 1950', for which members undertook detailed research work hunting out the correct chair and actual speeches for a scene that commemorated Queen Victoria's opening of Leeds Town Hall in 1858. The research led to the 'surprise' discovery that a woman, Elizabeth Beecroft, had been centrally involved in the history of Kirkstall Forge Iron Works from 1779.[77] Other historical pageants after the Second World War by the same organisation addressed such topics as 'Women Can Make Peace', a view said to represent the views of more than 2,150 members, alongside another pageant explicitly intending to address the theme of female citizenship. The latter explored what the *Sunderland Daily Echo* felt to be the guild's belief that '[w]omen's social responsibility began when they gained the right to vote, and if the world is still in a mess they must share the blame equally with the men'.[78]

During the era which heralded second-wave feminism, women were still using historical pageants and theatre as a powerful visual channel through which to fight patriarchal constructs. This generation of women appropriated many of the established tropes that had been developed across the century. 'The Brilliant and the Dark', for instance, an opera staged by the Women's Institute at the Royal Albert Hall in 1969, led the audience through a history of women's experiences. It featured women dressed as suffrage supporters, nuns, peasants and cooks, among other roles.

Conclusion

Historical pageants organised by British women's organisations of the interwar years reveal the range in priorities for these groups through their choice of characters and themes, influenced by marital status, religious belief, occupation, nationality, location, class, age and personal interest. Many women's groups were wedded to using pageants to show support for both nationalistic sentiment and 'progress' – two aims that can be difficult to reconcile. Yet these pageants do demonstrate that there was a coherent circulation, amidst mainstream organisations for girls and women, of the belief that it was essential to promote the active role that women had played in the past – and could play in the present and future.

Such performances offer a new chronology for conceptualising twentieth-century women's history, one that is more open to non-professional participation. Moving away from focus on the activities of those in the academy as a result of second-wave feminism, this essay has demonstrated that, across the first half of the twentieth century, a great many women's organisations were deeply interested in researching, performing and exploring the complexities of women's histories. A number of women even took care to include histories of everyday life in their pageants in order to make these productions more relevant for 'ordinary' women.

Historical pageants thus provided an informal way for women to engage – as little or as much as they wished – in disseminating stories about the historical adventures of women to their family, friends and communities. They legitimised active female involvement in public life and asserted a space for women's future involvement as citizens. Many women did not have the time, energy or desire to define themselves as feminists, but pageants provided an opportunity to engage actively in an acceptable process of perpetuating feminist ideals, while not necessarily consciously articulating this in their self-representation. Historical pageants demonstrate the dispersed, yet committed, nature of the endeavours towards improving women's lives during the interwar years; in doing so, they support a more pluralistic understanding of women's engagement in activism across Britain.

Notes

1. Mark Freeman, '"Splendid Display; Pompous Spectacle": Historical Pageants in Twentieth-Century Britain', *Social History* 30 (2013): 423–55; Paul Readman, 'The Place of the Past in English Culture, *c.* 1890–1914', *Past and Present* 186 (2005): 147–99.
2. Tom Hulme, '"A Nation of Town Criers": Civic Publicity and Historical Pageantry in Inter-War Britain', *Urban History* 44 (2017): 1–23.

3. Readman, 'Place of the Past'; Deborah Sugg Ryan, '"Pageantitis": Visualising Frank Lascelles' 1907 Oxford Historical Pageant', *Visual Culture in Britain* 8 (2007): 63–82; Ayako Yoshino, *Pageant Fever: Local History and Consumerism in Edwardian England* (Tokyo: Waseda University Press, 2011); Helen McCarthy, 'The League of Nations, Public Ritual and National Identity in Britain, c. 1919–56', *History Workshop Journal* 70 (2010): 108–32.
4. See also Zoë Thomas, 'Historical Pageants, Citizenship, and the Performance of Women's History before Second-wave Feminism', *Twentieth Century British History* 28 (2017): 319–43; Amy Binns, 'New Heroines for New Causes: How Provincial Women Promoted a Revisionist History through Post-Suffrage Pageants', *Women's History Review* 27 (2017): 1–26.
5. Newspapers even made special pleas for male participants. In the Manchester Centenary pageant of 1938 female volunteers outnumbered men by ten to one: 'Women Eager for Pageant', *Sunderland Daily Echo and Shipping Gazette*, 6 June 1938, 2.
6. 'Pageantry and Its Fascination', *Observer*, 17 June 1934, 26.
7. Sei Kosugi, 'Representing Nation and Nature: Woolf, Kelly, White', in *Locating Woolf: The Politics of Space and Place*, ed. Anna Snaith and Michael Whitworth (Basingstoke: Palgrave Macmillan, 2007), 81–96; Mick Wallis, 'Unlocking the Secret Soul: Mary Kelly, Pioneer of Village Theatre', *New Theatre Quarterly* 16 (2000): 347–58; Deborah Sugg Ryan, 'Lally, Gwen (1882–1963)', *Oxford Dictionary of National Biography* (Oxford: Oxford University Press, 2004).
8. Advertisements, reviews and photographs listing over 200 pageants staged by women's organisations were collated from the British Newspaper Archive digitisation project and through documentation at the Women's Library, London School of Economics (LSE). The actual number of women's interwar pageants is likely to have been substantially higher because some may not have been reported in the press and a number were repeated – nor is the digitisation project yet complete.
9. Freeman, '"Splendid Display; Pompous Spectacle"', 426.
10. In contrast, David Glassberg has argued that in North America women's contributions upheld patriarchal roles because – in his view – women were only represented in episodes depicting the social and domestic side of community life. As such, '[t]he pageant woman symbolizing the community resembled the idealized female … explicitly tied to images of both maternity and maturity through casting and surrounding imagery. The women commonly cast in this role were middle-aged and married'. David Glassberg, *American Historical Pageantry: The Uses of Tradition in the Early Twentieth Century* (Chapel Hill, NC: University of North Carolina Press, 1990), 135–7. In Britain, however, the women involved ranged in age, class, marital status and political motivation, as well as in the histories they wished to tell.
11. Billie Melman, 'Gender, History and Memory: The Invention of Women's Past in the Nineteenth and Early Twentieth Centuries', *History and Memory* 5 (1993): 5–41. See also Billie Melman, 'Changing the Subject: Women's History and Historiography, 1900–2000', in *Women in Twentieth-Century Britain*, ed. Ina Zweiniger-Bargielowska (Harlow: Longman, 2001), 16–35.
12. Hilda Kean, 'Searching for the Past in Present Defeat: The Construction of Historical and Political Feminism in the 1920s and 1930s', *Women's History Review* 3 (1994): 57–80.
13. *The Invention of Tradition*, ed. Eric Hobsbawm and Terence Ranger (Cambridge: Cambridge University Press, 1983), 12.
14. Caitriona Beaumont's research shows that mainstream women's organisations avoided using potentially divisive terms associated with suffragettes or feminists in favour of a more capacious and less challenging rhetoric of citizenship: Caitriona Beaumont, 'Citizens not Feminists: The Boundary Negotiated Between Citizenship and Feminism by Mainstream Women's Organizations in England, 1928–39', *Women's History Review* 9 (2000): 411–29; Caitriona Beaumont, *Housewives and Citizens: Domesticity and the Women's Movement in England, 1928–64* (Manchester: Manchester University Press, 2013). See also June Hannam and Karen Hunt, 'Towards an Archaeology of Inter-war Women's Politics: The Local and the Everyday', in *The Aftermath of Suffrage: Women, Gender, and Politics in Britain, 1918–1945*, ed. Julie V. Gottlieb and Richard Toye (Basingstoke: Palgrave Macmillan, 2013), 121–41; Julie V. Gottlieb, 'Introduction: "Flour Power" and Feminism Between the Waves', *Women's History Review* 23 (2014): 325–9; Tom Hulme, 'Putting the City Back into Citizenship: Civics Education and Local Government in Britain, 1918–45', *Twentieth Century British History* 26 (2015): 26–51.
15. Alison Light, *Forever England: Literature, Femininity and Conservatism between the Wars* (London: Routledge, 1991), 13–14.
16. Maxine Berg, *A Woman in History: Eileen Power 1889–1940* (Cambridge: Cambridge University Press, 1996), 63; Antoinette Burton, *Burdens of History: British Feminists, Indian Women,*

and Imperial Culture, 1865–1915 (Chapel Hill, NC: University of North Carolina Press, 1994), 56–7; Antoinette Burton, '"History" is Now: Feminist Theory and the Production of Historical Feminisms', *Women's History Review* 1 (1992): 25–39.

17. Sheila Stowell, *A Stage of Their Own: Feminist Playwrights of the Suffrage Era* (Ann Arbor, MI: University of Michigan Press, 1994); Irene Cockroft and Susan Croft, *Art, Theatre and Women's Suffrage* (Twickenham: Aurora Metro, 2010).
18. Rebecca Cameron, 'From Great Women to Top Girls: Pageants of Sisterhood in British Feminist Theater', *Comparative Drama* 43 (2009): 143–66.
19. In recent years there have been concerted efforts to show the vibrancy of the interwar women's movement. During the 1920s and 1930s, Pat Thane has argued, more women, from a wider range of backgrounds than ever before, were actively campaigning for gender equality: Pat Thane, 'What Difference Did the Vote Make? Women in Public and Private Life in Britain Since 1918', *Historical Research* 76 (2003): 272. See also Adrian Bingham, '"An Era of Domesticity"? Histories of Women and Gender in Inter-War Britain', *Cultural and Social History* 1 (2004): 225–33; Maria DiCenzo, '"Our Freedom and its Results": Measuring Progress in the Aftermath of Suffrage', *Women's History Review* 23 (2014): 421–40.
20. 'Women's War Procession: Pageant of the Allies', *Observer*, 23 June 1916, 11.
21. Woolf's novel is likely to have been influenced by her involvement in Women's Institute pageants in Rodmell, Sussex. See Ayako Yoshino, '*Between the Acts* and Louis Napoleon Parker – The Creator of the Modern English Pageant', *Critical Survey* 15 (2003): 49–60; Ben Harker, '"On Different Levels Ourselves Went Forward": Pageantry, Class Politics and Narrative Form in Virginia Woolf's Late Writing', *English Literary History* 78 (2011): 433–56; Clara Jones, *Virginia Woolf: Ambivalent Activist* (Edinburgh: Edinburgh University Press, 2016), 154–206. Of particular interest is Jones's exploration of how Woolf felt about the Women's Institute. Woolf felt it to have a nationalistic and patriotic agenda which led to her personal 'competing impulses of desire for inclusion and ironic detachment' (p.157).
22. Mary Kelly, *How to Make a Pageant* (London: Sir I. Pitman & Sons, 1936), 8.
23. 'Group Meeting of Women's Institutes', *Mid Sussex Times*, 20 October 1931, 2.
24. Constance Smedley, *Crusaders: The Reminiscences of Constance Smedley / Mrs Maxwell Armfield Smedley* (London: Duckworth, 1929), 204.
25. Smedley, *Crusaders*, 204.
26. Newspaper reports regularly reported on the involvement of different classes. At one pageant in Kenilworth in 1939 the reporter commented: '[g]lancing around the members of the cast at one of the performances this week, there seemed to be women, women everywhere. Young girls from Leamington High School, married women, mothers, grandmothers, grandchildren, and even one lady over 80 years of age … There are all ranks of women in the Pageant from titled ladies to young shop girls from nearby villages who have had to cycle to practices after their day's work was over': 'Women's Part in Kenilworth Pageantry', *Coventry Herald*, 15 July 1939, 2.
27. Gladys K. Arnold, 'I Can Smell Gas'. Undated and self-published; in the author's possession.
28. Maggie Andrews, *The Acceptable Face of Feminism: The Women's Institute Movement 1915–1960* (London: Lawrence & Wishart, 1997), 11. See also Lorna Gibson, *Beyond Jerusalem: Music in the Women's Institute, 1919–1969* (Aldershot: Ashgate, 2008).
29. 'Pageant at Worcester College, Oxford', *Banbury Guardian*, 24 May 1926, 7; 'In Lincolnshire', *Lincolnshire Echo*, 1 July 1939, 4.
30. Vivienne Richmond, '"It is not a Society for Human Beings but for Virgins": The Girls' Friendly Society Membership Eligibility Dispute 1875–1936', *Journal of Historical Sociology* 20 (2007): 304–27; Brian Harrison, 'For Church, Queen and Family, the Girls' Friendly Society, 1874–1920', *Past and Present* 61 (1973): 109.
31. A number of women's pageants decided to use famed male pageant-masters to enhance the prestige of their events. Louis N. Parker and Henry Millar, *The Quest: A Pageant of the Girls' Friendly Society* (London: The Girls' Friendly Society, 1925).
32. '"The Quest." Girls' Friendly Society', *The Sydney Morning Herald*, 5 December 1928, 15.
33. '"The Quest"', 15.
34. Parker and Millar, *The Quest*, 5–6.
35. Fiona Hackney, 'Quiet Activism and the New Amateur: The Power of Home and Hobby Crafts', *Design and Culture* 5 (2013): 169–93.
36. Andrews, *The Acceptable Face of Feminism*, 67–70.
37. International Council of Women pamphlet and tickets: Box 17 5ICW/C/02/04, 'International Council of Women Pageants.' Women's Library, LSE.

38. 'Women's Pageant', *Aberdeen Journal*, 7 May 1929, 6.
39. A Correspondent, 'Women's Festival: A Message of Good Will and Helpfulness', *Manchester Guardian*, 10 May 1929, 8.
40. A Correspondent, 'Women's Festival', 8.
41. 'Women Present Pageant: Appear as Leaders in Feminine Progress for London Council', *New York Times*, 5 May 1929, 33.
42. A Correspondent, 'Women's Festival', 8.
43. 'Women's Pageant', *Aberdeen Journal*, 7 May 1929, 6.
44. Joseph A. Collins, 'A "Surplus" Woman: Florence White Leads England's Spinsters in their Crusade for Old-Age Pensions at 60', *New York Times*, 5 May 1946, 15.
45. Collins, 'A "Surplus" Woman', 15.
46. 'Pensions for Spinsters at 55: M.P.s at London Rally', *Observer*, 6 June 1937, 28; 'Spinsters, Demanding Their Pension at 55, Cause Some Red Faces in House of Commons', *New York Times*, 12 February 1948, 15.
47. 'Million Spinsters to Petition', *Observer*, 25 July 1937, 8; 'Pensions at 55: Million Signatures to Petition', *Manchester Guardian*, 27 July 1937, 6.
48. 'Pageant of Famous Spinsters', *Yorkshire Evening Post*, 12 January 1937, 11.
49. NSPA pageant programme, Papers of Annie Marienne Marsland 7AMM Acc No 2002/30, Women's Library, LSE.
50. NSPA pageant programme, Papers of Annie Marienne Marsland 7AMM Acc No 2002/30, Women's Library, LSE.
51. 'Motherhood Down the Ages', *Derby Daily Telegraph*, 1 December 1938, 5.
52. 'City to See Lives of Famous Women', *Sheffield Independent*, 30 September 1938, 3.
53. 'Delightful Pageant at Beachborough', *Folkstone, Hythe, Sandgate and Cheriton Herald*, 30 June 1934, 16.
54. Barbara Caine, 'Feminist Biography and Feminist History', *Women's History Review* 3 (1994): 250.
55. Laura Carter, 'The Quennells and the "History of Everyday Life" in England, *c.* 1918–69', *History Workshop Journal* 81 (2016): 113.
56. H. K. C., 'Victorian Pageant: The Woman's Part', *Manchester Guardian*, 1 May 1934, 8.
57. 'Page from History: Sheffield Pageant of Noble Women', *Sheffield Independent*, 15 April 1936, 7.
58. 'Big Week for a Church', *Cheltenham Chronicle*, 16 April 1932, 8.
59. NSPA pageant programme, Papers of Annie Marienne Marsland 7AMM Acc No 2002/30, Women's Library, LSE.
60. 'Sharnbrook Women's Pageant: The Domestic Life of England', *Bedfordshire Times and Independent*, 30 July 1937, 3.
61. '1,000 Guild Members to Take Part in Pageant', *Sunderland Daily Echo and Shipping Gazette*, 3 May 1938, 6.
62. '1,000 Will Take Part', *Sunderland Daily Echo and Shipping Gazette*, 13 May 1938, 16.
63. 'Pageant in a Forest: A Women's Institute Production', *Manchester Guardian*, 19 July 1926, 6.
64. On pageants deriving 'authenticity from their setting', see Angela Bartie, Linda Fleming, Mark Freeman, Tom Hulme, Alexander Hutton and Paul Readman, '"History Taught in the Pageant Way": Education and Historical Performance in Twentieth-Century Britain', *History of Education* 48 (2019): 170.
65. Pamphlet, 'A Historical Pageant of Some of the Chief Events in the History of England Taking Place on Berkshire Soil', 5FWI/H/13 Box 274, Women's Library, LSE.
66. 'Women Present Pageant', 33.
67. Kean, 'Searching for the Past in Present Defeat', 60.
68. '1,000 Guild Members to Take Part in Pageant', 6.
69. '1,000 Will Take Part', 16.
70. Colin M. Coates and Cecilia Morgan, *Heroines and History: Representations of Madeleine de Verchères and Laura Secord* (Toronto: University of Toronto Press, 2002), 210.
71. Pamphlet, 'A Historical Pageant of Some of the Chief Events in the History of England Taking Place on Berkshire Soil', 5FWI/H/13 Box 274, Women's Library, LSE.
72. 'Looking Ahead', *Gloucester Citizen*, 17 August 1925, 11. 'Bangor Students "Rag": Women's Prominent Part', *Manchester Guardian*, 26 February 1932, 6.
73. A Special Correspondent, 'Bedford College Pageant "Time's Daughters"', *Observer*, 18 May 1930, 21.

74. The Bedford College Union Magazine noted that Miss fforde, a former student, wrote and produced the pageant alongside a large number of assistants: *Bedford College Union Magazine*, No.27, June 1930, 6. Bedford College Archive, Royal Holloway, University of London.
75. 'Regiment of Women', *Yorkshire Post*, 12 May 1930, 8.
76. A Special Correspondent, 'Bedford College Pageant', 21.
77. 'News-Notes for Women', *Yorkshire Post and Leeds Intelligencer*, 2 March 1950, 3.
78. 'Women Can Make Peace', *Sunderland Daily Echo and Shipping Gazette*, 3 July 1946, 5; 'Townswomen's Guilds at Festival Hall', *The Stage*, 17 June 1954, 10.

Bibliography

Andrews, Maggie. 1997. *The Acceptable Face of Feminism: The Women's Institute Movement 1915–1960*. London: Lawrence & Wishart.

Bartie, Angela, Fleming, Linda, Freeman, Mark, Hulme, Tom, Hutton, Alexander and Readman, Paul. 2019. '"History Taught in the Pageant Way": Education and Historical Performance in Twentieth-Century Britain', *History of Education* 48: 156–79.

Beaumont, Caitriona. 2000. 'Citizens not Feminists: The Boundary Negotiated Between Citizenship and Feminism by Mainstream Women's Organizations in England, 1928–39', *Women's History Review* 9: 411–29.

Beaumont, Caitriona. 2013. *Housewives and Citizens: Domesticity and the Women's Movement in England, 1928–64*. Manchester: Manchester University Press.

Berg, Maxine. 1996. *A Woman in History: Eileen Power 1889–1940*. Cambridge: Cambridge University Press.

Bingham, Adrian. 2005 '"An Era of Domesticity"? Histories of Women and Gender in Inter-War Britain', *Cultural and Social History* 1: 225–33.

Binns, Amy. 2017. 'New Heroines for New Causes: How Provincial Women Promoted a Revisionist History through Post-Suffrage Pageants', *Women's History Review* 27: 1–26.

Burton, Antoinette. 1992. '"History" is Now: Feminist Theory and the Production of Historical Feminisms', *Women's History Review* 1: 25–39.

Burton, Antoinette. 1994. *Burdens of History: British Feminists, Indian Women, and Imperial Culture, 1865–1915*. Chapel Hill, NC: University of North Carolina Press.

Caine, Barbara. 1994. 'Feminist Biography and Feminist History', *Women's History Review* 3: 247–61.

Cameron, Rebecca. 2009. 'From Great Women to Top Girls: Pageants of Sisterhood in British Feminist Theater', *Comparative Drama* 43: 143–66.

Carter, Laura. 'The Quennells and the "History of Everyday Life" in England, *c*.1918–69', *History Workshop Journal* 81: 106–34.

Coates, Colin M. and Morgan, Cecilia. 2002. *Heroines and History: Representations of Madeleine de Verchères and Laura Secord*. Toronto: University of Toronto Press.

Cockroft, Irene and Croft, Susan. 2010. *Art, Theatre and Women's Suffrage*. Twickenham: Aurora Metro.

DiCenzo, Maria. 2014. '"Our Freedom and its Results": Measuring Progress in the Aftermath of Suffrage', *Women's History Review* 23: 421–40.

Freeman, Mark. 2013. '"Splendid Display; Pompous Spectacle": Historical Pageants in Twentieth-Century Britain', *Social History* 38: 423–55.

Gibson, Lorna. 2008. *Beyond Jerusalem: Music in the Women's Institute, 1919–1969*. Aldershot: Ashgate.

Glassberg, David. 1990. *American Historical Pageantry: The Uses of Tradition in the Early Twentieth Century*. Chapel Hill, NC: University of North Carolina Press.

Gottlieb, Julie V. 2014. 'Introduction: "Flour Power" and Feminism Between the Waves', *Women's History Review* 23: 325–9.

Hackney, Fiona. 2013. 'Quiet Activism and the New Amateur: The Power of Home and Hobby Crafts', *Design and Culture* 5: 169–93.

Hannam, June and Hunt, Karen. 2013. 'Towards an Archaeology of Inter-war Women's Politics: The Local and the Everyday', in *The Aftermath of Suffrage: Women, Gender, and Politics in Britain, 1918–1945*, edited by Julie V. Gottlieb and Richard Toye. Basingstoke: Palgrave Macmillan, 121–41.

Harker, Ben. 2011. '"On Different Levels Ourselves Went Forward": Pageantry, Class Politics and Narrative Form in Virginia Woolf's Late Writing', *English Literary History* 78: 433–56.
Harrison, Brian. 1973. 'For Church, Queen and Family, the Girls' Friendly Society, 1874–1920', *Past and Present* 61: 107–38.
Hobsbawm, Eric and Ranger, Terence, eds. 1983. *The Invention of Tradition*. Cambridge: Cambridge University Press.
Hulme, Tom. 2015. 'Putting the City Back into Citizenship: Civics Education and Local Government in Britain, 1918–45', *Twentieth Century British History* 26: 26–51.
Hulme, Tom. 2017. '"A Nation of Town Criers": Civic Publicity and Historical Pageantry in Inter-War Britain', *Urban History* 44: 1–23.
Jones, Clara. 2016. *Virginia Woolf: Ambivalent Activist*. Edinburgh: Edinburgh University Press.
Kean, Hilda. 1994. 'Searching for the Past in Present Defeat: The Construction of Historical and Political Feminism in the 1920s and 1930s', *Women's History Review* 3: 57–80.
Kosugi, Sei. 2007. 'Representing Nation and Nature: Woolf, Kelly, White', in *Locating Woolf: The Politics of Space and Place*, edited by Anna Snaith and Michael Whitworth. Basingstoke: Palgrave Macmillan, 81–96.
Light, Alison. 1991. *Forever England: Literature, Femininity and Conservatism between the Wars*. London and New York: Routledge.
McCarthy, Helen. 2010. 'The League of Nations, Public Ritual and National Identity in Britain *c*. 1919–56', *History Workshop Journal* 70: 108–32.
Melman, Billie. 1993. 'Gender, History and Memory: The Invention of Women's Past in the Nineteenth and Early Twentieth Centuries', *History and Memory* 5: 5–41.
Melman, Billie. 2001. 'Changing the Subject: Women's History and Historiography, 1900–2000', in *Women in Twentieth-Century Britain*, edited by Ina Zweiniger-Bargielowska. Harlow: Longman, 16–35.
Readman, Paul. 2005. 'The Place of the Past in English Culture, *c*. 1890–1914. *Past and Present* 186: 147–99.
Richmond, Vivienne. 2007. '"It is not a Society for Human Beings but for Virgins": The Girls' Friendly Society Membership Eligibility Dispute 1875–1936', *Journal of Historical Sociology* 20: 304–27.
Ryan, Deborah Sugg. 2007. '"Pageantitis": Frank Lascelles' 1907 Oxford Historical Pageant, Visual Spectacle and Popular Memory', *Visual Culture in Britain* 8: 63–82.
Stowell, Sheila. 1994. *A Stage of Their Own: Feminist Playwrights of the Suffrage Era*. Ann Arbor , MI: University of Michigan Press.
Thane, Pat. 2003. 'What Difference Did the Vote Make? Women in Public and Private Life in Britain Since 1918', *Historical Research* 76: 268–85.
Thomas, Zoë. 2017. 'Historical Pageants, Citizenship, and the Performance of Women's History before Second-wave Feminism', *Twentieth Century British History* 28: 319–43.
Wallis, Mick. 2000. 'Unlocking the Secret Soul: Mary Kelly, Pioneer of Village Theatre', *New Theatre Quarterly* 16: 347–58.
Yoshino, Ayako. 2003. '*Between the Acts* and Louis Napoleon Parker – The Creator of the Modern English Pageant', *Critical Survey* 15: 49–60.
Yoshino, Ayako. 2011. *Pageant Fever: Local History and Consumerism in Edwardian England*. Tokyo: Waseda University Press.

6

Nobility, Duty and Courage: Propaganda and Inspiration in Interwar Women's and Girls' Pageants

Amy Binns

For women, the interwar years have often been seen as a period of conservative reaction. Women who had gone out to work during the war largely returned to the home: doing men's jobs was now widely seen as selfish, not patriotic. New civic organisations such as the Women's Institute (WI) upheld traditional gender roles and lauded 'responsibility', in contrast to the law-breaking militancy of the pre-war fight for the vote. The political dominance of the Conservative Party was partly due to its success in appealing to the newly enfranchised women, not least by means of innovative propaganda specifically addressing these voters.[1] Nor did the winning of the vote for women of property over 30 in 1918 herald the opening of many further doors. Women continued to face resistance at every stage in their advance: into political parties, trade unions and Parliament. Prior to 1945, there were never more than 15 women MPs in the House of Commons at any one time.[2]

But to paint these years as wholly reactionary is simplistic. Women were growing into their new roles as enfranchised citizens. They were searching for new identities without the comradeship of the fight for the vote; and they were reconciling their new status and opportunities with traditional roles as wives and mothers. Political energy still existed, but splintered into new campaigns, such as those for better housing and freely available contraception. The generation of 'war spinsters' fought for a better economic deal while finding creative ways of living without men.[3]

One reason for the prevalence of interpretations emphasising the regressive character of interwar society is the prominence, in the archival record, of material associated with large, extant institutions such as the WI. Hundreds of other smaller, informal or short-lived groups have left fainter traces, yet they represented a wider range of views.[4] Many of these varying women's groups produced historical pageants, as did the WI itself. These events, although largely neglected by historians,[5] give us a valuable window onto their ideas, as they created new narratives and celebrated forgotten heroines. There was no standard or accepted women's history, and so dozens of groups created their own. The organisation of pageants gave women a chance literally to step on to the public stage, using a large-scale and (sometimes) profitable format to promote their own visions of what has been and could be. The hustings, the debating halls and even the letters pages of newspapers were guarded by male gatekeepers, and gaining access demanded considerable confidence and assertiveness. Yet the staging of a pageant enabled women creatively to express political views on women's roles, freely or subtly, while supported by friends.

Pageants as a political statement had been well-known to the women's movement long before the First World War. Suffragettes used a pantheon of heroines as part of their justification for the right to vote. The Christian military figure of Joan of Arc was particularly popular; women personified her in parades in Britain and the United States, sometimes with other heroines such as Grace Darling, Charlotte Brontë, Jenny Lind and Harriet Martineau. The concept was formalised in Cicely Hamilton's 'Pageant of Great Women' which toured Britain from 1910.[6]

After the landmark of suffrage in 1918, however, these politics had to change. The suffragettes, always a loose and factionalised movement, moved into political parties on a wide spectrum from left to right.[7] In this context fresh – and often quite divergent – ideas about women's roles as citizens within the state began to be articulated. Thus women's postwar pageants were diverse in form and content. They encompassed the very traditional messages of the Girls' Friendly Society (to which only virgins were admitted), the unorthodox biblical heroines of the Methodist sisterhoods and the robot-servants of the future imagined by the Women's Institute.[8] Their choices of characters and framing give us an insight into the beliefs of women rarely seen in the male-dominated media of the day, reflecting a wide variety of perspectives on class, religious beliefs and education.

For some women, there was disappointment in the return to traditional roles after the excitement and profitability of war work. For others, however, these were buoyantly optimistic years. Even a partial enfranchisement was a huge step forward, and many women looked forward confidently to a future in which they would take a full part.[9] This future was not universally welcomed, however. Other women felt the pace of change was too fast, and they continued to promote a very traditional view of gender roles. The pageants of the Girls' Friendly Society (GFS), run by Church of England ladies predominantly for servant girls, reflect a concerted effort to promote the most traditional virtues. It is these to which we now turn.

The Girls' Friendly Society: purity propaganda

The 'propaganda plays' only make sense against the background of the GFS. Still running today, the society is one of the lesser-known youth organisations, despite once boasting more than 300,000 members in various categories. It was founded in 1875 by a group of Anglican ladies concerned to prevent virtuous working-class girls from falling into ruin. Though this may seem priggish and controlling from a twenty-first-century perspective, the founders of the GFS were working against a background of endemic venereal disease, not least syphilis. By the 1870s and 1880s there was increasing feminist indignation about male 'vice' and its effects on unsuspecting new brides and their infants.[10] With no reliable prophylactics or cure for syphilis, the purity organisations could be seen as public health campaigners.

The GFS ladies brought respectable working-class girls together to train them in religious and domestic duty and to ward off temptation through fun weekly meetings, cheap, female-only hostels and recommendations to good positions. Such efforts can be interpreted as being led by a social control agenda – a desire to keep these women in their place at a time when it was becoming difficult to find servants. The lady organisers had access to a pool of trained, unmarried girls who were being kept away from the chance to build their own relationships. Saving maids from unwanted pregnancies also saved their employers from having to find replacements. But the social control paradigm has its limitations, and the GFS was not entirely self-serving.[11] Long before the #MeToo movement, harassment by predatory men was recognised as an established feature of everyday life for women. Many novels, such as Elizabeth Gaskell's *Ruth*, describe older, wealthier men grooming unsuspecting, dependent girls.[12] In the interwar period abused women continued to have little recourse to the law; in a real sense, therefore, the GFS functioned as a protective sisterhood. Its success is shown in its numbers: at its peak in 1914 it had nearly 200,000 members and 80,000 younger 'candidates' in England and Wales, led by 40,000 'lady associates', with sister societies throughout the world.[13]

The GFS was always hierarchical, with two tiers of membership: working, unmarried girls and lady associates. As it mimicked the founders' own relationships with their servants, so it naturally attracted the huge domestic servant class, particularly girls who led a tough, lonely existence as maids-of-all-work. The society was uninterested in women's suffrage, devoted to imperial ideals and deeply conservative. Lady associates had to be Anglican (no Dissenters were allowed), girls had to be given written permission by their employers before they could join and all members had to be 'of good character' – usually interpreted as meaning virgins, though it is unclear how far this requirement was tested in practice.[14] Indeed, the virginity rule was highly contentious among clergymen in particular: some were in favour, while others argued that it went against the Christian ideal of forgiveness. This difference of opinion was partly the reason why the GFS never became an official Church of England organisation – which, in turn, meant that it remained entirely female-managed.

The conservatism of the GFS meant that it flourished best in rural areas and the south of England. The servant members repelled the urban shop and clerical young ladies while the northern mill girls were, according to a GFS report,[15] too 'undisciplined, impatient of reproof and entirely wanting in self-control'. Freed by a modest financial independence, as typified by the bold weaver Fanny Hawthorn in Stanley Houghton's stage play *Hindle Wakes*,[16] the mill girls were immune to the GFS ideals of modesty, thrift, and quiet, uncomplaining respectfulness. These ideals were promoted through the GFS's huge literature and propaganda department, produced as a counterattack on the evils of frivolous light literature. Harrison has argued that the influence of this propaganda should not be underestimated, either in ideological terms or in sheer weight of numbers – and there is no denying its considerable reach and popularity. The most popular of the four GFS monthly magazines, *Friendly Leaves*, sold 60,000 copies a month, double the circulation of the Women's Social and Political Union (WSPU)'s *Votes for Women*.[17] Dozens of tracts, leaflets, plays and pageants along the same lines were also produced. A few pageant titles held by the British Library give a flavour of this material: 'Burden-Bearers', 'The Prayer Book Pageant', 'A Pageant of Empire', 'A May Pageant of Oak Apple Day', 'A Jubilee Pageant', 'The Glorious Ranks' and 'The Signpost'.[18]

One of the most successful GFS productions was *The Quest*, written by the famous pageant-master Louis Napoleon Parker and first performed before Queen Mary at the Albert Hall in 1925. (The GFS, being firmly 'establishment' in its character, had royalty as patrons: first Queen

Figure 6.1 Margaret Tarrant, 'The High Way or the Low?' Frontispiece to Louis Napoleon Parker, *The Quest: A Pageant of the Girls' Friendly Society* (London: Girls' Friendly Society, 1925). Reproduced with kind permission of the Girls' Friendly Society.

Victoria, then Queen Alexandra, then Queen Mary. Their larger pageants were often attended by local dignitaries.)[19] *The Quest* followed the pattern of many pageants: its scene was set when a wise narrator met a young or ignorant character and taught them a lesson through a series of historical episodes (see chapter 5). *The Quest* opened with an old woman, wrapped in a shawl, huddled against a signpost. An exhausted girl then limped up (Fig. 6.1). On the left was the High Way: a rocky path leading up to a cleft in the rocks, through which poured a wonderful light. On the right was the Low Way, a gaudy path of gilded pillars and tinsel. The Old Woman urged the Girl to take the High Way, but the Girl replied that while men may be strong enough to climb it, she was weak and alone. The Old Woman asked if she had lost her way, to which the Girl responded by saying that she was wandering, seeking happiness. The Old Woman then declared:

> Only the impossible is worth a struggle.
> In every woman's life there comes an hour
> When she must choose her way: or this – or that.
> Some heed me not: elect the primrose path,
> And sink into the slough; but those who heed,
> And seek my help, achieve their happiness.
> You are disheartened. Rest. Your eyes shall see
> What joys those win to who believe in me.

Thus was introduced a series of inspirational figures: St Hilda of Whitby, St Elizabeth of Hungary, St Joan of Arc, Queen Elizabeth I, Elizabeth Fry and finally Florence Nightingale. Representations of England, Scotland, Wales and Ireland then appeared, followed by the founding members of the GFS from 50 years earlier and GFS members of the time in the uniforms of various professions. They in turn were followed by younger members: 'The Candidates; the Novices; white souls, / Eager to join, and keep their souls unspotted'.[20] Yet the Girl still doubted, saying that among all the throng she had no friend. At this the Old Woman threw off her disguise and revealed herself as Friendship: 'Oh! Hither to my arms! For I am Friendship! All the love that burns in all these hearts is symbolised in me!' After a hymn the whole crowd marched off, leaving the Girl, now radiantly happy, to move on easily up the rocky path with Friendship's arm about her.

The references to virginity are clear even to modern eyes: the weakness of women, the white souls of the youngest girls and the hour in every woman's life when she must choose between the difficulties of virtue and the primrose path to unhappiness. Of the six named heroines, four are unmarried, including the Virgin Queen. (It is perhaps worth noting here that one nickname for the GFS was the 'Godforsaken spinsters'.)[21] But though the pageant may seem patronising, it was more even-handed than it first appears. It concealed a clever secondary message worthy of Parker – one clearly inspired by Ophelia's reply to Laertes in Hamlet:

> Do not, as some ungracious pastors do,
> Show me the steep and thorny way to heaven,
> Whiles, like a puff'd and reckless libertine,
> Himself the primrose path of dalliance treads.[22]

Thus the pageant was not only a message and inspiration to the young girls. It also threw down a challenge to those in the audience educated enough to understand a Shakespearean reference. Did love burn in *their* hearts? Or did they recommend virtue for others while enjoying a life of luxury? What were they doing to help others keep to the 'steep and thorny way'? Such pageants, after all, often ended with an appeal for funds or assistance, and this one was partly a reminder of the duties of the better-off.

A similar message is given in *The Signpost*, written by J. A. S. Edwards in 1924. This shows the limits of the vision offered by the GFS to its members. Sitting down to rest by the signpost to a village was pretty young Virginia, surely named for the GFS's central tenet. She was bored with her routine and was bunking off the weekly meeting. While Virginia drowsed in the summer evening, a series of inspirational women walked past, all seeking to get on their way whatever the difficulties. These figures included the Sanskrit scholar Pandita Ramabai, the headmistress Dorothea Beale and the purity campaigner Josephine Butler. Virginia repeatedly suggested that they should choose different paths if the way ahead was so hard, but the women told her firmly that they could not 'pick and choose'. In the face of these responses, Virginia finally realised that the signpost no longer read 'To the village' but 'The way of love and duty'. 'Horribly ashamed' to realise she had deserted her own duty, she prayed at the foot of the signpost and was rewarded with a vision of the Virgin Mary. In this pageant, then, the parade of courageous, learned women is not shown as an inspiration for young girls to find their own adventures, but instead to enjoin their conformance to everyday duties, however dull. Having ideas beyond your station is presented as a sin.

Although aimed at servants, GFS pageants rarely commemorated working-class women. One example was a large-scale Essex production in 1925, which introduced a series of famous local women.[23] As with *The Quest*, the framework is pure GFS propaganda. Here the wise narrator was a GFS lady associate, while the younger character was a country girl alone and frightened at a London railway station, having foolishly agreed to meet a young male acquaintance who had stood her up. The lady associate sought to raise her interlocutor's spirits by telling her of Essex women who had made history, but here the taste of the upper-class organisers becomes plain. Their choices are skewed to commemorate elite and aristocratic women: Essex queens, abbesses, martyrs, scholars and authors, beauties and heiresses, philanthropists and, finally, burgesses and justices.

Indeed, in GFS pageants as whole, the only working-class woman featured was the devoted servant St Zita, whose best-known saying was 'a servant is not holy if she is not busy'. There were no suffrage campaigners. The ideals and qualities celebrated were of visionary Christianity and service; the women leaders were figures such as abbesses who worked within an unquestioned framework of male power. Only queens such as Boudica and Elizabeth I, empowered by man-made rules, slipped through the net. But in the interwar years the GFS hierarchical ideals were already starting to look dated. By 1931 membership had fallen by 42 per cent in 18 years.[24] Far less oppressive ideals were moving into the mainstream.

The Guiding spirit: courage and comradeship

The Girl Guide movement was very much of the zeitgeist. Though a girls' club like the GFS, it had a different ethos from its beginnings in 1910, when it was formed as a sister organisation to the Boy Scouts. The Guides' membership quickly overtook the declining GFS during the 'pageantitis' of the interwar years. By 1928 there were 430,000 Guides, Brownies and Rangers, all with a cross-class membership. Unlike the Anglican GFS, these groups commonly met at schools, synagogues and even factories, as well as churches of all denominations. And while the GFS had imperialism at its heart, the Guides took inspiration from the new League of Nations and aspired to a global sisterhood, although inevitably cultural and racial hierarchies crept in.[25]

The Guides' inception in 1910 came just as ideas of femininity had already been challenged by the New Woman and the suffragists. The war gave added impetus to its development as a practical movement which freed girls to take part in previously off-limits energetic activities such as camping. It was intended to 'appeal to the more adventurous type of girl', who would, as founder Robert Baden-Powell said, become men's 'partners and comrades, rather than dolls'.[26] However, this liberation was built on a bedrock of conservatism: it never challenged the idea that these girls' future roles were as wives and mothers. In fact, the Guides were promoted by Baden-Powell's wife Olave as being an antidote to the boy-mad, empty-headed flappers, aiming to take in girls of every type and turn them out as 'clear-headed happy women of trained character'.[27] This confusing mixture of freedom and control was reflected in their name: Girl *Guides*. Although named for the South Asian military guides' keenness, courage and resourcefulness, the name also reflected the founder's view that as adult women their role would be to influence men's actions and quality.

The Guides routinely took part in public events, such as the dedication of war memorials, wearing their distinctive, military-style uniforms. They were a reliable source of performers for large-scale town pageants, as well as producing their own pageants. Some of these latter were the typical mix of local happenings and characters, fables and fun that characterised the free approach to history adopted by many pageant-writers. One of the first was 'A Lancashire Pageant: Camp Fire Tales', performed by about 250 North East Lancashire Guides for a fête in the grounds of Gawthorpe Tower in 1925. The event was opened by the Marchioness of Aberdeen; the close of the fête included a march-past of 5,000 Guides and Scouts in front of Lady Olave Baden-Powell herself.

Gawthorpe Tower, now owned by the National Trust, is close to Pendle Hill, where a group of witches were famously arrested and tried in the seventeenth century. Thus the pageant begins with Witch Past, Witch Future and Witch Present chanting the well-known lines from *Macbeth*: 'Double, double, toil and trouble'. The witches then take us back to the invading Saxons and forward through a series of scenes, all using the motif of outdoor camps and fairs. They end with the arrival of the mills and canals and the famous local inventors of textile machinery.[28]

The pageant was a lavish and successful affair; it was followed by similar events throughout the country. These duly received glowing reviews in local newspapers, but they did not really depart from the standard fare of local pageants of the time. However, some Girl Guide pageants were more revealing of the movement's own beliefs and can be seen as propaganda aimed as much at the performers as the audience. One such was *The Amber Gate*. Produced by Girl Guide groups nationwide for more than 30 years, this pageant has a far more forward-looking feel to it than the GFS equivalents, reflecting the Guides' adventurous and determined spirit. The choices of heroes and heroines bear closer examination, representing as they do the spirit of this successful organisation. Male and female characters are presented in similar numbers and with equal respect, with Guides playing all the roles.

The Amber Gate was written by Kitty Barne, a Carnegie-medal-winning author and for several years the Girl Guides 'Commissioner for Music and Drama'. Published as a play with an alternative prologue for Girl Guide troops, it was first produced in 1923, in Eastbourne.[29] The story was then published as a children's book in 1933 and, after several editions, was still in print in the 1950s.[30] Like the GFS Essex pageant described above, *The Amber Gate* used a framework of a narrator who slowly convinces a sceptical listener, but these are not stock Victorian morality figures. An older, uncle-type figure ('Gaffer') addressed 11-year-old Eve, who was too bad-tempered and lethargic to join her Girl Guide friend on a 'supper hike' in the woods on a hot summer evening. He persuaded her to shut her eyes and see the Amber Gate leading to that country where children, including many Girl Guides, were playing, building and having fun. This was a kingdom of opportunity, inherited by the new generation. Eve climbed on to the arm of Gaffer's lounge chair and they jetted back through history to see the pioneering boys and girls who helped to push the gate open. These individuals are very different from the elite women of the GFS Essex pageant, celebrated for the queenly virtues of beauty, philanthropy, scholarship and religion. The overwhelming virtue extolled in the Girl Guides' pageant was courage, as Gaffer explained when they met the first character, David, who in the Bible slew Goliath:

> He opened it with his courage, you see. You'll find that all these children have courage. You can have all sorts of other qualities too, but you must have courage with them to open the Gate.[31]

Gaffer was a forthright character, learned enough to correct Eve's misnaming of Handel's Larghetto but dismissive of school poetry recitals and apocryphal tales such as the six-year-old George Washington's chopping down of his father's cherry tree. Gaffer praised 'tough girls' such as Grizel Home, who saved her Protestant father from King Charles's men, and was approving of the Guides' supper hike menu of sausages and eggs: 'Guides don't starve themselves'. For Gaffer, the days of feminine uselessness were consigned to the dustbin of history:

> Specially when girls were supposed to be silly little feeble things, as was the fashion then. It was not considered suitable in a female to do anything at all well, but Grace [Darling] knew how to manage a boat, didn't she? … No good being brave unless you know your job too.[32]

Toughness, loyalty, persistence and level-headedness in a crisis were all common themes, as personified by Flora Macdonald, William Tell's son, the Maid of Saragossa (who manned a cannon alone when all her comrades deserted) and Hans the Dutchman (who jammed his elbow in a leaking dyke). Commodore Casabianca's son (the boy who stood on the burning deck) was praised for 'obeying orders, sticking to your job whatever happens'.[33]

But the pageant was not militaristic in tone, nor just a celebration of physical courage. The inventiveness of Giotto, James Watt and child diarist Marjorie Fleming were also praised, along with the visionaries St Joan of Arc and Bernadette of Lourdes and the commitment and generosity of Dick Whittington. The most complex discussion was around Lady Jane Grey:

> 'Is she going to read her way through the Gate?' asked Eve, watching her. 'She can't do that, can she?'
>
> Gaffer pondered. 'Not exactly, I suppose. You can't open it with theories. But her books informed her, as they used to say ... Her death was all her father's fault, and she knew it, and yet the night before she died she wrote him a most beautiful and forgiving letter ... I think that's how she opened the Gate.'[34]

Not all the young heroes were famous, however. Nine-year-old Agnes Green, another 'nice, tough little thing, full of common sense', appeared on account of her caring for her five young siblings for four days when her parents lost their way and died in a blizzard near their remote Lake District home.[35] The Gaffer made the point that many nameless children have also helped open the gate, though they are unknown to history.

The final characters celebrated in the pageant were deaf-blind writer Helen Keller (then still living) and Jack Cornwell VC, a Boy Scout and sailor boy in the First World War. The gate was then opened wide and hordes of children rushed through. Eve was among them, now fired with enthusiasm to join her Girl Guide friend. But Gaffer was clear that the story was not yet over:

> Enjoy yourself ... and don't forget there's another Gate the other end that leads into another country. It'll want opening.[36]

Thus the pageant ends with a message to audience and participants alike – the work was not yet done and the duty of today's children was to build on the work of the past, showing the same courage as their forebears.

Missing manuscripts, missing voices: outside the Establishment

The pageants organised by large institutions were popular and influential. They were staged over and over, as guaranteed crowd-pleasers with a palatable message. For the historian, they are relatively straightforward to study because their books of words were published. The organisations producing them were well-disciplined, national bodies with archive facilities. Sometimes the pageants were written or produced by influential figures whose lives were well-documented and whose papers were preserved. In short, they benefit from 'survival bias'. Susan Mumm has described the greater body of academic work on larger and extant organisations in this way.[37] She explains that smaller, local philanthropic organisations may do a lot of work, but are less likely to leave a record trace.

One set of such organisations is made up of those associated with the many Nonconformist churches: the thousands of Presbyterian, Methodist, Baptist, Congregational, Quaker and other denominations that between them once had more members than the Church of England, but which saw precipitate mid-to-late twentieth-century decline.[38] A few of these churches were entirely independent; others existed under an umbrella body, such as the Methodist Connexion, but nevertheless prided themselves on being self-governing. The founding principles of the Free Churches included this right to self-determination. Their members, who had formed, paid for and built their own churches, were unwilling to be imposed upon from above.

Unfortunately, the fascinating and varied independence of Nonconformist churches and organisations presents difficulties for the historian. For one thing, they were less likely to submit records to archives, either during or at the end of their existence. Unlike the Church of England, which requires lengthy procedures before closing a church, many Nonconformist churches closed without fanfare, on the decision of their members and without leaving much of a documentary trace, if any. Hundreds have closed since the war as congregations shrank and the costs of maintaining ageing, outsize buildings increased – this is indeed a process that continues to this day. Their papers may sometimes be transferred to a council archive or central body, but they may also be reduced to a few handfuls of souvenirs kept by former members, and discarded as worthless on their deaths.

All this means that exploring their histories is a somewhat hit-and-miss affair, involving combing through the British Newspaper Archive and multiple county record offices. By this patchy process I have found 75 pageants by the female members of Nonconformist churches or organisations on the theme of 'Noble Women', held between 1915 and 1947 and featuring a great variety of heroines. (This figure of 75 is an underestimate, as the British Newspaper Archive is incomplete and many events will have gone unreported in the press.[39]) The 'Noble Women' theme was one used by other women's and youth organisations, but it was most popular with the Nonconformists and the associated Temperance movement (Fig. 6.2). Indeed, it is notable that it was largely the Free Churches that were most likely to produce pageants on this theme. These churches had granted power in the church to women far earlier than the Church of England and had a tradition of women preachers from the outset.[40] In contrast, I have not found a single Roman Catholic 'Noble Women' pageant.

The Nonconformists' progressive views were shown in their response to a government survey in the 1920s which revealed that the Free Churches supported the use of contraception (then opposed by both the Church of England and the Roman Catholic church).[41] Their stance on this issue was in part a function of a politically left-wing stance: Dissenters were usually working-class or recent arrivals in the middle class, with links in the Victorian era to the trade unions, the Chartist movement and radical liberalism, as well as a commitment to universal literacy through the Sunday School movement.[42] Yet this political progressiveness was married

Figure 6.2 Ladies of the Hatfield House Land Primitive Methodist Church, Sheffield, in a performance of 'A Pageant of Noble Women', *c.* 1930s. Photographer unknown. Reproduced by kind permission from the collection of Brian Woodriff.

to socially conservative principles. Some historians have even claimed that Methodism prevented a British revolution. The most influential of these, E. P. Thompson, castigated the Wesleyan 'anti-intellectualism' and described their Sunday schools as inculcating 'barbaric and evil superstitions'.[43] This amalgam of progressivism and conservatism is evident in the pantheon of heroines chosen by the Sisterhoods, Temperance branches and Dorcas societies that organised these Nonconformist pageants.[44] Alas, for all these dozens and perhaps hundreds of events I have not been able to locate a single entire script. Fortunately, thanks to the local newspaper practice of listing performers with their characters, we can at least learn which heroines they chose, even if it is impossible to gain much of a sense of how they were portrayed.

Of all the Nonconformist productions of 'A Pageant of Noble Women', 25 cast lists were printed in newspapers; from these we can rank the popularity of characters chosen. The top choices include many of the usual suspects who were doubtless fun to play: Florence Nightingale is the character most frequently mentioned, followed by Boudica, Grace Darling, Joan of Arc, Elizabeth I, Queen Victoria and Queen Bertha of Kent (the consort of Aethelbert whose influence in the sixth century helped lead to the Christianisation of England). But scattered among these popular favourites are Dissenter heroines: Elizabeth Fry, Quaker campaigner for prisoners' welfare; Susannah Wesley, mother of John and Charles; Catherine Booth, a campaigner for women preachers and co-founder of the Salvation Army; Harriet Beecher Stowe, Calvinist author of the anti-slavery novel *Uncle Tom's Cabin*; Alice of Lisle, executed for sheltering anti-Royalist soldiers; and Mary Slessor, a Presbyterian missionary who prevented many infanticides by confronting an African superstition that twins were possessed by demons. Learning is also highly valued. The Greek mathematician Hypatia is one of the most popular characters, while scientists Mary Somerville and pioneering sociologist Harriet Martineau also get several mentions each. Authors appear only as they support morality, with examples including Harriet Beecher Stowe (mentioned above), the campaigning poet Elizabeth Barrett Browning and religious poets Frances Havergal, Fanny Crosby and Anne Bradstreet.

The omissions are also revealing. Emmeline Pankhurst is honoured only once by a Nonconformist group – perhaps the Dissenters did not approve of militancy even while supporting suffrage. The Pankhursts' patriotism during the First World War was also at odds with Quaker pacifism. Novelists are rare: Charlotte Brontë, creator of the moral but passionate Jane Eyre, appears twice in Nonconformist productions, while Emily, author of the more Gothic *Wuthering Heights*, is mentioned just once and then only as Charlotte's sister. Jane Austen and Mary Shelley are entirely missing – idle husband-hunters and tragedians were apparently unpopular with this down-to-earth, hard-working audience. Actresses, singers and artists are likewise absent.

In stark contrast to the GFS's Essex production, nobility is defined without reference to beauty or wealth. The Nonconformist 'noble women' are strong-minded, opinionated and outspoken, but only in the service of Christian morality and the rights of the oppressed. They are educated above usual standards and use this to create a better world, even in the face of opposition. But women who break with convention for selfish reasons – whether gain, fame or sexual satisfaction – are excluded. Yet despite the exclusions and restrictions, there is evidence of much creativity and a wide range of opinion. Some scripts were obviously passed around – the Temperance *White Ribbon* magazine mentions that a script for their youth branch can be sent out but must be copied and returned promptly as it is in great demand[45] – but there is no evidence of published, generic pageants as in the Girl Guides or the GFS. No two lists of characters are the same. Each chapel had their own favourites and, as we will see, some were highly unorthodox.

An unusual grouping of biblical characters appeared in two pageants: one in a Baptist church in Hebden Bridge, West Yorkshire, and another in a Methodist church in Penzance, Cornwall. In both these pageants (and in common with Nonconformist pageants more generally), the best-known female Bible characters are missing: the Virgin Mary, Mary Magdalene, the sisters Martha and Mary and the Old Testament mothers are all absent, as are most of the best-known female saints. In the Cornish and Yorkshire pageants these figures are replaced with an entirely different group. This included two prophetesses, Miriam and the more warlike Deborah; mother- and daughter-in-law Ruth and Naomi, often used as an emblem of female friendship; and wealthy trader Lydia. But the most striking inclusion in this group is the five-times-wed Woman of Samaria – unashamedly shacked up with lover number six – who speaks with Jesus and testifies for him.[46]

These biblical characters were joined by many other less familiar historical figures, such as the suffragist and war medic Dr Elsie Inglis, the pioneering gynaecologist Mary Scharlieb, the working-class philanthropist Kitty Wilkinson and the Temperance campaigner Agnes Weston. These varied choices all speak of long debates in draughty Sunday schools between women seeking to commemorate a different pantheon to those they saw immortalised in church windows and civic statues. But although varied and creative in their content, these pageants were generally humble affairs compared to the full-blown spectacles of those most iconic of interwar organisations, the Women's Institute, and its sister, the Townswomen's Guilds.

The WI: diverse and feminist agendas

The WI was a secular organisation, originally created to help rural women help each other in Canada. It arrived in Britain in 1915. Although known for 'jam and Jerusalem', handicrafts and hobbies, the WI was also a successful lobbying group. Its campaigns included agitating for improvements to water supplies and rural housing. Branches spread quickly throughout the 1920s and their popularity led to the concept being copied for urban women with the formation of the Townswomen's Guilds in 1929.[47] Like the Girl Guides, the WI and Townswomen's Guilds would often join forces with other groups to produce large-scale civic events, as well as producing their own pageants. Some were small, but others used the county federation networks to produce spectacles involving many hundreds and even thousands of performers, including massed choirs. The pageant format lent itself naturally to this, with each local branch made responsible for a scene and the whole production being co-ordinated by the county federations. Though often thought of as conservative and 'respectable', the WI pageants show a surprising diversity, embracing women of all kinds from working-class northerners to powerful goddesses. They openly celebrated women's history and women's rights.

The WI and Townswomen's Guilds had access to vast resources in terms of skilled women with expertise in costume making and catering, with a mix from ladies of the manor to the wives of shopkeepers and labourers. They could create imaginative, lavishly staged events. While most of the Free Churches described above performed in a Sunday school or chapel, WI branches had aristocratic members who could supply glamorous locations, such as the grounds of stately homes. Many of their productions took the form of traditional historical pageants – but pageants in which women played all the roles, including male ones. This gave women the opportunity to play the 'best' parts. Pageant-master and actress Gwen Lally, who always wore masculine clothes and played male parts, began working with the WI from 1923. She encouraged other women to act in male roles (demanding, among other things, high standards of make-up and fake beards).[48]

Women's Institute pageants were more likely than mixed-sex civic pageants to include episodes from women's history and to give greater weight to female characters. One of their earliest, in 1926, was the Earlham Pageant, organised by the Norfolk Federation of Women's Institutes.[49] Due to the large number of branches taking part, there were two performances with a different set of scenes in the afternoon and evening. The afternoon performance told the history of the county from a more male perspective, but nevertheless included many romantic scenes foregrounding women. These included the romance between the Earl of Leicester and Amy Robsart and the marriage of John Rolfe to Princess Pocahontas. The evening performance told the history of Norfolk from a female perspective, featuring the queens Boudica, Eleanor, Anne Boleyn and Elizabeth I. It also incorporated stories from the famous cache of letters written by Margaret Paston in the fifteenth century, including 'The Love Story of Margery Paston'.[50]

Not everyone was impressed. In an odd piece of double-dealing, the *Yarmouth Independent* devoted two columns on page 7 to the usual detailed report, presumably written by a staff writer, which named many local worthies and contained much praise of the performers, costumes and organisations. On the same page, however, the newspaper gave almost as much room to a blistering review of the pageant's historical inaccuracies by Mr Walter Rye; he had used the programme sold in advance to write a point-by-point critique of its romantic touches.[51] Comments include 'too ridiculous', 'absurd', 'not the faintest evidence', 'the episode as described is fantastic and impossible' and 'the compiler has mixed up his [*sic*] dates sadly'. Rye's article is really a very strange inclusion. Local newspapers thrive on contention, but they also do well not to offend too many readers; one can imagine a sack-full of cancelled subscriptions landing on the editor's desk on Monday morning.

However, criticism certainly did not deter the WI, which continued to produce many major pageants over the next decades, and did so right across the country. These pageants also continued to feature strong female characters and – notwithstanding the strictures of Mr Rye and others – did not hesitate to include popular legend at the expense of historical scholarship. For example, Coleford WI used the 'Pageant of Noble Women' format so beloved of the Free Churches for their first public entertainment in 1936, but chose a very different set of characters.[52] This pageant portrayed the popular favourites of several queens, Elizabeth Fry, Grace Darling, Florence Nightingale, Catherine Booth and missionary Mary Slessor, but added many more romantic figures such as the actress Sarah Siddons, all the Brontë sisters, Kate Burless and other popular singers and Scottish darling, Flora Macdonald. The Native American environmental writer Anahareo, then still living, also made an appearance; so did the Pankhurst family.

There were also two characters of doubtful authenticity from narrative poems. One was Barbara Frietche, an old woman who refused to lower her Confederate flag when confronted with Union troops during the American Civil War, and the other was 'Bessie of Curfew fame'.[53] In this legend, dating back to the fifteenth century, Bessie was desperate to save her imprisoned lover, due to be hanged when the curfew bell tolled, even though a horseman was on his way from the king (or Oliver Cromwell, in later versions) with a pardon. After fruitlessly pleading with the curmudgeonly old sexton not to ring the bell, she saves her lover by climbing the tower and hanging on to the clapper until the pardon arrives. It is not known what music was used to accompany this episode, but there were several comic songs associated with the story ('As you swing to the left and swing to the right, remember curfew must not ring tonight!'), so perhaps the audience joined in with one of these. Altogether the pageant seems to have aimed more at entertainment than serious historical representation.

The representation of the Pankhurst family was unusual in a pageant of this type, but the Coleford ladies were not the only WI members to acknowledge a debt to the suffragettes. A larger-scale production in the same year, titled *Mother Earth*, was held by five branches in Northumberland. It was written and produced by Elsie Reed for about 200 performers, including a choir 100-strong. It had a similar 'great women' grouping of characters, from the Old Testament mother of Moses, Rebecca and Ruth, through to Florence Nightingale. However, unlike most pageants, it carried on through the suffragettes to the land girl, lady doctor and airwoman of the time.[54]

The framing of the pageant still feels contemporary today, with Mother Earth – a female deity and forerunner of Gaia – presiding over the action. First, she acknowledged the gifts of the fruit and flower bearers, declaring: '[t]hey are fruits of healing and love. The women of the world know the value of my fruits'. She was followed by flower bearers. One of these children carried 'the sad little poppy which speaks of little mounds in Flanders'. Mother Earth had a consoling message:

> Yes, the poppy speaks of our loved ones, but gives us too, the message of eternal life … The women of the world must see to it that such things must cease. There must be no more war and it is the duty of every woman to train every child to realise that war is contrary to all decent thinking.

The last, timid child sadly carried wild flowers and spoke of the thoughtlessness and cruelty of humanity:

> When they see a bank of primroses or a dell of bluebells, they cannot be content with a pretty bunch, but must pull up roots and destroy the plants.

Mother Earth again commented that it was the duty of women to see that such things cease, before making way for the entrance of characters through the ages. The final scene was of Northumberland's fisherwomen: this offered a template for modern working-class womanhood, seamlessly integrating traditional values with a practical attitude. As three of these fisherwomen explained,

> There are houses to keep clean, bairns to mind and all the jobs that good wives do ... But yet when we are needed we do not mind giving a hand to launch the lifeboat – aye – and to man it too, if we are needed ... Then we can always spare time to remember to pray for those at sea.

A pageant involving an even more forthright celebration of women's emancipation was held in nearby Sunderland only two years later. Written by the headmistress of a local girls' school, Miss W. J. E. Moul, and organised by the Sunderland Townswomen's Guild, this 'play-pageant' was staged in the Victoria Hall and was accompanied by a choir contest and handicraft exhibition (see chapter 5). More than 1,000 women took part.[55] The five scenes covered an impressive amount of ground, including the need for social and economic as well as legal independence across all classes, and the restrictive effect of public opinion. The action began with Lord Shaftesbury's inquiry into working conditions in mines and factories. Next came an episode depicting the awakening of social conscience among young middle-class women who wanted the freedom to go out and do their bit – and the resultant horror of the Victorian 'heavy father'. Then the need for married women's legal independence was shown through a dramatisation of Mrs Caroline Norton's fight for custody of her children from her violent, drunken husband. The *Sunderland Daily Echo* said that the fourth scene, featuring Florence Nightingale, showed 'that women's exclusion from power, position and employment is not based on any logical recognition or natural inferiority'.[56] The final part of the pageant, involving all the guilds, comprised a series of short scenes showing how women had got the vote, largely through their war work. The *Sunderland Daily Echo* concluded:

> Finally there is the plea that women are not afraid of work of any sort, however difficult or exacting; that, if they come to be

> recognized as having a natural right to share in the work creating a happier world for men and children, they are prepared to enter upon all the hazards and to pay all the penalties of life.[57]

In this way Moul's 'Play-pageant' culminated with a contemporary, future-oriented message.

Such messages were not unusual in pageants, but one extraordinary WI production in Preston went further, offering a vivid vision of the countrywoman of the twenty-first century, surrounded by appliances and wrestling with the new robotic servant problem. *Pedlar's Ware, or the Countrywoman's Life Through the Ages* was written by the vicar of Preston, Canon E. W. Wallis; it was performed by the Lancashire Federation of Women's Institutes in 1935. In this pageant Wallis sought to 'get away from the glorification of Queen Elizabeth and other stock figures, and the very trifling incidents of local history, magnified out of all proportion'. Instead, all the scenes focus on ordinary women of the past, living domestic lives which have messages for the present.[58] The pageant used the motif of the pedlar wandering through the centuries, renewed through seven episodes and 18 centuries into various characters including a travelling clock-mender and a female con-artist. In 2060 the last pedlar was a saleswoman from Saturn, selling 'autobetties' controlled by a keyboard. The naughty children took over the controls, the robots went berserk and attempted to kill them until disarmed by the parents. But despite the technology, little seemed to have changed for this countrywoman – the final scene ended with father asking mother what is for dinner as he has a golf match to go to on Neptune. It was a very original piece, requiring a huge amount of organisation by the producers who travelled to far-flung parts of Lancashire to rehearse the various branches. Only the WI would have been capable of such a feat of organisation or used such an imaginative production.

Conclusion

The interwar years have been represented as being conservative ones, in which women reacted against the hard-won rights of earlier feminists. The relative freedoms and progressiveness of the war years and the militancy of the suffragettes have been depicted as stalling in the face of a traditionalist backlash. However, a close examination of this generation's ideologies as shown through their pageants reveals that they were more feminist than previously thought. Even traditional organisations such as the Girl Guides and WIs were experimenting with new histories and projecting them into new and exciting futures. Indeed, the pageants staged by these groups often ended with a call for further progress. The Guides' paradise beyond the Amber Gate has a silver gate at the far end, one that is still to be opened; Mother Earth calls on the women in the audience to prevent future wars; the inclusion of living women, such as environmental campaigner Anahareo, shows that the work goes on.

Churches outside the establishment were consciously creating new pantheons of heroines, which challenged traditional views of female virtue. They ignored beauty, birth and the religious imperative of silent obedience. Though Christian, their new pantheon did not include traditional figures such as Martha and Mary, who served and listened to men. Rather these women celebrated education, the single life and the practical achievements of working women. Their heroines were Elizabeth Fry, Mary Slessor and Harriet Beecher Stowe – women who were devout but outspoken. In this way, the Nonconformist women of the interwar generation used pageantry as a means of celebrating the disruptive influences which – embodied in the activism of their heroines – had done so much to change society.

Reading the reports of these interwar pageants, it does seem that women sidelined their most recent history. They largely ignored the Pankhursts and other suffragist campaigners, but this is not evidence of a reaction against their ideals. The bitter divisions associated with the suffragists may still have been too raw to be staged. On a more personal level, the omission is understandable. What woman wants to be endlessly reminded of her mother's glory days? No generation wants to give too much credit to the one immediately before. For 'Generation X', the ageing babyboomers' endless reminiscing about the 1960s was annoying, boring, dispiriting and often unbelievable. Many interwar women may well have felt the same way about the suffragettes.

These, then, were years not of conservatism but consolidation. Through pageants, women took stock of their new position and their history, reframing the past as leading up to their new freedoms and futures. Through history, they showed themselves as deserving of their new citizenship. They claimed as their forebears many generations of extraordinary women. Perhaps paradoxically, these were also years of diversity. The fight for the vote had been a focus of energy. Now that energy could diverge into multiple streams, forming new channels and spreading over wider territories.

These groups did not all agree on what was worthy of veneration. Rather they selected various heroines, scenes and virtues in varying, imaginative reconstructions of the past. Indeed it is this imagination that sets apart the productions by women's and girls' groups of the interwar years. From the grandest county pageant to the smallest Free Church event, their pageants included surprising, novel elements that show widening perspectives on what history and culture could mean. Arranged as an historical pageant, by now a 'traditional' form, these new perspectives were given legitimacy. The groups that expounded them, from the WI to the Guides to Nonconformist churches, claimed the right for their heroines and stories to be included as a part of British national history. And by performing in symbolically significant spaces, such as stately homes, churches and public halls, they literally planted their banners in the territory of the establishment.[59] Thus the pageants conceived and organised by women's groups served many purposes. They created a new pantheon of role models for women as they adjusted to great social and political changes, they promulgated these new ideas to wider audiences and they confirmed the new social order as being part of a reassuring continuum of British and local history. Above all, they did so in a format that the women themselves could own.

Notes

1. David Jarvis, 'Mrs Maggs and Betty: The Conservative Appeal to Women Voters in the 1920s', *Twentieth Century British History* 5 (1994): 129–52.
2. Brian Harrison, 'Women in a Men's House: The Women MPs 1919–1945', *Historical Journal* 29 (1986): 623–54.
3. Jane Lewis, 'The Ideology and Politics of Birth Control in Inter-War England', *Women's Studies International Quarterly* 2 (1979): 33–48; Virginia Nicholson, *Singled Out: How Two Million British Women Survived Without Men After the First World War* (Oxford: Oxford University Press, 2005).
4. Susan Mumm, 'Women and Philanthropic Cultures', in *Women, Gender and Religious Cultures in Britain, 1800–1940*, ed. Sue Morgan and Jacqueline DeVries (London and New York: Routledge, 2010), 54–71.
5. Though see Zoë Thomas, 'Historical Pageants, Citizenship, and the Performance of Women's History before Second-Wave Feminism', *Twentieth Century British History* 28 (2017): 319–43.
6. The script by Cicely Mary Hamilton, published in 1910 by the Suffrage Shop, was digitised by Google from the University of Michigan's copy and is available at https://archive.org/details/apageantgreatwo00hamigoog/page/n13/mode/2up (accessed 28 June 2019). See also Katharine Cockin, 'Cicely Hamilton's Warriors: Dramatic Reinventions of Militancy in the British Women's Suffrage Movement', *Women's History Review* 14 (2005): 527–42.
7. Helen Lewis, 'Why the Suffragettes Still Matter', *Guardian*, 19 September 2015, https://www.theguardian.com/books/2015/sep/19/suffragettes-why-still-matter-abi-morgan-film-writers-reflect (accessed 31 May 2020).
8. For these robot-servants (the 'autobetties'), see p. 151.
9. Alison Light, *Forever England: Femininity, Literature and Conservatism between the Wars* (London and New York: Routledge, 1991); Adrian Bingham, 'An Era of Domesticity? Histories of Women and Gender in Interwar Britain', *Cultural and Social History* 1 (2004): 225–33; Maria DiCenzo, 'Our Freedom and Its Results: Measuring Progress in the Aftermath of Suffrage, *Women's History Review* 23 (2014): 421–40, and other articles from this special edition of *WHR*; Caitriona Beaumont, *Housewives and Citizens: Domesticity and the Women's Movement in England, 1928–64* (Manchester: Manchester University Press, 2013).

10. Judith R. Walkowitz, *Prostitution and Victorian Society: Women, Class, and the State* (Cambridge: Cambridge University Press, 1982), 50, 256.
11. For a still-pertinent critique of 'social control' interpretations, applicable to the twentieth quite as much to the nineteenth centuries, see F. M. L. Thompson, 'Social Control in Victorian Britain', *Economic History Review*, new series 34 (1981): 189–208.
12. Elizabeth Gaskell, *Ruth* (London: Chapman & Hall, 1853).
13. Vivienne Richmond, '"It is not a Society for Human Beings but for Virgins": The Girls' Friendly Society Membership Eligibility Dispute 1875–1936', *Journal of Historical Sociology* 20 (2007): 304–27; Brian Harrison, 'For Church, Queen and Family: The Girls' Friendly Society 1874–1920', *Past and Present* 61 (1973): 107–38.
14. Richmond, '"It is not a Society for Human Beings but for Virgins"'.
15. This report from the Chester diocese in 1881 is quoted in Harrison, 'For Church, Queen and Family', 116–17. He also quotes a Cleckheaton Branch secretary who wrote in the *Associates Journal* of August 1896 that associates had little idea of the work situation, courting customs or modes of speech of the girls they were trying to guide (p.120).
16. Stanley Houghton, *Hindle Wakes* (1910). It was first performed in 1912 and was made into a film in 1952.
17. Harrison, 'For Church, Queen and Family'.
18. Many are held in the British Library as a collection: *Miscellaneous Pamphlets, Leaflets etc.*, Girls' Friendly Society (England and Wales) (London, 1920–?). These include: Mrs Hubert Edwards, *Burden-bearers – A Jubilee Pageant for Five Characters and Ten Groups* (1925); Henry Millar and Louis N. Parker, *The Quest – A Pageant* (1925); Mrs Aylmer Astley, *A May Pageant – Oak Apple Day, 1661* (1927); M. F. Unwin, *A Jubilee Pageant for a GFS Country Branch* (1930); J. A. S. Edwards, *The Signpost: A Play for GFS Members, based on the Characters in the GFS Calendar* (1924); Margaret Cropper, *The Glorious Ranks – A Pageant with Scenes in Mime* (1936). Further titles are given in the same file under the pamphlet, *GFS List of Recommended Plays, Pageants, Dialogues* (1921).
19. *Birmingham Daily Post*, 3 July 1939, 13; *Western Daily Press*, 5 October 1931, 7.
20. Louis N. Parker. *The Quest: A Pageant of the Girls' Friendly Society* (London: Girls' Friendly Society, 1925), 7.
21. Miriam Glucksmann, *Cottons and Casuals: The Gendered Organisation of Labour in Time and Space* (Durham: Sociology Press, 2000), 101.
22. William Shakespeare, *Hamlet*, Act 1, Scene 3.
23. *Chelmsford Chronicle*, 15 May 1925, 5.
24. Richmond, '"It is not a Society for Human Beings but for Virgins"'.
25. Kristine Alexander, 'The Girl Guide Movement and Imperial Internationalism During the 1920s and 1930s', *Journal of the History of Childhood and Youth* 2 (2009): 37–63.
26. Tim Jeal, *Baden-Powell: Founder of the Boy Scouts* (London: Hutchinson, 1989), 470.
27. *Daily Mirror*, 15 July 1918, quoted in Richard A. Voeltz, 'The Antidote to "Khaki Fever"? The Expansion of the British Girl Guides during the First World War', *Journal of Contemporary History* 27 (1992): 627–38.
28. Angela Bartie, Linda Fleming, Mark Freeman, Tom Hulme, Alex Hutton, Paul Readman, 'A Lancashire Pageant: Camp Fire Tales', *The Redress of the Past*, http://www.historicalpageants.ac.uk/pageants/1112/ (accessed 29 December 2018).
29. Angela Bartie, Linda Fleming, Mark Freeman, Tom Hulme, Alex Hutton, Paul Readman, 'The Amber Gate', *The Redress of the Past*, http://www.historicalpageants.ac.uk/pageants/928/ (accessed 29 December 2018). See also *The Stage*, 5 July 1923, 6 and Kitty [Marion Catherine] Barne, *The Amber Gate: A Pageant-Play of Episodes in Lives of Children Famous in History with Prologue and an Alternative Special Prologue for Girl Guides* (London, n.d.; Bratton Collection, Roehampton University).
30. Kitty [Marion Catherine] Barne, *The Amber Gate* (London: T. Nelson and Sons, 1936).
31. Barne, *Amber Gate* (1936), 21.
32. Barne, *Amber Gate* (1936), 277.
33. Barne, *Amber Gate* (1936), 277.
34. Barne, *Amber Gate* (1936), 84.
35. Dorothy Wordsworth later took in one of the bereaved children. The story is included in Edmund Lee, *Dorothy Wordsworth, The Story of a Sister's Love* (London: James Clarke & Co., 1886).
36. Barne, *Amber Gate* (1936), 280.

37. Mumm, 'Women and Philanthropic Cultures', 54–71.
38. Held on a Sunday in 1851, Britain's only religious census held in 1851 revealed 'to the horror and anguish of the Victorian Establishment that more people had gone to Chapel than to Church that day'. Nonconformity remained very vibrant into the early decades of the twentieth century, but while in 1932 there were 32,000 Methodist chapels in England and Wales, fewer than 7,500 remained by 1980. See Ken Powell, *The Fall of Zion: Northern Chapel Architecture and its Future* (London: SAVE Britain's Heritage, 1980), no pagination [pp. i, 16]. The quotation is from the foreword ('A Conspiracy of Silence') by Marcus Binney [p. i].
39. Amy Binns, 'New Heroines for New Causes: How Provincial Women Promoted a Revisionist History through Post-suffrage Pageants', *Women's History Review* 27 (2018): 221–46. Full spreadsheets detailing the pageants are available on the University of Central Lancashire's CLoK online archive: see https://doi.org/10.17030/uclan.data.00000122 (accessed 20 February 2019).
40. Olive Anderson, 'Women Preachers in Mid-Victorian Britain: Some Reflexions on Feminism, Popular Religion and Social Change', *Historical Journal* 12 (1969): 467–84; Pamela J. Walker, '"With Fear and Trembling": Women, Preaching and Spiritual Authority', in *Women, Gender and Religious Cultures*, ed. Morgan and DeVries, 94–116; Deborah M. Valenze, *Prophetic Sons and Daughters: Female Preaching and Popular Religion in Industrial England* (Princeton, NJ: Princeton University Press, 1985).
41. Sue Morgan, '"The Word Made Flesh": Women, Religion and Sexual Cultures', in *Women, Gender and Religious Cultures*, ed. Morgan and DeVries, 159–87.
42. D. W. Bebbington, *The Nonconformist Conscience: Chapel and Politics, 1870–1914* (London: Allen & Unwin, 1982).
43. E. P. Thompson, *The Making of the English Working Class* (London: Victor Gollancz, 1963).
44. Dorcas Societies were small philanthropic groups who sewed together and provided clothes for the poor. They are named for Dorcas of Acts 9:36.
45. *White Ribbon*, February 1916. The White Ribbon magazines of the British Women's Temperance Association are held in archive by the White Ribbon Association.
46. John 4:29.
47. Maggie Andrews, *The Acceptable Face of Feminism: The Women's Institute as a Social Movement* (London: Lawrence & Wishart, 2015 [1997]).
48. 'Women's Institute Drama Festival', *Warwickshire Advertiser*, 12 April 1930, 8.
49. Angela Bartie, Linda Fleming, Mark Freeman, Tom Hulme, Alex Hutton, Paul Readman, 'Norfolk Federation of Women's Institutes Pageant', *The Redress of the Past*, http://www.historicalpageants.ac.uk/pageants/1388/ (accessed 29 December 2018).
50. The Pastons were a Norfolk gentry family. Margery (b. *c.*1450) was the daughter of Margaret (1421/2–84); her love affair with and subsequent marriage to Richard Calle, steward of the Paston estates (and therefore a servant), caused a major scandal.
51. *Yarmouth Independent*, 12 June 1926, 7.
52. *Gloucester Journal*, 16 May 1936, 14.
53. Angela Williams, writing at http://www.literaryplaces.co.uk/?p=351 (accessed 29 December 2018), describes the various versions of the story, including a narrative poem by Rose Hartwick Thorpe (1867) and a play and short story by Albert Smith (1842).
54. Angela Bartie, Linda Fleming, Mark Freeman, Tom Hulme, Alex Hutton, Paul Readman, 'Mother Earth', *The Redress of the Past*, http://www.historicalpageants.ac.uk/pageants/1264/ (accessed 28 June 2019). Quotes are from a partial script contained in 'Papers Relating to WI Pageant at Blagdon Hall, 1936', Northumberland Archives, Ashington, ref. PC20/22.
55. *Sunderland Daily Echo and Shipping Gazette*, 13 May 1938, 16; and 26 May 1938, 8.
56. *Sunderland Daily Echo and Shipping Gazette*, 13 May 1938, 16.
57. *Sunderland Daily Echo and Shipping Gazette*, 13 May 1938, 16.
58. Angela Bartie, Linda Fleming, Mark Freeman, Tom Hulme, Alex Hutton, Paul Readman, 'Pedlar's Ware', *The Redress of the Past*, http://www.historicalpageants.ac.uk/pageants/1241/ (accessed 28 June 2019).
59. The use of symbolic space is discussed in George A. Tresidder, 'Coronation Day Celebrations in English Towns 1685–1821: Elite Hegemony and Local Relations on a Ceremonial Occasion', *British Journal of Eighteenth Century Studies* 15 (1992): 1–32. See also Michael Woods, 'Performing Power: Local Politics and the Taunton Pageant of 1928', *Journal of Historical Geography* 25 (1999): 57–74.

Bibliography

Alexander, Kristine. 2009. 'The Girl Guide Movement and Imperial Internationalism During the 1920s and 1930s', *Journal of the History of Childhood and Youth* 2: 37–63.

Anderson, Olive. 1969. 'Women Preachers in Mid-Victorian Britain: Some Reflexions on Feminism, Popular Religion and Social Change', *Historical Journal* 12: 467–84.

Andrews, Maggie. 2015 (2nd ed.), 1997 (1st ed.). *The Acceptable Face of Feminism: The Women's Institute Movement 1915–1960*. London: Lawrence & Wishart.

Beaumont, Caitriona. 2013. *Housewives and Citizens: Domesticity and the Women's Movement in England, 1928–64*. Manchester: Manchester University Press.

Bebbington, D. W. 1982. *The Nonconformist Conscience: Chapel and Politics, 1870–1914*. London: Allen & Unwin.

Bingham, Adrian. 2005 '"An Era of Domesticity"? Histories of Women and Gender in Inter-War Britain', *Cultural and Social History* 1: 225–33.

Binns, Amy. 2017. 'New Heroines for New Causes: How Provincial Women Promoted a Revisionist History through Post-Suffrage Pageants', *Women's History Review* 27: 1–26.

Cockin, Katharine. 2005. 'Cicely Hamilton's Warriors: Dramatic Reinventions of Militancy in the British Women's Suffrage Movement', *Women's History Review* 14: 527–42.

DiCenzo, Maria. 2014. '"Our Freedom and its Results": Measuring Progress in the Aftermath of Suffrage', *Women's History Review* 23: 421–40.

Glucksmann, Miriam. 2000. *Cottons and Casuals: The Gendered Organisation of Labour in Time and Space*. Durham: Sociology Press.

Harrison, Brian. 1973. 'For Church, Queen and Family, the Girls' Friendly Society, 1874–1920', *Past and Present* 61: 107–38.

Harrison, Brian. 1986. 'Women in a Men's House: The Women MPs 1919–1945', *Historical Journal* 29: 623–54.

Jarvis, David. 1994. 'Mrs Maggs and Betty: The Conservative Appeal to Women Voters in the 1920s', *Twentieth Century British History* 5: 129–52.

Jeal, Tim. 1989. *Baden-Powell: Founder of the Boy Scouts*. London: Hutchinson.

Lewis, Jane. 1979. 'The Ideology and Politics of Birth Control in Inter-War England', *Women's Studies International Quarterly* 2: 33–48.

Light, Alison. 1991. *Forever England: Literature, Femininity and Conservatism between the Wars*. London and New York: Routledge.

Morgan, Sue. 2010. '"The Word Made Flesh": Women, Religion and Sexual Cultures', in *Women, Gender and Religious Cultures in Britain, 1800–1940*, edited by Sue Morgan and Jacqueline DeVries. London and New York: Routledge, 159–87.

Morgan, Sue and DeVries, Jacqueline, eds. 2010. *Women, Gender and Religious Cultures in Britain, 1800–1940*. London and New York: Routledge.

Mumm, Susan. 2010. 'Women and Philanthropic Cultures', in *Women, Gender and Religious Cultures in Britain, 1800–1940*, edited by Sue Morgan and Jacqueline DeVries. London and New York: Routledge, 54–71.

Nicholson, Virginia. 2005. *Singled Out: How Two Million British Women Survived Without Men After the First World War*. Oxford: Oxford University Press.

Powell, Ken. 1980. *The Fall of Zion: Northern Chapel Architecture and its Future*. London: SAVE Britain's Heritage.

Richmond, Vivienne. 2007. '"It is not a Society for Human Beings but for Virgins": The Girls' Friendly Society Membership Eligibility Dispute 1875–1936', *Journal of Historical Sociology* 20: 304–27.

Thomas, Zoë. 2017. 'Historical Pageants, Citizenship, and the Performance of Women's History before Second-wave Feminism', *Twentieth Century British History* 28: 319–43.

Thompson, E. P. 1963. *The Making of the English Working Class*. London: Victor Gollancz.

Thompson, F. M. L. 1981. 'Social Control in Victorian Britain', *Economic History Review*, new series 34: 189–208.

Tresidder, George A. 1992. 'Coronation Day Celebrations in English Towns 1685–1821: Elite Hegemony and Local Relations on a Ceremonial Occasion', *British Journal of Eighteenth Century Studies* 15: 1–32.

Valenze, Deborah M. 1985, *Prophetic Sons and Daughters: Female Preaching and Popular Religion in Industrial England*. Princeton, NJ: Princeton University Press.

Voeltz, Richard A. 1992. 'The Antidote to "Khaki Fever"? The Expansion of the British Girl Guides during the First World War', *Journal of Contemporary History* 27: 627–38.

Walker, Pamela J. 2010. '"With Fear and Trembling": Women, Preaching and Spiritual Authority', in *Women, Gender and Religious Cultures in Britain, 1800–1940*, edited by Sue Morgan and Jacqueline DeVries. London and New York: Routledge, 94–116.

Walkowitz, Judith R. 1982. *Prostitution and Victorian Society: Women, Class, and the State*. Cambridge: Cambridge University Press.

Woods, Michael. 1999. 'Performing Power: Local Politics and the Taunton Pageant of 1928', *Journal of Historical Geography* 25: 57–74.

7
Historical Pageants, Neo-Romanticism and the City in Interwar Britain

Tom Hulme

In the 1920s and 1930s historical pageantry was especially popular in the urban heartlands of Britain.[1] Before 1914 only two major cities in England (Liverpool and London) had staged an historical pageant and there are examples of urban pageants failing to take off due to a lack of local interest, particularly from the urban working classes.[2] By 1939, however, the picture was strikingly different, with 14 of the 20 biggest cities having staged at least one pageant. Northern and Midlands manufacturing cities had now emerged as pageantry's new and appreciative home, while casts of thousands were regularly raised with ease in the name of civic history. Accompanying this shift to cities was the rise of a new breed of pageant-master and producer, particularly inspired (or at least influenced) by Frank Lascelles and straddling the worlds of theatre, government and business. From their earliest days pageants had possessed a commercial motive, as small historic towns tried to stimulate a growing market for tourism.[3] But interwar coalitions of city councils and industrialists took this to a new level, using historical pageantry to encourage the local economy in a time of economic depression. This tactic arguably emerged from the nascent 'civic publicity' movement, which originated in wartime government propaganda, but was catalysed especially by the 1924 British Empire Exhibition in London. Municipally-led 'Civic Weeks' held at the Exhibition then spread across heavily industrialised areas of Britain, joining popular entertainment with economic boosterism – of which pageants became an important element.[4]

In this chapter I expand more specifically on the historical themes and ideas that were portrayed in the episodes of urban pageants in the late 1920s and 1930s. In doing so I argue that the vogue for the performance of the past can tell us much about a complex and often contradictory topic: the place of Neo-Romanticism, and its relationship to modernity, in mid-twentieth-century urban Britain.

The Neo-Romantic city

When Romanticism emerged as an artistic, literary and intellectual movement in the late eighteenth and early nineteenth centuries, it was primarily rooted in commitments to nature, natural life and the medieval past. As such, it can be seen as a reaction to rapid industrialisation and accompanying urbanisation, as well as to scientific rationalisation and the Enlightenment.[5] However, Romanticism also shaped the experience of the burgeoning modern city to which it could seem diametrically opposed. The city, in turn, set the stage for many of Romanticism's achievements in literature and culture. Romanticism was therefore 'not a movement against the city', but rather 'an aesthetic that developed along with – and contributed to – the ascendancy of metropolitan life'.[6]

A key concern of Romantic thinking was thus the mutual interdependence of the individual and society, and the search for solutions to the individual's alienation from, and in, the city. William Wordsworth, for example, was not just the 'Poet of Nature' and extoller of the supposedly untainted Lake District, but also an 'avid metropolitan' who could find stimulation and beauty in London. Meanwhile William Blake, perhaps more obviously a 'city poet', could see the urban as 'a node, a fissure, through which the true nature of society can be glimpsed' – which included 'a vision of the new, renovated millennial city of the New Jerusalem established through a "mental fight" in the minds of "England's green & pleasant Land"'.[7] Transcendental Romantic art, shaped through collaborative networks of often city-based or visiting artists, actualised the urban and rural tension. Yet at the same time it could also function as a site and symbol of inclusion, in a moment of rapid social change, by envisaging an 'ideal' city.[8]

Urbanisation continued unabated in the nineteenth century and, at the turn of the twentieth century especially, was accompanied by debates about the effects of the city on the life, morality and health of its inhabitants. As Britain's ability to compete in an age of global economic and military competition came under increasing scrutiny, these debates grew in intensity.[9] In the ensuing intense search for an ideal society, in which ideal 'citizens' could live healthy, happy and co-operative lifestyles, anti-urban 'Neo-Romantic' artists and social reformers looked again to the landscape. More than just a muse for art and literature, the countryside was seen both as a fruitful source of a usable identity based on idealistic notions of 'Englishness', and a recuperative environment, which fostered health and community.[10] For the proponents of rural preservation or the advocates of increasingly popular leisure 'rambling', the 'degenerative' city was thus in tension with the romantic countryside.[11] Accordingly there were 'loud and influential' calls for a reversal of urbanisation and a concurrent revival of traditional rural communities. These were led by organisations such as the National Trust (formed 1895) and the Council for the Preservation of Rural England (formed 1926) and individual campaigners, such as the architect Clough Williams-Ellis.[12] A significant part of the logic of Neo-Romanticism, then, was its turn towards 'home' and history, as artists and writers – in reaction to the revolutionary artistic manifestos of modernist groups such as the Futurists, or their British counterpart the Vorticists – wondered how to 'reconnect with the heavily abandoned past'.[13]

As with the original Romantics, however, the relationship between Neo-Romanticism, modernity and urban life could be a complex one. The city, of course, did not disappear in the twentieth century – neither in reality nor in representation – and an anti-urban and anti-modern notion of 'Englishness' was not embraced by all.[14] Rural preservationists, too, were not always exclusively motivated by anti-modernism.[15] Both Neo-Romantics and vociferous urban critics, and individuals who belonged to both categories, could accept that they were inescapably living in an urban-industrial age; pragmatists realised that simply 'dispersing urban life' to idealistic rural communities was not feasible.[16]

Alternatives included the construction of new sorts of cities and the changing of cities from within. The former category included Ebenezer Howard's turn-of-the-century 'Garden City' model, which attempted to reconcile the benefits of country and city in a new synthesis and informed town planning discourse until the mid-twentieth century, and, in a similar vein, William Morris's vision, in his utopian novel *News from Nowhere* (1890), of a socialist society where London and other large centres of manufacturing had been replaced by smaller, better-built and more cohesive urban settlements: here inhabitants were liberated, rather than enslaved, by the beneficent use of mechanisation.[17] In the latter category, on the other hand, we could see the 1930s demolition of inner-city slums and the concurrent enthusiasm for 'cottage-style' social housing – or, as will be argued here, the staging of popular and participatory theatre. Such events sought to locate present-day cities in their pre-industrial and rural history, thus providing a sense of belonging and continuity at a time of change and dislocation. Indeed, targeted at urban and suburban audiences, the emotive power of the interwar 'conjured village of the mind's eye' was harnessed just when the values and traditions of the country were arguably being lost.[18] Rural-inflected ideals of Englishness, then, despite often being conceived as anti-industrial and anti-modern, could also be found in various methods of regenerating the city and its culture.[19]

Historical pageantry and adaptive modernity

Scholarly debates about the contradictions and complexities of the relationship between modernity and Neo-Romanticism have been reflected, if only implicitly, in the growing historiography of historical pageantry. Performances of a utopian, pre-industrial and 'Merrie England' past could be seen as conservative reactions to change. Louis Napoleon Parker, the inventor of modern pageantry, moved in early Neo-Romanticist circles (particularly those clustered around the folk revival). He was open about his hope that the 'community bonanza' of pageantry would both relieve class tensions and kill off 'the modernising spirit' that he believed was destroying 'all loveliness and has no loveliness of its own to put in its place' and which signalled the 'negation of poetry [and] romance'.[20]

Into the interwar period, pageantry could certainly be 'an ideal bedfellow to expressions of rural nostalgia and the projections of a bucolic "deep" England' – expressed particularly in the pageants of villages and towns that feared the urban 'ribbon development' famously lamented in rural preservationist tracts such as Williams-Ellis's *England and the Octopus* (1928).[21] David Glassberg has seen the Parkerian tradition as a protest against modernity by means of the deployment of 'historical imagery in a format that glorified a remote golden handicraft past'.[22] Although Parker may have originated the format, however, his version of pageantry was only the beginning rather than the end of the movement. Indeed it underwent several divergent evolutions – almost as soon as it had been 'invented' – which complicate a simplistic conservative/modern binary.

Deborah Sugg Ryan, for example, has shown how the actor and director Frank Lascelles, who staged huge and popular pageants from 1907, developed his own distinctive style of visual spectacular. Unlike Parker, Lascelles prioritised the dramatic movement of large groups of people in colourful dances and processions rather than spoken dialogue, and arguably 'embraced modernity' instead of rejecting it.[23] His pageants, Ryan posits, should be seen in the context of other contemporaneous mass events that depended on the visual impact of thousands of people gathered together in one space – such as the spectacle plays of Max Reinhardt, 'toga plays', huge exhibitions and the cinema epics of D. W. Griffith and Cecil B. DeMille.[24] Also in contrast to Parker, who had a tendency to downplay the importance of scenery (he thought it was often a distraction), Lascelles encouraged the creation of entire historical landscapes, informed by his practice as a painter, his interest in the Pre-Raphaelites and his enthusiasm for the Arts and Crafts movement.[25]

From a somewhat different perspective, Jed Esty has shown how authors associated with the English late-modernism of the 1930s, such as Virginia Woolf, E. M. Forster and T. S. Eliot, actually found the pageant-play format a means of composing 'valedictions' to modernist modes of thought. In the performance of the past, they believed, was a positive 'spontaneous folk authenticity' and an 'acceptable' version 'of national art' – one that responded to their increasing sense of cultural isolation.[26] New political organisations, too, from the internationalist League of Nations Union to the Women's Institute, were able to adapt the basic elements of pageantry to promote progressive and forward-looking ideas.[27]

Historical pageantry as a form, then, can arguably be better defined by its sheer adaptability and malleability than by any inherent conservatism. In Britain's industrial cities during the Great Depression, pageantry could accordingly be used to stimulate the local economy and – more importantly for the argument put forward here – provide a rooted sense of continuity, stability and future prosperity.[28] To achieve this, pageant-masters of the interwar period adopted a Neo-Romantic perspective. In doing so, they attempted to overcome potential contradictions or tensions between the reality of modern urban life and the pre-modern historical past(s) that their pageants celebrated.

As Kitty Hauser has shown in her study of archaeological photography from the 1920s to the 1950s, 'Neo-Romanticism may be thought of as a way of seeing as well as a style', encompassing 'Neo-Romantic viewers as well as Neo-Romantic artists'. For Hauser, this Neo-Romantic 'way of seeing' entailed the ways in which contemporaries could identify the Romantic symbolic importance of the depiction of topics such as local scenes, nature and landscape in a variety of media forms. Hauser further delineates what might be seen as the two prevalent – and antithetical – discourses of Neo-Romanticism: a strictly 'preservationist' mindset on the one hand and a more reflexive 'archaeological imagination' on the other. In the former, modernity is deemed an 'irremovable barrier in the way of aesthetic pleasure'; in the latter, it is 'a barrier that can be seen through, over, or round': the past may have lost visibility in the modern landscape, but it was not 'sensuously un-recoverable'. The past could, consequently, operate as a 'consoling sensibility' in the present. Modernity, by the same token, could be reconciled with an increasingly impossible ideal historical landscape or culture, so long as the essential destructibility of history and historical culture was recognised or – better still – portrayed. It was this function of historical pageantry, its 'archaeological imagination', which enabled or allowed pageant-masters to stage historical spectaculars that looked both backwards and forwards in a way that Neo-Romantic viewers may have recognised. As Hauser points out, modernity did not remove the historicity of a place; it was simply the latest stage in that place's history.[29]

Historical pageantry, I would argue, was a visual representation of this reality. Indeed, as Paul Readman and others have shown, the interest in the past signified by the pageant movement did not necessarily imply a wish actually to *return* to a pre-industrial society or its values. On the contrary: the past provided inspiration for a new future, positively accommodating rapid and frightening change and progress alongside the preservation of historic landscapes, customs and culture.[30] Mick Wallis, for example, has demonstrated how historical pageantry in village settings was seen as having the potential to create a new rural community through recourse to the life and history of the common labourer, rather than the landed gentry. The interwar village pageant-master Mary Kelly, 'unlike many of her more nostalgic contemporaries', still 'recognised the class conflicts and history of deprivation of the rural poor, and blended such elements into the pageants she devised.'[31] At a time when the countryside, idealised by some, did not tally with the impression from others of continuing economic and moral rural malaise, Kelly's pageants arguably bridged this gap.[32]

For the great urban pageants of the late 1920s and 1930s, however, the evocation of the rural and pre-industrial worked in other ways. By this point Parker had all but stopped producing historical pageants. In his 1928 autobiography he complained that a whole host of unworthy imitators had sprung up and commercialised his invention, with only one 'honourable exception': Charles Hawtrey, who had died in 1910 after acting as pageant-master for only three pageants.[33] Other new and ambitious pageant impresarios were still connected to Parker's ethos in many respects, but they arguably had more in common – both personally and professionally – with Lascelles. He was now responsible for many of the hugely successful pageants in the cities of the Midlands and the North until his death in 1934.[34]

Municipal autonomy

For an industrial town or city, dependent on trade and thus suffering hard times, the romantic pre-industrial past needed to serve as a reassurance that the place could survive – and indeed prosper – through the vicissitudes of the present. In tune with pre-1914 pageants, the historical events of pre-modern civic life were celebrated – not because authors and participants yearned to turn the clock back, but because including a long chronological range enabled the construction of a genealogical lineage for contemporary civic institutions and the power that such institutions now wielded. What may have seemed unique or atemporal was instead portrayed as the cumulative result of a process that had begun many centuries before. Pageants in cities were thus often staged to commemorate their past incorporation, with episodes demonstrating the historical roots of government and urban growth.

The massive Pageant of Manchester in 1938, part of the city's centenary celebrations, which had 10,000 performers and was seen by perhaps 100,000 people, offers a notable example. It was directed by Nugent Monck, the pageant-master and creator of the Norwich Maddermarket Theatre, who claimed to have developed his style without influence from Parker. Assisting Monck was Edward Baring, a businessman and pageant producer with 30 years of experience; in the 1920s and 1930s he had formed something of a double act with Lascelles. Episodes in Manchester's pageant included the founding of a Roman fort at 'Mancunium' in AD 79; the inclusion of 'Mameceaster' in the dominions of Edward the Elder, king of the Anglo-Saxons, in AD 924; and Manchester's receipt of its first charter from Thomas Gresley in 1301.[35] In an era of central state growth, with fears mounting of a declining societal interest in municipal matters, the celebration of the bestowal of charters in medieval times – with all their associated pomp and ceremony – was aimed at encouraging local people to think of their municipal government as a body with both a long and a noble history.[36] Choosing medieval episodes that demonstrated a city's importance and autonomy reflected the continuing power of what David Matthews has dubbed the 'civic Middle Ages' – despite his contention that this aspect of British culture had declined in the early twentieth century.[37]

Other pageants also highlighted the medieval heritage of urban governance, but demonstrated its evolution in later periods as well – especially when there was a charter anniversary to be celebrated. The Pageant of Birmingham in 1938, for example, was organised explicitly to commemorate the centenary of the granting of the town's civic charter: its second episode portrayed the granting of a market charter to Peter de Birmingham in 1156, while the penultimate scene showed the ceremonial welcome that the mayor and council gave Queen Victoria upon her visit in 1858.[38] The pageant had a cast of 8,000 and was seen by almost 140,000 people. It was directed by Gwen Lally, an increasingly important pageant-master in the 1930s. Lally had strong connections with Lascelles: as an actress under the management of Sir Herbert Beerbohm Tree (himself Lascelles' mentor), she had performed in Lascelles' 1907 Oxford pageant and took on board his preference for minimal dialogue and maximum spectacle.[39] A similar ethos was apparent in the Salford pageant of 1930, staged by a cast of 6,000 in the year of the 700th anniversary of the granting of a charter to make the town a 'free borough'.[40] Unsurprisingly one episode featured 'Ranulf the Good' (Ranulph de Blondeville), the sixth Earl of Chester (1153–1232), conferring this charter. Other episodes also showed the royal patronage that confirmed both Salford's long and more recent history of autonomy – from King Alfred the Great declaring the town to be the 'capital of Salfordshire' in the ninth century, to Bonnie Prince Charlie being blessed at Salford Cross in the eighteenth.

'Inventing' a history of local governmental autonomy proved particularly attractive for towns in the home counties. In the late nineteenth and early twentieth centuries transport developments and suburbanisation fuelled the rapid expansion of 'Outer London'.[41] At first critics were wary of the impact this might have on non-urban Britain. C. F. G. Masterman, a settlement house worker and later Cabinet-ranking politician, ably brought these fears together in *The Heart of the Empire* (1901). When Masterman described London's suburbia as a 'gigantic plasmodium: spreading slimy arms over the surrounding fields', he vividly evoked contemporary worries that the capital's evils were seeping out beyond its borders.[42] Less dramatic analyses of London's growth, such as those of the planner Patrick Geddes, called instead for more comprehensive governmental systems to join together urban areas within reach of the capital.[43] Some of the politicians and administrators of the London County Council (LCC) agreed. During the First World War the coalition between the Progressives and the Municipal Reform Party included a commitment to extending the boundaries of the County. In response to the passing of a resolution to this effect in 1919, a new Royal Commission was set up to consider how London's government might be expanded.[44]

With the expansionist tendencies of the LCC now more apparent, district councils increasingly petitioned for new charters of municipal borough incorporation as a way to provide 'freedom from attack by a neighbouring authority'.[45] Such efforts were informed by a desire to encourage local inhabitants to think less of their town as a 'dormitory' of London and more as a discrete place with a venerable and important history, with local pageants being the perfect demonstration of such a history.[46] In the Walthamstow pageant of 1930, performed by 600 children to commemorate the granting of the municipal borough charter the previous year, episodes aimed to demonstrate the length of time that the settlement had existed – all the way from the Normans and Lord Ralph de Toni of the Manor of Wilcumestou to 'the Coming of the Charter' in 1929, an event presented as a 'notable landmark in Walthamstow's progress'.[47] Scenes in between the main episodes emphasised the importance of Walthamstow to the nation as a whole, particularly through portraying the visits or residence of famous figures (Samuel Pepys, Richard Turpin, Benjamin Disraeli and William Morris).

The Barking pageant of 1931 was likewise staged to celebrate the granting of a municipal charter of incorporation, which in this case had taken place in the same year as the pageant.[48] Directed by Lascelles, with a relatively small cast of 2,000, the pageant made much of Barking's

Figure 7.1 Postcard of the Pageant of Barking (1931). Reproduced by kind permission of the Ellie Reid Collection.

glorious past. Episodes included the foundation of Barking Abbey, a visit from Charles I and the Great Barking Fair of 1746 (Fig.7.1), patronised by the Lord Mayor of London and other notables such as Captain Cook (who had married locally, in St Margaret's Church). But its epilogue consisted of a march-past by the costumed performers, finally joined by municipal representatives of the new borough, as 'Long Live Barking' was cried out. This was an obvious attempt to connect the great deeds and men of the past with the successful corporation and councillors of the present. A very similar ethos was evident in the episodes of the Dartford pageant (1932), which featured William the Conqueror being forced to accept terms of privilege by Kentishmen in 1066, Edward the Black Prince visiting Bexley Hall and praising the area, and Henry VIII enjoying local revelries on May Day 1515.[49] Thus although not as large as the civic pageants of Northern and Midlands cities, 'Outer London' pageants shared with them a desire to demonstrate how present-day power and prestige rested on a much longer historical record.

Economic boosterism

Parker would perhaps have recognised and approved of this continued emphasis on the origins and autonomy of local civic institutions. But there were other developments of which he might have been less appreciative. Pageants, in the interwar period, became far more comfortable with portraying the industrial past and present – and highlighting (implicitly and sometimes explicitly) the connection between the two. In doing so they contributed to a growing desire to boost the fortunes of the local economy, while simultaneously cooling the temperature of working-class discontent. Lascelles' Bradford pageant of 1931, for example, which had 7,500 performers and was seen by around 120,000 people, was organised by the city's elites in the context of the socio-economic instability of the Great Depression.[50] After a narrative that started in Roman times, and passed through the Normans, Plantagenets and Stuarts, the final episode featured 'Bradford of the Industrial Revolution'. Scenes depicted the development of woollen production in the late eighteenth and nineteenth centuries, as well as the triumphant election of the town's first MPs after the 1832 Great Reform Act (Fig.7.2). In presenting such a story, the organisers hoped to rally a fractious local society around the city and its governors.

Birmingham's centenary pageant (mentioned above) offers an even more striking example of this agenda in action. Here the second episode

Figure 7.2 Election Scene: *Historical Pageant of Bradford Souvenir Programme* (Bradford: Percy Lund, Humphries and Co., Ltd, 1931). Reproduced by kind permission of the Ellie Reid Collection.

showed the granting of a market charter followed by a scene from the buoyant market that resulted. The final scene also returned to the economy of the city, but this time it portrayed 'Birmingham Today', complete with representations of the important trades of the city such as electrical trades, firearms and motor vehicles.[51]

In Stoke-on-Trent's pageant of 1930, staged by Lascelles with 5,000 performers, the historical narrative proved a useful way of connecting the manufacturing innovators of the past with the industrial power of the present. The story told how 'a one-time insignificant spot', as the pageant handbook put it, came 'to be one of the most famous industrial centres of the world'.[52] The first half of the pageant was fairly standard fare, depicting early Britons resisting Romans, John of Gaunt (a powerful figure in Staffordshire) at Tutbury Castle in 1374, and the dissolution of Hulton Abbey in 1549. However, given that the year of its performance was also the bicentenary of the birth of Josiah Wedgwood, the second half concentrated on the rise of the pottery industry in the Midlands town. One episode showed the 'personalities' associated with pottery, as 'pioneer peasant potters' were depicted 'at work and play' in the seventeenth and eighteenth centuries; another showed some of the 'incidents in the life and time of Josiah Wedgwood'; and a third offered an 'allegorical portrayal of the modern potteries industry'. As the handbook explained, allegory was necessary in this episode – the final one in the pageant – both because it was 'impossible to depict the development of the Potteries by referring to individuals, or even individual firms', and also because 'the drab facts of the industrial machine' were better brought to life through 'the play of the imagination and the skill of the artist'.[53] Thus instead of direct depictions of industries such as ceramics, coal mining and metallurgy, the episode featured a Ceramic Queen with attendants, King Coal and his 'offsprings' and Tubal Cain (the biblical blacksmith). The Stoke pageant was, as the president of the North Staffordshire Chamber of Commerce put it, an attempt to 'help' local industry as it went through 'hard times' and became ever more 'in desperate need' of business.[54]

Perhaps the apotheosis of industrial depiction in historical pageants came with Matthew Anderson's Lancashire Cotton Pageant, performed by 12,000 performers in 1932. Staged in Manchester in the Belle Vue stadium, it was a county-wide affair led by regional industrial bodies such as the Cotton Trade Organisations.[55] When Ellis Green, the Lord Mayor of Manchester, opened the pageant, he declared that 'behind all' the 'showmanship was' an 'underlying' idea: Lancashire's cotton industry had to be 'advertised, and advertised flamboyantly, [and] vociferously … The industry had to "bang the drum", and bang it hard'.[56] To achieve this perspective, the pageant offered a hotchpotch of events, themes, countries and fiction. It featured a Persian cotton market in 'Ancient Times' and Flemish weavers being welcomed to England by William the Conqueror, before skipping eight centuries to 'Lancashire at the Dawn of the Industrial Revolution', which bizarrely included Macbeth-style witches flying on broomsticks and casting magic spells before being driven off by Lancashire farmers. Other scenes featured the North American cotton fields (with actors in blackface) and the achievements of famous inventors in the textile industry such as John Kay, Richard Arkwright and Samuel Crompton.[57] As the *Manchester Guardian* quipped, the pageant 'stuck to cotton all the time … The thread is never off the bobbin'.[58]

The common people

Evocations of historical continuity could also go beyond the city's institutions and industries. Parker had been keen for his pageanteers to take historical roles that reflected their current social positions – a mayor playing a mayor of the past, a vicar or priest playing a monk, an agricultural labourer playing a medieval peasant, and so forth. Parker's pageants thus gave attention to all sections of local society. But the focus was on what he saw as the most important historical actors – kings, queens, archbishops and the like – and on confirming social hierarchies rather than challenging them.[59] In the interwar period, however, it became increasingly common to celebrate the lives of ordinary folk. They were given enhanced visibility and more speaking roles, and were also depicted as having a key importance in the unfolding of local life. In Anderson's cotton pageant, for example, barely a real historical figure was portrayed. Instead, in the second half, scenes such as 'Market Day', 'Lancashire at Work' and 'Lancashire at Play' concentrated on the lives of representative working people. For Edward Genn, Anderson's producer, the change in style was about producing a lively, people-oriented production that would 'bear no resemblance' to the 'artistic abomination' of the 'civic history pageant' and its 'tiresome … tradition of Romans, Saxons, monks and knights, wandering like lost, unshepherded sheep across a field in front of a flimsy property castle'. Instead he wanted the pageant to show 'Lancashire as a great province of heroic achievement built up on the struggles, sufferings and sacrifices of the men, women and children'.[60]

Genn's somewhat flippant disregard for civic history may have been out-of-tune with broader interwar trends, but his emphasis on 'the people' had greater resonance. Indeed, according to Nugent Monck, the 'central theme of modern pageantry' in the 1930s was the increased importance accorded to the 'influence of the crowd in municipal government':

> From law and order by the Romans, through the breaking of the Feudal Barons, the establishment of the Constitution, and so gradually to universal suffrage and state ownership, it is the increasing power of the man in the street to organise his life and it is these men and women who become the principal performers in pageants.[61]

F. E. Doran, a local theatre producer, clergyman and pageant-master, made similar points to Monck. His Manchester pageant in 1926, seen by around 100,000 people, aimed to

> symbolise the growing power of the people through the centuries, to indicate the part played by Manchester people in moulding the thought, institutions and commerce of the country, to emphasise that beyond the veil of smoke and the forest of chimneys our civic life is based on heroic and romantic incidents, the endeavours and struggles of the common people.[62]

As the Lord Bishop of Rochester said of the Dartford pageant of 1932, re-enactment helped 'to recall the splendour of past history, the great deeds that had made this country what it is to-day' – including those of the 'common or ordinary men and women of days gone by who had done their share towards making this nation of ours what it is'.[63] In one sense, scenes of pre-urban life also reflected an already established tendency to identify the peasant as 'the nostalgic embodiment of noble, Anglo-Saxon virtues and an exemplary figure in an authentic and stable golden age entirely unaffected by change'.[64] But interwar pageants also reflected a more recent growth of interest in histories of 'everyday life', one propagated by social historians such as the Quennells and institutions such as the BBC.[65] Romanticising the role of the common man was about creating an affinity between the present-day urban-industrial worker and his (or, less consistently, her) rural forebears in the past, as well as projecting such values forward in time.

Monck's mentioning of suffrage and signalling of the role of women, in addition, is instructive. By the interwar years, and in contrast to the pre-war period, women had a much higher visibility in the organisational structure of pageant committees; they also increasingly made up a larger proportion of the cast. Both individual women and women's organisations saw the pageant format as one way of fitting themselves into a non-contentious role of active citizenship following suffrage extension in 1918 and 1928.[66] As one local newspaper put it in 1929, pageants were 'probably the ideal form of dramatic expression for Women's Institutes', since both sought to 'bring a wider culture and a comradeship to the countryside' as well as providing a chance for women to develop their practical skills in the making of costumes and properties, and offering an opportunity to express teamwork. Organising a pageant was thus 'the dramatisation' of the Institute's 'ideals'.[67]

At the same time pageants in both rural and urban areas could draw attention to the domestic lives of women and the parts they had played in past conflict and politics; they could even signal contemporary women's associational opposition to varied issues, such as hunting or war.[68] Romanticising the common people was also an exercise in demonstrating a less elitist sense of society in the context of the mass participation and sacrifice of the First World War. Such an aim coalesced with hopes and fears about the supposed susceptibility of the working classes to political radicalism in the context of continental fascism and communism.[69]

In an often class-torn society, the authors and organisers of historical pageants tended to emphasise common history and achievements, while smoothing over antagonistic debates and interests. Not all performers or spectators, it should be said, were either fooled or even necessarily interested in this narrative. Pageant-masters could face challenges from left-wing organisations if it was felt they had occluded urban working-class history or revolt. During the 1938 Manchester Pageant, for example, much debate took place over the omission of Peterloo from the narrative; the Communist Party eventually staged their own alternative pageant that celebrated the labour movement's role in the life of the city.[70] Similarly, at Bradford in 1931, there was controversy over the depiction of the Luddites, with the local Communist Party claiming that the pageant attempted to subvert the goal of workers' rights.[71]

Mainstream pageants were not always shy about including still-sore conflicts, however. The Lancashire Cotton Pageant, for example, also included Luddites attacking factories, as well as a surprisingly bloody re-enactment of Peterloo (which ended with 'dead and dying men and women, and items of clothing scattered across the scene').[72] Moreover, we must acknowledge the multiplicity of responses that pageants could engender in spectators and performers – from fun and adventure to subverting the message for their own ends. Crowds could misinterpret serious scenes for humorous ones; use the gathering of masses of people for social or criminal behaviour; or, quite simply, enjoy the spectacle rather than the educational ethos.[73]

Conclusion

I have argued here that the performance or re-enactment of the past did not result solely from backward-looking and anti-modern impulses. For cities dealing with difficult problems in the present – whether they be challenges to municipal autonomy, the expansion of the citizenry at the same time as a perceived decline in civic interest or the fluctuations in economic fortunes caused by depression – the past provided a wellspring of usable evidence for how towns and cities had adapted throughout their history.[74]

To make this argument, I have demonstrated how the specifically modern city – with its democratic government and industrial basis – could rest upon both the pre-urban and pre-industrial. Curating a 1987 exhibition on the Neo-Romantic imagination in Britain between 1935 and 1955, David Mellor usefully opened out the definition of Neo-Romanticism from a narrow history of art to include a wide range of media, such as photography, poetry and films, thus illustrating the prevalence of a more general Neo-Romantic sensibility throughout British culture.[75] Urban pageantry, as I have shown here, can be added to this list. Pageant-masters, authors and organisers may not have been Neo-Romantic in any strict or self-defining sense, but they were dealing with – and overcoming – similar shifts in thought and artistic practice. Historical pageantry could achieve a balancing act by allowing a Neo-Romantic rural or conservative impulse to be expressed within the modern city, rather than only beyond its borders.

Seeing the 'traditional' and 'the modern' as binary opposites in the interwar period has proved to be simplistic in a variety of cases – from the cultural memory of the First World War to the branding of the London Underground. This also holds true for urban culture more broadly.[76] The place of the city in interwar Neo-Romanticist currents of thought was a complex one, but it was not necessarily wholly negative or contradictory. Andrew Radford has rightly noted that both the definition and cultural legacies of Neo-Romanticism are 'notoriously tricky to delimit, given the tangle of the movement's theoretical strands and elusive periodisation'.[77] In a different vein, Alan Powers has pointed out the dangers of always associating certain motifs or symbols with a cultural tradition – such as landscape or countryside being always a 'cipher for conservatism and nostalgia'.[78] By the same token, it is now worth pointing out that industrial cities in the 1920s and 1930s were not always associated with the death of romantic ideas of the national or local past – despite the prevalence and power of the English countryside in the construction of 'Englishness'.

Notes

1. This chapter is an expansion of an article published in *Informationen zur modernen Stadtgeschichte* 2 (2016): 19–34. The author wishes to acknowledge and thank the editors of that journal for their permission to reprint here.
2. See, for example, the failure of the Nottingham pageant to get off the ground in 1908 – seemingly a victim of the apathy of the 'workers' rather than the 'gentlemen' who had committed the guarantee money needed: 'District Intelligence', *Grantham Journal*, 23 November 1907, 3.
3. Angela Bartie, Linda Fleming, Mark Freeman, Tom Hulme and Paul Readman, 'Performing the Past: Identity, Civic Culture and Historical Pageants in Twentieth-Century Small Towns', in *Small Towns in Europe in the 20th and 21st Centuries: Heritage and Development Strategies*, ed. Luda Klusakova (Prague: Karolinum Press, 2017), 24–51. See also Ayako Yoshino, *Pageant Fever: Local History and Consumerism in Edwardian England* (Tokyo: Waseda University Press, 2011).
4. For more discussion of this shift to cities, see Tom Hulme, '"A Nation of Town Criers": Civic Publicity and Historical Pageantry in Inter-War Britain', *Urban History* 44 (2017): 270–92.
5. See Joanne Schneider, *The Age of Romanticism* (Westport, CT: Greenwood, 2007), 71–3.
6. James Chandler and Kevin Gilmartin, 'Introduction: Engaging the Eidometropolis', in *Romantic Metropolis: The Urban Scene of British Culture, 1780–1840*, ed. James Chandler and Kevin Gilmartin (Cambridge: Cambridge University Press, 2005), 1, 19.
7. Eugene Stelzig, 'Wordsworth's Invigorating Hell: London in Book 7 of *The Prelude* (1805)', in *Romanticism and the City*, ed. Larry H. Peer (Basingstoke: Palgrave Macmillan, 2011),

181–196; Andrew Winckle, 'William Blake and the Urban Landscape of Apocalypse', conference paper, International Conference on Romanticism, New York, NY, 6 November 2009: see https://18thcenturyculture.wordpress.com/conference-papers/william-blake-and-the-urban-landscape-of-apocalypse/ (accessed 28 September 2016). See also Mark Lussier, 'Blake's Golgonoosa: London and/as the Eternal City of Art', in Peer, *Romanticism and the City*, 197–207. For the classic work on the city–country tension, see Raymond Williams, *The Country and the City* (London: Chatto & Windus, 1973).

8. See Larry H. Peer, 'Introduction: The Infernal and Celestial City of Romanticism', in Peer, *Romanticism and the City*, 2–3. For the network of Romantic artists, see Daisy Hay, *Young Romantics: The Shelleys, Byron and Other Tangled Lives* (London: Bloomsbury, 2010).
9. See Geoffrey R. Searle, *The Quest for National Efficiency: A Study in British Politics and Political Thought, 1899–1914* (Oxford: Oxford University Press, 1971); David Peters Corbett, Ysanne Holt and Fiona Russell, 'Introduction', in *The Geographies of Englishness: Landscape and the National Past 1880–1940*, ed. David Peters Corbett, Ysanne Holt and Fiona Russell (New Haven and London: Yale University Press, 2002), ix–xix.
10. See Frank Trentmann, 'Civilization and its Discontents: English Neo-Romanticism and the Transformation of Anti-Modernism in Twentieth-Century Western Culture', *Journal of Contemporary History* 29 (1994): 583–625; Paul Ward, *Britishness since 1870* (London: Routledge 2004), 55; Corbett, Holt and Russell, 'Introduction'; Ben Anderson, 'A Liberal Countryside? The Manchester Ramblers' Federation and the "Social Readjustment" of Urban Citizens, 1929–1936', *Urban History* 38 (2011): 84–102.
11. Martin J. Wiener has been particularly influential in cementing the notion that the countryside was the place in which the British looked for their values: see Martin J. Wiener, *English Culture and the Decline of the Industrial Spirit, 1850–1980* (2nd ed., Cambridge: Cambridge University Press, 2004 [1981]).
12. Alexandra Harris, *Romantic Moderns: English Writers, Artists and the Imagination from Virginia Woolf to Jon Piper* (London: Thames & Hudson, 2010), 169.
13. Harris, *Romantic Moderns*, 11.
14. Peter Mandler, especially, has made a convincing case for challenging the assumptions of Wiener's thesis: 'Against "Englishness": English Culture and the Limits to Rural Nostalgia, 1850–1940', *Transactions of the Royal Historical Society*, 6th ser. 7 (1997): 155–75. For a more recent critique, see the discussion in Paul Readman, *Storied Ground: Landscape and the Shaping of English National Identity* (Cambridge: Cambridge University Press, 2018), esp. introduction.
15. See David Matless, *Landscape and Englishness* (2nd ed., London: Reaktion, 2016 [1998]). Nor, arguably, had they been before the First World War: Paul Readman, 'Preserving the English Landscape, *c.*1870–1914', *Cultural and Social History* 5 (2008): 197–218.
16. Ward, *Britishness*, 60.
17. See Stephen V. Ward, 'The Garden City Introduced', and Frederick H. A. Aalen, 'English Origins', in *The Garden City: Past, Present and Future*, ed. Stephen V. Ward (London: Spon, 1992), 1–27, 28–51; William Morris, *News from Nowhere: or, an Epoch of Rest, Being some Chapters from a Utopian Romance* (London: Reeves & Turner, 1891 [1890]).
18. Harris, *Romantic Moderns*, 174.
19. For example, as managing director of the London Underground in the 1920s, Frank Pick encouraged the use of medieval motifs in the advertising of the Tube as a way of restoring harmony, stability and spirituality to an urban world that seemed increasingly fragmentary, transitory and secular: Michael T. Saler, *The Avant-Garde in Interwar England: Medieval Modernism and the London Underground* (Oxford: Oxford University Press, 1999).
20. Louis N. Parker, 'Historical Pageants', *Journal of the Society of Arts* 54 (1905): 142–3. Parker's comments also reflected a wider viewpoint from those interested in the past and in folk culture. Hubert Parry's inaugural address to the Folk-Song Society shared much in common with the language used by Parker: Parry, 'Inaugural Address', *Journal of the Folk-Song Society* 1 (1899): 1–3.
21. See entries on pageants in Selborne (1926 and 1938), Abinger (1934), Ashdown (1929) and Chittlehampton (1936) in Angela Bartie, Paul Caton, Linda Fleming, Mark Freeman, Tom Hulme, Alex Hutton, Paul Readman, *The Redress of the Past*, http://www.historicalpageants.ac.uk/pageants (accessed 22 January 2019). Somewhat ironically, villages and towns staging these pageants that idealised the rural in opposition to London often depended on metropolitan authors and spectating visitors, enabled by the development of comprehensive modern rail and road networks.

22. Glassberg contrasts this with the American style of pageantry, which he sees as being much more future-orientated: see David Glassberg, *American Historical Pageantry: The Uses of Tradition in the Early Twentieth Century* (Chapel Hill, NC: University of North Carolina University Press, 1990), 149–50. H. V. Nelles, writing about Canadian pageantry, makes much the same point: Nelles, *The Art of Nation-Building: Pageantry and Spectacle at Quebec's Tercentenary* (Toronto: Toronto University Press, 1999), 144.
23. Deborah Sugg Ryan, '"Pageantitis": Visualising Frank Lascelles' 1907 Oxford Historical Pageant, Visual Spectacle and Popular Memory', *Visual Culture in Britain* 8 (2007): 68–9.
24. Deborah Sugg Ryan, 'Staging the Imperial City: The Pageant of London, 1911', in *Imperial Cities: Landscape, Display and Identity*, ed. Felix Driver and David Gilbert (Manchester: Manchester University Press, 1999), 118.
25. Ryan, 'Staging', 120.
26. Joshua D. Esty, 'Amnesia in the Fields: Late Modernism, Late Imperialism, and the English Pageant-play', *ELH* 69 (2002): 250.
27. Mick Wallis, 'Pageantry and the Popular Front: Ideological Production in the "Thirties"', *New Theatre Quarterly* 10 (1994): 132–6; Helen McCarthy, 'The League of Nations, Public Ritual and National Identity in Britain c.1919–56', *History Workshop Journal* 70 (2010): 108–32.
28. Hulme, '"A Nation of Town Criers"'.
29. Kitty Hauser, *Shadow Sites: Photography, Archaeology and the British Landscape* (Oxford: Oxford University Press, 2007), 11, 4, 281, 5.
30. Paul Readman, 'The Place of the Past in English Culture *c.*1890–1914', *Past and Present* 186 (2005): 191; Angela Bartie, Linda Fleming, Mark Freeman, Tom Hulme and Paul Readman, 'Commemoration through Dramatic Performance: Historical Pageants and the Age of Anniversaries, 1905–1920', in *The Age of Anniversaries: The Cult of Commemoration, 1895–1925*, ed. T. G. Otte (Abingdon and New York: Routledge, 2018), 195–218.
31. Mick Wallis, 'Unlocking the Secret Soul: Mary Kelly, Pioneer of Village Theatre', *New Theatre Quarterly* 16 (2000): 348.
32. It is worth noting that an entirely negative interpretation of interwar agriculture and rural life has been challenged recently, with historians emphasising regeneration as well as decline. See *The English Countryside between the Wars: Regeneration or Decline?*, ed. Paul Brassley, Jeremy Burchardt and Lynne Thompson (Woodbridge: Boydell Press, 2006).
33. Louis Napoleon Parker, *Several of My Lives* (London: Chapman & Hall, 1928), 297–8.
34. For Matthew Anderson and Lascelles, see Hulme, "A Nation of Town Criers"; for Lascelles and Lally, see Ryan, '"Pageantitis"' and Deborah Sugg Ryan, 'Lally, Gwen (1882–1963)', *Oxford Dictionary of National Biography* (Oxford: Oxford University Press, 2004).
35. See Angela Bartie, Linda Fleming, Mark Freeman, Tom Hulme, Alex Hutton, Paul Readman, 'The Manchester Pageant', *The Redress of the Past*, http://www.historicalpageants.ac.uk/pageants/1125/ (accessed 21 January 2019).
36. For these aspects of pageantry in relation to small towns in Britain in particular, see Bartie et al., 'Performing the Past'.
37. David Matthews, *Medievalism: A Critical History* (Cambridge: D. S. Brewer, 2015), 30. For more extensive discussion of the medieval content of historical pageantry, see Angela Bartie, Linda Fleming, Mark Freeman, Tom Hulme, Alexander Hutton and Paul Readman, 'Historical Pageants and the Medieval Past in Twentieth-Century England', *English Historical Review* 133 (2018): 866–902.
38. Angela Bartie, Linda Fleming, Mark Freeman, Tom Hulme, Alex Hutton, Paul Readman, 'Pageant of Birmingham', *The Redress of the Past*, http://www.historicalpageants.ac.uk/pageants/994/ (accessed 21 January 2019).
39. Ellie Reid, 'Gwen Lally: A Pageant Master in the Making' (13 August 2014), http://historicalpageants.ac.uk/blog/pageanteers-archives-1-gwen-lally/ (accessed 20 September 2016).
40. Angela Bartie, Linda Fleming, Mark Freeman, Tom Hulme, Alex Hutton, Paul Readman, 'Salford Historical Pageant', *The Redress of the Past*, http://www.historicalpageants.ac.uk/pageants/1181/ (accessed 21 January 2019).
41. See, as an introduction, Peter Hall, 'Metropolis 1890–1940: Challenges and Responses', in *Metropolis 1890–1940*, ed. Anthony Sutcliffe (London: Mansell, 1984), 19–66.
42. C. F. G. Masterman [and others], *The Heart of the Empire: Discussions of Problems of Modern City Life in England* (London: Unwin, 1901).
43. Patrick Geddes, *Cities in Evolution: An Introduction to the Town Planning Movement and to the Study of Civics* (London: Williams & Norgate, 1915), 28–34.

44. John Davis, 'The Government of London', in *Debating Nationhood and Governance in Britain, 1885–1945: Perspectives from the Four Nations*, ed. Duncan Tanner, Chris Williams, W. P. Griffith and Andrew Edwards (Manchester: Manchester University Press, 2006), 211–32.
45. According to Willliam F. Blay, former chair of the Urban District Council of Dartford: 'The Effect of Incorporation', *West Kent Advertiser,* 17 March 1933, 3. In reality, however, the collapse of the wartime coalition in the post-war period greatly dampened the Council's political desires for expansion.
46. 'Municipal Energy', *The Times,* 20 September 1933, 11.
47. Angela Bartie, Linda Fleming, Mark Freeman, Tom Hulme, Alex Hutton, Paul Readman, 'The Walthamstow Pageant 1930', *The Redress of the Past*, http://www.historicalpageants.ac.uk/pageants/1232/ (accessed 21 January 2019).
48. Angela Bartie, Linda Fleming, Mark Freeman, Tom Hulme, Alex Hutton, Paul Readman, 'The Barking Historical Pageant', *The Redress of the Past*, http://www.historicalpageants.ac.uk/pageants/981/ (accessed 21 January 2019).
49. Angela Bartie, Linda Fleming, Mark Freeman, Tom Hulme, Alex Hutton, Paul Readman, 'Dartford Division of Kent Historical Pageant', *The Redress of the Past*, http://www.historicalpageants.ac.uk/pageants/1047/ (accessed 7 March 2019).
50. Angela Bartie, Linda Fleming, Mark Freeman, Tom Hulme, Alex Hutton, Paul Readman, 'Historical Pageant of Bradford', *The Redress of the Past*, http://www.historicalpageants.ac.uk/pageants/1000/ (accessed 21 January 2019).
51. Bartie et al., 'Birmingham Historical Pageant'.
52. Angela Bartie, Linda Fleming, Mark Freeman, Tom Hulme, Alex Hutton, Paul Readman, 'Stoke-on-Trent Historical Pageant', *The Redress of the Past*, http://www.historicalpageants.ac.uk/pageants/1214/ (accessed 21 January 2019).
53. *Handbook of the Stoke-on-Trent Historical Pageant, Military Tattoo, Pottery Exhibitions, and Bicentenary Celebrations* (Stoke-on-Trent, n.p. 1930).
54. Sir Francis Joseph, 'Stoke-on-Trent's Great Opportunity', *Evening Sentinel*, 10 May 1930, 1.
55. Angela Bartie, Linda Fleming, Mark Freeman, Tom Hulme, Alex Hutton, Paul Readman, 'The Lancashire Cotton Pageant', *The Redress of the Past*, http://www.historicalpageants.ac.uk/pageants/1111/ (accessed 22 January 2019).
56. 'The Pageant Opens', *Manchester Guardian*, 27 June 1932, 11.
57. Bartie et al., 'Lancashire Cotton Pageant'.
58. 'The Pageant Opens', *Manchester Guardian*, 27 June 1932, 11.
59. Wallis, 'Popular Front Pageant'. This aspect certainly continued in some interwar pageants with Taunton being one example: Michael Woods, 'Performing Power: Local Politics and the Taunton Pageant of 1928', *Journal of Historical Geography* 25 (1999): 57–74.
60. Cited in Bartie et al., 'Lancashire Cotton Pageant'.
61. W. Nugent Monck, 'English Fond of Pageantry', *Portsmouth Evening News*, 7 June 1938, 6.
62. F. E. Doran, Producer's preface, in *Historical Pageant of Manchester* (Manchester, 1926), 4.
63. 'Kent's Great Historical Pageant', *West Kent Advertiser,* 22 July 1932, 2.
64. Corbett et al., 'Introduction', xiii.
65. Laura Carter, 'The Quennells and the "History of Everyday Life" in England c.1918–69', *History Workshop Journal* 81 (2016): 106–34.
66. Caitriona Beaumont, 'Citizens not Feminists: The Boundary Negotiated between Citizenship and Feminism by Mainstream Women's Organisations in England, 1928–39', *Women's History Review* 9 (2000): 411–29; Zoë Thomas, 'Historical Pageants, Citizenship, and the Performance of Women's History Before Second-Wave Feminism', *Twentieth Century British History* 28 (2017): 319–43.
67. 'Pageant of Dorset History', *Bridport News,* 26 July 1929, 4.
68. See, for example, the entries for Dorset (1929) and Dorset (1939) in Bartie et al., *Redress of the Past.*
69. The Association for Education in Citizenship, for example, was formed by the politician, industrialist and philanthropist E. D. Simon due to his belief that the young needed to be guided away from the temptations of fascism: Guy Whitmarsh, 'The Politics of Political Education: An Episode', *Journal of Curriculum Studies* 6 (1974): 133–42. It is also notable that many pageants depicted the First World War in this period from an angle that commended the bravery and sacrifice of both soldiers and mourners. On this, see Angela Bartie, Linda Fleming, Mark Freeman, Tom Hulme, Paul Readman and Charlotte Tupman, '"And Those Who Live, How Shall I Tell Their Fame?" Historical Pageants, Collective Remembrance and the First World War, 1919–1939', *Historical Research* 90 (2017): 636–61.

70. Bartie et al., 'Manchester Pageant'.
71. Bartie et al., 'Historical Pageant of Bradford'.
72. Bartie et al., 'Lancashire Cotton Pageant'.
73. For more on responses to pageants, see Ryan, 'Staging the Imperial City', 128–30.
74. See Tom Hulme, *After the Shock City: Urban Culture and the Making of Modern Citizenship* (Woodbridge: Royal Historical Society/Boydell & Brewer, 2019), for a broader perspective on this notion of historical continuity.
75. *A Paradise Lost: The Neo-Romantic Imagination in Britain 1935–1955*, ed. David Mellor (London: Lund Humphries/Barbican Art Gallery, 1987). See also the discussion in Hauser, *Shadow Sites*, 10–11.
76. See Jay Winter, *Sites of Memory, Sites of Mourning: The Great War in European Cultural History* (Cambridge: Cambridge University Press, 1996), 3–4.
77. Andrew Radford, *Mary Butts and British Neo-Romanticism: The Enchantment of Place* (London: Bloomsbury, 2014), xii.
78. Alan Powers, 'The Reluctant Romantics: Axis Magazine 1935–37', in Corbett, Holt and Russell, *Geographies of Englishness*, 262.

Bibliography

Aalen, Frederick H. A. 1992. 'English Origins', in *The Garden City: Past, Present and Future*, edited by Stephen V. Ward. London: Spon, 28–51.

Anderson, Ben. 2011. 'A Liberal Countryside? The Manchester Ramblers' Federation and the "Social Readjustment" of Urban Citizens, 1929–1936', *Urban History* 38: 84–102.

Bartie, Angela, Fleming, Linda, Freeman, Mark, Hulme, Tom, Hutton, Alexander and Readman, Paul. 2018. 'Historical Pageants and the Medieval Past in Twentieth-Century England', *English Historical Review* 133: 866–902.

Bartie, Angela, Fleming, Linda, Freeman, Mark, Hulme, Tom and Readman, Paul. 2017. 'Performing the Past: Identity, Civic Culture and Historical Pageants in Twentieth-Century Small Towns', in *Small Towns in Europe in the 20th and 21st Centuries: Heritage and Development Strategies*, edited by Luda Klusakova. Prague: Karolinum Press, Charles University, 24–51.

Bartie, Angela, Fleming, Linda, Freeman, Mark, Hulme, Tom and Readman, Paul. 2018. 'Commemoration through Dramatic Performance: Historical Pageants and the Age of Anniversaries, 1905–1920', in *The Age of Anniversaries: The Cult of Commemoration, 1895–1925*, edited by T. G. Otte. Abingdon and New York: Routledge, 195–218.

Bartie, Angela, Fleming, Linda, Freeman, Mark, Hulme, Tom, Readman, Paul and Tupman, Charlotte. 2017. '"And Those Who Live, How Shall I Tell their Fame?" Historical Pageants, Collective Remembrance and the First World War, 1919–1939', *Historical Research* 90: 636–61.

Beaumont, Caitriona. 2000. 'Citizens not Feminists: The Boundary Negotiated Between Citizenship and Feminism by Mainstream Women's Organizations in England, 1928–39', *Women's History Review* 9: 411–29.

Brassley, Paul, Burchardt, Jeremy and Thompson, Lynn, eds. 2006. *The English Countryside between the Wars: Regeneration or Decline?* Woodbridge: Boydell Press.

Carter, Laura. 2016. 'The Quennells and the "History of Everyday Life" in England c.1918–69', *History Workshop Journal* 81: 106–34.

Chandler, James and Gilmartin, Kevin. 2005. 'Introduction: Engaging the Eidometropolis', in *Romantic Metropolis: The Urban Scene of British Culture, 1780–1840*, edited by James Chandler and Kevin Gilmartin. Cambridge: Cambridge University Press, 1–41.

Corbett, David Peters, Holt, Ysanne and Russell, Fiona. 2002. 'Introduction', in *The Geographies of Englishness: Landscape and the National Past 1880–1940*, edited by David Peters Corbett, Ysanne Holt and Fiona Russell. New Haven and London: Yale University Press, ix–xix.

Davis, John. 2006. 'The Government of London', in *Debating Nationhood and Governance in Britain, 1885–1945: Perspectives from the Four Nations*, edited by Duncan Tanner, Chris Williams, W. P. Griffith and Andrew Edwards. Manchester: Manchester University Press, 211–32.

Esty, Joshua D. 2002. 'Amnesia in the Fields: Late Modernism, Late Imperialism, and the English Pageant-play', *ELH* 69: 245–76.

Glassberg, David. 1990. *American Historical Pageantry: The Uses of Tradition in the Early Twentieth Century*. Chapel Hill, NC: University of North Carolina Press.

Hall, Peter. 1984. 'Metropolis 1890–1940: Challenges and Responses', in *Metropolis 1890–1940*, edited by Anthony Sutcliffe. London: Mansell, 19–66.

Harris, Alexandra. 2010. *Romantic Moderns: English Writers, Artists and the Imagination from Virginia Woolf to John Piper*. London: Thames & Hudson.

Hauser, Kitty. 2007. *Shadow Sites: Photography, Archaeology, and the British Landscape*. Oxford: Oxford University Press.

Hay, Daisy. 2010. *Young Romantics: The Shelleys, Byron and Other Tangled Lives*. London: Bloomsbury.

Hulme, Tom. 2017. '"A Nation of Town Criers": Civic Publicity and Historical Pageantry in Inter-War Britain', *Urban History* 44: 270–92.

Hulme, Tom. 2019. *After the Shock City: Urban Culture and the Making of Modern Citizenship*. Woodbridge: Royal Historical Society/Boydell & Brewer.

Lussier, Mark. 2011. 'Blake's Golgonoosa: London and/as the Eternal City of Art', in *Romanticism and the City*, edited by Larry H. Peer. Basingstoke: Palgrave Macmillan, 197–207.

McCarthy, Helen. 2010. 'The League of Nations, Public Ritual and National Identity in Britain c.1919–56', *History Workshop Journal* 70: 108–32.

Mandler, Peter. 1997. 'Against "Englishness": English Culture and the Limits to Rural Nostalgia, 1850–1940', *Transactions of the Royal Historical Society*, 6th ser., 7: 155–75.

Matless, David. 2016 (2nd ed.); 1998 (1st ed.). *Landscape and Englishness*. London: Reaktion Books.

Matthews, David. 2015. *Medievalism: A Critical History*. Cambridge: D. S. Brewer.

Mellor, David, ed. 1987. *A Paradise Lost: The Neo-Romantic Imagination in Britain 1935–1955*. London: Lund Humphries/Barbican Art Gallery.

Nelles, H. V. 1999. *The Art of Nation-Building: Pageantry and Spectacle at Quebec's Tercentenary*. Toronto: University of Toronto Press.

Peer, Larry H., ed. 2011. *Romanticism and the City*. Basingstoke: Palgrave Macmillan, 2011.

Peer, Larry H. 2011. 'Introduction: The Infernal and Celestial City of Romanticism', in Peer, *Romanticism and the City*, 1–8.

Powers, Alan. 2002. 'The Reluctant Romantics: Axis Magazine 1935–37', in *The Geographies of Englishness: Landscape and the National Past 1880–1940*, edited by David Peters Corbett, Ysanne Holt and Fiona Russell. New Haven and London: Yale University Press, 249–74.

Radford, Andrew. 2014. *Mary Butts and British Neo-Romanticism: The Enchantment of Place*. London: Bloomsbury.

Readman, Paul. 2005. 'The Place of the Past in English Culture, *c*. 1890–1914', *Past and Present* 186: 147–99.

Readman, Paul. 2008. 'Preserving the English Landscape, c.1870–1914', *Cultural and Social History* 5: 197–218.

Readman, Paul. 2018. *Storied Ground: Landscape and the Shaping of English National Identity*. Cambridge: Cambridge University Press.

Ryan, Deborah Sugg. 1999. 'Staging the Imperial City: The Pageant of London, 1911', in *Imperial Cities: Landscape, Display and Identity*, edited by Felix Driver and David Gilbert. Manchester: Manchester University Press, 117–35.

Ryan, Deborah Sugg. 2007. '"Pageantitis": Frank Lascelles' 1907 Oxford Historical Pageant, Visual Spectacle and Popular Memory', *Visual Culture in Britain* 8: 63–82.

Saler, Michael T. 1999. *The Avant-Garde in Interwar England: Medieval Modernism and the London Underground*. Oxford: Oxford University Press.

Schneider, Joanne. 2007. *The Age of Romanticism*. Westport, CT: Greenwood.

Searle, Geoffrey R. 1971. *The Quest for National Efficiency: A Study in British Politics and Political Thought, 1899–1914*. Oxford: Oxford University Press.

Stelzig, Eugene. 2011. 'Wordsworth's Invigorating Hell: London in Book 7 of *The Prelude* (1805)', in *Romanticism and the City*, edited by Larry H. Peer. Basingstoke: Palgrave Macmillan, 181–96.

Thomas, Zoë. 2017. 'Historical Pageants, Citizenship, and the Performance of Women's History before Second-wave Feminism', *Twentieth Century British History* 28: 319–43.

Trentmann, Frank. 1994. 'Civilization and its Discontents: English Neo-Romanticism and the Transformation of Anti-Modernism in Twentieth-Century Western Culture', *Journal of Contemporary History* 29: 583–625.

Wallis, Mick. 1994. 'Pageantry and the Popular Front: Ideological Production in the "Thirties"', *New Theatre Quarterly* 10: 132–56.

Wallis, Mick. 2000. 'Unlocking the Secret Soul: Mary Kelly, Pioneer of Village Theatre', *New Theatre Quarterly* 16: 347–58.
Ward, Paul. 2004. *Britishness since 1870*. London: Routledge.
Ward, Stephen V., ed. 1992. *The Garden City: Past, Present and Future*. London: Spon.
Ward, Stephen V. 1992. 'The Garden City Introduced', in Ward, *The Garden City*, 1–27.
Whitmarsh, Guy. 1974. 'The Politics of Political Education: An Episode', *Journal of Curriculum Studies* 6: 133–42.
Wiener, Martin J. 2004 (2nd ed.); 1982 (1st ed.). *English Culture and the Decline of the Industrial Spirit 1850–1980*. Cambridge: Cambridge University Press.
Williams, Raymond.1973. *The Country and the City*. London: Chatto & Windus.
Winter, Jay. 1996. *Sites of Memory, Sites of Mourning: The Great War in European Cultural History*. Cambridge: Cambridge University Press.
Woods, Michael. 1999. 'Performing Power: Local Politics and the Taunton Pageant of 1928', *Journal of Historical Geography* 25: 57–74.
Yoshino, Ayako. 2011. *Pageant Fever: Local History and Consumerism in Edwardian England*. Tokyo: Waseda University Press.

8
'A Chorus of Greek Poignancy': Communism, Class and Pageantry in Interwar South Wales

Daryl Leeworthy

> The men and women of the mining villages show ... some part of their traditions and their pride. Banners, bands[,] gaiety, and besides the brass bands, the colourful character bands are an interesting echo of the gazooka bands of the 1926 period. A day of explosive joy. History marches here, these men asking for security and peace. The names of their lodges are a fanfare of heroic conflict for the achievement of a saner social set-up, for greater happiness and peace.[1]
>
> Gwyn Thomas, 1960

Compared with the other large coalfields of Britain, notably Durham and Yorkshire, where miners' galas and picnics were annual events from the 1870s, the miners of South Wales were not traditionally disposed to pomp and pageantry. Galas such as that held in Blaenavon in 1873, with its displays of minstrelsy, sporting endeavour, massed bands and marching banners, were relatively rare before the middle decades of the twentieth century.[2] Following the creation of the National Union of Mineworkers (NUM) in 1944 and the nationalisation of the coal mining industry in 1947, the executive committee of the South Wales Area (formerly the South Wales Miners' Federation) set about moulding a 'more politically conscious lodge and area leadership' and as a consequence 'embarked on an ambitious policy of educating its membership'.[3] These efforts resulted in new district-wide cultural events such as the South Wales Miners' Eisteddfod, established in 1948, and the South Wales Miners' Gala, which followed five years later. It also led, in the early 1950s, to the creation of a Youth Advisory Committee and the revival of *The Miner*, the Area's glossy magazine detailing industrial, political and cultural activities.

Superficially, the slow development of a cultural programme might be explained by the relative strength of religious Nonconformity and the importance of chapel-based cultural institutions, notably the eisteddfod and the *gymanfa ganu* (a festival of sacred hymns, usually sung in Welsh).[4] However, such an explanation is inadequate and inaccurate. The labour movement organised an array of artistic and sporting activity in South Wales from at least the 1890s; drama groups, choirs and various musical ensembles, as well as concerts and performances, were commonplace.[5] The coalfield likewise responded to the working-class education movement with considerable enthusiasm, producing notable works of labour history, proletarian literature and attempts to work out left-wing historical and literary theory (both, of course, informed by Marxism).[6] The absence of galas and other large-scale cultural events akin to the Durham Miners' Gala, established in 1871, should be understood less as the absence of a tradition of the arts in the South Walian labour movement than as a lack of immediate need for regionalised forms of cultural policy.

The left-wing pageants held in South Wales in the 1930s, which provide the key focus of the present chapter, were therefore part of a transition in cultural activity from localised efforts of branch-level acting troupes and musical ensembles under the auspices of the Independent Labour Party (ILP) to regionalised (and internationalist) expressions of collective struggle and working-class cultural and political identity organised by the South Wales Miners' Federation (SWMF) and its successor, the South Wales Area of the NUM. Moreover, it is important to note that these new activities were inspired by the communism of those most responsible for its implementation. Indeed, for some of those involved in the creation of post-war cultural policy in the miners' union, such as Dai Dan Evans, Will Paynter and Dai Francis, enthralled by the great May Day displays they saw on visits to Moscow, Berlin, Prague, Budapest and Belgrade, the pageants and the later galas, eisteddfods and sports days were evocative of a spirit of working-class fellowship – a small slice of what could be truly possible in the workers' state to which they aspired. Such a view may not have been universally shared across the labour movement, even within the ranks of the South Wales miners, but it was strongly and genuinely held. It was also quite distinct in form from what had come before.

South Wales Labour and artistic endeavour

In 1909 the Mountain Ash branch of the ILP organised what appears to have been the first eisteddfod under a Labour banner in South Wales. With the patronage of Keir Hardie, the local MP, the event enjoyed a relatively high profile in the press. The prize-winning poem by the Cardiff-based poet Daniel Owen, an epic on the life of Hardie and his role as a hero of the labour movement, added to its prestige.[7] A further eisteddfod of this kind was held that year at Pontycymmer, organised by the local ILP branch.[8] The embrace of the eisteddfod as a legitimate mechanism for expressing cultures of labour continued into the 1920s, as did organised musical activity, before the decline of the ILP denuded the South Walian labour movement of a swathe of cultural activity, at least in a party political sense – since Labour instituted a rich array of artistic endeavour municipally.[9] In 1925, the ILP could record in its annual report that 'in Wales and London ILP choirs are beginning [to win high recognition]', with musical festivals being held at Briton Ferry and Neath.[10] The same year a large-scale eisteddfod, sponsored by the Newport Labour Party and held in the town, was chaired by Ramsay MacDonald.[11] In his chairman's address he offered his own thoughts on the importance of culture to the organisation of a left-wing political movement, at one point remarking that he had little love for the *Red Flag* because it was 'not good enough. We still want our great Labour song, a Labour song which is not a ditty'. He continued: 'The "Red Flag" to me is too much of a ditty ... We want fine, pulse-stirring music which does not require to have sentiments to apologise for it'.[12]

MacDonald, who rarely missed an opportunity to stress his Scottishness, argued that Labour should embrace the great 'love songs of Burns, not silly music-hall pitter-patter', and would do well to institute a competition between Welsh and Scottish tunesmiths to produce 'the best Labour marching song which would really enshrine in itself the fighting spirit of the Labour Movement'. He regarded the relationship between Labour and the arts to be an essential one, and a relationship which capitalism sought to sunder. He drew a sharp conclusion:

> Labour has got an inheritance to cherish in popular song and folk music. It is just as essential for us to revive folk music and get our working men and women singing as it is for us to build houses and revive trade. In your workshop, in your homes there is much less song than there used to be. One of the reasons is that capitalism, with its oppressive burdens of uncertainty, with its soullessness,

> with its crushing materialism, is making us both mute of mouth and silent of heart. If the Labour Movement succeeds at all, it will make our industrial towns once again nests of singing birds. The distinction between Labour and other Parties is that the root of the Labour Party goes right into the lives of the people.[13]

Ramsay MacDonald was by no means alone in believing in the necessity of linking culture with the labour movement. No less a figure than Keir Hardie had written songs of his own for precisely the purpose which MacDonald had presented in Newport in 1925.[14] The Clarion movement had promoted artistic endeavour through initiatives such as the National Clarion Players before the First World War, and in the summer of 1925 the ILP launched its Arts Guild.[15] Neither the Clarion Players nor the Arts Guild had much of a presence in South Wales, however, although by 1926 the latter claimed as many as 100 affiliated groups.[16] Among those which can be traced in the South Wales context were the ILP male voice choirs of Neath and Briton Ferry, the Cardiff East Labour Brass and Reed Band, the Cardiff Labour Dramatic Group and the Merthyr Tydfil ILP Dramatic Society, all of which were in existence in the 1920s and were members of the Arts Guild.[17] Alongside them were co-operative choirs for adults and children, as well as various faltering attempts at establishing co-operative dramatic societies. As William Hazell noted of the Ynysybwl Co-operative Society (one of the largest in South Wales), 'drama seems to have been a difficult proposition: there was a "Wheatsheaf Dramatic Group" in 1933, largely an employees' effort'.[18]

But by what means did this ostensibly localised activity within the labour movement transform itself into regionalised cultural policy, and thus into the historical pageantry evident at the end of the 1930s? Scholars have followed Mick Wallis in arguing that this 'turn' marked a fuller incorporation of left-wing politics into the historical and dramatic narrative.[19] As Tom Hulme has noted, the pageants of the period depicted 'working-class history from a more political angle'; they 'mostly [eschewed] the ecclesiastical and royal focus of Edwardian pageants, [and] were organized by groups such as the Co-operative Society and the Communist Party of Great Britain [CPGB]'.[20] Likewise, there was the advent of more stridently theorised ideas about the arts as a mechanism for working-class expression. In the *Sunday Worker*, organ of the CPGB from 1925 until 1929, Huntly Carter and Rutland Boughton wrote columns entitled, respectively, 'Workers and the Theatre' and 'Music and the Class War'. These offered critiques of contemporary bourgeois cultural production and sought to theorise a workers' culture by which it could be replaced. However, the prospects for this kind of activity in South Wales in the late 1920s and early 1930s were somewhat limited. This being the case, the emergence of the left-wing pageants in the second half of the 1930s needs to be set alongside the relatively fallow period which preceded it – a period that has not been fully excavated by historians in their commentary on the 1939 Pageant of South Wales.

Intellectually there was little difference between circumstances in South Wales and those in London. Indeed the writings of Ness Edwards, notably his *The Workers' Theatre* (1930), were part of the same artistic developments exemplified by Huntly Carter and others.[21] Edwards's perspective was enriched by the Marxian education he received at the Central Labour College in London, which he attended on an SWMF scholarship in 1919. On returning to South Wales he experienced a lengthy period of unemployment and took a series of short-term jobs to make ends meet, including a stint as a door-to-door encyclopaedia salesman, before being appointed as a full-time miners' official in 1927.[22] It was in this period that Edwards began writing and tutoring for the Plebs League near his home in Abertillery, and the books and pamphlets he wrote, including *The Workers' Theatre*, bore the hallmarks of the radical perspective of the Plebs League.[23] *The Workers' Theatre* was thus 'intentionally provocative' and dismissive of most forms of existing theatre as irretrievably hostile to the working class. Even Shakespeare was regarded as having dignified royalty. Instead of bourgeois culture, Edwards insisted, what was needed was a new workers' drama that presented contemporary problems in class terms. As he argued,

> The workers' drama is an agitational force, it is propaganda by a dramatization of facts ... What the drama was able to do for the Catholic Church, the guilds and the ruling classes, it can be made to do for the working class. No longer will it be confined to a professional clique, no longer will it be merely entertainment.[24]

Alongside his scorn for Shakespeare, Edwards was full of praise for the activities of the ILP's Arts Guild for producing plays of 'a definite working-class character' – although he was keen that this go further, as it had done in the Soviet Union. He argued that workers' theatre should be put on in 'labour halls, club rooms, hired concert halls and in the open air', with work that pointed the way to the 'destruction of capitalism and the creation of a workers' republic' to be warmly encouraged (George Bernard Shaw and Henrik Ibsen were among those playwrights whom Edwards promoted as ideal). After all, he concluded, [t]he object of the workers' drama is to organise the working class for the conquest of power, to justify this conquest of power, and arouse the feelings of the workers to intensify this struggle'.[25]

Yet these ideas do not seem to have been put widely into practice. Those plays which can be identified as having been performed by workers' theatre groups in South Wales included *Twelve Pound Look* by J. M. Barrie (1920), Monica Ewer's *Best of Both Worlds* (1925) and Stephen Schofield's popular satire *The Bruiser's Election* (1925), all of which were staples of the ILP Arts Guild in the 1920s. In the coalfield there also appears to have been some attempt at improvisatory play writing during the 1926 miners' lockout, although this was not sustained in the longer term.[26] In London, by contrast, the workers' theatre movement performed Soviet plays, adaptations of works by the American writer Upton Sinclair and the Czech writer Karel Čapek, and a theatrical version of Robert Tressell's *Ragged-Trousered Philanthropists* – all of which had more in common with the artistic ambitions of left-wing writers and activists.[27] The differences were made even more apparent when, with much of the Labour and ILP effort fading away and the CPGB at its lowest ebb (membership in 1930 fell to fewer than 300), South Wales became the 'target' of travelling left-wing theatre groups in the early 1930s – and thus a consumer rather than a producer of politically-orientated proletarian culture: Proletkult.

Towards Proletkult

Radicalised by the political and economic circumstances of the Depression and endowed with the rhetoric of 'class against class' (some of the worst of which was reserved for the Labour Party, who were denounced as 'social fascists'), the workers' theatre movement turned consciously towards agitprop and street drama after 1930. Itinerant troupes went on tours to various parts of Britain to encourage Proletkult and to build support for the CPGB and its front organisations, such as the National Unemployed Workers' Movement. These troupes sang politically-charged songs, burned effigies of political opponents and eschewed the forms and functions of bourgeois theatre.[28] One such tour, by the London-based Red Pioneer Troupe, came to South Wales in January 1932, visiting various parts of the Rhondda. According to press reports, however, the tour struggled to engage with audiences who were little disposed to the CPGB's current perspectives.[29] One of the sketches performed by the Red Pioneer Troupe, *The Two Paths*, provides a case in point. Tom Thomas, the workers' theatre movement secretary, explained what audiences could expect from the 30-minute sketch in the movement's journal *Red Stage*:

> To interest the workers by dealing with their own experiences, it first shows the recent election and the contrast between what was promised and what has resulted. The points are made rapidly in short, self-contained scenes, using often a semi-naturalistic method. A Court of Referees [Debtor's Court] – the PAC [Public Assistance Committee] – the victims of the Means Test – police batoning unemployed – wage cuts in all industries, and the drive to tariffs, follow one another in quick succession.[30]

Yet, although the sketch presented a rigorous and theoretically sound Proletkult narrative, it lacked immediate appeal to audiences not used to the form. And in any case, those who remained in the CPGB in South Wales in the early 1930s tended towards an austere and theoretical Marxism which seemed remote from the day-to-day realities of life for working people.[31] The audience for Proletkult agitprop in South Wales was thus limited.

Marginally more successful were the efforts of the workers' film society branch, established in Cardiff by the spring of 1930, and the contemporary drive by members of the National Unemployed Workers' Movement to establish libraries, musical bands and sports clubs.[32] The upturn in communist fortunes came with the abandonment of Third Period rhetoric after 1934.[33] It resulted in a communist football league in the Rhondda, as well as workers' choirs, workers' film societies, a large number of Left Book Club branches and a Left Theatre group in Cardiff. The city also had a successful branch of Collet's bookshop and a branch of Kino Films.

Yet for all that there remained a sense within communist circles that the CPGB in South Wales was too austere and lacking in popular appeal. To inject colour into the movement and to make Party activity 'attractive not only to the politically conscious workers, but the mass of unthinking workers as well', the District Committee sought to strike a more populist note. It was with this in mind that they set about creating a 'Pageant of History', performed for the first time in the Rhondda on 21 March 1937.[34] Now entirely overshadowed by the 1939 Pageant of South Wales, sponsored by the SWMF in conjunction with the Labour Research Department (LRD), the 1937 event nevertheless pioneered the translation of moments of South Wales's industrial and working-class history into theatre for a contemporary audience. 'We are confident that this Pageant will become the talk of the whole of South Wales', remarked Idris Cox, the South Wales District organiser. He added that

> we need more colour and style and music in the whole of our activity, and this should be the keynote of our public meetings so that communist meetings become the centre of attraction with all progressively thinking people.[35]

Contemporary critics were less enthused, however. The conservative *Western Mail* observed that

> South Wales Communists demonstrated at Tonypandy on Sunday afternoon, when they gave what they termed a pageant of history. The description of the event as a pageant was a flattering one, for all it proved to be was a march with banners through the streets of Mid-Rhondda.[36]

The success of the 1937 Pageant of History lay in awakening the South Walian left to the possibilities of mass spectacle for propaganda purposes – as opposed to traditional demonstrations and marches. In this, as with the subsequent pageant held in Pontypool in 1938 and the 1939 Pageant of South Wales, it was a distinctive form of cultural production, at least in the Welsh context, placing an emphasis on history as a collective experience. This was an act of remembrance and a visual presentation of history from below, then rare in printed form (except primarily for the works of Ness Edwards). It was to have a lasting impact on *how* the past was conceived and written about in the region. History became theatre; reportage and journalism became theatre; and the lives which people had led and the events which punctuated them, such as the General Strike, the hunger marches or key campaigns such as that led by the SWMF against silicosis, also became theatre.[37] This was theatre which had, on the one hand, some roots in the workers' theatre movement and the intellectual currents of the 1920s, but – more importantly – it satisfied the needs of the Popular Front politics of the CPGB and the SWMF in the second half of the 1930s. The two came together in the Pageant of South Wales, performed on May Day 1939.

Pageant of people's history

Recalling the Pageant of South Wales, which he conducted, André van Gyseghem described it as a 'form of mass theatre I found tremendously satisfying, using the people themselves to play to the people, so linking theatre and audience in a very real way'.[38] This was the spirit in which

Gyseghem approached the 'mass spectacular pageants of the Popular Front', as Mick Wallis has called the left pageants of the late 1930s.[39] An active member of the Communist Party, Gyseghem was a key figure in the Unity Theatre (founded in London in 1936), serving as president of its management committee. Together with the playwright Montagu Slater, the composer Benjamin Britten and others, Gyseghem professionalised and modernised the workers' theatre movement in London, drawing inspiration from a series of visits to the Soviet Union and the cultural developments in the United States resulting from the New Deal.[40] The Pageant of South Wales, formally organised by the SWMF in conjunction with the LRD, was both an extension of these activities and a fulfilment of their social, political and cultural aims.

The origins of the Pageant of South Wales lay in the artistic response of Slater and Britten to a series of stay-down strikes that took place in 1935 as the last phase in a fierce, decade-long struggle between the SWMF and the company union, the South Wales Miners' Industrial Union.[41] Slater had travelled to Cwmfelinfach near Caerphilly to report on and record events at Nine Mile Point Colliery. His observations were published the following year as *Stay Down, Miner*.[42] This provided the narrative basis for a play of the same name, performed by the Left Theatre at the Westminster Theatre in May 1936; the music was provided by Britten. Following revisions, the play was published in 1937 as *New Way Wins*.[43] Most of the action in the play took place underground or at the colliery, shifting to a courtroom struggle in the final act. In many respects this was typical workers' theatre and involved the audience as part of the dramatic context. One of the stage directions, for instance, called for 'a metronome set at largo in the orchestra pit. A drum takes up rhythm, various percussions die away into the sound of the metronome again'.[44] The insistent tick-tocking recalled a number of sounds underground: the dripping of water, the creaking of pit props, the conveyor belt that took waste to the coal tips on the mountainsides and, of course, the rain.

Britten wrote only a small amount of incidental music for the play together with one major chorus – the 'Wind Song'. He thought the script 'really good – very dry and terse, with a strong sense of comedy'.[45] But his enthusiasm was not shared by the critics. They scratched their heads in either bemusement, as in the case of W. A. Darlington in the *Daily Telegraph*, or confusion, as in the case of *The Times*'s critic. In the view of the *Manchester Guardian*, the play was seen as having failed to achieve its objectives.[46] L. A. Butt, writing in the more sympathetic *Left Review*, was more enthusiastic than the national press, declaring it to be 'a very enjoyable show' – but he still felt that Slater had failed to give full life to the stay-down strikes as a mass action. 'We don't get the small shopkeepers, or the bus drivers, or any of the other sections who must have clustered round the mining village', Butt complained, noting that

> I know the cast had to be kept small, and that their influence or presence would have had to be indicated obliquely, but it could have been done, and it would have added to the convincingness of the play as well as to the political moral.[47]

Whether or not Slater took these criticisms much to heart is not easily established (Britten, certainly, was dismissive of the *Telegraph*'s review). However, the Pageant of South Wales, his next project about the South Wales miners, took the idea of mass participation to its obvious conclusion.

On 1 December 1938 a group of four members (two Communist, two Labour) of the SWMF executive met to discuss holding a pageant on May Day to mark the Chartist centenary.[48] The following day Oliver Harris, the Federation's general secretary, wrote to the LRD for assistance in 'suggesting some twenty outstanding phases of incidents in the working class movement during the late hundred years which would be suitable for representation in a pageant'.[49] W. H. Williams, the LRD's secretary, replied a few weeks later offering a range of possible events which could be covered, from the martyrdom of Dic Penderyn in 1831 to the battles against company unionism which had only recently been concluded. 'The problem', Williams reflected, 'is the elimination of data so as to get a simple and vivid portrayal of incidents, which at the same time is historically accurate'.[50] One synopsis considered by the South Wales committee had 24 separate events, with approximately 100 people needed for each![51]

As the *Redress of the Past* database entry for this pageant notes, eventually it was 'decided that a simpler pageant of two scenes would be more effective than an attempt at depicting the entirety of [South Walian] history since the Industrial Revolution'.[52] Historical advice was sought from Robin Page Arnot, the LRD's director of research and a key figure in the Communist Party; Ness Edwards, whose writings had established a working-class history of the South Wales coalfield; and David Williams, a history lecturer at the University College of South Wales and Monmouthshire in Cardiff. Williams's book *John Frost: A Study in Chartism* was the first academic study of Welsh labour history.[53]

The decision to involve Montagu Slater as librettist, Pegaret Keeling as costume designer and Gyseghem as pageant-master was taken relatively early – although initially there had been some thought that the programme would be led by the districts of the SWMF, with the union's executive taking responsibility for arranging banners and liaising with the Chartist Centenary Committee.[54] On his appointment, Slater set about putting together a major spectacle – one that would tell the history of workers' struggle from the Chartists to the Hunger Marches (and eventually to the Spanish Civil War and the return of the International Brigades), and that could be performed simultaneously in three different locations.[55] Each of the performances ended with the following words, spoken by a volunteer in the International Brigade, whose fight against fascism was regarded as honest and true and whose death would be honoured as the sacrifice of a martyr (in a manner similar to Len Roberts in Lewis Jones's 1939 novel, *We Live*):

> I am one of the little band that went out from South Wales to fight in the International Brigades in Spain. I am going to ask you to rise, all of you, and swear with me this oath of victory.
>
> In the name of Wales and its people, in the name of our high-wrought past, in the name of our traditions, in the name of all our battles in the fight for freedom, on this day, 1st May 1939, we solemnly swear not to relax until freedom, and the prosperity that can only be brought by the power of the people bring back the sunshine to our land.[56]

The crowds were then to sing the *Internationale* – at least, that was the intention. In the event, rain, high winds and even snow (this being Wales in spring) dampened the effect. The Pontypool performance, intended for May Day evening, had to be postponed until the following weekend.[57] Writing to Slater's wife Enid a few weeks later, Britten offered his 'heartiest condolences on the rain fiasco in Wales – I cannot think why people do these things out of doors'.[58]

In many respects the Pageant of South Wales was enormously successful – not least in bringing communities together with almost military precision. Applications for the speaking parts were so numerous, recorded the *Western Mail*, that three rounds of auditions were held in Abertillery and a further two in Pontypool. Many of those who were successful came from the region's flourishing amateur dramatic societies.[59] The Federation's headquarters in St Andrew's Crescent, Cardiff, seemed to take on the appearance of a draper's shop; more than 600 costumes made to Keeling's designs were stored there, along with the 'thousands of yards of material' used in their creation.[60] Spectators and participants alike wrote to congratulate both the SWMF and the LRD for their organisation.

One of those who saw the Pageant of South Wales in May 1939 was Benjamin Farrington, professor of Classics at University College, Swansea and a leading figure in the Left Book Club in that city. He attended the event with his wife Ruth Schechter. In a letter to the Miners' Federation executive, Farrington described what he had witnessed:

> In spite of the appalling weather, there was a great interest and animation in the large gathering; both actors and audience entered into the spirit of the representation, and it seems clear that if the performance became an annual institution it would enrich the cultural life of the people and strengthen their democratic outlook.[61]

One local councillor was similarly enthusiastic, telling W. H. Williams that

> I am convinced that we reached our object and that it was a change from the old tradition of speeches and demonstrations which was out of date … the Pageant is certainly stimulating to our knowledge of history. It would be very educative if a pageant could be devised teaching local history. Our children are not so well informed on the history of these valleys.[62]

Williams, for his part, considered the pageant to be 'a new form of dramatic expression which will be of incalculable value to the labour movement'.[63] The press, which had some qualms with the political ethos of the event, were nevertheless supportive.[64] The *Western Mail* recorded that 'the pageant was impressive … It was thrilling to hear hundreds of mining folk singing the anthem of their Fatherland'.[65] The *Midland Daily Telegraph*'s Welsh column was equally impressed, noting that:

> These pageants … presented a message far more effectively than a spate of oratory regarding the collective sacrifice and activity of the people from the hills and valleys of South Wales … The SWMF will do a national service if it can elevate these pageants into a new form of Welsh art.[66]

That, however, did not come to pass.

Aftermath

The pageants of 1937, 1938 and 1939 were rarely repeated, although pageantry of a different kind continued to be a feature of South Walian social life into the 1960s (as it had been before the CPGB got involved).[67] But the spirit of cultural engagement lived on. The establishment of the miners' eisteddfod and miners' gala after the Second World War removed the need for mass spectacle of the sort that pageantry provided, and the South Wales Area executive committee found other ways of teaching history and politics to its members – notably through education classes and the presentation of memory and purpose on marching banners, most of which, in the South Wales context, date from the 1950s. In this way the pageants achieved their aim of firmly establishing both the necessity of large-scale regionalised social and cultural activity and embedding an historical narrative of working-class achievement and struggle into the popular consciousness. Other elements were involved in this transformation, too, such as the successful courting of singer and actor Paul Robeson. This led not only to his appearance at the 1938 'welcome home' ceremony for Welsh International Brigaders held in Mountain Ash, but also to the making of the Ealing Studios film *This Proud Valley* (1940) and to high-profile post-war events – most notably Robeson's appearance at the 1958 National Eisteddfod in Ebbw Vale and his performance (down a telephone line) at the 1957 South Wales Miners' Gala in Porthcawl.[68]

Another successful artistic relationship was with the prominent director and documentary film-maker Humphrey Jennings. He made three films in South Wales during the Second World War: *Spare Time* in 1939, *The Silent Village* (about the Nazi destruction of the Czech town of Lidice) in 1943 and *A Diary for Timothy* in 1945.[69] The production of *The Silent Village*, as Jennings observed, relied especially on advice given by Dai Dan Evans (who was to star in the film) and Arthur Horner; it was filmed in the village of Cwmgiedd (near Ystradgynlais), using Welsh language elements to mirror the impact of Nazi rule on Czechoslovakia.[70] Jennings, although never formally a member of the Communist Party, had become a fellow traveller during the Popular Front period. As Kevin Jackson has noted, he 'often sympathized with its analyses at this time and became ... a thoughtful student of the classical texts of Marx and Engels, as well as their elaborations by Lenin and others'.[71]

A Diary for Timothy, of which the Welsh elements were filmed in Ynysybwl, near Pontypridd, typified these communist connections to the coalfield. The film's Welsh miner, Goronwy Jones, was presented in the script as a 'leading light in what is a truly socialistic community'.[72]

Although never fully identified, Jones was in fact the chairman of the Lady Windsor Lodge of the SWMF. At the time of filming he was also chair of the miners' institute committee – positions which he had held for a number of years. As John E. Morgan, who served as lodge secretary and who also featured in the film, recalled, Jones was

> perhaps the best all-round chairman in the Lodge history. Self-reliant, he impressed one as having authority, not only in Lodge meetings, but also on deputations and in price-list negotiations. No grievance reported to him was unattended to, and that often before the complainant left the colliery premises. Any workman in trouble generally inquired 'Where's Gronow?'[73]

Jones and Morgan had been expelled from the Labour Party because of their involvement in the People's Vigilance Committee (established in summer 1940) and their active support for the People's Convention (held in London in January 1941 to call for friendship with the Soviet Union and the formation of a people's government).[74] Jones subsequently joined the Communist Party, becoming 'leader of the local branch ... and prominent in its advocacy'. He stood as the Party's candidate for elections to Mountain Ash Urban District Council in 1946, with his campaign constituting the first meaningful opposition to Labour since the 1920s. In the event he won more than 500 votes but trailed the successful Labour candidates by more than 1,000.[75]

In contrast to pageantry, workers' theatre continued into the 1940s and 1950s, with branches of the Unity Theatre in Cardiff and the Rhondda maintaining this tradition of cultural activity.[76] The London Unity Theatre also toured the region in 1946.[77] Unity's repertoire included Karel Čapek's *Power and Glory*, Sean O'Casey's *Juno and the Paycock*, J. B. Priestley's *They Came to a City*, Ena Lamont Stewart's *Starched Aprons* and George Landen Dann's *Fountains Beyond*.[78] Such performances led the nationalist poet Harri Webb, active in the Cardiff Unity Theatre, to complain in 1948 about the lack of Welsh material. 'Why', he wrote, 'should the Mid-Rhondda Unity Group be doing "Juno and the Paycock"? Why should the Arts Council with whatever good intentions have the field to itself with its subsidised company peddling Priestley in those quaint places whose names they probably can't pronounce?'[79]

For others, the concern was that workers' theatre was too political and too close to certain parts of the left. In 1947 Cardiff Unity Theatre split in two. The non-political members went on to form the Everyman Dramatic Society, which described itself as both 'non-political and independent'.[80]

Although Unity continued into the early 1950s, the split marked the denouement of the workers' theatre movement in South Wales.

Conclusion

In retrospect, and despite the attention of historians, the pageants held in South Wales at the end of the 1930s were highly unusual events – typical of the cultural endeavours of the Communist Party, the Labour Party and the Co-operative Society in London, to be sure, but with little direct ancestry in the communities in which they were held. Yet, as this chapter has demonstrated, in order fully to appreciate the significance and legacy of these pageants it is important to recognise their distinctiveness, and to place them in the wider context of debates about the purpose of cultural production for left-wing politics. For communist adherents of workers' theatre, such as Idris Cox, combining the arts with politics meant fostering class consciousness through something other than the electoral machine, and the presentation of collective struggle in accordance with prevailing theoretical perspectives. For Labour men such as Ramsay MacDonald and Keir Hardie, this meant the fusion of national with working-class identities and the manifestation of cultures of labour which were as folkish as they were proletarian. For Harri Webb and others who shared his Welsh nationalist instincts, it meant the creation, through workers' theatre, of a genuinely national form – one that presented Welsh art, rather than productions of English or Irish art.

Together with workers' theatre, pageants provided one answer to the question of how the left could and should encourage the arts for political purposes; but they did not provide *the* answer. There were too many political variations from which to choose. Likewise the Popular Front, which provided the impetus for the most high-profile pageants and workers' theatre performances at the end of the 1930s, as well as the cinematic work of Humphrey Jennings in the early 1940s, did not survive the stresses and strains of the early Cold War intact. By then a new generation had moved into the leadership of the South Wales Area of the NUM. They took inspiration from the Popular Front pageantry and workers' theatre of the interwar years and established the Miners' Gala and the Miners' Eisteddfod.

These annual events were the descendants of earlier waves of left-wing art forms, setting South Walian proletarian culture alongside the mass staging of Proletkult found in the communist countries. The 'chorus of Greek poignancy', as the Pageant of South Wales was called in 1939, was not silenced or abandoned entirely, but translated into a new enterprise. In this way it provided the foundations of a cultural platform for left-wing internationalist politics, ranging from the anti-apartheid movement to support for democracy in Eastern and Southern Europe and Latin America.[81] In this way, the cultural activism of the later twentieth century left owed much to the interwar political pageant.

Notes

1. Gwyn Thomas, 'Commentary for Promotional Film of South Wales Miners' Gala, 1960', cited in Hywel Francis and David Smith, *The Fed: A History of the South Wales Miners in the Twentieth Century* (London: Lawrence & Wishart, 1980), 427.
2. *South Wales Daily News*, 9 August 1873. A notable exception to this rule was the institution of 'Mabon's Day', the monthly Monday holiday instituted in 1888. See Andy Croll, 'Mabon's Day: The Rise and Fall of a Lib-Lab Holiday in the South Wales Coalfield, 1888–1898', *Labour History Review* 72 (2007): 49–68. The relatively late establishment of a miners' gala in South Wales nevertheless mirrored circumstances in Scotland, where the Scottish Area of the NUM inaugurated the Scottish Miners' Gala in 1947.
3. Francis and Smith, *The Fed*, 446.
4. These rich traditions have been examined in Gareth Williams, *Valleys of Song: Music and Society in Wales, 1840–1914* (Cardiff: University of Wales Press, 2003) and Gareth Williams, *Do You Hear the People Sing? The Male Voice Choirs of Wales* (Llandysul: Gomer, 2015).
5. Daryl Leeworthy, *Labour Country: Political Radicalism and Social Democracy in South Wales, 1831–1985* (Cardigan: Parthian, 2018); Daryl Leeworthy, 'Partisan Players: Sport, Working-Class Culture and the Labour Movement in South Wales, 1920–1939', *Labor History* 55 (2014): 580–93. On the wider debates around leisure and recreation in the Labour Party at this time, see Chris Waters, *British Socialists and the Politics of Popular Culture, 1884–1914* (Stanford: Stanford University Press, 1990) and Duncan Hall, *'A Pleasant Change from Politics': Music and the British Labour Movement Between the Wars* (London: New Clarion Press, 2001).
6. On the working-class education movement, see Richard Lewis, *Leaders and Teachers: Adult Education and the Challenge of Labour in South Wales, 1906–1940* (Cardiff: University of Wales Press, 1993).
7. *Merthyr Express*, 27 March and 19 June 1909; Daniel Owen, *J. Keir Hardie MP: The Prize Epic at the Mountain Ash ILP Eisteddfod, March 22 1909* (Mountain Ash: Saunders, 1909): copy consulted at Cardiff University Special Collections and Archives.
8. *Evening Express*, 8 June 1909; *Glamorgan Gazette*, 11 June 1909.
9. For instance, the Blaenavon Labour Eisteddfod of 1924 (*Daily Herald*, 17 November 1924). Labour's municipal encouragement of the arts included the Three Valleys Festival, created by Mountain Ash Urban District Council in 1930.
10. Independent Labour Party, *The Report of the Annual Conference held at Gloucester, April 1925* (London: Independent Labour Party, 1925), 27.
11. Ramsay MacDonald's cultural ideas were discussed in various of his writings, notably *The Socialist Movement* (London: Williams & Norgate, 1911), 178–85.
12. *Daily Herald*, 11 May 1925.
13. *Daily Herald*, 11 May 1925.
14. Namely the *Banner of Freedom*, written by Hardie for an ILP gathering at Porthcawl: *Evening Express*, 6 June 1908.
15. W. Miles Malleson, *The ILP Arts Guild* (London: ILP, 1925). Malleson, a playwright and West End actor, served as the National Director. The ILP Arts Guild gave way to the Masses Stage and Film Guild in 1929. For the history of the guild, see Ros Merkin, 'The Religion of Socialism or a Pleasant Sunday Afternoon? The ILP Arts Guild', in *British Theatres Between the Wars, 1918–1939*, ed. Clive Barker and Maggie B. Gale (Cambridge: Cambridge University Press, 2000), 162–89.
16. Independent Labour Party, *Report of the Annual Conference held at Whitley Bay, April 1926* (London: Independent Labour Party, 1926), 25.

17. *Daily Herald*, 1 March 1926. The Cardiff Labour Dramatic Group was noted in the *Western Mail*, 1 April 1926, and the Merthyr Tydfil ILP Dramatic Society was recorded in the *Daily Herald*, 7 January 1926. The Cardiff East Labour Brass and Reed Band was formed in 1920 and was organised by John S. Price, the divisional agent: *Daily Herald*, 5 July, 4 October and 22 December 1920; 4 May and 30 June 1921. See also Ros Merkin, 'The Theatre of the Organised Working Class, 1830–1930' (unpublished PhD diss., University of Warwick, 1993). Neath ILP Orpheus Male Voice Choir and the Briton Ferry ILP Male Voice Party were particularly renowned, performing all over the country: *Radio Times*, 8 March 1930, 50; 13 March 1931, 659; 25 March 1932, 811.
18. William Hazell, *The Gleaming Vision: Being the History of the Ynysybwl Co-Operative Society Ltd, 1889–1954* (Pontypridd: Ynysybwl Co-Operative Society, 1954), 134–5. Although much remains to be written about the culture of co-operative societies in Wales, the wider history of co-operative culture in Britain is discussed in Peter Gurney, *Co-Operative Culture and the Politics of Consumption in England, 1870–1930* (Manchester: Manchester University Press, 1996) and Nicole Robertson, *The Co-Operative Movement and Communities in Britain, 1914–1960: Minding Their Own Business* (Aldershot: Ashgate, 2016).
19. Mick Wallis, 'Pageantry and the Popular Front: Ideological Production in the "Thirties"', *New Theatre Quarterly* 10 (1994): 132–56; Mick Wallis, 'The Popular Front Pageant: Its Emergence and Decline', *New Theatre Quarterly* 11 (1995): 17–32.
20. Tom Hulme, '"A Nation of Town Criers": Civic Publicity and Historical Pageantry in Inter-War Britain', *Urban History* 44 (2017): 271.
21. Ness Edwards, *The Workers' Theatre* (Cardiff: Cymric Federation Press, 1930). Edwards was to serve as Labour MP for Caerphilly from 1939 until his death in 1968. Claire Warden notes, for instance, Edwards's engagement with Huntly Carter's 1929 study *The New Spirit in Russian Theatre, 1917–1928*: see Warden, *Migrating Modernist Performance: British Theatrical Travels Through Russia* (London: Palgrave Macmillan, 2016), 79.
22. Wayne David, *Remaining True: A Biography of Ness Edwards* (Caerphilly: Caerphilly Local History Society, 2006).
23. Raphael Samuel, 'Documents and Texts from the Workers' Theatre Movement (1928–1936)', *History Workshop* 4 (1977): 104–5.
24. Edwards, *The Workers' Theatre*; cited in Samuel, 'Documents', 105.
25. Edwards, *The Workers' Theatre*; cited in Samuel, 'Documents', 105.
26. *Sunday Worker*, 11 July 1926.
27. *Daily Herald*, 4 October 1928, 11 July 1929 and 28 November 1929.
28. Stephen G. Jones, *Workers at Play: A Social and Economic History of Leisure, 1918–1939* (London: Routledge, 1986), 154–5.
29. *Daily Worker*, 22 January, 29 January and 30 January 1932. The Red Pioneer Troupe comprised members of the Hackney Red Radio group (formerly the Hackney Workers' Theatre group) and the Streatham-based Red Front. For a wider sense of Labour–Communist tensions in the Rhondda in this period, see Leeworthy, *Labour Country* and Chris Williams, *Democratic Rhondda: Politics and Society, 1885–1951* (Cardiff: University of Wales Press, 1996).
30. *Red Stage* 4 (March 1932): 2.
31. Although there were exceptions, notably Arthur Horner. See Nina Fishman, *Arthur Horner: A Political Biography, Volume I, 1894–1944* (London: Lawrence & Wishart, 2010) and Nina Fishman, 'Horner and Hornerism', in *Party People, Communist Lives: Explorations in Biography*, ed. John McIlroy, Kevin Morgan and Alan Campbell (London: Lawrence & Wishart, 2001), 122–42.
32. *Daily Worker*, 25 February 1930.
33. The 'Third Period' was ushered in by the Communist International in the summer of 1928 and proposed a rhetoric of 'class against class'. Social democrats and reformist socialists were denounced as 'social fascists'. The phase lasted until the mid-1930s when the Comintern moved to embrace the Popular Front.
34. *Daily Worker*, 23 March 1937; Communist Party of Great Britain, *Report of the Central Committee to the Fourteenth National Congress* (London: Communist Party of Great Britain, 1937), 18.
35. Russian State Archive of Socio-Political History (RGASPI), Moscow, 495.14.239: 'A United Labour Movement Depends on the Number of Recruits to the Communist Party – Summary of Speech given at the South Wales Communist Congress by Idris Cox (February 1937)'.
36. *Western Mail*, 22 March 1937.
37. Richard Burton Archives, Swansea University [RBA], SWCC, SC546/1: 'Poster for 1939 Silicosis Pageant'; SC569: 'Speeches and Notes from the Silicosis Pageant'. For a wider sense of the

struggle for workmen's compensation for silicosis, see Arthur McIvor and Ronald Johnston, *Miners' Lung: A History of Dust Disease in British Mining* (Aldershot: Ashgate, 2007) and Francis and Smith, *The Fed*, 438–41.

38. André van Gyseghem, 'British Theatre in the Thirties: An Autobiographical Record', in *Culture and Crisis in Britain in the 30s*, ed. Jon Clark, Margot Heinemann, David Margolies and Carole Snee (London: Lawrence & Wishart, 1979), 218.
39. Wallis, 'Popular Front Pageant', 25.
40. The Left Theatre's council included Harold Laski, John Strachey, Victor Gollancz, Fenner Brockway, Vera Brittain, Paul Robeson and Ellen Wilkinson. For aspects of Popular Front literary culture see esp. Andy Croft, *Red Letter Days: British Fiction in the 1930s* (London: Lawrence & Wishart, 1990) and Andy Croft, 'Authors Take Sides: Writers and the Communist Party, 1920–56', in *Opening the Books: Essays on the Social and Cultural History of the British Communist Party*, ed. Nina Fishman and Kevin Morgan (London: Pluto Press, 1995), 83–101.
41. The circumstances of this are described in Francis and Smith, *The Fed*, 278–98.
42. Montagu Slater, *Stay Down, Miner* (London: Martin Lawrence, 1936).
43. Montagu Slater, *New Way Wins* (London: Lawrence & Wishart, 1937).
44. Slater, *New Way Wins*, 46. In music, 'largo' means a very slow tempo.
45. Benjamin Britten, *Journeying Boy: The Diaries of the Young Benjamin Britten, 1928–1938*, ed. John Evans (London: Faber & Faber, 2009), 352. A copy of the score and the script are held as part of the Britten-Pears Foundation Archives in Aldeburgh. See esp. BBM/stay_down_miner and PG/1936/0510. A digital version of the programme is at https://www.bpfcatalogue.org/archive/PG-1936-0510 (accessed 1 June 2020).
46. *Daily Telegraph*, 11 May 1936; *The Times*, 12 May 1936; *Manchester Guardian*, 11 May 1936.
47. *Left Review* 2 (June 1936): 475–6.
48. These were W. J. Saddler (Labour, the Federation's then Vice President), Will Paynter (Communist, President 1951–9 and General Secretary of the National Union of Mineworkers 1959–68), W. H. Crews (Labour, General Secretary 1951–8) and Dai Dan Evans (Communist, General Secretary 1958–63). The notes of the meeting are to be found in RBA, SWCC, MNA/NUM/3/4/45: Report of May Day Committee, 1 December 1938.
49. Labour Research Department Archives, London Metropolitan University, LRD/1/E/08/3: 'Letter from Oliver Harris to W. H. Williams, 2 December 1939'.
50. LRD/1/E/97/4: 'Letter from W. H. Williams to Oliver Harris, 6 January 1939' and 'Letter from W. H. Williams to Oliver Harris, 8 February 1939'.
51. RBA, SWCC, MNA/NUM/3/4/45: Report of May Day Committee, 1 December 1938.
52. Angela Bartie, Linda Fleming, Mark Freeman, Tom Hulme, Alex Hutton, Paul Readman, 'Pageant of South Wales', *The Redress of the Past*, http://www.historicalpageants.ac.uk/pageants/1315/ (accessed 22 November 2018). This was the form of the pageant as first advertised in March 1939. See *Western Mail*, 4 March and 22 March 1939; *Scotsman*, 7 April 1939; *Daily Mirror*, 8 April 1939.
53. David Williams, *John Frost: A Study of Chartism* (Cardiff: University of Wales Press, 1939).
54. RBA, SWCC, MNA/NUM/3/4/45: Report of May Day Committee, 1 December 1938; LRD/1/B/1/11: Labour Research Department Executive Committee, Minutes, 6 February 1939. For a discussion of Keeling's involvement, see *Hendon and Finchley Times*, 5 May 1939. Keeling was responsible for the artistic design of the 1938 Birmingham Centenary Pageant.
55. André van Gyseghem, 'A Pageant for Welsh Miners', *Theatre Arts Monthly* 23 (1939): 642.
56. South Wales Miners' Federation, *May Day, 1st May 1939: Pageant of South Wales* (Cardiff: South Wales Miners' Federation, 1939).
57. *Western Mail*, 8 May 1939. Although this considerably improved the audience, with as many as 9,000 turning out in addition to nearly 800 performers: Gwent Archives, Ebbw Vale (GwA), Britannia Lodge Records, D845/109: May Day Pageant, Pontypool, 1939.
58. Benjamin Britten, *Letters from a Life, Volume 2: 1939–45*, ed. Donald Mitchell (London: Faber & Faber, 2011), 663–4.
59. *Western Mail*, 27 March 1939.
60. *Western Mail*, 14 April 1939.
61. RBA, SWCC, MNA/NUM/3/4/45: 'Letter from Benjamin Farrington, 4 June 1939'.
62. LRD/1/E/08/18: 'Letter from Councillor Evan T. Lewis to W. H. Williams, 5 May 1939'.
63. LRD/1/E/08/19: 'Letter from W. H. Williams to David Harris, 6 May 1939'.
64. For political commentary, see, for example, *Daily Worker*, 2 May 1939 and, in a different vein, *Daily Herald*, 2 May 1939.

65. *Western Mail*, 2 May 1939.
66. *Midland Daily Telegraph*, 11 May 1939.
67. For instance, the Children's Pageant held to mark the centenary of Salem Baptist Chapel, Blaina, in September 1941 (GwA, D4267/3); the Gower Pageant and Fair held at Penrice Castle in 1969 (West Glamorgan Archives, Swansea, D/D z 565/18/1–4); the pageant held to mark the centenary of Methodist worship in Penarth in 1960 (Glamorgan Archives, Cardiff [GA], DWESB/36/1/22); and various pageants staged in 1951 to mark the Festival of Britain, not least the 'Pageant Play of Wales' held at the Sophia Gardens Pavilion, Cardiff and starring, among others, Kenneth Williams (GA, D977/3).
68. For a wider sense of Robeson's story, see Paul Robeson Jr, *The Undiscovered Paul Robeson: An Artist's Journey, 1908–1939* (New York: Wiley, 2001) and Robeson, *The Undiscovered Paul Robeson: Quest for Freedom, 1939–1976* (Hoboken, NJ: Wiley, 2010). A useful study of Robeson's relationship with Britain, in particular, can be found in Jeff Sparrow, *No Way But This: In Search of Paul Robeson* (London: Scribe, 2018).
69. On *Spare Time*, see The National Archives, Kew (TNA), Central Office of Information Records, INF 6/1025. On *The Silent Village*, see TNA, Central Office of Information Records, INF 5/90, INF 6/1916, INF 12/119; British Film Institute Archives, Central Office of Information Records, INF 33/23.
70. Humphrey Jennings, 'Radio Talk: *The Silent Village* (26 May 1943)', reprinted in *The Humphrey Jennings Film Reader,* ed. Kevin Jackson (London: Carcenet, 1993), 67–75. See also 'Did You Hear That?', *The Listener*, 17 June 1943, 717.
71. Kevin Jackson, *Humphrey Jennings* (London: Picador, 2004), 190.
72. TNA, Central Office of Information Records, INF 6/1917: 'A Diary for Timothy'.
73. John E. Morgan, *A Village Workers' Council* (Pontypridd: Celtic Press, 1950), 9.
74. The People's Vigilance Committee is discussed in Andrew Thorpe, 'Locking out the Communists: The Labour Party and the Communist Party, 1939–46', *Twentieth Century British History* 25 (2014): 221–50; Angus Calder, *The People's War: Britain, 1939–1945* (London: Pimlico, 1969), 244–5; and Nina Fishman, *The British Communist Party and the Trade Unions, 1933–45* (London: Scolar Press, 1995), 272.
75. Morgan, *A Village Workers' Council*, 47–8. Jones's expulsion from the Labour Party is noted in a series of letters sent by the constituency secretary, Edmund Stonelake, in January and February 1941 (National Library of Wales, Aberystwyth, GB 0210 PONERS, Pontypridd Miners' Agents' Papers, Goronwy R. Jones, File 1 and RBA, SWCC: MNA/PP/61/5). For Jones's Communist Party activities, see RBA, SWCC, MNA/PP/61/9.
76. The former as the Cardiff Unity Theatre, the latter as the Mid-Rhondda Unity Players.
77. *Neath Guardian*, 22 November 1946.
78. *Western Mail*, 17 June 1943, 7 December 1944, 31 March 1945, 30 August 1948, 16 March 1949, 18 October 1949, 31 January 1950, 25 April 1950 and 5 September 1950. Aspects of the Cardiff Unity Theatre Group's activities can be found in University of Glasgow, Special Collections, Scottish Theatre Archive, STA Ar 4: Cuttings, Correspondence and Programme for Cardiff Unity Theatre Group's production of *Starched Aprons*, July 1946; University of Queensland, Fryer Library, George Landen Dann Collection, UQFL 65/A8: 'Correspondence from Cardiff Unity Theatre to George Landen Dann regarding performance of *Fountains Beyond*, 1950'; V&A Department of Theatre and Performance Archives, London, Unity Theatre Collection, THM/9/6/1/6; 'Letters from Norman Draper regarding history of Cardiff Unity, 1984'; GA, D and J Exports Collection, D953/6/1: 'Clifford Janes Scrapbook'. The Richard Burton Archives at Swansea University holds a 1942 poster advertising the Mid-Rhondda Unity Players' performance of a Soviet play.
79. Harri Webb, 'A Theatre for Wales', *Wales* 29 (1948): 552–3.
80. *Western Mail*, 28 July 1947.
81. South Wales Miners' Federation, *Pageant of South Wales*; Smith and Francis, *The Fed*, 429.

Bibliography

Calder, Angus. 1969, *The People's War: Britain, 1939–1945*. London: Pimlico.
Croft, Andy. 1990. *Red Letter Days: British Fiction in the 1930s*. London: Lawrence & Wishart.

Croft, Andy. 1995. 'Authors Take Sides: Writers and the Communist Party, 1920–56', in *Opening the Books: Essays on the Social and Cultural History of the British Communist Party*, edited by Nina Fishman and Kevin Morgan. London: Pluto Press, 83–101.

Croll, Andy. 2007. 'Mabon's Day: The Rise and Fall of a Lib-Lab Holiday in the South Wales Coalfield, 1888–1898', *Labour History Review* 72: 49–68.

David, Wayne. 2006. *Remaining True: A Biography of Ness Edwards*. Caerphilly: Caerphilly Local History Society.

Fishman, Nina. 1995. *The British Communist Party and the Trade Unions, 1933–45*. London: Scolar Press.

Fishman, Nina. 2001. 'Horner and Hornerism', in *Party People, Communist Lives: Explorations in Biography*, edited by John McIlroy, Kevin Morgan and Alan Campbell. London: Lawrence & Wishart, 122–42.

Fishman, Nina. 2010. *Arthur Horner: A Political Biography, Volume I, 1894–1944*. London: Lawrence & Wishart.

Francis, Hywel and Smith, David. 1980. *The Fed: A History of the South Wales Miners in the Twentieth Century*. London: Lawrence & Wishart.

Gurney, Peter. 1996. *Co-Operative Culture and the Politics of Consumption in England, 1870–1930*. Manchester: Manchester University Press.

Hall, Duncan. 2001. *'A Pleasant Change from Politics': Music and the British Labour Movement Between the Wars*. London: New Clarion Press.

Hazell, William. 1954. *The Gleaming Vision: Being the History of the Ynysybwl Co-Operative Society Ltd, 1889–1954*. Pontypridd: Ynysybwl Co-Operative Society.

Hulme, Tom. 2017. '"A Nation of Town Criers": Civic Publicity and Historical Pageantry in Inter-War Britain', *Urban History* 44: 270–92.

Jackson, Kevin. 2004. *Humphrey Jennings*. London: Picador.

Jones, Stephen G. 1986. *Workers at Play: A Social and Economic History of Leisure 1918–1939*. London: Routledge.

Leeworthy, Daryl. 2014. 'Partisan Players: Sport, Working-Class Culture and the Labour Movement in South Wales, 1920–1939', *Labor History* 55: 580–93.

Leeworthy, Daryl. 2018. *Labour Country: Political Radicalism and Social Democracy in South Wales, 1831–1985*. Cardigan: Parthian Books.

Lewis, Richard. 1993. *Leaders and Teachers: Adult Education and the Challenge of Labour in South Wales, 1906–1940*. Cardiff: University of Wales Press.

McIvor, Arthur and Johnston, Ronald. 2007. *Miners' Lung: A History of Dust Disease in British Mining*. Aldershot: Ashgate.

Merkin, Ros. 1993. 'The Theatre of the Organised Working Class, 1830–1930.' Unpublished PhD diss., University of Warwick.

Merkin, Ros. 2000. 'The Religion of Socialism or a Pleasant Sunday Afternoon? The ILP Arts Guild', in *British Theatres Between the Wars, 1918–1939*, edited by Clive Barker and Maggie B. Gale. Cambridge: Cambridge University Press, 162–89.

Robertson, Nicole. 2016. *The Co-Operative Movement and Communities in Britain, 1914–1960: Minding Their Own Business*. Aldershot: Ashgate.

Robeson, Paul Jr. 2001. *The Undiscovered Paul Robeson: An Artist's Journey, 1908–1939*. New York and Chichester: John Wiley & Sons.

Robeson, Paul Jr. 2010. *The Undiscovered Paul Robeson: Quest for Freedom, 1939–1976*. Hoboken, NJ: Wiley.

Samuel, Raphael. 1977. 'Documents and Texts from the Workers' Theatre Movement (1928–1936)', *History Workshop* 4: 102–42.

Sparrow, Jeff. 2018. *No Way But This: In Search of Paul Robeson*. London: Scribe.

Thorpe, Andrew. 2014. 'Locking out the Communists: The Labour Party and the Communist Party, 1939–46', *Twentieth Century British History* 25: 221–50.

van Gyseghem, André. 1979. 'British Theatre in the Thirties: An Autobiographical Record', in *Culture and Crisis in Britain in the 30s*, edited by Jon Clark, Margot Heinemann, David Margolies and Carole Snee. London: Lawrence & Wishart, 209–18.

Wallis, Mick. 1994. 'Pageantry and the Popular Front: Ideological Production in the "Thirties"', *New Theatre Quarterly* 10: 132–56.

Wallis, Mick. 1996. 'The Popular Front Pageant: Its Emergence and Decline', *New Theatre Quarterly* 11: 17–32.

Warden, Claire. 2016. *Migrating Modernist Performance: British Theatrical Travels Through Russia*. London: Palgrave Macmillan.

Waters, Chris. 1990. *British Socialists and the Politics of Popular Culture, 1884–1914*. Stanford, CA: Stanford University Press.

Williams, Chris. 1996. *Democratic Rhondda: Politics and Society, 1885–1951*. Cardiff: University of Wales Press.

Williams, David. 1939. *John Frost: A Study of Chartism*. Cardiff: University of Wales Press.

Williams, Gareth. 2003. *Valleys of Song: Music and Society in Wales, 1840–1914*. Cardiff: University of Wales Press.

Williams, Gareth. 2015. *Do You Hear the People Sing? The Male Voice Choirs of Wales*. Llandysul: Gomer Press.

9

The 'Quite Ordinary Man' at the Pageant: History, Community and Local Identity in the 1951 Festival of Britain

Alexander Hutton

The Festival of Britain in 1951 sought to represent and celebrate Britain as a nation carefully balanced between past and present, tradition and modernity, community and technology, collectivism and individual values. In representing their vision of a collective future for the country, the Festival organisers were acutely aware of the weight of tradition and history. History, as many scholars have pointed out, was represented throughout the official Festival, from the 1851 Centenary Pavilion and the representations of the 'Instinct for Liberty' of the British people in the Lion and the Unicorn Pavilion on London's South Bank through to the various touring exhibitions and regional Festival sites.[1] These representations of history have often been viewed as somewhat self-serving attempts by the Labour government to craft a teleological and progressive historical narrative – one that was by and large rejected by a population who greatly preferred the Festival's evocations of modernity, from the famous Skylon to the promise of plentiful consumer goods in the labour-free house of tomorrow at the Dome of Discovery, and who returned the Conservative Party to government only a few months after the Festival's end.[2]

More recent studies have focused on local contexts away from London, examining how the Festival was viewed in the provinces in the context of continued economic austerity and an increasingly unpopular Labour government.[3] Although bookended by the victory celebrations of 1945 and the seemingly ubiquitous street parties celebrating the 1953 coronation, the Festival of Britain marked a highpoint of community participation in post-war Britain. The Festival, intended to lift the lingering post-war gloom and to shine a 'beacon for change' across British society, was experienced not merely by the millions of people who flocked to the South Bank but also by the tens of millions more who participated in thousands of small- and medium-sized, community-organised events held in almost every part of the country. Memorably described in J. B. Priestley's novel *Festival at Farbridge* (1951), these were bewildering in their variety. They included bazaars, concerts, gymkhanas, beauty contests, floral displays, sporting events, drama festivals, parades and much else besides.[4]

Priestley's novel also included one of the most prominent local events held in conjunction with the Festival of Britain: an historical pageant, of which at least 150 were staged during the Festival year (see Appendix, pp. 218–19). They ranged from spectacles with thousands of performers (such as the Carlisle Festival of Border History Pageant, which featured 5,000 performers and was viewed by 120,000 spectators) to small village pageants with casts of fewer than a hundred apiece.

The year 1951 saw the greatest number of historical pageants held at any time since the 1920s and such levels of 'pageant fever' were never again matched, not even during the coronation celebrations two years later.[5] Crucially, almost all these pageants were organised by local communities and voluntary groups, without any assistance from central government or the Festival's organising committee. Held across all four nations of Britain (plus the Isle of Man), they stressed the strength of local and regional identities – to the extent that imperial themes and overarching British historical narratives were almost completely excluded. It was the numerous small- and medium-scale pageants, arranged by enthusiastic local people far from the organisational grasp of the Festival in London, which reflected the local and collective spirit of the Festival and post-war Britain in presenting a new and optimistic relationship between past, present and future. In opening the festivities in May, George VI singled out for praise 'the pageants and displays which have been prepared in our ancient cities and throughout the countryside', and congratulated 'all those who will help to make our history live before us and send us forward with faith in our future'.[6]

Many pageants held during the Festival year foregrounded a history of the common people over kings, queens and nobles – often presenting radical critiques of British history that drew on earlier socialist pageants of the 1930s. As Claire Langhamer has argued, the positive and democratic connotations of 'ordinariness' largely emerged in the wake of the Second

World War (reframed as 'the People's War') and were exemplified by the films of Humphrey Jennings and the radio broadcasts of J. B. Priestley. While Langhamer argues that 'ordinariness' later became adopted as a conservative virtue, the Festival of Britain was, in many ways, a celebration of the social democratic potential of the 'ordinary people'.[7]

Planning and opposition

Many more pageants would have been held during the Festival year had it not been for significant reluctance, opposition and apathy. In June 1951 the *Daily Mail* reported that 18 local authorities were refusing to organise Festival celebrations, with many others threatening to cancel plans. The newspaper gave the following reasons for refusal: '1) They did not agree with the concept of the Festival; 2) It would mean a rise in rates; 3) Local apathy'.[8] If 18 local authorities had publicly refused to mark the Festival, however, many more were distinctly half-hearted in their planning of celebrations, having already cancelled expensive events. Pageants were often the first thing to be cancelled on the grounds of expense, unfeasibility or lack of public interest.[9] The *Daily Express*, a staunch critic of the Festival throughout, published a number of stories cautioning against towns holding pageants. One article warned that 50 of the men playing Chaucer's pilgrims at the Canterbury pageant were liable to be called up for military service, and as such ought not to grow beards; another quoted a Richmond councillor who warned that, 'what with the cost of living soaring to the stratospheric, the international situation plunging in the opposite direction, and the English Summer, he could see no hope' for the borough's upcoming pageant.[10] Several authorities were wary of holding a pageant after recent highly-publicised fiascos. Bradford's 1947 centenary pageant, beset by poor management and scandals, had lost the city £13,000 (equivalent to almost £400,000 today); the council pointedly refused to spend any money on the Festival.[11] Bradford's earlier failure was given as a reason by several nearby authorities for not holding pageants or other major events during the Festival year.[12]

With the decline of pre-war elite networks, which had previously organised, hosted and offered financial guarantees to many pageants, councils took the lead in organising most larger-scale post-war pageants. Conservative and Liberal councillors, as well as taxpayers, were often reluctant to stage what might prove to be costly failures resulting in rate increases. At a time of continuing austerity and rationing, pageants were accused by their opponents of being spendthrift vanity projects, wasting public money and leaving nothing of lasting worth. Iain Wilton has rightly argued that Conservative opposition to the Festival was more equivocal than is generally presumed, with local councils and national politicians (including Winston Churchill) tacitly accepting or even cautiously welcoming the celebrations.[13] Nonetheless, opposition to the Festival's financial outlay and supposed socialist bias formed part of a wider Conservative discourse of localism and government efficiency – one that Matthew Cragoe argues proved highly effective in the elections of 1950 and 1951.[14]

Much Conservative reaction to pageant schemes was consistent with this discourse. Discussing the proposed pageant in Sevenoaks in December 1949, one member of the local Conservative association approved of the venture in principle but 'with the proviso that the pageant must do nothing to increase the rates'. Warning that the cost of insuring pageants against loss had risen precipitously, he insisted that no decision be taken 'until a report as to the possible cost had been sent to the council'.[15] The decision was duly delayed until the following September, when it became clear that the council would not venture the £2,500 required to stage a pageant.[16] At the other end of the country, in Hartlepool, there was widespread uproar when it emerged that the council were paying the pageant producer £150 while refusing similar funds to guarantee the preservation of a local landmark, Sir Cuthbert Sharp's house. An anonymous 'Citizen' proposed several scenes of a satirical pageant depicting the council's various philistine efforts to erase the city's history before themselves being obliterated by an atomic bomb.[17]

At Bath, one of 13 regional Festival centres given limited government funds to stage events, local people remained reluctant – even after the council hired the prominent pageant-master Lawrence du Garde Peach, who had previously staged major pageants at Sheffield, Nottingham and Wolverhampton. There was trouble finding a venue with suitable seating; and when the Education Committee refused to guarantee an anticipated £500 deficit, the Festival Committee asked the Bath Assembly to accept liability. This prompted one alderman, who sat on both the Festival Committee and the board of the Bath Assembly, to complain that the council was trying to impose pageantry by diktat.[18] A reorganisation by the Assembly caused the pageant to be dropped quietly with little explanation, with Bath instead favouring a music festival and exhibition of Georgian architecture.[19] At Cannock in Staffordshire, where Peach was also contracted as pageant-master, the council cancelled the pageant two weeks before it was due to be performed, after only 40 locals volunteered; £2,000 of council money had already been spent.[20] Paignton in

Devon had initially intended to produce a large civic pageant to attract foreign tourists, but was forced to cancel its plans when anticipated government aid was not forthcoming and when nobody in the locality volunteered to act as pageant-master for free.[21]

A lack of volunteers terminated several pageants at their planning stage; this generally indicated a low interest that might well have led to small audiences. In December 1950 Daventry council proposed holding an inexpensive pageant, calling for 200 volunteers out of a town of over 35,000 residents. The council stressed that the pageant would go ahead 'only if full co-operation is forthcoming from every organisation in the town' and that it would only guarantee finances 'provided there is sufficient support'. The pageant was cancelled in April 1951 after only six volunteers from Daventry plus a further 20 from surrounding rural districts came forward.[22] The contract for the Brighton pageant-master A. L. Gilmore (formerly pageant-master to the King of Siam) allowed the council to cancel the pageant at short notice if sufficient local interest failed to materialise.[23] Yet although by mid-April 1951 only 539 performers had been recruited (one-third of the number hoped for), Gilmore assured the committee that he 'did not anticipate any difficulty in completing the cast in time'. Despite widespread local criticism the pageant ultimately went ahead, losing £3,480.[24] The Carlisle pageant, eventually staged with great success, was almost ruined by a lack of male volunteers, caused in part by the City Employers Committee refusing to offer paid leave for Festival performers.[25]

Before the Dartford pageant, several companies and organisations pledged to give financial support as well as to organise individual episodes, with performers drawn from among their employees and members. These, however, proved supremely reluctant to volunteer. L. Lack, secretary of the Inner Wheel Women's Voluntary Club, wrote on 4 July that their members would not now be performing, 'in view of holidays and other commitments'; the Red Cross and the Congregational Church Recreation Club also withdrew. On 25 July, barely a month before the first performance, F. Brumby of the Dartford Industrial Co-operative Society wrote to inform the town clerk that 'there is now very little possibility of our being able to complete the arrangements'; the Society had 'not even been able to recruit sufficient men for the speaking parts'. Brumby explained that 'few of our members or employees are prepared to give seven evenings, including two Saturdays', and that the pageant coincided 'with the Society's stock-taking period'.[26] While a number of young children wrote to the pageant organisers personally to offer their services, adults proved indifferent, with local schoolteachers refusing to surrender their holidays to supervise pupils at the pageant.[27] The Dartford Young Conservatives ultimately stepped in to ensure that all the scenes at least had sufficient speaking parts, although their Parliamentary candidate, Margaret Roberts, had recently declared the Festival to be a waste of time and money. These inauspicious signs indicated that the public was unlikely to turn out in great numbers; in the event the pageant lost £480.[28]

Whereas many pre-war pageants had been organised and financially guaranteed by networks of wealthy and aristocratic backers (who had often allowed pageants to go ahead in the grounds of stately homes), wartime upheavals and taxation saw the nadir of the landed elite. Quite apart from now being unwilling to bankroll pageants, many aristocrats had sold their mansions and sprawling grounds. The National Trust, which often received these cast-off estates (as well as their former owners), proved unwilling, perhaps surprisingly, to host pageants.[29] One of the reasons given for the cancellation of the 1951 Sevenoaks pageant in Knole Park was that the Trust, which had taken over the property from the Sackville family in 1946, refused to forgo the admissions charges for a week.[30] Whereas the 1923 Arundel pageant had been a lavish affair held in the grounds of Arundel Castle, featuring a depiction of all 36 Dukes of Norfolk up to the present, the 1951 pageant was held in the considerably less grandiose setting of the nearby, council-owned Arundel Park. Despite a visit from Princess Elizabeth, it was a decidedly non-aristocratic, low-key affair staged by children from schools and youth clubs. The Carlisle pageant likewise had conspicuously fewer titled patrons and committee members than its previous instance in 1928.[31] Only the Alnwick and Blenheim pageants were held in private residences and had significant aristocratic involvement (the latter featured Lord Saye and Sele playing his illustrious royalist ancestor, as well as the Duke and Duchess of Marlborough and Lady Rosemary Churchill).[32] Despite this, the Festival year saw many visits to pageants by members of the royal family. As well as Elizabeth's attendance at Arundel, Princess Margaret went to Blenheim, Carlisle and Drum Castle, while Queen Mary saw pageants at Hitchin and Hampton Court.

History for the common man

Such pageants, which nostalgically evoked spectacular histories, as well as reminding audiences of the glory days of pre-war pageantry, were rather different from the majority held during the Festival year. Most pageants in 1951 foregrounded the role of ordinary men and women in history, as well as celebrating regional and non-English cultures. Pageants took inspiration from popular social history books such J. L. and Barbara Hammond's *Village Labourer* (1911) and *Town Labourer* (1917), which had recently been reprinted with great success; A. L. Morton's *A People's History of England* (1938); G. D. H. Cole and Raymond Postgate's *The Common People* (1938, new edition 1946); and, most prominently, G. M. Trevelyan's phenomenally successful *English Social History* (1944), directly quoted by the narrator of the Basingstoke pageant.[33]

Many Festival pageants drew on an earlier tradition of radical pageantry during the 1930s and 1940s. Examples included the Pageant of Labour (1934), the communist-inspired 'Music for the People' (1939), the South Wales Miners' Pageant (1939; discussed in chapter 8), the Pageant of Chartism (1939) and the Co-operative Centenary Pageant (1944).[34] However, with the emergence of the Cold War, communist and radical pageant organisers – such as the composer Alan Bush and the director André van Gyseghem – had become ostracised from the cultural mainstream, with the Communist Party ignoring the Festival.

Nonetheless, many of those behind the Festival celebrations continued to celebrate a social democratic account of people's history, instanced in Humphrey Jennings's film *Family Portrait* or in the 'Lion and Unicorn Pavilion' at the Festival's South Bank site. The latter presented an ingrained 'Instinct for Liberty': it featured 12 scenes 'representing the growth of freedom in British history', including Milton's *Areopagitica*, the Tolpuddle Martyrs and women's suffrage campaigners.[35] The pageant at Rushden in Northamptonshire focused exclusively on the 'simple theme' of 'Rushden and its people'.[36] Its writer, L. V. Elliott, declared in the programme that spectators would 'look in vain for the crown or chopping-block, as the passing story reveals only the life and characters of a quiet village that was for several centuries even obscure'. Instead the pageant provided

> room for the gentler side of history; to observe how a useful, industrious town can evolve from simple living; to feel that some remote incident or celebrity need not be quoted or canonised as a justification for our survival.[37]

Rushden was typical of many pageants that embraced the lives of the common people. Those organised by religious groups often included episodes depicting the social work of the church among local communities. The Methodist 'Church Marches On' pageant in Colne, Lancashire, for example, had scenes on 'The Church and Social Service' (depicting the work of Elizabeth Fry and Charles Kingsley) and 'The Church and Social Justice' (featuring the Peasants' Revolt and the Tolpuddle Martyrs, three of whom were Methodists).[38]

Although few seemed to miss the pomp and spectacle of aristocratic high-living and visits by Elizabeth I, which had been a common feature of interwar pageants, some commentators felt that the emphasis on the 'ordinary' past was leading pageant organisers to omit some of the heroic passages of local history, while lively scenes featuring executions, riots and persecutions focused excessively on the negative aspects of this history, showing different classes pitted against one another. Reviewing the Boston pageant, which featured a scene where townspeople discussed the incorporation of the town, one critic complained that '[w]ith a history as rich as that of Boston, there must be, I felt, not a few incidents whose recounting would have provided more spectacular entertainment than some of those chosen' – although the pageant also included the grisly execution of several pirates who had previously terrorised the town.[39] Recounting a particularly graphic pageant in one Cotswold village, the correspondent for the *Manchester Guardian* remarked that although 'it may do some good to be reminded that barbarity did not begin with Belsen and atomic bombs … witch-burning supported by children as footpads and highwaymen still seems a slightly unexpected frolic'.[40]

Despite these criticisms, however, pageants that foregrounded the historical experiences of the common people were generally well received. These pageants projected the hopes of organisers that the Festival of Britain would herald in a new collective ethos, making Britain's obsession with class distinctions a thing of the past.

An 'Everyman' figure who narrated or commentated on the events was a feature of many Festival pageants, Rushden being one example.[41] These 'common people' narrators set the scenes, interpreted the actions (which in several cases were mimed rather than spoken) and explained or responded to events to break down the dramaturgical distance between the audience and the performance. Often they sought to relate historical events to audiences' own experiences. Alongside mythical patronal figures such as the 'Spirit of the Thames' at Hampton Court or 'Father Witham' at Boston, pageants were narrated or introduced by figures such as 'John Smith', a blacksmith at Dudley, 'upon whose labours and skill the industrial wealth of the town has been created'; the Smith family at Dartford; and a schoolboy at Wollaston, who, unable to stay awake during dull history lessons, dreamed the incidents of the pageant.[42] There were no 'Everywoman' figures.

Figure 9.1 Ronald Searle, 'The Festival Out of Town'. At East Grinstead, a modern-day gardener narrated the pageant in dialogue with a medieval herald: cartoon from *Punch*, July 1951. Reproduced by kind permission of the Punch Cartoon Library/Topfoto.

At East Grinstead in Sussex, the pageant was narrated by the 'Quite Ordinary Man' (Fig. 9.1). This figure of a modern-day gardener with his wheelbarrow (played by a local van driver) served, according to one reviewer, 'as a stabilizing element in so much curveting history'. Across six episodes, the pageant told a sweeping story. Beginning with the Norman occupation, it went on to depict the imperious visit of Edward I (shown ignoring the plight of the commoners), the burning of the Sussex Martyrs in 1556, a rigged parliamentary election, romantic highwaymen who were brutally hanged and finally the 1830 Agricultural Riots. The 'Quite Ordinary Man' provided a narrative chorus that took the side of the common people against their oppressive rulers – for instance lamenting

Figure 9.2 Ronald Searle, 'The Festival Out of Town': performers at the Pageant of East Grinstead. Cartoon from *Punch*, July 1951. Reproduced by kind permission of the Punch Cartoon Library/Topfoto.

the blatant corruption at the election, where the anti-government candidate had his legitimate victory struck down by the bailiff. In each scene the 'Quite Ordinary Man' described his outrage and sadness at the town's history of bloodshed, injustice and oppression. Despite its relatively small scale, East Grinstead's pageant gained national prominence after it was featured in a positive review of 'The Festival Out of Town' in the satirical magazine *Punch*, with cartoons by Ronald Searle (see Figs 9.1 and 9.2).[43]

These pageants, which often had strong links to the local Labour Party, presented a progressive people's history as a slow but inexorable struggle, by the people, against injustice and tyranny and towards freedom and equality. This was not always popular with local elites. At East

Grinstead, for example, the local chamber of commerce – which declared itself to be 'against the festival in principle' – forced the council to strip the pageant's funding; the event only went ahead after hundreds of local people themselves guaranteed the £800 required.[44] The Pageant of Headley in Hampshire also proceeded only with donations from 250 people who gave a pound each. Like that of East Grinstead, Headley's pageant told a bleak narrative of exploitation, violence and oppression, with scenes presenting the dispossession of Headley mill by invading Normans, peasants after the Black Death protesting for higher wages and a group of local people hiding the radical writer and MP William Cobbett from the authorities (who had come to arrest him and search the house for seditious materials). The final scene imagined a utopian vision of 2051, in which the leaders of the world meet in Headley to discuss collective efforts at finally eradicating disease, having previously outlawed poverty and the atomic bomb; they declared that '[t]here will be differences, but we shall reach a compromise and all will share the outcome equally'.[45] While these pageants were exceptional in their radical presentations of history, they reflected a wider celebration of the history of the common man and woman during the Festival of Britain, which often saw Labour's post-war Britain as the culmination of many centuries of social struggle.

The quite ordinary woman

Among the many organisations involved in pageants, women's groups were the most prominent. Festival pageants were organised by Women's Institutes (WIs) at Blenheim, Leek Wootton in Warwickshire, Horden in County Durham, Sollarshope in Herefordshire and Raglan in Monmouthshire; by Townswomen's Guilds at Weston in Somerset, Croydon and Southampton; and by the Women's Co-operative Guild at Leiston in Suffolk. Many other pageants featured scenes staged by women's groups or relied on women to provide the bulk of the organisational work; it was also easier to enlist women as volunteer performers, with men proving reticent in many cases.

There were also several prominent female pageant-masters at the time. None was more renowned than Gwen Lally, who produced pageants at Malvern and Dudley during the Festival year. Pageants produced by women, perhaps unsurprisingly, foregrounded women's roles in history, but others did so too. The Southampton 'Pageant of Womanhood', a Festival event produced by Arthur Black, included episodes depicting the seduction of a local widow by Henry VIII, persecuted women boarding the *Mayflower* and the contribution of women volunteers during the Second World War (it was one of many pageants that referred directly to the wartime endurance and sacrifices of ordinary people). As the prologue declared,

> We conjure back from the past a few of the multitude of women who have lived within our stout grey battlemented walls, who loved, laughed and feared as they trod our streets, who knelt in our churches and knew both weal and woe, the workers, the housewives and mothers, the wives of our rich merchants, the lay sisters of God's House, the Puritan women no less than the queens and princesses[.][46]

The Monmouth pageant, one of the largest in Wales and held at Raglan Castle, was organised by 47 WIs across Monmouthshire. It told the story of the medieval *Mabinogion,* including scenes foregrounding the female protagonists, including the Lady of Shalott, and the story of Enid, who proved her faithfulness and loyalty to her husband Geraint by joining him on a quest for the Holy Grail.[47]

By far the most prominent woman appearing in any pageant during Festival year was Anne Wrigg, star of the Coventry pageant. This regular event, held every decade or so since the seventeenth century, traditionally featured a procession through the city headed by a young woman portraying Lady Godiva, dressed in a flesh-coloured body stocking.[48] Lady Godiva's ride had last happened in 1936, and it was considered essential that she again rode through Coventry as a symbol of the city's spiritual reconstruction after its wartime devastation, as well as advertising to the world that Coventry was open for business. The *Chicago Tribune*, one of several American newspapers to cover the spectacle, quoted a city spokesman as saying that '[t]his time, Godiva rides, not only for Coventry, but for all Britain. She will be, the city council hopes, one of the prime features of the festival of Britain'.[49]

A lot of careful consideration went into choosing an appropriate Godiva, with the Council rigidly suppressing any hint of titillation or levity, declaring that applicants must be of 'mature age, cultured, of good physique and appearance'. This prompted the *Manchester Guardian* to muse as to whether this meant that 'she must be able to quote from ancient charters to prove her existence and look as if she fully realised that her ride is in protest against excessive taxes' – as well as to express the hope that the current 'Siberian weather' would be gone by June.[50] Matters were not helped when Gaumont released a comedy film shortly after the pageant, 'Lady Godiva Rides Again'. Directed by Frank Lauder, the film reveals how a young girl chosen to play the eponymous character during the Festival is subsequently thrust into the murky world of professional beauty pageants.[51]

Although Wrigg was indisputably the star of the show, seen by an estimated half a million onlookers, the pageant also featured episodes and tableaux celebrating the citizens of Coventry throughout history. These included displays of the history of local industries, from textiles to watchmaking, the struggle for women's rights, the successful campaign of eighteenth-century freemen for the franchise (which caused the sheriff to be put in the stocks) and, most recently, the Coventry Blitz.[52] As with the pageants held at Dudley and Carlisle, which revived the scripts of former pageants (held in 1908 and 1928 respectively), Coventry sought to channel earlier successful pageants while cautiously celebrating the social changes of post-war Britain.

National stories

In Wales and Scotland, historical pageants were important vehicles for expressing national identity and for stressing their autonomy from England. (Belfast, Londonderry, Carrickfergus and the Isle of Man also held pageants, with the first three resolutely loyalist in sentiment and the latter celebrating its Celtic and Norse heritages within an avowedly pro-British framework.)[53] The Cardiff pageant 'Land of My Fathers' featured many prominent Welsh cultural figures such as actor and film star Clifford Evans, novelist Jack Jones, poet and writer A. G. Prys-Jones and playwright David Monger. 'Land of My Fathers' was intended as an active contribution to Welsh culture, with the producer looking forwards to a future in which 'Wales may one day achieve a National Theatre of her own ... that will draw upon all the talent in Wales'. The pageant was framed by a Welsh boy explaining the importance of the Welsh national anthem, Welsh language and literature – and of course Welsh rugby – to an English boy; he declared that the true guardians of Welsh culture had always been the common people. The central scene of the pageant featured the rising of Owain Glyndŵr (*c*.1359–*c*.1416), whose ultimate defeat was presented as a rallying cry to modern Welsh nationalism.[54] The Pageant of Anglesey took the unprecedented step of conducting many scenes in Welsh, described by the *Holyhead and Anglesey Mail* as 'a labour of love ... which would help the children of Holyhead to preserve their glorious heritage in the history and language of Wales'. However, this caused it to be omitted from the national Festival guide and denied official Festival status, reserved for events performed solely in English.[55]

While Scottish pageants were less concerned with linguistic heritage, they also foregrounded a Scottish historical narrative separate from Britain. Arbroath's regular pageant (discussed in chapter 10) – which depicted the story of Scotland's struggle for independence from the execution of William Wallace to the signing of the Scottish Declaration of Independence in Arbroath Abbey in 1320 – was particularly freighted with nationalist sentiment during the Festival year. In April 1951 the Stone of Scone, which had been taken from Westminster Abbey the previous year, was deposited in the grounds of Arbroath Abbey by three anonymous men who – it later transpired – had been aided by the pageant's producer, F. W. A. Thornton, and treasurer, D. A. Gardner, although the organisers sought to distance these events from the pageant itself.[56]

All pageants were fiercely proud of their own local history, with several also using it as a means of emphasising local and non-national identities. Carlisle's pageant, for example, championed its liminal position between England and Scotland, its self-definition as a sturdily independent 'border city' being a marker of civic distinctiveness worthy of celebration.[57] Weston's pageant was at pains to stress its historical independence from Bath, whose boundaries had been redrawn earlier that year to subsume the village.[58] In Scotland several pageants celebrated a Highland or even a Norse identity rather than a Scottish-wide one.[59]

Although the peculiarities of disparate national and local identities were foregrounded in pageants, imperial and international scenes were noticeably absent, reflecting a wider lacuna across the Festival as a whole.[60] Relatively few pageants were held in port cities, previously the sites of the most overt displays of imperial-themed pageantry. Those that *were* held conspicuously avoided reference to historical events beyond the British Isles.[61] Likewise, in contrast to the major Festivals of Empire in 1911 and 1924, both of which featured huge pageants in London celebrating the British Empire, the Three Towns Pageant at Hampton Court avoided any reference to the empire; instead it focused on a blend of monarchical and social history pertaining to the Borough of Richmond.[62] If empire was mentioned at all in pageants, it tended to be presented as a further instance of ruling-class injustice, such as the Scrooby Puritans' flight from persecution to America in the Boston pageant or, at the East Grinstead pageant, James Stephen's resignation as the local MP during the Napoleonic War in protest against slavery.

Scenes which did present international themes were added to several pageants in the hope of appealing to American and other overseas tourists, who it was thought would travel to Britain during the Festival year in great numbers. It was hoped that Americans would be especially interested in British history and would make the trip to pageants in towns where their ancestors came from, or which had some connection to US cities. The Dartford pageant featured two American tourists who were told about the history of the town by their hosts.[63] The Boston pageant included scenes relating to the founding of Boston, Massachusetts, as well as speeches stressing the friendship between the two places and even a promotional film aimed at attracting visitors from its famous namesake. However, despite an extensive magazine advertising campaign for the Festival in America, there is little evidence that these strategies worked: the only Americans reported at Boston were the pilots of three fighter aircraft, whose unanticipated flyover disrupted one of the scenes.[64] Some commentators saw these desperate ploys for hard currency as a reflection of Britain's diminished global status. In the run up to the Festival one correspondent to the *Yorkshire Post* suggested

> that a suitable pageant to celebrate the achievements of our country at the opening of the Festival of Britain would be for Mr Attlee to come by water to the [South Bank] site, travelling in a replica of Nelson's Victory, and hand over the British Navy to Mr. Truman.[65]

Legacies of the Festival

While 7,000 people saw the East Grinstead pageant (at a time when the population of the town was less than 11,000), it made a loss of £392. To make matters worse, several guarantors refused to pay up, forcing the council and members of the public to pay the rest.[66] Despite the Quite Ordinary Man's exhortations to the people of East Grinstead to shake off the shackles of oppression, the town's Conservative MP was returned with an increased majority in the October general election which swept away the Attlee government.[67] The newly-elected Conservative government continued in the vein of previous hostility to the Festival of Britain by dismantling much of the South Bank site. For its supporters, the Festival represented the high-water mark of socialist Britain; its detractors saw it as costly hubris. In both cases, the perceived results were equivocal. As critics of the 'affluent' 1950s noted, the working classes seemed much happier enjoying consumer goods and supposedly mindless mass entertainment than celebrating their shared history and collective future.[68]

Several pageants lost money due to the exceptionally poor weather throughout the summer which ruined or forced the cancellation of performances at Alnwick,[69] Anglesey,[70] Arbroath,[71] Barton-under-Needwood,[72] Bedale,[73] Brandanes,[74] Cambridge,[75] Dartford,[76] Drum Castle,[77] Dudley[78] and Rothesay.[79] Even where performances went ahead, the most civic-minded of audiences often proved unwilling to sit in a cold grandstand exposed to the elements for three or four hours, and attendances fell below expectations. The Ipswich pageant was dogged by poor plumbing and foul odours, prompting a letter to the *Ipswich Evening Star* suggesting that the town would have better spent its money on upgrading the sewerage works, with another local wit declaring that 'Ipswich for their pageant have included a festival of smells'.[80]

Many pageants, particularly larger ones, struggled due to their proximity to London. Earlier pageants had benefited from being on a direct train line to the capital and had often advertised discount fares to audiences yearning to escape the city to witness a depiction of the picturesque history of the English countryside – but during the Festival year precisely the reverse happened. Eight-and-a-half million people visited the South Bank exhibition during 1951, with roughly the same number visiting the Battersea Pleasure Gardens, of whom 56 per cent travelled from areas of Britain outside London. By contrast barely one million visited other official Festival sites or exhibitions around the country.[81] 'It's too remote' and 'it's London's show' were widely-held local views offered to the *Birmingham Daily Gazette*, explaining the failure of many pageants and other Festival events in the West Midlands.[82]

At a time when pageants had a hard time encouraging local residents to attend, hopes for visitors from the rest of Britain and overseas proved optimistic at best. Provision was made for 85,000 spectators at the Rochester Dickens Pageant (across 14 performances), but only 19,000 turned out to watch, losing the city £6,100. The meagre turnout could hardly have been helped by the price of admission being higher than at the South Bank.[83] Even East Grinstead, which put on late buses and a special 'midnight train' to London, struggled to attract substantial numbers of visitors.[84] Amateur presentations of often obscure local history, with unconvincing wooden swords and knitted chain mail, could not compete with the presentation of gleaming modernity on offer at the South Bank site. Those that attempted to offer such competition fell short by comparison.

The well-publicised failure of large-scale pageants did much to dissuade potential organisers in subsequent years. Only two pageants with more than 2,000 performers were held for the coronation in 1953 – at St Albans and Warwick (which respectively lost £1,206 and £6,349) – down from six held during the Festival.[85] During the 1950s pageants gradually ceased to be a mainstay of the British summertime. Michael Frayn's celebrated essay on the Festival outlined two competing visions of Britain in the early 1950s: that of the 'Herbivores' – 'philanthropic, kindly, whimsical, cosy, optimistic, middlebrow' – who had organised the Festival and who had been eclipsed by the 'Carnivores', exemplified by the Conservative Party.[86] The successes and failures of the thousands of well-meaning do-gooders, almost all from the progressive middle classes, who staged pageants during the Festival in the hope of demonstrating to people the radical nature of their own history, seem to confirm Frayn's reading.

While the Festival of Britain did not create a new citizenry, as some of its more optimistic or even utopian planners had hoped, it did succeed in restoring and stimulating many local communities. The most successful pageants, which tended to be in places remote from London, actively presented themselves as offering visions of local authenticity and community, in stark contrast to the expensive and slightly baffling pseudo-utopia constructed in the capital. Writing to the *Monmouthshire Beacon* after the Raglan pageant, W. Allen John thanked the organisers 'for choosing to attempt something so ambitious and "out of the run"'; he contrasted their efforts with 'the obvious, and somewhat lightweight' celebrations offered at the South Bank site (for example, 'the Fun Fair at Battersea Park').[87] Enthusiastic participants in several pageants went on to restage them in subsequent years and even formed local dramatic groups to put on plays. After the Monmouth pageant, for example, the Buckholt WI announced that it was forming a permanent dramatic section.[88] Pageanteers from Headley went on to form the Headley Theatre Club, which staged subsequent shows, including pageants for the coronation of Elizabeth II and, much later, the millennium; its stated mission was '[t]o unite the village in good fellowship', continuing the Festival's communitarian ideals.[89]

Pageants and other Festival events raised substantial sums for local buildings and charities that were otherwise forced to go without during a prolonged period of austerity. At Wollaston over £70 was raised, which went towards building tennis courts and a children's playground.[90] Chippenham raised money to build homes for older people, and the Ewelme pageant in Oxfordshire raised over £200, which was used to provide plumbing for the local school. Ewelme was also, like Bradgate in Leicestershire, one of several pageants which successfully raised funds to restore church bells or clocks.[91] While few pageants raised significant sums of money – indeed, almost every large pageant made a considerable loss – they were often fondly remembered long after the acrimonious disputes about who would pay for the losses had been forgotten: several places, including Chippenham, have recently staged exhibitions to remember their Festival celebrations.[92]

Despite widespread scepticism and apathy, local celebrations of the Festival – of which pageants were the largest and most culturally significant examples – showed that many people in post-war Britain had taken its themes of community, localism and citizenship to heart. Although these 'Herbivores' may not have quite succeeded in their peaceful revolution, the Festival did reflect the altered culture and class structure of post-war Britain. Above all, pageants held during the Festival demonstrated that history belonged, first and foremost, to the 'ordinary people'. Despite a return to more traditional depictions of the monarchy and aristocracy during the coronation year, subsequent pageants would continue to include depictions of the ordinary sorts, echoed by the growing popularity of new forms of social history from the 1960s onwards. The era in which the upper classes possessed both the leisure and money to dress up as their ancestors and demonstrate their social superiority had passed, and Britain had become more equal: something which the incoming Conservative government was quick to note. Speaking to the children who performed in the Arundel pageant, only a year before her accession to the throne, Princess Elizabeth declared that

> they who portrayed the past, held the future in their hands, and would all in some degree affect the course of history. By learning now to be good citizens, their influence could not fail to be good.[93]

It was an utterance that reflected a new sense of popular history, and one that the Festival pageants had done much to promote.

Appendix

Pageants held for the Festival of Britain

For villages and small towns, the county is given.

Cancelled pageants

Bath, Burton-on-Trent, Buxton, Cannock (Staffordshire), Daventry, Lennoxtown (Dunbartonshire), Paignton, Sevenoaks, Stroud, Swynnerton (Staffordshire), Tewkesbury, Turriff (Aberdeenshire).

Fewer than 500 performers

Abbotshall (Fifeshire), Alnwick, Anglesey, Astley (Warwickshire), Aylesbury, Barrow-upon-Humber, Barton-under-Needwood (Staffordshire), Basingstoke, Bathgate (West Lothian), Birmingham, Bolton Castle, Bradgate (Leicestershire), Brandanes, Bungay, Burnley, Cambridge, Canvey Island, Carmarthenshire, Chesterfield, Chichester, Chippenham, Colne (two pageants), Croston (Lancashire), Croxley Green (Hertfordshire), Croydon, Derby, Diss (Norfolk), Ditchling (Sussex), Eastwood (Nottinghamshire), Edwardstone (Suffolk), Eltham (Kent), Ely, Ewelme (Oxfordshire), Glamorgan, Glastonbury, Grimsby, Hambledon Hill (Dorset), Harrow, Hartlepool, Hawes, Headley, Hellesdon (Norfolk), Helmsley (North Yorkshire), Horden (County Durham), Hunmanby (North Yorkshire), Inverness, Kettering, Kirkcudbright (Dumfries), Leek Wootton (Warwickshire), Leicester, Leiston (Suffolk), Llandaff, London (Friend's House), London (East End), Longlevens School (Gloucestershire), Maidenhead, Monmouthshire, Morpeth (Northumberland), Newcastle, Padiham (Lancashire), Penrith, Portsmouth, Rushden (Northamptonshire), Sandwell (Staffordshire), Sollarshope (Herefordshire), South Norwood, Southampton, Southbourne (Dorset), St Andrews, Streatham, Thorncliffe (West Yorkshire), Todmorden, Uxbridge, Walsall, Welshpool (Montgomeryshire), Westminster, Walsgrave on Sowe (Warwickshire), Weston (Somerset), Whitby, Wollaston (Northamptonshire), Wraysbury (Buckinghamshire).

Between 500 and 1,000 performers

Barmouth (Gwynedd), Belfast, Blenheim, Boston, Canterbury, Carrickfergus, Colchester, Dagenham, Drum Castle (Aberdeenshire), Dudley, East Grinstead, Herefordshire, Isle of Man, Liverpool, Londonderry, Malvern, Paulsgrove (Hampshire), Newcastle, Rhondda Valley, Rothesay (Argyllshire), Swansea, Walsall.

Between 1,000 and 2,000 performers

Arundel, Bedale (North Yorkshire), Brighton, Dartford, Hitchin, London (Albert Hall, two pageants), Raglan.

More than 2,000 performers

Cardiff, Carlisle, Coventry, Hampton Court, Ipswich, Rochester.

Notes

1. Becky Conekin, *'The Autobiography of a Nation': The 1951 Festival of Britain* (Manchester: Manchester University Press, 2003), 84–100.
2. Steven Fielding, Peter Thompson and Nick Tiratsoo, *'England Arise!': The Labour Party and Popular Politics in 1940s Britain* (Manchester: Manchester University Press, 1995), 217; Steven Fielding, '"To Make Men and Women Better than They Are": Labour and the Building of Socialism', in *Labour's Promised Land?: Culture and Society in Labour Britain*, ed. Jim Fryth (London: Lawrence & Wishart, 1995), 16–27; Becky E. Conekin, '"No Glorious Assurance": The 1951 Festival of Britain Looks at the Victorian Past', in *The Victorians Since 1901: Histories, Representations and Revisions*, ed. Miles Taylor and Michael Wolff (Manchester: Manchester University Press, 2004), 138–49; Becky Conekin, '"Here is the Modern World Itself": The Festival of Britain's Representation of the Future' in *Moments of Modernity: Reconstructing Britain, 1945–1964*, ed. Frank Mort, Becky Conekin and Chris Waters (London: Rivers Oram, 1999), 228–46.
3. Barry Turner, *Beacon for Change: How the 1951 Festival of Britain Helped to Shape a New Age* (London: Aurum Press, 2011); Harriet Atkinson, *The Festival of Britain: A Land and Its People* (London: I. B. Tauris, 2012); R. C. Richardson, 'Cultural Mapping in 1951: The Festival of Britain Regional Guidebooks', *Literature and History* 24 (2015): 53–72; Simon Featherstone, *Englishness: Twentieth-Century Popular Culture and the Forming of English Identity* (Edinburgh: Edinburgh University Press, 2008), 50–4; Inyang Isola Ime Ebong, 'The Origins, Organisation and Significance of the Festival of Britain' (Unpublished PhD diss., University of Edinburgh, 1986).
4. *Daily Mail, Festival of Britain 1951: Preview and Guide* (London: *Daily Mail*, 1951), 58–78; J. B. Priestley, *Festival at Farbridge* (London: William Heinemann, 1951).
5. Of the information on over 100 pageants held during the Festival year, I have found one, 'Truth On the March', a communist pageant held to commemorate the twenty-first anniversary of the *Daily Worker*, which was not explicitly part of the Festival celebrations: Angela Bartie, Linda Fleming, Mark Freeman, Tom Hulme, Alex Hutton, Paul Readman, '"Truth on the March": A Pageant of the Press in the Struggle for Peace', *The Redress of the Past*, http://www.historicalpageants.ac.uk/pageants/1372/ (accessed 25 February 2019).
6. *Manchester Guardian*, 4 May 1951, 3.
7. Claire Langhamer, '"Who the Hell Are Ordinary People?": Ordinariness as a Category of Historical Analysis', *Transactions of the Royal Historical Society* 28 (2018): 175–95; Alan Sinfield, 'The Government, the People and the Festival', in *Labour's Promised Land?*, ed. Jim Fryth, 181–96.
8. *Daily Mail*, 13 June 1951, 23.
9. On fears of public apathy in the 1950s, see Lawrence Black, *The Political Culture of the Left in Affluent Britain, 1951–64: Old Labour, New Britain?* (Basingstoke: Palgrave Macmillan, 2003); *An Affluent Society?: Britain's Post-War 'Golden Age' Revisited*, ed. Lawrence Black and Hugh Pemberton (Aldershot: Ashgate, 2004).
10. *Daily Express*, 17 January 1951, 5 and 6 February 1951, 3.
11. *Yorkshire Post and Leeds Intelligencer*, 7 July 1951, 8.
12. *Halifax Daily Courier and Guardian*, 3 January 1948, 2; *Yorkshire Evening Post*, 21 April 1948, 4. Although Leeds was a regional centre of the Festival, hosting the touring exhibition, the council did relatively little aside from organising 'Festival' football matches: Conekin, *'Autobiography of a Nation'*, 180–1.
13. Iain Wilton, '"Continuous Abuse" or "A Unanimous Blessing"? Reassessing the Conservative Party's Stance on the 1951 Festival of Britain', *Contemporary British History* 31 (2017): 546–67.
14. Bryan Keith-Lucas and Peter G. Richards, *A History of Local Government in the Twentieth Century* (London: G. Allen & Unwin, 1978), 12, 52, 149–50; Matthew Cragoe, '"We Like Local Patriotism": The Conservative Party and the Discourse of Decentralisation', *English Historical Review* 122 (2007): 979–80.
15. *Sevenoaks and Kentish Advertiser*, 23 December 1949, 1.
16. *Sevenoaks and Kentish Advertiser*, 1 September 1950, 3.
17. *Hartlepool Northern Daily Mail*, 12 March 1951, 2.
18. *Bath Chronicle and Weekly Gazette*, 29 July 1950, 7.

19. *Bath Chronicle and Weekly Gazette*, 21 October 1950, 1 and 16 December 1950, 5; *Manchester Guardian*, 22 May 1951, 5.
20. *Birmingham Daily Gazette*, 21 July 1951, 3.
21. Peter Pindar, 'Paignton Talk', *Torbay Express and South Devon Echo*, 6 December 1949; 30 September 1950, 4; 2 October 1950, 2.
22. *Northampton Mercury*, 8 December 1950, 6; 15 December 1950, 8; 15 February 1951, 2; 13 April 1951, 7.
23. East Sussex Record Office, DB/B/262/4, Council Minutes, 11 September 1950. On the link with Siam, see *Manchester Guardian*, 30 July 1951, 4.
24. East Sussex, DB/D/62/60, Minutes Festival of Britain Publicity Sub-Committee, 13 April 1951 and DB/B/262/4, Council Minutes, 15 October 1951; Clifford Musgrave, *Life in Brighton* (London: Faber, 1970), 397; Angela Bartie, Linda Fleming, Mark Freeman, Tom Hulme, Alex Hutton, Paul Readman, 'Brighton Pageant 1951', *The Redress of the Past,* http://www.historicalpageants.ac.uk/pageants/1266/ (accessed 28 June 2019).
25. *Newcastle Journal*, 10 April 1951, 5.
26. Kent Local History Centre, DA/Ac/74, Literature and correspondence concerning the Festival of Britain Dartford Historical Pageant, L. Lack to T. Armstrong, 4 July 1951.
27. Kent, DA/Ac/74, Grace Blakes to Armstrong, 24 June 1951.
28. Kent, DA/Ac/74, A. E. Allison to Armstrong, 1 August 1951; Margaret Thatcher [née Roberts], 'Speech in Crayford', 6 February 1950, https://www.margaretthatcher.org/document/100863 and 'Speech to Belvedere Conservatives', 6 July 1951, Margaret Thatcher Foundation, http://www.margaretthatcher.org/document/100907 (both accessed 19 April 2020); Angela Bartie, Linda Fleming, Mark Freeman, Tom Hulme, Alex Hutton, Paul Readman, 'Festival of Britain Dartford Historical Pageant 1951', *The Redress of the Past*, http://www.historicalpageants.ac.uk/pageants/1274/ (accessed 21 June 2018).
29. David Cannadine, *Making History Now and Then* (Basingstoke: Palgrave Macmillan, 2008), 123–7; David Cannadine, *Decline and Fall of the British Aristocracy* (New Haven and London: Yale University Press, 1990), 644.
30. *Sevenoaks and Kentish Advertiser*, 29 September 1950, 1.
31. Angela Bartie, Linda Fleming, Mark Freeman, Tom Hulme, Alex Hutton, Paul Readman, 'Carlisle Historical Pageant 1951', *The Redress of the Past,* http://www.historicalpageants.ac.uk/pageants/1024/ (accessed 21 June 2018).
32. *The Stage*, 26 July 1951, 13.
33. *Festival of Britain 1951: A Pageant of Basingstoke History* (Basingstoke: Hankin's Duplicating Service, Basingstoke, 1951), unpaginated, copy in Hampshire Record Office, 50A07/E27.
34. Mick Wallis, 'Pageantry and the Popular Front: Ideological Production in the "Thirties"', *New Theatre Quarterly* 10 (1994): 132–56; Mick Wallis, 'The Popular Front Pageant: Its Emergence and Decline', *New Theatre Quarterly* 11 (1995): 17–32.
35. Ian Cox, *The South Bank Exhibition: A Guide to the Story It Tells* (London: His Majesty's Stationery Office, 1951), 68; Conekin, '*Autobiography of a Nation*', 84–7, 98–100; Conekin, 'No "Glorious Assurance"'.
36. Cyril G. Faulkner, 'Civic Foreword', in *Pageant of Rushden, 1951* (Rushden: n.p., 1951), unpaginated.
37. L. V. Elliott, 'Introduction', in *Pageant of Rushden*, unpaginated; Angela Bartie, Linda Fleming, Mark Freeman, Tom Hulme, Alex Hutton, Paul Readman, 'Pageant of Rushden', *The Redress of the Past,* http://www.historicalpageants.ac.uk/pageants/1180/ (accessed 21 June 2018).
38. *Barnoldswick and Earby Times*, 17 August 1951, 5.
39. *Lincolnshire Standard and Boston Guardian*, 9 June 1951, 10.
40. *Manchester Guardian*, 4 May 1951, 3.
41. *Rushden Echo and Argus*, 12 October 1951 and 16 November 1951.
42. *The Pageant of Dudley* (Dudley: n.p., 1951), unpaginated; *Northampton Mercury*, 6 July 1951, 2.
43. *East Grinstead Through the Ages* (East Grinstead: n.p., 1951), unpaginated, copy in West Sussex History Centre, Lib 5341–2; 'The Festival Out of Town', *Punch*, 18 July 1951, 62.
44. *East Grinstead Through the Ages* (East Grinstead: n.p., 1951), unpaginated, copy in West Sussex History Centre, Lib 5341–2; *Punch*, 18 July 1951, 62; 'Pageant Celebrates', *Crawley News,* 15 July 2010; Angela Bartie, Linda Fleming, Mark Freeman, Tom Hulme, Alex Hutton, Paul Readman, 'A Pageant of East Grinstead', *The Redress of the Past*, http://www.historicalpageants.ac.uk/pageants/1056/ (accessed 25 February 2019).

45. Eveline Clarke, *Pageant of Headley* (Farnham: n.p., 1951), 2, 29, 47, copy in Surrey Local History Centre, PSH.HED/22/33–4; Angela Bartie, Linda Fleming, Mark Freeman, Tom Hulme, Alex Hutton, Paul Readman, 'Pageant of Headley', *The Redress of the Past,* http://www.historical pageants.ac.uk/pageants/1091/ (accessed 25 February 2019).
46. *Pageant of Womanhood* (Southampton: n.p., 1951), unpaginated, copy in Hull History Centre, U DCW/8/4/f.
47. *Monmouthshire Beacon*, 13 July 1951, 3. On the presentation of women's history in pageants see Zoë Thomas, 'Historical Pageants, Citizenship, and the Performance of Women's History before Second-Wave Feminism', *Twentieth Century British History* 28 (2017): 319–43.
48. Ronald Aquilla Clarke and Patrick A. E. Day, *Lady Godiva: Images of a Legend in Art and Society* (Coventry: City of Coventry Leisure Services, Arts and Museums Division, 1982).
49. Leonard Turner, 'Foreword', in *Coventry Festival of Britain Godiva Pageant* (Coventry: n.p., 1951), 20; *Chicago Tribune*, 15 February 1951, 99.
50. *Manchester Guardian*, 17 February 1951, 4.
51. *Manchester Guardian*, 28 October 1951, 6; 'Lady Godiva Rides Again', Internet Movie Database, https://www.imdb.com/title/tt0043719/ (accessed 21 June 2018).
52. *Godiva Pageant*, 35; Angela Bartie, Linda Fleming, Mark Freeman, Tom Hulme, Alex Hutton, Paul Readman, 'Coventry Festival of Britain Godiva Pageant', *The Redress of the Past,* http://www.historicalpageants.ac.uk/pageants/1043/ (accessed 21 June 2018).
53. *Observer*, 24 June 1951, 5; *Daily Mail, Festival of Britain*, 58; Conekin, *'Autobiography of a Nation'*, 169, 171–2; Maurice Powell, 'The Isle of Man Festival of Britain Pageants, 1951', http://www.manxmusic.com/media/News%20images%202017/The%20Pageant%20of%20the%20Isle%20of%20Man%20or%20Manx%20Pageant.pdf (accessed 21 June 2018).
54. Clifford Evans, 'A Message from the Producer', in *'The Land of My Fathers': A Pageant Play of Wales* (Cardiff: William Lewis, 1951), unpaginated, copy at National Library of Wales, 2011 XC 1327; Conekin, *'Autobiography of a Nation'*, 170–1; Angela Bartie, Linda Fleming, Mark Freeman, Tom Hulme, Alex Hutton, Paul Readman, 'The Land of My Fathers', *The Redress of the Past,* http://www.historicalpageants.ac.uk/pageants/1116/ (accessed 21 June 2018).
55. *Holyhead and Anglesey Mail*, 22 June 1951, 6; Atkinson, *Festival of Britain*, 129–31.
56. *Manchester Guardian*, 12 April 1951, 5; *The Times*, 12 April 1951, 6; J. N. Graham Ritchie, 'Images of the Declaration: The Arbroath Pageant', in *The Declaration of Arbroath: History, Significance, Setting*, ed. Geoffrey Barrow (Edinburgh: Edinburgh University Press, 2003), 86–107; Angela Bartie, Linda Fleming, Mark Freeman, Tom Hulme, Alex Hutton, Paul Readman, 'Arbroath Abbey Pageant 1951', *The Redress of the Past,* http://www.historicalpageants.ac.uk/pageants/959/ (accessed 21 June 2018).
57. See 'A Festival of Border History: the Carlisle Pageant, 1951', http://www.historical pageants.ac.uk/featured-pageants/festival-border-history-carlisle-pageant-1951/ (accessed 21 February 2020)
58. *A Weston Miscellany* (Weston: Weston Village Townswomen's Guild, 1999), 37–8.
59. *A Pageant of the Brandanes to Mark the 550th Anniversary of the Granting of the Royal Charter to the Burgh of Rothesay, Souvenir Programme* (n.p., [1951]), unpaginated; Angela Bartie, Linda Fleming, Mark Freeman, Tom Hulme, Alex Hutton, Paul Readman, 'A Pageant of the Brandanes, 1401–1951', *The Redress of the Past,* http://www.historicalpageants.ac.uk/pageants/1176/ (accessed 21 June 2018).
60. Conekin, *'Autobiography of a Nation'*, 183–202; Alayna Heinonen, 'A Tonic to the Empire?: The 1951 Festival of Britain and the Empire-Commonwealth', *Britain and the* World 8 (2005): 76–99; Jo Littler, '"Festering Britain": The 1951 Festival of Britain, National Identity and the Representation of the Commonwealth', in *Visual Culture and Decolonisation In Britain*, ed. Anandi Ramamurthy and Simon Faulkner (Farnham: Ashgate, 2006), 21–42; Wendy Webster, *Englishness and Empire 1939–1965* (Oxford: Oxford University Press, 2007), 93.
61. Paul Readman, 'Commemorating the Past in Edwardian Hampshire: King Alfred, Pageantry and Empire', in *Southampton: Gateway to the British Empire*, ed. Miles Taylor (London: I. B. Tauris, 2007), 95–113.
62. Angela Bartie, Linda Fleming, Mark Freeman, Tom Hulme, Alex Hutton, Paul Readman, 'The Three Towns Pageants', *The Redress of the Past*, http://www.historicalpageants.ac.uk/pageants/1324/ (accessed 21 June 2018); Deborah Sugg Ryan, 'Staging the Imperial City: The Pageant of London, 1911' in *Imperial Cities: Landscape, Display and Identity*, ed. Felix Driver and David Gilbert (Manchester: Manchester University Press, 1999), 117–35.

63. *Daily Mail*, *Festival of Britain 1951*, 58; Mariel Grant, '"Working for the Yankee Dollar": Tourism and the Festival of Britain as Stimuli for Recovery', *Journal of British Studies* 45 (2006): 581–601; Atkinson, *Festival of Britain*, 21–3; *Festival of Britain Dartford Historical Pageant 1951* (Dartford: n.p., 1951), unpaginated; Turner, 'Foreword', 20.
64. *Lincolnshire Standard and Boston Guardian*, 9 June 1951, 8; 'A Boston Story (1951)', BFI Archive, http://www.bfi.org.uk/films-tv-people/4ce2b6f7d39d1 (accessed 21 June 2018); *Lincolnshire Standard and Boston Guardian*, 9 June 1951, 10.
65. *Yorkshire Post and Leeds Intelligencer*, 27 February 1951, 2.
66. *Crawley and District Observer*, 26 October 1951, 14; M. J. Leppard, *A History of East Grinstead* (Chichester: Phillimore & Co. Ltd, 2001), 165.
67. Brian R. Mitchell and Klaus Boehm, *British Parliamentary Election Results 1950–1964* (Cambridge: Cambridge University Press, 1966), 42.
68. Conekin, *'Autobiography of a Nation'*, 232–6; Atkinson, *Festival of Britain*, 190–3.
69. *Morpeth Herald*, 10 August 1951, 4.
70. *Holyhead and Anglesey Mail*, 15 June 1951, 8.
71. *Dundee Courier*, 20 August 1951, 2.
72. *Staffordshire Advertiser*, 15 June 1951, 3.
73. *Yorkshire Post and Leeds Intelligencer*, 18 July 1951, 8.
74. *Glasgow Herald*, 21 June 1951, 4.
75. 'Rain (Almost) Stopped Play: Cambridge and the 1951 Festival of Britain', https://musicb3.wordpress.com/2011/07/13/rain-almost-stopped-play-cambridge-and-the-1951-festival-of-britain/ (accessed 21 June 2018).
76. Kent, DA/Ac/74, Armstrong to F. H. Ager, 30 August 1951.
77. *Aberdeen Evening Express*, 27 August 1951, 4.
78. Michael Pearson, *The Little Book of the Black Country* (Stroud: The History Press, 2014), 125; *Staffordshire Advertiser*, 15 June 1951, 5.
79. *Glasgow Herald*, 21 June 1951, 4.
80. *Ipswich Evening Star*, 12 June 1951, 4 and 14 June 1951, 4; Angela Bartie, Linda Fleming, Mark Freeman, Tom Hulme, Alex Hutton, Paul Readman, 'The Ipswich Pageant', *The Redress of the Past*, http://www.historicalpageants.ac.uk/pageants/1100/ (accessed 21 June 2018).
81. Conekin, *'Autobiography of a Nation'*, 4, 223 n. 92; Richardson, 'Cultural Mapping in 1951', 54.
82. *Birmingham Daily Gazette*, 3 May 1951, 4.
83. *The Times*, 21 September 1951, 3; Conekin, *'Autobiography of a Nation'*, 46–67.
84. *West Sussex County Times*, 15 June 1951, 4.
85. Figures from the *Redress of the Past* database: http://www.historicalpageants.ac.uk/pageants/ (accessed 21 June 2018).
86. Michael Frayn, 'Festival', *Age of Austerity, 1945–51*, ed. Michael Sissons and Philip French (London: Hodder & Stoughton, 1963), 320; Robert Hewison, *Culture and Consensus: England, Art and Politics since 1940* (London: Routledge, 1995), 62.
87. *Monmouthshire Beacon*, 13 July 1951, 3.
88. *Monmouthshire Observer*, 15 February 1952, 6.
89. John Owen Smith, 'A Brief History of Headley Theatre Club', http://www.johnowensmith.co.uk/htc/history.htm (accessed 21 June 2018).
90. *Northampton Mercury*, 20 July 1951, 2.
91. South Oxford Diocesan Guild of Church Bell Ringers, http://southoxonodg.co.uk/html/february-2010-newsletter.html (accessed 21 June 2018); 'Church clock – All Saints – Newtown Linford, Leicestershire, UK Historical Markers, http://www.waymarking.com/waymarks/WMY3JE_Church_clock_All_Saints_Newtown_Linford_Leicestershire (accessed 21 June 2018).
92. 'Exhibition Revisits Festival of Britain in Chippenham 65 Years on', *Gazette and Herald*, 12 October 2016: http://www.gazetteandherald.co.uk/news/headlines/nostalgia/14797003.Exhibition_revisits_Festival_of_Britain_in_Chippenham_65_years_on/ (accessed 21 June 2018).
93. *The Times*, 21 May 1951, 2.

Bibliography

Atkinson, Harriet. 2012. *The Festival of Britain: A Land and Its People*. London: I. B. Tauris.

Black, Lawrence. 2003. *The Political Culture of the Left in Affluent Britain, 1951–64: Old Labour, New Britain?* Basingstoke: Palgrave Macmillan.

Black, Lawrence and Pemberton, Hugh, eds. 2004. *An Affluent Society?: Britain's Post-War 'Golden Age' Revisited*. Aldershot: Ashgate.

Cannadine, David. 1990. *Decline and Fall of the British Aristocracy*. New Haven and London: Yale University Press.

Cannadine, David. 2008. *Making History Now and Then*. Basingstoke: Palgrave Macmillan, 2008.

Clarke, Ronald Aquilla and Day, Patrick A. E. 1982. *Lady Godiva: Images of a Legend in Art and Society*. Coventry: City of Coventry Leisure Services, Arts and Museums Division.

Conekin, Becky. 1999. '"Here is the Modern World Itself": The Festival of Britain's Representation of the Future', in *Moments of Modernity: Reconstructing Britain, 1945–1964*, edited by Frank Mort, Becky Conekin and Chris Waters. London: Rivers Oram, 228–46.

Conekin, Becky. 2003. *'The Autobiography of a Nation': The 1951 Festival of Britain*. Manchester: Manchester University Press.

Conekin, Becky. 2004. '"No Glorious Assurance": The 1951 Festival of Britain Looks at the Victorian Past', in *The Victorians Since 1901: Histories, Representations and Revisions*, edited by Miles Taylor and Michael Wolff. Manchester: Manchester University Press, 138–49.

Cragoe, Matthew. 2007. '"We Like Local Patriotism": The Conservative Party and the Discourse of Decentralisation', *English Historical Review* 122: 965–85.

Ebong, Inyang Isola Ime. 1986. 'The Origins, Organisation and Significance of the Festival of Britain.' Unpublished PhD diss., University of Edinburgh.

Featherstone, Simon. 2008. *Englishness: Twentieth-Century Popular Culture and the Forming of English Identity*. Edinburgh: Edinburgh University Press.

Fielding, Steven. 1995. '"To Make Men and Women Better than They Are": Labour and the Building of Socialism', in *Labour's Promised Land?: Culture and Society in Labour Britain*, edited by Jim Fryth. London: Lawrence & Wishart, 16–27.

Fielding, Steven, Thompson, Peter and Tiratsoo, Nick. 1995. *'England Arise!': The Labour Party and Popular Politics in 1940s Britain*. Manchester: Manchester University Press.

Frayn, Michael. 1963. 'Festival', in *Age of Austerity, 1945–51*, edited by Michael Sissons and Philip French. London: Hodder & Stoughton, 319–38.

Fryth, Jim, ed. 1995. *Labour's Promised Land?: Culture and Society in Labour Britain*. London: Lawrence & Wishart.

Grant, Mariel. 2006 '"Working for the Yankee Dollar": Tourism and the Festival of Britain as Stimuli for Recovery', *Journal of British Studies* 45: 581–601.

Heinonen, Alayna. 2005. 'A Tonic to the Empire?: The 1951 Festival of Britain and the Empire-Commonwealth', *Britain and the World* 8: 76–99.

Hewison, Robert. 1995. *Culture and Consensus: England, Art and Politics since 1940*. London: Routledge.

Keith-Lucas, Bryan and Richards, Peter G. 1978. *A History of Local Government in the Twentieth Century*. London: G. Allen & Unwin.

Langhamer, Claire. 2018. '"Who the Hell Are Ordinary People?": Ordinariness as a Category of Historical Analysis', *Transactions of the Royal Historical Society* 28: 175–95.

Littler, Jo. 2006. '"Festering Britain": The 1951 Festival of Britain, National Identity and the Representation of the Commonwealth', in *Visual Culture and Decolonisation in Britain*, edited by Anandi Ramamurthy and Simon Faulkner. Farnham: Ashgate, 21–42.

Mitchell, Brian R. and Boehm, Klaus. 1966. *British Parliamentary Election Results 1950–1964*. Cambridge: Cambridge University Press.

Pearson, Michael. 2014. *The Little Book of the Black Country*. Stroud: The History Press.

Readman, Paul. 2007. 'Commemorating the Past in Edwardian Hampshire: King Alfred, Pageantry, and Empire', in *Southampton: Gateway to the British Empire*, edited by Miles Taylor. London: I. B. Tauris, 95–113.

Richardson, R. C. 2015. 'Cultural Mapping in 1951: The Festival of Britain Regional Guidebooks', *Literature and History* 24: 53–72.

Ritchie, J. N. Graham. 2003. 'Images of the Declaration: The Arbroath Pageant', in *The Declaration of Arbroath: History, Significance, Setting*, edited by Geoffrey Barrow. Edinburgh: Edinburgh University Press, 86–107.

Ryan, Deborah Sugg. 1999. 'Staging the Imperial City: The Pageant of London, 1911', in *Imperial Cities: Landscape, Display and Identity*, edited by Felix Driver and David Gilbert. Manchester: Manchester University Press, 117–35.

Sinfield, Alan. 1995. 'The Government, the People and the Festival', in *Labour's Promised Land?: Culture and Society in Labour Britain*, edited by Jim Fryth. London: Lawrence & Wishart, 181–96.

Thomas, Zoë. 2017. 'Historical Pageants, Citizenship, and the Performance of Women's History before Second-Wave Feminism', *Twentieth Century British History* 28: 319–43.

Turner, Barry. 2011. *Beacon for Change: How the 1951 Festival of Britain Helped to Shape a New Age*. London: Aurum Press.

Wallis, Mick. 1994. 'Pageantry and the Popular Front: Ideological Production in the "Thirties"', *New Theatre Quarterly* 10: 132–56.

Wallis, Mick. 1996. 'The Popular Front Pageant: Its Emergence and Decline', *New Theatre Quarterly* 11: 17–32.

Webster, Wendy. 2007. *Englishness and Empire 1939–1965*. Oxford: Oxford University Press, 2007.

Wilton, Iain. '"Continuous Abuse" or "A Unanimous Blessing"? Reassessing the Conservative Party's Stance on the 1951 Festival of Britain', *Contemporary British History* 31: 546–67.

10
'The Scots' Pageant': The Arbroath Abbey Pageants 1947–2005

Linda Fleming

The Arbroath Abbey Pageant – which celebrated the Declaration of Scottish Independence of 1320, popularly known as the Declaration of Arbroath – has two claims to fame when considered within the overall framework of British historical pageantry. First is its longevity: initially performed in the ruins of Arbroath Abbey in 1947, the pageant has been held 18 times between 1947 and 2005.[1] Its status as the most frequently staged pageant in the UK is to date unbeaten. Its second hallmark relates to its politics. Most historical pageants in twentieth-century Britain were political in some sense, in that they incorporated often contested issues of local, national and imperial identities; a good number were even organised by political parties and activist pressure groups, from the Communist Party of Great Britain to the Tory Primrose League. However, the Arbroath Pageant provides a particularly clear example of how the questions of identity addressed in pageant performances might relate to the politics of nationalism. Although it began as a modest fundraiser, Arbroath's pageant very quickly came to rejoice in the title of the 'Scots' Pageant'.[2] The pageant's subject matter centred on the claims for national self-determination made during the Wars of Independence against England (*c.* 1296–1328); in doing so, it intersected with contemporaneous debates about Scotland's status within the United Kingdom.

The Arbroath Pageant never incorporated any of the usual mass signifiers of Scottish identity popular in the mid-twentieth century: there were no bagpipes, tartan or sentimental songs about Highland glens. Instead there was religiosity, solemnity and a clarion call to defend national autonomy. For many involved, Scotland's fourteenth-century struggle to remain an independent nation was a story of much relevance in post-war Britain, when economic and social planning and policymaking had become increasingly centralised in London.[3] This development formed an important backdrop to the pageants. Without doubt some of the more romantic readings of the significance of the declaration played to the views of those concerned about a governmental system in which major decisions affecting Scotland were being made in England. Certainly accusations that the pageant was a vehicle for this critique of increasing Anglo-centricity would dog the event, though its organisers always hotly denied charges of separatist political nationalism. What they do seem to have taken advantage of, however, was 'the chance to write their own history, rather than being passive consumers of a predetermined argument'.[4] Before the later 1940s pageants staged in Scotland had shied away from challenging the established, celebratory and teleological narrative of ever-closer Union:[5] Arbroath changed this.

Alongside exceptionalism, however, are features that reveal much about the nature of changes within the pageant movement more generally. The first of these must be technical innovation, which the Arbroath Pageant embraced with enthusiasm. The second is the pageant's narrow gaze on one specific aspect of Scottish medieval history. This focus was unmoveable because the performance always took place in Arbroath Abbey, said to be the place where the declaration was drafted and authorised – the building was therefore integral to the drama and alerts us to the growing status of heritage-based tourism. Third, the event's inauguration in the post-war period highlights pageantry's widespread resurgence in the late 1940s, but specifically within the context of a part of the United Kingdom where this development has received little concentrated scholarly attention. Indeed, this oversight is remarkable given that 1947, the year of the first pageant, also saw the opening of the now world-famous Edinburgh International Festival – an event which, as Angela Bartie has argued, 'encapsulated many of the new values given to culture in the immediate post-war world'.[6] The town of Arbroath wanted to put itself on the cultural map of Scotland alongside Edinburgh, and pageant organisers concluded that their event, like Edinburgh's, could carry an international message. Arbroath's performance aimed to show that as a small nation that had for centuries battled to maintain its own distinct identity, Scotland was uniquely placed to teach others about the value of liberty.

As it turned out, however, over the course of the various Arbroath performances this international message – however sincerely meant – often stood in contrast with other ambitions regarding national self-determination that were closer to home. This is not to say that the organisers openly used the pageant as a rallying point for nationalist votes; indeed, the same organisers stoutly denied that the pageant had *any* party-political affiliation. Yet as will be seen, calls for greater devolution of government to Scotland, and later for complete independence, tended to be raised whenever the declaration was celebrated; there can be no doubt that some involved with the pageant saw it as a cultural conduit for contemporary political demands. For them, present-day needs and future hopes could be effectively expressed through the dramatic exposition of events in the past. Those needs and hopes were foregrounded by anxieties about Scotland's place within the United Kingdom and its continued status as a nation with its own distinct economic, social and cultural complexion.

Beginnings: 1947

In 1947 the economic fortunes of Arbroath were on the wane. Arbroath was by no means unique in this respect; the 'staple' industries that had been established in nineteenth-century Scotland were now in long-term decline. High levels of unemployment and emigration had caused social dislocation in many Scottish communities across much of the early twentieth century, and in the context of post-war austerity the problem returned with a vengeance. For although wartime conditions had done something to suspend the economic qualms of the interwar years, fear that mass unemployment might return emerged at the coming of peace.[7] One industry that did have a potential future was tourism, and Arbroath Town Council had an eye to developing this. While the idea for a pageant in Arbroath originated with the YMCA, seeking to raise money to support the welfare needs of British servicemen still stationed overseas, Arbroath's Council was quick to give the proposal official support. In giving the initiative their blessing, multiple benefits were envisaged: the pageant would be commercial in that it would be good for attracting visitors, but it was also true to the roots of the pageant movement in that any surplus made would go to a good cause. In addition the pageant, as it was first conceived, intended to raise the profile of what the town had to offer in terms of its industrial heritage by recounting the history of its traditional trades.[8]

Armed with the support of the council, the YMCA then took its idea to two well-known local figures with interests in amateur theatre: the journalist George Shepherd and the businessman and local politician Frank Thornton. What they thought about the idea of basing the drama on Arbroath's industrial history is not recorded; but it was quickly dropped in favour of something less workaday.[9] Manufacturing industry in this northeast coastal town had once been vibrant, but by the mid-twentieth century much of the local textile and machine manufacturing trades had an uncertain future in the face of automation and international competition. As stalwarts of local theatre, Shepherd and Thornton probably knew that there was little in the way of entertaining drama to be had from placing this sad fact centre stage. Instead they reached further into Arbroath's past. In doing so they introduced into the storyline a key figure in many Scottish pageants – the heroic warrior king, Robert the Bruce – and made the focus of the drama a visit by the Bruce to Arbroath Abbey on 6 April 1320, the date stated on the declaration.

Founded in 1178 by King William the Lion of Scotland, the ancient abbey dominates the skyline of Arbroath.[10] In common with most medieval religious houses in Scotland, it fell into rapid ruin following the Reformation. That the shell survives at all, in what is still an impressive state, is probably a consequence of the building's totemic role in the creation of the Declaration of Arbroath, which – in the form of a letter from the king and commonweal of Scotland addressed to Pope John XXII – had been despatched from the abbey in 1320. The pageant organisers annexed the drama that this famous missive conjured up through the reiteration of a longstanding story about a parliament held at Arbroath in 1320.[11] The pageant thus described an imagined ceremony wherein King Robert, accompanied by barons and bishops, all lined up to 'sign' the declaration while its alleged author – Abbot Bernard de Linton – supervised the proceedings.

In the early twenty-first century all kinds of tourist ephemera can be found depicting facsimiles of the declaration. Whether on a tea towel, T-shirt or bookmark, images of the numerous wax seals appended to the parchment are familiar to a wide audience. Yet the central scene of the pageant depicted king and nobles taking quilled pen in hand to sign – not seal – the letter, an 'inauthentic' detail which has been the source of sneering by some medieval historians. Yet such dismissiveness may miss the point of the theatrical performance of the scene: historical pageantry does not necessarily aim for perfect authenticity in re-enactment. Rather, part of its success lies in its ability to re-create scenes from the past in an accessible and engaging manner for a contemporary audience while not losing sight of the essential differences between past and present.

Authenticity in this light takes on a different meaning. The truth of the Declaration of Arbroath is that in modern times it has become a powerful signifier of Scottish nationhood; for at the time when it was written, Scotland's independence was under assault from England – its larger and more powerful neighbour.[12] Inauthentic quill pen or no, this historical parallel spoke to a growing faction in Scottish society that worried about the increasing centralisation of power in the UK, and the threat that this might pose to the fortunes of Scotland – which seemed to be emerging from war as a mere 'region of the UK, and a peripheral one at that'.[13]

Often described as Scotland's 'Magna Carta', owing to the strident message it contains about liberty, the declaration's most quoted passage affirms that

> It is in truth not for glory, nor riches, nor honours that we are fighting, but for freedom – for that alone, which no honest man gives up but with life itself.

Such poetic language carries its own drama and allegedly has influenced other freedom fighters, most notably the authors of the American Declaration of Independence (although this claim remains unproven, many in Scotland and North America accept it readily).[14] Moreover, the abbey itself lends dramatic power by providing an evocative stage, with its huge round aperture facing out to sea – named locally as the 'round-O' – visible from across the town.[15] For these reasons Thornton probably did not feel he had to do much to assert historical validity within a narrative that carried words of national and international historical significance and was set in the very place they were written.

All that was needed to underscore the drama were some active signifiers of medieval religious life: these were provided by a local male voice choir dressed as monks, whose plainsong chanting echoed within the abbey's ancient walls. The choir was joined by a colourful procession of nobles and bishops headed by the striking figure of the king. In 1947, and in many subsequent years, the Bruce was played by a local vet; he was said to suit the role perfectly, being tall and powerfully built.[16] The abbot and monks were seen first at worship; this was interrupted by the stately arrival of the king and his entourage; then followed the solemn ceremony of the signing of the document. The pageant ended with the departure of the king and his companions and the return of Abbot Bernard and monks to religious devotions. All this drama was fictional; there is no evidence that any such gathering took place.[17] Throughout the action Thornton provided a live commentary, summarising the ongoing wars and Scotland's beleaguered condition, while also conveying an impression of the 'majesty and magnificence of the monastery church of those days'.[18]

During the signing ceremony, the voiceover included a reading of the words of the declaration – translated from the Latin, but notably into English not Scots. In these early years the political interests of many associated with the pageant were concerned with devolution rather than separation. The event was, therefore, just as replete with the usual expressions of British patriotism found in pageants across the UK: the national anthem was sung and Union flag bunting adorned the town.

Apart from four women dressed as pages within the king's entourage, the entire cast of around 130 players comprised adult men.[19] In part at least, this was likely due to a shortage of funds available for the costuming of a more diverse cast. As one correspondent to the *Scotsman* newspaper rather unkindly suggested, the far-from-authentic garb worn by the monks of Arbroath Abbey in the pageant could be attributed to a 'lack of clothing coupons'.[20] Despite such constraints, however, the inaugural Arbroath Abbey Pageant was a critical success: post-war austerity or no, there was still a considerable appetite for this kind of communal activity in 1940s Scotland.

Indeed, there was an appetite for culture more generally – culture being viewed as integral to post-war reconstruction. Opening an art exhibition that followed on from pageant week, Sir Frank Mears, president of the Royal Scottish Academy, acknowledged 'that we were at present passing through a period of austerity, and some people might wonder why anyone found time to organise such an exhibition'. However, as Mears went on to point out,

> one could not live on bread alone ... One wanted other things to think about. Arbroath had just finished celebrating with a pageant the signing of the great Declaration of Independence, which [was] one of the noblest documents in our language, proving it was not a dead thing, but something that meant much to them in these days. Soon they were to have an exhibition of the future planning and development of the town ... It might mean the altering of the whole of our lives and lead to a brighter period, when we would not depend on a central authority to push us along, but would get at things ourselves, in our own localities, and in our own ways ... It might be that we were now moving from that heavy industry age into one of lighter-hearted approach to life in some ways.[21]

The exhibition had been arranged by Arbroath Art Society in conjunction with the Arts Council of Great Britain. Such sponsorship of high culture in a predominately working-class town such as Arbroath perhaps explains the tone adopted within the pageant; neither the art exhibition nor the pageant was frothy entertainment. The Abbey Pageant was earnest, dignified theatre, high-brow in its artistic approach, albeit situated within what had become a popular medium. At a time of optimism about cultural renaissance in Scotland, there evidently was little fear that this kind of pageant would fail to find an audience. Neither was there much fear that Mears's message about the need to 'get at things' themselves in Scotland might be lost.

Yet, in comparison with most Scottish pageants, even those staged in small communities, the Arbroath Pageant of 1947 took a decidedly abbreviated approach to re-enacting history. Performed in a single episode encompassing four scenes, it would have been a relatively quick performance had it not been for lengthy preliminary elements. These consisted of a welcome by a local notable and a speech by a well-known public figure, both of whom were then accorded a vote of thanks by a third dignitary. The speechmaking was followed by a short religious service. This introductory programme was hardly heart-stopping drama set to appeal to tourists. But it should be remembered that Scotland in the 1940s and 1950s was, in many senses, a country of conservative values where the Presbyterian religion continued to exert a huge influence over the population as a whole, as well as its governing structures.[22]

The presence of a Church of Scotland minister and accompanying prayers and hymns were, in any case, necessary foils to what came after. In what may have been a slightly surprising sight, the drama did little to underplay the Catholicism of the medieval abbey. Roman Catholic bishops were resplendent in their robes and mitres of office, and genuflection was even performed – not a sight to gladden the hearts of diehard Calvinists. Yet authenticity in this mode trumped Presbyterian sensibilities and underlines Bartie's argument that after centuries of fire and brimstone fulminating against the theatre, the Church of Scotland had begun to see the possibilities of blending culture and religion.[23]

What undoubtedly helped make this pageant more of a mass-market festival were the 'parades and revelries' added to pageant week.[24] For example, many spectators saw the king and his entourage without benefit of a ticket, as they rode through the town on their way to the abbey.[25] Further attractions included the re-enactment of a traditional wedding performed by members of the fishing community; the re-creation of an old-style Highland village by the local branch of the Women's Rural Institute; a mile-long pageant procession with bands and floats, held after the final Saturday afternoon performance; and a grand fireworks display funded by the town council to close the week. All these saved the day financially, for pointedly, despite high attendance, the pageant itself lost money. The collections taken at these additional events having raised an overall profit to the benefit of the YMCA, the association quickly applied to hold the pageant again in 1948 (Fig. 10.1), stating that it had received acclaim from all parts of Scotland, and the YMCA Council were very proud that they could be regarded as pioneers of a pageant which had such a moral and educational value … Apart from any financial profit we feel that the service rendered to Arbroath and to Scotland, and the prestige we have gained by being associated with this most successful presentation, make our efforts worthwhile.[26]

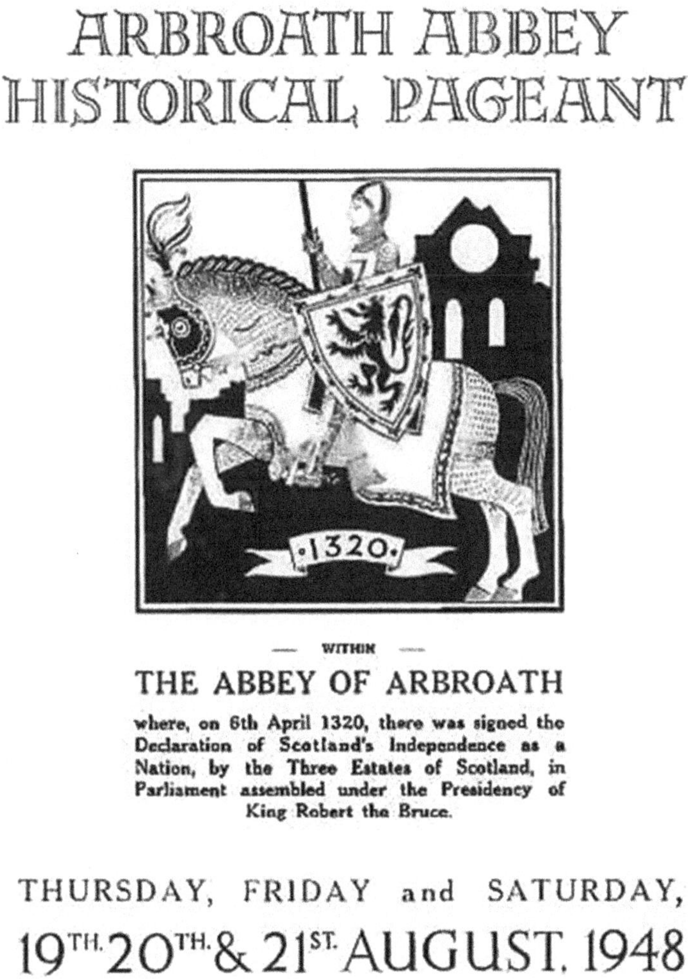

Figure 10.1 Front cover of the Arbroath Abbey Pageant programme, 1948. Much of the iconography that became closely associated with this pageant was prominent on the 1948 programme cover: the momentous 1320 date, the Bruce in full warrior mode and, overlooking all, Arbroath Abbey's famous 'Round O'. Reproduced by kind permission of the Arbroath Pageant Society.

In future years the pageant, although run ostensibly without ambition to make a profit, withdrew from being a fundraiser through the setting up of the Arbroath Pageant Society. This was an independent organisation with its own committee, but on which sat a statutory number of representatives from the town council.[27] The Society was so named only after some consideration: an earlier suggestion had been the Arbroath Independence Pageant Society.[28] The stage was thereafter set for a long-running pageant, but – as we shall see – one with a contest of ambitions between the cultural and the political at its centre.

Five years on: 1951

As we see in chapter 9, 1951 was a bumper year for pageants staged as part of the Festival of Britain. In Arbroath, however, this was simply year five of what had become an annual event. The Festival met with a lukewarm response in some parts of Scotland, being viewed by many as just another leftist-inspired, London-centric scheme that undermined local autonomy and would do little but drain the strained coffers of Scottish towns. In Inverness, for example, the plan to hold a Festival pageant was sternly opposed by the local council. The town's provost thought otherwise, however, pushing ahead with it as a boost to Highland tourism. As it turned out, the provost's instincts proved well-founded: performed by an amateur dramatic society, the 1951 Pageant of Inverness went on to be a huge success.[29] So far as Arbroath was concerned, its pageant was going ahead, Festival or no, but the question for its organisers was whether they should make it a Festival of Britain event? Like Inverness, they did.

Since 1947 additional features had been incorporated into the action. Following the introductory speeches and religious service a prologue was performed; then came a curtain-raiser for the main scene in the form of a one-act play entitled *The Laurel Crown*. Also written by Thornton, this play enacted the infamous trial of William Wallace at the hands of his English foes. Something of a pageant favourite in Scotland, Wallace, the brave and doomed hero of the people, tended to gather a good deal more popular adulation than did high-born Robert the Bruce, who featured in the pageant's main scene.[30] Wallace stirred the patriotic blood of Scots, but he also raised the spectre of something much more contentious: anti-Englishness.

This complementary drama seemed to work, creating a synthesis that built anticipation for the main declaration episode. The speeches also played a part; in 1948, for example, the guest speaker at the closing performance was the journalist and home-rule supporter Lewis Spence.[31] Spence's speech reminded the audience that the values articulated in the Arbroath declaration made Scotland 'the most venerable nation in Europe', where men could 'speak forthrightly and not under the compulsions of terrorism'.[32] Both Wallace and Bruce obtained their reputations, of course, for standing up to English aggression, and the implicit nationalism of Spence's presentation would not have been lost on the audience. While nationalist sensibilities may have operated in a low-key and more subtle way within the drama performed, it was often in the preliminary speeches that the political message of the pageant was most obviously delivered. Many of the speakers invited to Arbroath in the post-war years were, like Spence, vocal about present-day threats to Scotland's sense of national autonomy. Such sentiments were received with interest; Scots were certainly becoming more receptive to calls for greater devolution, even if the majority were sceptical about outright independence.

The 1949 performance saw an effort to broaden the historical chronology with the addition of more episodes, but this experiment was never repeated.[33] In 1950 the programme returned to that of 1948, with Wallace eloquently defying the English yet again from the pageant stage. In other respects, however, significant changes had been made. Enhancements had been applied to the costumes, though most were still made locally: for example, an Arbroath sheet metal worker made authentic helmets for the Bruce and his barons.[34] Acoustic improvements were achieved with 'the introduction of new apparatus and skilful placing of loudspeakers'.[35] This technological advance made appreciation of dialogue in *The Laurel Crown* possible, and it was what probably encouraged the Pageant Society to inaugurate an evening performance in addition to those held in the afternoons – an initiative that achieved further impact through the use of innovative lighting. The scale of the production had increased to still greater proportions by the time Festival year came around, the Abbey Pageant Society having amassed props and costumes to the value of £800.[36]

There were good reasons why the Pageant Society embraced being a Festival of Britain production. The first of these was to maintain good audience numbers. Visitor numbers in 1950 were said to be the highest yet, the organisers claiming that the pageant had 'given Arbroath a place in Scotland which no other event could have done'.[37] Indeed in 1950 the pageant had been used as backdrop to an episode of a hugely popular BBC radio series, *The McFlannels*.[38] The society's second motive was, so it seems, to distance itself from accusations of political nationalism and make the pageant more inclusive.[39] It was certainly true that the Pageant Society was beginning to be seen as an elite clique with its own particular nationalist agenda. Famously, in 1950 the Stone of Scone (removed from Scotland by Edward I during the Wars of Independence) was stolen from Westminster by some youthful nationalists. It was recovered in April 1951 at Arbroath Abbey, a move that further cemented this building's association with the nationalist cause. Members of Arbroath Town Council sympathetic to home rule facilitated this recovery. These councillors included Frank Thornton, the pageant's writer, director and performer.[40]

For the 1951 Festival pageant more technological innovation was used in order to move the evening performance to later at night. In the context of Scottish towns in the early 1950s, where pubs shut at 10 p.m. and were closed entirely on Sundays, the very notion of public entertainment at midnight on the eve of the Sabbath was nothing short of revolutionary. Furthermore, the idea that the pageant itself was quasi-sacred had been promoted by the Church, with one local minister preaching in 1949 that

> Our Pageant was young in years ... But the originators were wise. They decreed that each performance should open with an act of worship ... should the pageant be divorced from the worship of God and degenerate into mere miming of sacred things, should these hallowed walls be desecrated by being turned into a place of mere interest and entertainment, then the pageant is doomed. Spiritually it must die. Only a spiritual impulse will keep our Pageant alive.[41]

The minister's predictions were off the mark. The religiosity of the pageant was to be outstripped by an artistic agenda and the need to increase audience numbers through the novelty of late-night performances. This outdoor lighting ingeniously created *son et lumière* effects that produced the illusion of pillars and gave 'a roofed effect' to the abbey ruins.[42] With Presbyterian strictures about the Sabbath losing some of their grip, and the days of austerity coming to an end, the midnight spectacles proved popular. However, new audio and lighting technology created hefty expenses. These, together with bad weather, contributed to financial losses despite the late-night closing performance being over-subscribed:

> After the close of the Floodlight performance, a large concourse of spectators gathered in the vicinity of the Abbey to witness the firing of the beacon in the lancet window underneath the famous Round O ... Even after this symbolic ending of Pageant Week, crowds still

> hovered around the Abbey where the 'House' lighting illumined the nave, and gave to those not fortunate enough to be present during the performance some inkling of the departed glories of an unforgettable night.[43]

The popularity of the floodlit performance meant that it became Arbroath's trademark in future years, with late-night stagings largely replacing those in the afternoon.

Yet while some types of innovation were embraced, other elements of the pageant were steadfastly preserved. Many translations of the declaration exist, but from 1947 the one used at Arbroath was the work of the popular historian Agnes Mure Mackenzie, a staunch supporter of the pageant.[44] Mackenzie took her turn at delivering the pageant's introductory addresses and in 1951 provided a rousing opening speech at the inaugural floodlit performance. That same year the Saltire Society published an analysis of the declaration written by her.[45] In this Mackenzie mentioned Arbroath's annual celebration, stating that it 're-affirmed' rather than 're-enacted' the spirit of the document; she also commented that the declaration was 'as much to the point today, for all the world, as it was for the Scotland of six hundred years since'.[46] She was not alone in her beliefs.

Led by John MacCormick and bringing together politicians from all parties who favoured greater devolution for Scotland, the Scottish Covenant movement became prominent after the war.[47] In 1949 it famously canvassed Scottish public opinion, collecting two million signatures (two-thirds of the Scottish electorate) on a petition calling for a Scottish Assembly. Yet after this high point, hopes for an assembly rapidly receded.[48] The Covenant movement failed, as Ian Levitt has pointed out, 'to translate a deeply held cultural distinctiveness to the level of political awareness and significance'.[49] In making this argument Levitt draws on the most influential analyses of Scottish national identity in recent decades. These have tended to rest upon notions of a common civic identity and sense of place rather than any attachment to ancient ethnic origins.

One of the best-known accounts of this view has been proffered by David McCrone, who claims that it complicates any possible 'relationship between cultural and political nationalism' – by which he means that while 'cultural concerns provide some material for nationalism', they 'are rarely its *raison d'être*'.[50] More recently, however, this scholarly consensus has been charged with creating a false divide between the 'ethnic/cultural' and the 'civic/political' in explanations of Scottish identity and – more particularly – with underplaying the role played by popular discourses of the past in Scottish people's everyday understandings of their identity. Indeed it has been argued that politicians, and even academics, cannot entirely escape discourses that are

> laden with atavistic tendencies, historical references and irrational collectivism. Even when the stories are about the heritage of the Scottish Enlightenment, proud educational traditions or respected legal institutions these civic narratives cannot escape an emotive presentation.[51]

It was exactly this type of 'emotive presentation' of the past that many involved with Arbroath's pageant hoped to exploit and transfer into the political consciousness of their audience. Yet the devolution campaign retreated in the early 1950s amid relative – albeit short-term – economic stability and welfare improvements within Scottish society, while Arbroath's pageant struggled on, with the annual effort coming under increasing stress.

End of an era? 1956

In the years after the Festival, further changes were made to Arbroath pageant arrangements. In 1953 the number of performances was increased in the hope that ticket sales would create a profit. Seven performances were given – five at night-time and fully illuminated. For the year of the Queen's coronation Arbroath also went to town with street decorations and all was said to be 'gay and exhilarating' with 'a Continental air' in this 'staid Scots Seaport town'.[52] This fulsome publicity hid the truth, however, which was that the pageant had lost local support; and just as they had with the Covenant, the Scottish public had shifted their attention away from arguments about national self-determination. Challenging this climate of indifference, Thornton was belligerent: 'we are not providing entertainment ... but commemorating a historic event'. With the encroaching Cold War on everyone's minds, Thornton claimed that as 'the lights are going out all over Europe' the message of the pageant that 'each small nation should be allowed self-determination' remained of critical contemporary importance.[53]

In addition to increasing the number of performances, changes were also made in the script. From 1952 the performances of *The Laurel Crown* alternated with another one-act play written by Thornton. This piece, entitled *Of Their Own Experience*, dramatised a fictional visit by Edward I to Arbroath Abbey. The pageant was also now bookended by a new prologue and epilogue. These features aimed to deflect accusations of nationalism by extolling

> a spirit which contrasts the unity of the nations of this island in the present with the disruption of the past, and proves to be an effective answer to the critics who label the pageant ultra-nationalistic in tone.[54]

The prologue and epilogue featured an ancient warrior, who in the prologue declaimed:

> I knew this abbey once when like a rock it rose above this ancient town. Roofless and crumbled it stands today, but there is still a spirit in these broken walls … Secure in this island, united under one crown, you know a happiness I and my comrades never knew. Your Border keeps are empty ruins … Britain is a land of peace … I belong to the old Scotland, and from the past I rise … to honour the men who choose Freedom and led me to victory. You should not forget them now, even though you are members of a wider community of Freedom. They helped to make the Scotland you love to-day – a nation within a United Kingdom, proud of her past, but not dwelling in it. But had proud Edward crushed us, then what a rancour might have been stored in the hearts of a conquered people! Come back with me to those days when even this proud abbey was no refuge from fear … here in Aberbrothock, we hear the shout of tyranny.[55]

Whether this type of programme tweak put a stop to accusations of aggressive nationalism and anti-Englishness is a moot point, however.

In 1955 further concessions to modern audiences were introduced when a change was made in the timing of the pageant and the religious service was dropped. The August schedule had been seen as a means of extending the summer season and encouraging visitors to combine Edinburgh's festivities with a trip north to Arbroath; but that year the pageant was moved to July to coincide with the annual trades holiday for Glasgow and much of west central Scotland when Arbroath had many more 'Glasgow Fair' visitors. All such change was for nought, however, for despite glorious weather, following the 1955 season, the Pageant Society was left with an overdraft of £125.[56]

After fervent fundraising by the Pageant Society's 'Ladies' Committee', what was viewed as a final farewell was given in 1956. Accordingly the performers pulled out all the stops and the concessions previously made to those who accused the pageanteers of being over-zealous nationalists were abandoned: William Wallace strode the stage once again in *The Laurel Crown*. Further technological innovation allowed Thornton to recite the declaration from 'a ramp so ingeniously contrived and cleverly lit that it gave the impression of the commentator being suspended in the air'. This upped the drama further and Thornton, a trouper to the last, gave his all, delivering the prologue 'in ringing tones that at once set the atmosphere for all that followed'.[57] In 1957 the *National Geographic* ran an article about many of the literary landmarks of Scotland, the climax of which described a visit to the 1956 pageant. Labelling the declaration as 'the Scottish Magna Carta', the article offered a romantic description of the drama:

> Darkness again filled the ruins. A monk bearing a lighted torch crossed the nave. His light flickered up narrow stairs in the south wall. Soon he reappeared high overhead at 'Arbroath's O', an empty circular window space, and plunged the burning torch into a cresset – an iron vessel filled with oil – such as used to blaze out over the North Sea to guide mariners home … a great glow of flame crackled skyward. It was the Light of Freedom, Scotland's message to the world.[58]

The anniversary year: 1970

In the event, 1956 was not the end. The pageant returned first in 1964, to critical acclaim (though once more incurring massive financial losses), and again in 1966, when it was opened by Lord Kilbrandon, a known 'arch-devolutionist'.[59] As borne out by Kilbrandon's presence, questions of home rule (and even independence) remained and were given a profile whenever the pageant was performed. In 1966 one letter to the press congratulating the pageant went on to ask, 'is it necessary to play the anthem of the country whose aggression against Scotland made the Declaration of Arbroath necessary?' The editor replied in the affirmative, stating that it was perfectly appropriate since the Queen was the Queen of Scots and '[o]nly English history books curtail Her Majesty's lineage by taking it back through the Tudors to the Norman Conquerors'.[60] Just the same, this would be the last time the national anthem was played at Arbroath. Also around this time Frank Thornton, who had regularly fended off accusations of nationalism, evidently gave up any pretence of neutrality and joined the Scottish National Party (SNP).[61] He did so when support for the party was in decline, although – in keeping with the volatile fortunes of political nationalism in Scotland – it would enjoy more electoral success with the turn of the 1970s and the coming of North Sea oil.[62]

There could never have been any doubt that the pageant would reappear in 1970 – the 650th anniversary year of the declaration. Among many educational initiatives planned across Scotland to celebrate the anniversary, including exhibitions and commemorative publications, those taking place in Arbroath held extra significance.[63] For its special anniversary staging the poet, playwright and known nationalist Sydney Goodsir Smith agreed to adapt part of his verse-play, *The Wallace*, as an episode for the pageant, and accordingly a book of words was published for the first time.[64] Smith's work provides a version of the Wallace story in which the Earl of Carrick (the future King Robert the Bruce) is an opportunist, and the lowlier-born Wallace emerges as the real man of courage. Dialogue in the pageant adaptation was delivered by two chroniclers – one English, one Scottish – with the latter telling his side of the story in broad Scots. This juxtaposition was meant to underline the differences in historical interpretation of the Wars of Independence.

All performances held that August were at night – and none of these included civic or religious ceremonies or speeches. This may have been because of the controversy that had preceded the commemorative ceremony held on the anniversary date of 6 April to open Arbroath's year of declaration celebrations. Attended by the great and good from all over Scotland – including the Secretary of State for Scotland, William Ross, and the Moderator of the General Assembly of the Church of Scotland – this event had been mostly religious in tone, with mass choirs and prayers as well as speeches. But only two days beforehand the SNP had held their own celebration, attracting 2,000 party members.[65]

The venue for this party political rally was the lawn outside the abbey, the Secretary of State having refused permission for it to take place within the ruins. Frank Thornton, in his capacity as a local SNP organiser, presided over the occasion and read the words of the declaration, after which there were several minutes of silence. This was followed by a speech from the SNP leader William Wolfe, who declared that his party sought to 'give back to the people of Scotland their responsibilities and opportunities as a nation'. Railing against increasing 'centralisation', Wolfe announced that 'we must grow up as a human community in Freedom. This was Arbroath's message of 1320. It is also Arbroath's message of 1970'. After Wolfe had finished, an actor then read out 'a new Declaration':

> To-day we reaffirm our nationhood in the words and in the spirit of the Declaration of Arbroath … Scotland is no northern appendage

> of England, but a kingdom in treaty relations with a neighbouring kingdom … Scotland's nationhood is as real as England's or that of any other nation; as deeply rooted in history; as fully expressed in national institutions and as completely embodied in a distinctive national genius and character … Scotland had survived, refusing to be submerged into a region, because a fierce democratic spirit and love of freedom have burned in this land for centuries, in spite of all the most consistent and determined efforts to quench them.[66]

As further remonstration for the rally being denied access to the abbey, many SNP supporters paid a shilling to enter as visitors; they took their flags with them and soon the 'Lion Rampant and the Saltire … flew from every embrasure'.[67] News of the colourful protest spread and even made the *New York Times,* thus eclipsing coverage of the formal commemoration two days later.[68]

For all the brouhaha that had attended the April commemorations, the organisers of the pageant saw 1970 as a new beginning. Reflecting on the August performances, the event's then co-producer, Tom Walker, felt that 'Arbroath could become known as Scotland's Oberammergau … There is no point in being under-ambitious … we have a production and setting that is unparalleled anywhere is Scotland'.[69] These were sanguine words: pageants were out of vogue by this point and moreover their version of history might be challenged. Dr Grant Simpson of Aberdeen University gave a lecture to Arbroath's antiquarian society in October 1970 in which he tactfully stated that 'the traditional story of an Assembly in the Abbey could not be proved or disproved; events were more involved'. Simpson further argued that 'any comparison with Magna Carta' was inaccurate, though the declaration was 'one of the masterpieces of political rhetoric of all time'.[70] Simpson's diplomatic insights on matters of historical interpretation fell on deaf ears, however. The organisers were determined that the pageant's version of the declaration story should continue as it had done.

During the 1960s no consideration appears to have been given to making the pageant drama less highbrow in tone, despite changing tastes in an era where television was in the ascendancy. In 1965 the nearby town of Forfar had held a pageant to celebrate the tercentenary of its charter. Written by the talented playwright Robert Kemp, who also wrote prolifically for radio and television in such popular series as *Dr Finlay's Casebook*, Forfar's pageant was a sold-out triumph; it struck an excellent balance between thoughtful depictions of history and the familiar tropes of TV entertainment.[71] Though it may have pained Arbroath pageanteers to see their nearest civic rival succeed in this way, in 1970 and into the future they continued to see the declaration narrative as a timeless commemoration and as such immune to changing tastes. Indeed by 1970 the pageant had accumulated a history of its own – a pub situated on the main route to the Abbey is even named the 'Pageant Bar'. Another pageant week was planned for 1975, but rising production values were costly and, despite its stated ambition, the Society struggled to raise the funds required.

A long wait: 1980

Concerted planning to reinstate the pageant only began in early 1979. While it is tempting to think this resurrection after nine years was finally achieved because of the politics of the time – a long-awaited referendum on Scottish devolution was held on 1 March 1979 – this was only one probable prompt. The death throes of Scottish heavy industries during the 1970s encouraged interest in other types of economic activity, including tourism. Thus as the Pageant Society entered the 1980s, it had no difficulty attracting generous funding from the local authority and the Scottish Tourist Board.[72]

This kind of investment was unprecedented, arriving after the dark days of the mid-1970s when statutory arts funding had been severely constrained.[73] However, the 'bucket-and-spade' popularity that Arbroath had enjoyed in the 1940s had emigrated to the Mediterranean and 'heritage' was now meant to replace it. External funding galvanised the Pageant Society. It began a year-long campaign on 6 April 1979, with 'principal characters in the pageant attired in the costumes they will wear next year' processing through Arbroath to the abbey where their arrival was proclaimed:

> six hundred and fifty nine years ago this day, in the great hall above that arch yonder, the Estates of Scotland gathered under their king Robert Bruce, and sent forth a clarion declaration of the Scottish people's will to maintain their nation in freedom.

A crowd numbering several hundreds gathered to hear this clarion call and the BBC filmed the occasion.[74] The same actors were despatched by the Tourist Board as far away as Newcastle-upon-Tyne to publicise their pageant at a trade exhibition entitled 'Enjoy Scotland'.[75] This enthusiasm was infectious: a new generation of local people showed interest where there had previously been indifference. The new pageant producer, Bill Shaw, commented that 'Arbroath still had more than a spark of community spirit'.[76] The street procession was also resurrected and 90 local businesses each donated £10 to pay for street bunting.[77] The performance

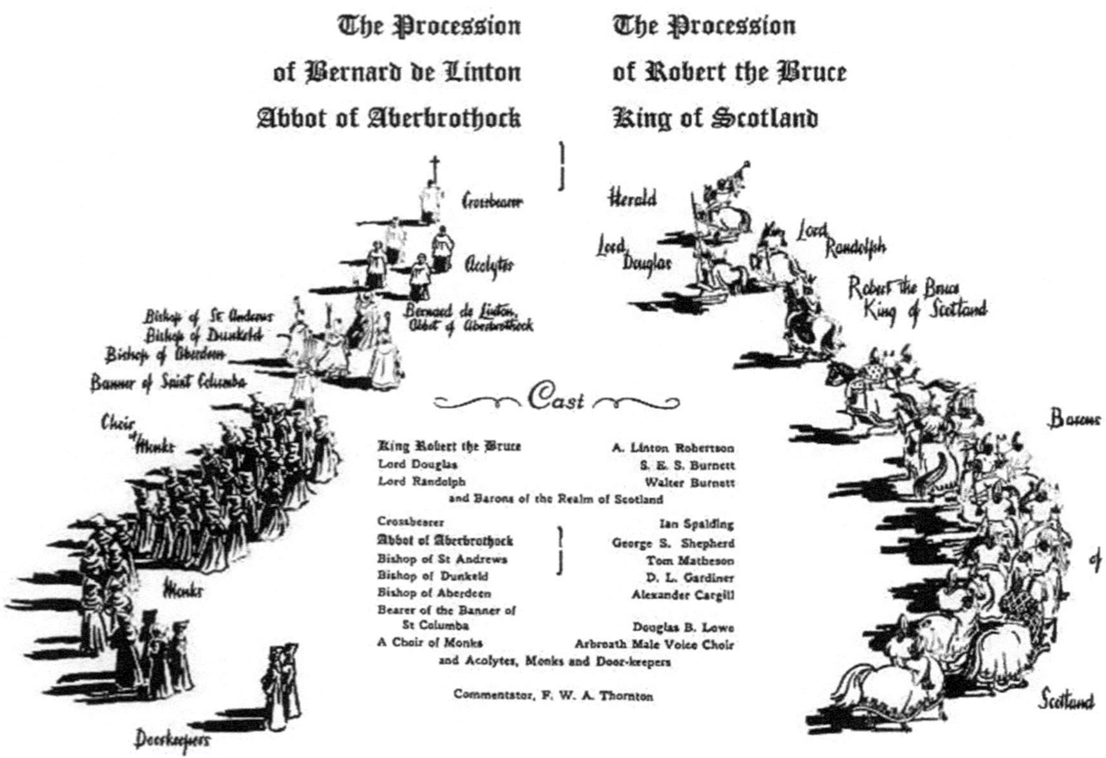

Figure 10.2 The procession of Bernard de Linton and Robert the Bruce with cast list. From the programme of the Arbroath Abbey Pageant, 1949. Reproduced by kind permission of the Arbroath Pageant Society.

itself had changed little, but even greater application of spectacular lighting effects was used 'to create the effect of a giant roof over the Abbey'.[78] Dundee University's audiovisual department also recorded a soundtrack of *The Laurel Crown*, so that in 1980 the entire drama of the pageant was mimed to a pre-recorded audio track.[79]

Press reports stressed, nonetheless, that tradition was at the heart of the event. From the cloak worn year-on-year by Robert the Bruce to Mackenzie's translation of the declaration, many features of the pageant were the same as those employed in the late 1940s. The illustration above, which appeared as the centre pages within the 1949 programme, shows the procession through the abbey of the pageant's main characters; this would have been just as familiar to audiences in the 1980s as it was to those attending over 30 years earlier (Fig. 10.2). Indeed, a 14-year-old recording of Frank Thornton's rousing reading of the Declaration of Independence was reused in the 1980 pageant.[80]

The Tourist Board's chairman, Alan Devereux, officially opened the 1980 pageant. He was new to the job, previously having been chairman of the Confederation of British Industry in Scotland, in which capacity he had also been a vocal opponent of devolution. In his speech at the first performance, Devereux did not shy from stating what he thought were the merits of Scottish traditions for the wider economy, nor from dipping his toes in political waters in order to underline this view:

> Whatever your political persuasion and whichever your country of birth, you cannot fail to be moved by the sheer beauty of Scotland, by the timeless traditions of its people and their courage in the face of adversity ... The world's images of the kilt, heather, clans and bagpipes are essential parts of the timeless traditions and the reality of Scotland. May we never feel any sense of shame in displaying these traditions in the shop window of the world ... Scotland is a nation, not in any narrow sense of some cobbled-together Devolutionary Act of Parliament, but in the greater sense of enjoying a unique history and a unique birthright of values. Much has been made of the Declaration of Arbroath. Let us now pledge ourselves to a new Arbroath. Let us affirm our faith in ourselves ... Our future does not lie in joining a queue of begging bowls in England but rather with building our own greater society free from the sleazy overcrowding of our neighbours – a future based on hope and optimism, increasingly free from the worthless bounds of centralisation. By all means revel in our history tonight, but tomorrow let us be determined to go forward to strengthen Scotland's economic might through its major industries of the future – the industries of tourism, banking and electronics.[81]

The performances were well-attended and accorded praise, although once again no profit was made. Nonetheless, pageant organisers were buoyed by artistic success and news that the Tourist Board had agreed to support the pageant for two more years. Any UK-wide decline in historical pageantry was not considered relevant: Arbroath was evidently viewed as a case apart. If the direction in which the pageant was being pushed – to engage with heritage as a straightforward commodity within a Scottish economy increasingly based on service industries – was noted, no heed was given to the possible price to be paid. Pageant organisers took the Tourist Board's money and kept their own counsel where Devereux's views were concerned, for surely tartan and bagpipes had never been a part of this pageant. An invitation to the 1981 opening was extended to Wendy Wood, the infamous campaigner for Scottish independence, but she died a few months before her planned appearance.[82] Nevertheless her invitation tells us much about the politics that still pervaded this pageant. The local press reported that Wood had written her introductory speech before her death, and quoted part of it:

> When you leave this holy place, may the spirits of Sir William Wallace and King Robert the Bruce be in you, to achieve the independence of Scotland from English rule. Soara [*sic*] Alba! May the Pageant proceed.[83]

The decision to invite Wood was probably an act of defiance against the marriage of convenience that the pageant had entered into with the Tourist Board, and the commercially exploitative view of Scottish culture promoted by the likes of Devereux. The 1981 pageant was less successful and plans for 1982 were cancelled. A fire in 1984, which destroyed valuable props, then contributed to the pageant's longest absence, for it did not re-emerge until the end of the century – by which time much of the Scottish electorate had lost all faith in the Unionist philosophy and centralising policies of successive Conservative governments.

The twenty-first-century pageants

The ostensible occasion for a pageant revival was Arbroath's charter anniversary in 1999. However, this was also the year in which Scottish devolution was at last achieved, with a new parliament being installed in Edinburgh. In the first elections to this body, held in May of that year, Angus returned an SNP candidate with a large majority.[84] The 1999 pageant was a major success, selling out at most of its five performances. Yet, while Arbroath seemingly defied the eclipse of historical pageants in the twentieth century, probably because many of its stalwart organisers had their own political agenda, this would not be the case in the twenty-first.

All along, it was an open secret that many, if perhaps not all, of those involved with the Arbroath Pageant were nationalist sympathisers. Yet, even when discussed in the SNP's monthly newspaper, more mileage was made of the pageant's cultural value than any possible political capital:

> Anyone who has ever taken part in a pageant will tell you of the special feeling they get as they help to re-enact that scene of 679 years ago. There is a unique magic in watching the ancient sandstone walls of the abbey growing upwards from ground level as the floodlights rebuild the abbey in the mild August darkness, and shafts of 'sunlight' shine through the long mullioned windows of the nave as it would have done all those centuries ago. The monks' chorus (supplied by the Arbroath Male Voice Choir) has the uncanny effect of helping to transport the cast and the audience back through the centuries and, for an hour or two, Arbroath and its abbey are again centre stage in Scotland's struggles with its southern neighbour.[85]

As many descriptions of the drama reveal, the pageant's appeal went beyond mere propaganda. The 'uncanny effect' of transporting the viewer back in time was the source of its enduring fascination for audiences, and it is hard to escape the conclusion that as a political mission it failed to make much impact. Indeed, the persistence of Arbroath's pageant points to the complexity of any possible relationship between the type of identity politics celebrated within historical pageants and effective politicking.

Emerging again in 2000 amid a rash of Millennium celebrations and supported by the Heritage Lottery Fund, the pageant took its last bow in 2005 – when audience turnout was poor. A Pageant Society – now called Arbroath Abbey Timethemes – still exists in Arbroath, but it is unlikely that a full production will be attempted again. (A processional pageant had been planned for April 2020, to mark the septuacentenary of the Declaration, but this was postponed due to the coronavirus outbreak in the early part of the year.) In the judgement of one present member of the society, a large dramatic pageant on the model of the 1947 original 'would be just impossible'.[86] Rising costs and difficulties with use of the historic site, as well as doubts about attracting enough local involvement and a sufficiently large audience, are all relevant considerations; but so too are the politics always lurking in the shadows of this pageant.

There is no doubt that many organisers did support devolution and/or independence, and their involvement with the pageant reflected the spectrum of nationalist views that evolved during the latter part of the twentieth century.[87] Yet if within this timeframe some Scots steered clear of a cultural event that smacked of a particular political agenda, that problem has obtained an even bigger profile in the twenty-first century; questions about independence have now inspired even sharper – and often angrier – divisions in Scottish political opinion. Certainly members of the Society today are shy of the pageant's potential as a political tool, while being keenly adamant about the declaration's significance in relation to local and national identities. For one member, the declaration's main message is that 'we are a people'; she saw the pageant as not 'so much nationalist as just Scottish. I mean, true, patriotic Scots'.[88]

Nonetheless, any perceived failures of the Arbroath Abbey Pageant should not blind us to its many successes. Without doubt, it became a trailblazer for technical innovation, often years ahead of other such community spectacles. Moreover, in its post-war heyday – and occasionally beyond this – it fulfilled the most critical mainstay of successful pageanteering: that of engendering community enthusiasm. Throughout all its history the pageant has also provided an exemplar of local heritage taking centre stage in a national story. Surely the Arbroath Pageant, not least through its very persistence, does indeed deserve the title of *the* Scots' Pageant.

Notes

1. The pageant was performed annually, usually in August, from 1947 to 1956. Thereafter performances took place in 1964, 1966, 1970, 1980, 1981, 1999 and 2000, with the last full performance given in 2005. Since then, in some years, there have been abbreviated performances of the pageant's central scene. The latter have taken place at the Abbey on 6 April – the date of the Arbroath Declaration of 1320 and the date assigned to the annual 'Tartan Day' celebrations in North America.
2. This origin of this title can probably be attributed to the historian Agnes Mure Mackenzie, who stated in a piece published in the 1949 pageant programme that the pageant had begun as 'a burgh commemoration. By its second performance it belonged to Scotland'. Subsequently the notion of the 'Scots' Pageant' was used for publicity purposes. See Arbroath Abbey Pageant Society, *Pageant of the Declaration of Independence Souvenir Programme* (1949), 14. When the script of the pageant was published in 1970 it was entitled 'The Scots' Pageant'.
3. David McCrone, 'Cultural Capital in an Understated Nation: The Case of Scotland', *British Journal of Sociology* 56 : 67–9.
4. Juliet Kinchin, 'Art and History into Life: Pageantry Revived in Scotland', *Journal of the Scottish Society for Art History* 2 (1997): 50.
5. For a brief discussion of 'unionist-nationalism' in historical pageants, see Angela Bartie, Linda Fleming, Mark Freeman, Tom Hulme and Paul Readman, ' Commemoration through Dramatic Performance: Historical Pageants and the Age of Anniversaries', in *The Age of Anniversaries: The Cult of Commemoration, 1895–1925*, ed. T. G. Otte (Abingdon and New York: Routledge, 2018), 201–2.
6. Angela Bartie, *The Edinburgh Festivals: Culture and Society in Post-War Britain* (Edinburgh: Edinburgh University Press, 2014), 2.

7. W. W. Knox, *Industrial Nation: Work, Culture and Society in Scotland 1800–Present* (Edinburgh: Edinburgh University Press, 1999), 254–6.
8. *Dundee Courier*, 11 March 1947, 2.
9. These two were the mainstay of the pageant as its co-producers. In addition both performed, and Thornton was scriptwriter. Both remained active in the pageant until at least the 1960s, with Thornton's script continuing to be used until 2005.
10. The abbey was dedicated to the memory of William's friend, Thomas Becket, Archbishop of Canterbury. It housed Tironesian monks until the Reformation.
11. J. N. Graham Ritchie, 'Images of the Declaration: The Arbroath Pageant', in *The Declaration of Arbroath: History, Significance, Setting*, ed. Geoffrey Barrow (Edinburgh: Society of Antiquaries of Scotland, 2003), 90–1.
12. Dauvit Broun, 'The Declaration of Arbroath: Pedigree of a Nation?', in Barrow, *Declaration of Arbroath*, 1.
13. Duncan M. Ross, 'Diminishing Dividend: The Union and the Economy', in *Nation in a State: Independent Perspectives on Scottish Independence*, ed. Rob Brown (Dunfermline: Ten Book Press, 2007), 64.
14. For discussion of the significance of the declaration, see Edward J. Cowan, *'For Freedom Alone': The Declaration of Arbroath, 1320* (Edinburgh: Birlinn Ltd., 2008).
15. The 'round O' is the circular window in the south transept gable of the Abbey. It became a landmark for shipping.
16. *Dundee Evening Telegraph,* 16 August 1947, 2.
17. Cowan discusses existing problems with establishing the declaration's authorship, including the mistaken identity of the abbot in question – not Bernard de Linton, but Abbot Bernard of Arbroath, Chancellor of Scotland during Bruce's reign. See Cowan, *For Freedom Alone*, 54–5 and J. N. Graham Ritchie, 'Images of the Declaration', 102.
18. *Arbroath Guide,* 23 August 1947, 6.
19. *Arbroath Guide,* 23 August 1947, 6.
20. Letter from Peter F. Anson, *Scotsman,* 27 August 1947, 4.
21. *Arbroath Herald,* 5 September 1947, 4.
22. Callum G. Brown, *Religion and Society in Scotland since 1707* (Edinburgh: Edinburgh University Press, 1997).
23. Bartie, *Edinburgh Festivals*, 48–9.
24. *Arbroath Guide,* 30 August 1947, 6.
25. *Scotsman,* 22 August 1947, 6.
26. *Arbroath Herald,* 12 September 1947, 7.
27. *Arbroath Guide,* 13 December 1947, 3.
28. *Arbroath Herald,* 12 September 1947, 7.
29. Angela Bartie, Linda Fleming, Mark Freeman, Tom Hulme, Alex Hutton, Paul Readman, 'Pageant of Inverness', *The Redress of the Past,* http://www.historicalpageants.ac.uk/pageants/1293/ (accessed 7 April 2019).
30. James J. Coleman, *Remembering the Past in Nineteenth-Century Scotland: Commemoration, Nationality and Memory* (Edinburgh: Edinburgh University Press, 2014), 39–87.
31. Michael Fry, 'Spence, (James) Lewis Thomas Chalmers (1874–1955)', *Oxford Dictionary of National Biography* (Oxford: Oxford University Press, 2004).
32. Quoted in 'Abbey Historical Pageant: Closing Scenes in Memorable Week in Arbroath', *Arbroath Guide*, 28 August 1948, 6.
33. Angela Bartie, Linda Fleming, Mark Freeman, Tom Hulme, Alex Hutton, Paul Readman, 'Pageant of the Declaration of Independence, Arbroath 1949', *The Redress of the Past*, http://www.historicalpageants.ac.uk/pageants/957/ (accessed 7 April 2019).
34. *Dundee Courier*, 5 August 1950, 4.
35. *Dundee Courier*, 11 August 1950, 4.
36. *Dundee Courier*, 27 October 1950, 4.
37. Editorial comment, *Arbroath Guide*, 19 August 1950, 4.
38. *Arbroath Guide,* 28 October 1950, 4. The *McFlannels* was a BBC radio series about a Glasgow family (1939–53).
39. Comments made by Archie Robertson, *Dundee Courier*, 28 September 1951, 2.
40. 'Return of the Stone', *Guardian*, 12 April 1951. A short newsreel clip about the Stone's discovery at Arbroath Abbey, featuring Thornton, can be viewed at the British Pathé website: https://www.britishpathe.com/video/the-stone-returns (accessed 21 March 2019).

41. *Arbroath Herald*, 26 August 1949, 9.
42. *Dundee Courier*, 11 August 1951, 2.
43. *Arbroath Herald*, 24 August 1951, 8.
44. Angela Bartie, Linda Fleming, Mark Freeman, Tom Hulme, Alexander Hutton and Paul Readman, '"History Taught in the Pageant Way": Education and Historical Performance in Twentieth-Century Britain', *History of Education* 48 (2019): 168.
45. Agnes Mure Mackenzie, *On the Declaration of Arbroath* (Edinburgh: Saltire Society, 1951).
46. Mackenzie, *Declaration of Arbroath*, 3, 24.
47. For a short explanation of the movement and its leader, see MacCormick's obituary, 'Champion of Scottish Nationalism', *Glasgow Herald*, 14 October 1961.
48. Ian Levitt, 'Britain, the Scottish Covenant Movement and Devolution, 1946–50', *Scottish Affairs* 22 (1998): 33–57.
49. Levitt, 'Britain, the Scottish Covenant Movement and Devolution', 35.
50. David McCrone, *Understanding Scotland: The Sociology of a Stateless Nation* (London: Routledge, 1992), 212.
51. Murray Stewart Leith and Daniel P. J. Soule, *Political Discourse and National Identity in Scotland* (Edinburgh: Edinburgh University Press, 2012), 143.
52. *Arbroath Guide*, 22 August 1953, 4.
53. *Arbroath Guide*, 8 August 1953, 6.
54. *Arbroath Herald*, 22 August 1952, 7.
55. *Arbroath Abbey Pageant 1953: Souvenir Programme* (n.p., 1953). Aberbrothock is the archaic name for the Arbroath settlement.
56. *Arbroath Herald*, 23 September 1955, 7.
57. *Arbroath Herald*, 24 August 1956, 8.
58. Isobel Wylie Hutchison, 'Poets' Voices Linger in Scottish Shrines', *National Geographic Magazine* 112 (October 1957): 480.
59. Kilbrandon was chair of the Scottish Law Commission at the time and a well-known public figure because of his involvement with reform of juvenile justice. The description of him as a supporter of devolution is from his obituary in the *Glasgow Herald*, 12 September 1989.
60. *Arbroath Herald*, 26 August 1966, 14.
61. Thornton set up a local branch of the SNP and was its secretary: *Arbroath Herald*, 25 November 1966, 7. George Shepherd's strong belief in Scottish independence is discussed in his obituary: *Arbroath Herald*, 1 December 2000.
62. McCrone, *Understanding Scotland*, 164–8.
63. For discussion of these activities see Ritchie, 'Images of the Declaration', 101–6.
64. *The Scots' Pageant: The Script of the Arbroath Abbey Pageant* (n.p., 1970).
65. *Arbroath Herald*, 10 April 1970, 6.
66. *Arbroath Herald*, 10 April 1970, 6; the actor was Stuart McGugan.
67. *Arbroath Herald*, 10 April 1970, 6.
68. 'America Hears About Arbroath', *Arbroath Herald*, 7 August 1970, 17.
69. *Arbroath Herald*, 16 October 1970, 9.
70. *Arbroath Herald*, 2 October 1970, 8.
71. Angela Bartie, Linda Fleming, Mark Freeman, Tom Hulme, Alex Hutton, Paul Readman, 'Farfar Will Be Farfar Still: A Cavalcade of Forfar's Story', *The Redress of the Past*, http://www.historicalpageants.ac.uk/pageants/1343/ (accessed 7 April 2019).
72. *Arbroath Herald*, 2 March 1979, 17; *Arbroath Herald*, 18 May 1979, 14.
73. Bartie, *Edinburgh Festivals*, 215.
74. *Arbroath Herald*, 13 April 1979, 12.
75 *Glasgow Herald*, 5 January 1980, 3.
76. *Arbroath Herald*, 21 November 1980, 11.
77. *Arbroath Herald*, 12 September 1980, 13.
78. *Arbroath Herald*, 29 September 1980, 20.
79. '"Laurel Crown" Sound Track Recorded', *Arbroath Herald*, 29 August 1980, 20.
80. *Arbroath Herald*, 29 September 1980, 20.
81. 'Cheers for the Pageant', *Arbroath Herald*, 5 September 1980, 17.
82. Wood obtained notoriety for her subversive activities and was a high profile (if slightly eccentric) exponent of Scottish independence, gaining respect from institutions such as the Church of Scotland for her principled views. See entry for Wood in *New Biographical Dictionary of Scottish Women*, ed. Elizabeth Ewan and Rose Pipes (Edinburgh: Edinburgh University Press, 2018), 262–3.

83. *Arbroath Herald*, 28 August 1981, 20. 'Saor Alba' is generally translated as 'Free Scotland'.
84. *Arbroath Herald*, 14 May 1999, 1. The MSP was Andrew Welsh.
85. *Scots Independent*, August 1999, 7–8.
86. Interview with Pageant Society President, Anita Walker; interviewed by the author, 16 June 2016.
87. T. M. Devine, 'The Death of the Union?', in *Scotland and the Union 1707–2007*, ed. T. M. Devine (Edinburgh: Edinburgh University Press, 2008), 175–94.
88. Interview with Anita Walker.

Bibliography

Barrow, Geoffrey, ed. 2003. *The Declaration of Arbroath: History, Significance, Setting*. Edinburgh: Society of Antiquaries of Scotland.

Bartie, Angela. 2014. *The Edinburgh Festivals: Culture and Society in Post-War Britain*. Edinburgh: Edinburgh University Press.

Bartie, Angela, Fleming, Linda, Freeman, Mark, Hulme, Tom, Hutton, Alexander and Readman, Paul. 2019. '"History Taught in the Pageant Way": Education and Historical Performance in Twentieth-Century Britain', *History of Education* 48: 156–79.

Bartie, Angela, Fleming, Linda, Freeman, Mark, Hulme, Tom and Readman, Paul. 2018. 'Commemoration through Dramatic Performance: Historical Pageants and the Age of Anniversaries, 1905–1920', in *The Age of Anniversaries: The Cult of Commemoration, 1895–1925*, edited by T. G. Otte. Abingdon and New York: Routledge, 195–218.

Broun, Dauvit. 2003. 'The Declaration of Arbroath: Pedigree of a Nation?', in *The Declaration of Arbroath: History, Significance, Setting*, edited by Geoffrey Barrow. Edinburgh: Society of Antiquaries of Scotland, 1–12.

Brown, Callum G. 1997. *Religion and Society in Scotland since 1707*. Edinburgh: Edinburgh University Press.

Coleman, James J. 2014. *Remembering the Past in Nineteenth-Century Scotland: Commemoration, Nationality and Memory*. Edinburgh: Edinburgh University Press.

Cowan, Edward J. 2008. *'For Freedom Alone': The Declaration of Arbroath, 1320*. Edinburgh: Birlinn Ltd.

Devine, T. M. 2008. 'The Death of the Union?', in *Scotland and the Union 1707–2007*, edited by T. M. Devine. Edinburgh: Edinburgh University Press, 175–94.

Kinchin, Juliet. 1997. 'Art and History into Life: Pageantry Revived in Scotland', *Journal of the Scottish Society for Art History* 2: 42–51.

Knox, W. W. 1999. *Industrial Nation: Work, Culture and Society in Scotland 1800 – Present*. Edinburgh: Edinburgh University Press.

Leith, Murray Stewart and Soule, Daniel P. J. 2012. *Political Discourse and National Identity in Scotland*. Edinburgh: Edinburgh University Press.

Levitt, Ian. 1998. 'Britain, the Scottish Covenant Movement and Devolution, 1946–50', *Scottish Affairs* 22: 33–57.

McCrone, David. 1992. *Understanding Scotland: The Sociology of a Stateless Nation*. London: Routledge.

McCrone, David. 2005. 'Cultural Capital in an Understated Nation: The Case of Scotland', *British Journal of Sociology* 56: 65–82.

Mackenzie, Agnes Mure. 1951. *On the Declaration of Arbroath*. Edinburgh: Saltire Society.

Ritchie, J. N. Graham. 2003. 'Images of the Declaration: The Arbroath Pageant', in *The Declaration of Arbroath: History, Significance, Setting*, edited by Geoffrey Barrow. Edinburgh: Society of Antiquaries of Scotland, 86–107.

Ross, Duncan M. 2007. 'Diminishing Dividend: The Union and the Economy', in *Nation in a State: Independent Perspectives on Scottish Independence*, edited by Rob Brown. Dunfermline: Ten Book Press, 61–79.

11

After the Show is Over ... Souvenirs and Mementos: The Material Culture of Historical Pageants

Ellie Reid

Sources for the study of historical pageantry include a remarkable array of items that have survived from the events themselves. Found in museums and archives, or held in private ownership, pageant-related artefacts range from unique objects such as costumes, props, scrapbooks and handmade souvenirs to mass-produced items such as posters, postcards, badges, medallions, souvenir china and paper ephemera. These material remnants complement documentary sources such as published scripts (usually known as 'books of words'), official programmes, newspaper reports, administrative records, diaries, biographies, oral histories and film footage in providing insights into how pageants have been organised, performed, experienced and commemorated by participants, spectators and local communities. This chapter gives a context to the surviving material culture of historical pageants and seeks to provide an aid to its interpretation. The original purpose, design and creation of publicity materials and souvenirs are described to reveal their role in the staging of pageants. Mass-produced, pageant-related souvenirs are located within the wider context of their genre. The post-pageant afterlife of the objects is examined to explore their legacy. Finally, personal mementos are considered for their evidence of individual experience of participation.

Making local history

Louis Napoleon Parker's 'modern pageantry' established a fashionable way of engaging with local history – one that sought to offer an immersive and memorable experience for both participants and spectators.[1] His first pageant, at Sherborne in Dorset in 1905, was not simply a nostalgic 1,200-year retrospective, but also a commemoration that aimed to make a deliberate and lasting impact on the community. As Parker wrote in his introduction to the souvenir book, published in the following year:

> In my mind's eye I see many an old man and many an old woman, too, for that matter, years and years hence, opening its battered cover and calling the children, and crooning: 'This is what we did in the year 1905 to show honour to our dear town and to the dear school which is the glory of the town'.[2]

He had hoped that 'pageant towns' would repeat their pageant in the style of, for example, Rothenburg's annual performance of 'Der Meistertrunk' or the Oberammergau passion play, thereby creating a cycle of events that might establish a tradition.[3] Although proposals to repeat successful pageants did emerge in some communities during the Edwardian wave of 'pageant fever', it soon became apparent that the idea was impractical. Organisers could not sustain the enthusiasm and supply of financial and logistical support needed from their local communities.[4] Civic pageants, being large undertakings and – unlike stage plays – place-specific in content and staging, were not easily repeatable in new locations. So although some historical pageants were reprised, and some towns and cities did hold more than one pageant during the century, large pageants were usually staged as one-off events, the pageant ending after the last performance. Cast members and spectators were therefore being recruited to participate in a unique event in and about local history. This 'uniqueness' is a theme that can be identified in the study of pageant artefacts.

Most civic pageants took months or even years to prepare. Although the pageants staged across the twentieth century varied in size, purpose, location and content, the organisers did use common approaches, and these were outlined in literature on pageant-making.[5] When Parker confirmed his retirement as pageant-master in 1909, he gave a brief outline of his methods and announced that he proposed to write a 'little handbook on the subject'.[6] He eventually set out his advice in his 1928 autobiography, emphasising the importance of engaging the 'goodwill and co-operation of all the townsfolk'.[7] Regarding the 'Material' used in pageants, he insisted that 'every article of whatever kind used in the performance must be invented, designed, and made in the town; out of material purchased from local purveyors'. Not only would the money spent on the pageant be spent within the town, but also, 'more important than this commercial consideration, the

Pageant becomes a school of Arts and Crafts' to interest and benefit the local community.[8] Although Parker spoke against the staging of pageants solely for fundraising, he was conscious as a theatre professional of the need for pageants at least to break even, and cited financial considerations as influencing his decision to retire from the scene.[9] His advice was therefore astute and practical, including recommendations for the financial arrangements that should be put in place. Parker advocated the sourcing of local expertise on costume, armour and heraldic devices. He acknowledged that a pageant was only possible with volunteers prepared not only to perform in but also to administer it, and to make the costumes and props.

The scheme and methods that Parker described were expanded and developed by other pageant-masters. In 1936 Mary Kelly, pioneer of village drama, published her handbook *How to Make a Pageant*, designed to assist amateur producers.[10] Kelly's advice concentrated on theatrical considerations: she sought to raise the level of the artistry of historical pageants by, for example, promoting the dramatic possibilities of crowd work. She discussed all aspects of staging pageants, including costume and stage design, business management and publicity. In 1954 Anthony Parker, grandson of Louis Parker and an experienced pageant-master himself, published *Pageants: Their Presentation and Production*.[11] His detailed guide, which concentrated on the practical aspects of arranging a pageant, reflected both the advances in technology since Louis Parker's first pageants and an evolution of his grandfather's methods.

While pageant-masters and their committees each brought their own ideas to the performances they staged, guides such as Parker's and Kelly's provide a useful context in which to consider the commonality of material remnants that have survived from individual pageants. More particularly, their detailed advice on souvenir publications, approaches to publicity and administration, utilising of voluntary participation and the handcrafting of pageant artefacts can do much to shed light on specific items in hand.

Establishing a pageant identity

Pageant organisers had to promote their idea from its first inception in order to attract volunteers prepared to invest time, money and energy in the project. Distinguished persons, preferably with aristocratic connections, were courted as patrons. Financial backers were also required at the outset, as subscribers to loan up-front funds and as guarantors to underwrite the pageant in the event of losses. Hundreds of volunteers were needed to serve as committee members, costume and prop makers, as well as to take performing parts. Positive publicity was found necessary to counter naysayers' objections to any costs to ratepayers and the disruption to daily life that a pageant might entail. Thus in order to promote the idea of a pageant and keep interested parties informed, public meetings were staged and newspaper coverage was sought. This publicity effort often drew on the personal contacts of the (usually well-connected) pageant organisers.

Communication by post was the norm in the first half of the twentieth century. Once a 'pageant committee' had been established, the organisers commissioned official stationery, including headed notepaper; this gave the formal name of the pageant and the address of their headquarters (frequently termed 'Pageant House'). Standard letters or leaflets with a reply slip were often issued to recruit volunteers from the local community. Pre-printed postcards such as pro-forma rehearsal invitations were produced to ease the administrative burden of organisation. To create an identity for the pageant the adoption of a pageant logo was recommended. Mary Kelly suggested using a 'decorative badge' for notepaper and programmes, while Anthony Parker advocated a badge or trademark with a simple, recognisable design.[12]

Subsequently used on advertising brochures, leaflets, souvenir publications and postcards, the logos designed or adopted to symbolise the pageant were often based on civic heraldry. Indeed, historic heraldic symbols were important tools used by pageant-makers to create their spectacle of an imagined past, and municipal coats of arms were convenient symbolic expressions of both history and place. Civic heraldry, however, was a more recent innovation than personal armorial bearings. Although historically some places, for example London and Hull, depicted their seals on a heraldic shield, it was not until the sixteenth and seventeenth centuries that the Royal Herald recorded and sanctioned many such arms or granted new civic arms. By the turn of the eighteenth century 90 cities and towns had acquired armorial bearings – relatively few compared to the 500 that local authorities recorded as bearing arms by right in 1953, of which around three-quarters had been adopted in the preceding 100 years. Civic heraldry was therefore largely modern, reflecting a trend in local government to obtain seemingly historic emblems that gave Crown-sanctioned affirmation of authority.[13] Its use in pageants was part of a wider promotion of civic identity through association with the history of localities.

Promoting the pageant

Devising a logo was the first step in creating an identity for a pageant. But it was only a small part of a much larger advertising strategy – one that aimed to attract spectators by combining historical authenticity with popular appeal. Once the dates of a proposed pageant were settled and the details of the episodes to be enacted were agreed, a preliminary brochure or leaflet was issued as a prospectus to be sent to VIPs, newspapers and travel companies to advertise the pageant beyond its immediate locality. Large colour posters were another key part of this promotional campaign. Their design not only communicated the essentials – date, time, place, ticket office and so on – but also placed before the public a graphic that represented, or at least hinted at, the kind of colourful spectacle that was planned. Reflecting common practice, Anthony Parker recommended two poster campaigns: one to stimulate advance bookings and a second prior to the commencement of performances.[14]

The early twentieth century saw the birth of commercial graphic design. Recent advances in large-scale lithographic printing combined with the influences of the Arts and Crafts movement and Art Nouveau to stimulate the rise of artist-designed posters.[15] In this febrile, commercial-creative context, prominent pageant-masters such as Louis Parker and Frank Lascelles could use their personal connections to enlist design professionals. At Bury St Edmunds in 1907, for example, decorative posters designed by the late Pre-Raphaelite Byam Shaw were praised for their 'romantic and powerful artistry'.[16] The staff and students of local schools of art were often major contributors to all aspects of a pageant's design, including the advertising. At St Albans, also in 1907, Robert Groves, headmaster of the St Albans School of Art and Master of Properties for the forthcoming pageant, produced a striking poster design depicting a 'pageanteer' in the costume of the narrative chorus. Competitions were commonly used to source poster designs. Pageant-master Gwen Lally received 300 entries for an open competition held for the 1932 Battle Abbey Pageant. The prize of £10 10s. was won by a Leeds College of Art student whose poster, depicting a Norman warrior, had been inspired by the work of artist and graphic designer Maurice Greiffenhagen.[17] Students from Thanet School of Art at Margate won prizes of between one and five guineas (£1 1s. to £5 5s.) for poster and stamp designs to publicise the 1934 Ramsgate Historical Pageant and Charter Jubilee Celebrations.[18] Local professional expertise was also drawn upon. At Leicester in 1932 the designers and printers Nutt & Stevens Ltd – a firm based in the city – proudly advertised in the official handbook that four of the five poster designs used to promote the pageant, staged to boost the local economy, had been 'executed at home' by their staff.[19]

Seeking to limit costs by choosing an amateur poster design or cheap reproduction methods could prove a false economy if the advertising failed to produce ticket sales. The Dover pageant in June 1908, which was competing with the widely advertised Chelsea and Winchester pageants, was hampered by a finely-detailed poster; while deemed an artistic success, it was not considered sufficiently eye-catching.[20] Similarly, Ayako Yoshino notes that pageant-master Frank Benson had to persuade the 1907 Romsey Pageant Committee to replace their monochrome poster design with a more striking coloured image.[21] Perhaps paradoxically, posters needed to embrace popular contemporary graphic styles to promote these historical spectacles successfully. Using professional artists and art students helped to avoid 'old fashioned' designs. Pageant posters issued during the Edwardian period reflected popular taste for Arts and Crafts- and Art Nouveau-inspired designs. By the 1930s, however, developments in professional graphic design showed the influence of modernism – as reflected in the stylised images and modern typographic style of the advertising designs for pageants such as those held at Leicester in 1932, Nottingham in 1935 and Chester in 1937.[22] As Mary Kelly warned, '[a]n ordinary poster with a herald blowing a trumpet will suggest an ordinary pageant, and those who do not like pageants will stay away'.[23] That said, the adoption of a style considered too modern for popular taste risked inciting criticism. In order to portray the 1947 pageant of Bradford as a departure from its interwar predecessor, a Cubist-inspired advertising design was adopted for posters and programmes. Rather than attracting an audience, however, this design (controversially printed by a non-local firm) simply gave rise to complaints.[24]

To complement posters and other publicity materials, organisers often issued labels bearing the pageant logo or the poster design. Now known as 'Cinderella stamps', these labels resembled postage stamps but were solely decorative, intended to be affixed to letters and other items to advertise the pageant. They also provided individuals and businesses with a visible means of showing their support. Examples from Edwardian, interwar and post-war periods have survived and can be found on correspondence and in scrapbooks. Pageant committees' minutes and newspaper reports reveal the extent of their use. In 1951, for example, 60,000 stamps advertising the Pageant of Dudley (one of many held in connection with the Festival of Britain) were issued for use by local businesses on overseas post.[25]

The use of 'Cinderella stamps' as an advertising medium was superseded in the 1960s, when a relaxation of Post Office regulations permitted the use of slogan postmarks to promote local events and anniversaries.[26] The new arrangements allowed organisers to pay for a bespoke postmark to be added to local post. This new, cost-effective approach to advertising was adopted by the organisers of both the Bedford and Berkhamsted pageants in 1966. And in 1971 a hand-stamped postmark, promoting the pageant held as part of York's 1,900th anniversary celebrations, formed just one aspect of a postal advertising campaign that also included decorative envelopes and postcards.

Postcards

Postcards are the most numerous and diverse form of surviving pageant ephemera.[27] The Edwardian craze for pageants coincided with 'the golden age of postcards'; in the year 1908–9 the British Post Office reportedly handled 860 million cards. Although the Post Office had issued plain, pre-stamped postcards from 1870, privately printed cards were only permitted from 1894, with postal regulations confining any message or image to the front of the card. The introduction of the divided back in Britain in 1902 (and the US in 1907) permitted the address and message to be written on one side, so freeing the whole of the other for a picture. Advances in printing technology and photography enabled the production of attractive but affordable images, and postcards could be posted at a reduced rate (a halfpenny less than the lightest letter to inland addresses).

Postcards therefore offered an inexpensive means both of communicating and of sharing and collecting images. After the First World War a rise in all postal charges and the wider availability of telephones reduced their appeal for essential communications, but the preferential postage rate was retained until 1968, after which postcards were used primarily by tourists and businesses.[28] Reflecting these national trends, the publication of pageant postcards was most common before 1914; it continued to be popular during the interwar years, but usage went into sharp decline after 1945. Pageant postcards could be official publications of the pageant committee, but many others were unofficially or privately produced.

Postcards based on pageant posters were often the first issued by committees as a form of advertisement. Other 'official' publications included sets of coloured postcards reproducing specially commissioned paintings of the planned episodes; yet others featured reproductions of the costume designs. These met the need to create images of the pageant in advance of its staging in order to recruit volunteers and attract potential spectators; they also generated revenue through their sale as souvenirs. The leading publisher of artist-drawn postcards in Britain was Raphael Tuck & Sons

Ltd – a firm with a prolific output. By 1903 it had more than 10,000 individual designs in print and encouraged the postcard boom by running collecting competitions, for which they awarded significant prizes.[29] Tuck's produced the official postcards for the St Albans and Oxford pageants in 1907, with 18 different, artist-drawn designs of scenes and characters issued in three sets for each pageant. At Oxford the original designs were exhibited in the run-up to the actual performances.[30] To appeal to the broadest range of collectors, the cards were promoted in newspapers and issued in two qualities of colour prints (the superior version boasting gilt edges) and as black-and-white photographic reproductions. Tuck's also issued a single set of six images for the 1908 Gloucestershire pageant, which comprised reproductions of original paintings by Sydney Herbert, Master of Designs for that pageant.[31] Tuck's cards continued to circulate long after the pageant in question had passed into history. The Oxford pageant designs, for example, were issued from 1909 as jigsaws in the company's 'Playtime Picture Puzzles' series.[32] Other publishers issued similar sets of cards for virtually every major pageant before 1914, and some were also produced for many of the pageants of the interwar period – one notable example being Frank Lascelles' 1931 Pageant of Bradford.

Many postcards were reproductions of photographs showing scenes being performed. These were usually taken by the official photographer, often at a dress rehearsal, and so were available to buy when the pageant opened to the public. Close examination of these images can occasionally reveal some performers lacking their costume – so although a more accurate depiction of the pageant than artist-drawn cards, they may not represent eventual performances. Photographs of the entire scene from above, including all the participants, were usually taken from the pageant-master's 'crow's nest' control room on the top of the grandstand. In some cases, particularly for large Edwardian pageants, dozens of postcard designs and formats were produced; the same images were often made available as 'real photographs' printed on photographic paper or more cheaply on plain card. Composite postcards, combining several miniature reproductions of photographs, attempted to capture the essence of the pageant on a single postcard. Since many more photographs could be issued as postcards than might be published in souvenir books or programmes, these images can provide valuable additional information on the costumes, properties and staging of the pageant.

Some official postcards depicted portraits of performers in the principal roles. These can provide close-up views of individual costumes not readily seen in other images. Portrait postcards of pageant-masters reflected their celebrity status during the pageant, but cards of other committee members are less common. Postcards showing groups of performers may also give details of costumes; moreover, combined with cast lists or annotations by the original owner, they sometimes constitute the only identifiable images of individual participants.

These postcards provided participants with a memento of those who made or shared their pageant experience. For many of the 'pageanteers', dressing up and performing to a paying audience would have been a novel episode in their lives, one enhanced by appearing on a postcard that was for sale to the public. Copies of such postcards that have messages on the back can reveal a participant's or spectator's thoughts on the pageant, often expressing personal views in contrast to those in official reports (Figs. 11.1 and 11.2).

Figure 11.1 Photographic postcard of Edith Holloway, performer in the Bath Historical Pageant, 1909. Author's collection.

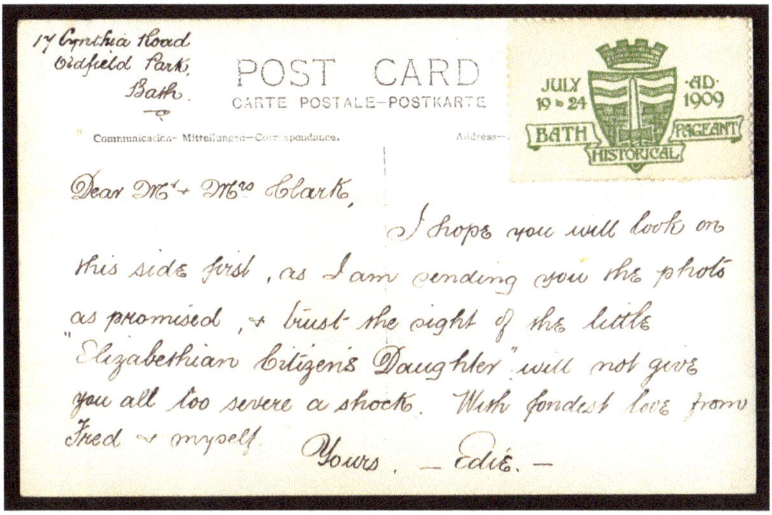

Figure 11.2 Reverse of Edith Holloway's postcard, with her message and an example of a 'Cinderella stamp'. Author's collection.

In the Edwardian period, the popularity of postcards and the limited availability of home photography prompted performers to have studio portraits taken and reproduced as postcards. While some official photographers offered portrait sittings on the pageant ground, others offered incentives for performers to visit their studio in costume. At Watford in 1907, for example, Messrs Downer & Sons prepared a backdrop imitating the St Albans pageant ground to entice performers into their studio. These postcards (such as those shown in Figs. 11.1 and 11.2) may be the only surviving images of pageanteers who performed in minor roles.

Other postcards captured views of the audience, taking care to include notable persons whose attendance was advertised as both a draw to and a seal of approval for the pageant.[33] Photographers (especially those without permission to take pictures on the pageant ground) also found opportunities in street scenes, capturing costumed performers heading to or from the pageant. One popular tactic was the juxtaposition of the old and the new, through images like that of a costumed cast-member on a bicycle. This incongruity was exploited by cartoonists who produced unofficial postcards, such as those published by Davis's of Oxford in 1907 which satirised their fellow citizens' enthusiasm for the pageant of that year.

Pageant publications: souvenir programmes, books of words and cast lists

Official publications produced by the committees of large Edwardian pageants, as described by Yoshino, usually included a souvenir programme and 'book of words' – often lavishly illustrated – to enable spectators to familiarise themselves with the script or to follow the performance.[34] Books of words for scripted pageants were published in advance of the performances, sometimes in a cheap edition for performers as well as in standard and (on occasion) deluxe editions for spectators. Pageants as eventually performed were not infrequently at variance with their published scripts, as overly-long performances or poor weather could necessitate changes. Individual copies of books of words annotated by performers or spectators can provide additional evidence for a pageant as eventually performed.

Souvenir programmes often incorporated not only a synopsis of the scenes, but also an explanation of the local history from which the scenes were drawn, as well as extensive notes on heraldry. Evidence that heraldic designs used in a pageant were based on historical research lent authenticity to the proceedings and enabled the organisers to promote the educational benefits of attendance. Heraldic symbols were an important means by which pageant-makers created the spectacle of an imagined past. Their use on shields, banners, armour, scenery and other properties also enabled spectators to identify the roles being played by the performers, often at considerable distance from the audience enclosure or grandstand. Advising on the introduction of important characters into a scene, Mary Kelly gave the example of Richard II. His formal entrance, she declared, should involve 'the appearance of the Royal Herald', together with 'his coat-armour and trumpeter' and the procession of his retinue 'in which the King's colours, and his famous device of the White Hart are constantly repeated'. All of this served as a visual prompt to accompany his verbal introduction. By such means, Kelly explained, the inherent difficulties in communicating with an audience at a distance outdoors might be overcome. In doing so the original use of armorial bearings to identify nobles or signify the allegiance of combatants, whether on the battlefield or in chivalric tournaments, might be recovered.[35]

Official publications for Louis Parker's 1909 York Pageant included an *Historic and Heraldic Guide* which gave the historical background to each scene enacted, followed by biographical profiles of the members of the nobility portrayed and illustrated notes on their heraldry.[36] It included a four-page index listing the documentary authority for every coat of arms used. The heraldic banners of the 20 city guilds and companies that featured in one of the episodes (set in 1483) were also listed and their arms described. Sold for 8d., the guide's purpose was educational, as the audience were expected to find it difficult fully to appreciate the pageant's content without such a supplement to the published script. Furthermore, the lavishly produced *Book of the York Pageant 1909* included full-colour illustrations and extensive descriptions of the banners. Such attention to detail caused the *Yorkshire Post* to remark that '[t]he Heraldic Committee are purists and the display of banners and equine trappings in the mediaeval scenes will entitle their creators to graduate in heraldry'.[37]

Although post-1918 pageant programmes and souvenir books were rarely as extensively detailed and illustrated as their predecessors, most large pageants still produced substantial publications. Mary Kelly advocated publishing just a souvenir book of words:

> With good organization quite an elaborate book can be made to pay well, and the importance of getting it sold well in advance is that your audience may come with some knowledge of the history, and so be prepared to watch the pageant intelligently.[38]

Sales of these and the advertising they contained typically contributed around 5–10 per cent of the income used to offset staging costs.[39] Complete cast lists were not always included in the programmes or official souvenirs, which tended to credit only the principal organisers, patrons, financial backers, scriptwriters, composers and committee members. There were two schools of thought on this matter. Louis Parker and Mary Kelly both promoted the idea that performers should shed their identities and become the characters they were portraying. Kelly's view was that 'the list programme is not necessary if the players are sufficiently *in* the pageant; they should be prepared to act anonymously'.[40] Others, Anthony Parker included, saw listing all the performers in the programme as an incentive for them or their families to buy a copy.[41] The scale of a pageant in part dictated whether it was practical to produce a full cast list; the production of an accurate list was virtually impossible owing to the inevitable changes in line-up.

Local newspapers responded to the popular demand for a recognition of the performers' contributions by publishing their own lists of the people involved.[42] At Oxford in 1907 an unofficial published list, *The Pageant Record*, pointedly rejected the style of the official publications, declaring:

> Instead, we will try to be useful, and give you at a fair price a list as complete as we can make it, of those who perform in the ceremonies, and who at great sacrifice of time and expense have given their services. In appreciation of their efforts we think that any work on the Pageant should include the names of those who take smaller parts, as well as those who are the leaders in the show.[43]

Elsewhere performers found their own solutions to the lack of a complete cast list by adding the names of those who took part to books of words or programmes, or by seeking autographs of fellow performers, pageant organisers and distinguished guests. These uniquely annotated copies can be a source of otherwise unrecorded information, while also representing a performer's endeavour to create a personal souvenir of their experience.

Manufactured souvenirs I: badges, medals, spoons

From the mid-nineteenth century an expanding market for royal and historical commemorative and tourist souvenirs saw a boom in their manufacture, aided by advances in technology and new ideas from abroad. Studies of souvenirs produced for Queen Victoria's Diamond Jubilee, the women's suffrage campaign and tourists to Stonehenge, for example, offer useful parallels to the vast array of items manufactured for pageants, which ranged from ceramics and silverware to paper napkins.[44] In *Pageant Fever*, Yoshino discusses the commercial and touristic aspects of Edwardian historical pageants. She identifies the nature and extent of both the consumer market for pageant souvenirs and the advertising strategies of pageant organisers, and explores the apparent contradictions in the commercialisation of 'authentic' experiences.[45] Although commercial pageant souvenirs were rarely manufactured locally, their design, production and consumption provides an important insight into the culture of historical pageantry.

Where pageants were held in locations already established as tourist destinations, existing products such as heraldic silverware could readily be promoted as fitting souvenirs. However, badges, medallions, spoons and trophies were all commissioned specifically for historical pageants. Most were made in Birmingham. The city was a notable centre for the manufacture of mayoral regalia and civic insignia, medals and other such items, and a place where jewellers also applied their specialised metalworking and enamelling skills to fulfilling the increasing demand for souvenirs and commemorative goods.[46]

Badges are among the most commonly found of these pageant artefacts. They have survived in part because they are attractive, small, robust and not readily re-purposed. Some will have been acquired as tourist souvenirs; others were kept as mementos by participants. At the beginning of the twentieth century Birmingham manufacturers were producing thousands of enamel metal badges for clubs and societies, as well as political, trade and professional bodies.[47] Several firms produced badges for pageants, including Thomas Fattorini Ltd, a leading supplier of both enamel and button badges. Enamel badges, produced by stamping a blank of gilding metal to leave a raised outline design that could be enamelled in colour by hand, were made for many Edwardian and interwar pageants. Those produced for Bath in 1909 and the 1935 Pageant of England were designed as badges of office, indicating the specific roles of participants (Fig. 11.3).

Button badges were patented in America in the 1890s and produced in Britain from 1902. Transparent celluloid was used to protect the printed paper design, both layers then being secured to the tin backing. The button badges produced for the 1909 York Pageant provide an early example of their use in a pageant context. In the interwar period this more ephemeral style of badge was increasingly common; examples included the 1934 Pageant of Runnymede performers' badges and badges made for the 1938 Pageant of Birmingham (Fig. 11.3). Fattorini's 1939 catalogue, which featured the 1932 Battle Abbey Pageant celluloid badge design, marketed them as products for children ('by nature badge wearers'), with the firm claiming that '[b]adges are an unqualified success as money raisers at Carnivals, Pageants, etc.'[48]

Figure 11.3 Badges of Bath Historical Pageant 1909, Pageant of England 1935, Pageant of Birmingham 1938. Author's collection.

While badges could be bought as souvenirs or worn to show support and encourage participation, some authorised access to the pageant ground. At Esher in 1932 admittance could be gained by purchasing one of the four styles of badge for committee members, performers, helpers, Scouts, Guides and schoolchildren, with prices ranging from 3d. to 1s.[49] Badges were also among the rewards and presentation pieces given to individuals in acknowledgement of their contribution to pageants. At York in 1909 £52 19s. 6d. was spent on badges for officials and performers. The sum included the cost of two nine-carat gold enamelled (medallion-style) badges by Robert Chandler of Birmingham, given to Princess Louise and the Duke of Argyll as patrons of the pageant.[50] At Colchester in 1909 individually inscribed enamel pendant badges were commissioned from B. H. Joseph, another Birmingham manufacturer. Depicting Boudica in her chariot, these were presented to ladies who took leading roles in the organisation of the pageant, among them Eveline Stanyon, a former milliner, who was Honorary Secretary of the Headdresses Committee.[51] Where these items survive, with provenance and sometimes oral history, they provide clear documentary evidence of an organised intention to reward participation.

Commemorative medals, commonplace souvenirs during the nineteenth and early twentieth centuries, were often issued in connection with historical pageants. These small portable items could be mass-produced and made in various qualities. Examples include the 1910 Chester pageant medals, struck in gold, silver and bronze and designed by leading medallist John R. Pinches of London (who also produced the 1911 Festival of Empire medals).[52] The official pageant medal made for the 1907 Bury St Edmunds pageant was a copy of an original coin of St Edmund. It was produced in gold, silver, silver gilt and bronze in two sizes, with prices ranging from 21s. to 1d. The jeweller stocking the medallion also held the original, probably to enable purchasers to verify the authenticity of the replicas.[53] Reading's reproduction of the Seal of Reading Abbey as a medal for their 1920 pageant reinforced the pageant's claims to historical authenticity. At York in 1909 two designs of medal were made available, both depicting Saint Helena: one reproduced an image found on Roman coins while the other depicted 'Mrs Shaw of Welburn as Saint Helena'.[54]

Rather less common than medals were pageant teaspoons. Spoons have a long history as gifts and souvenirs; early examples of commemorative spoons recorded London's Great Plague of 1665 and the 1683–4 Frost Fairs held on the frozen River Thames.[55] Teaspoons were among the souvenirs produced for the 1851 Great Exhibition. In America the hundreds of souvenir teaspoon designs produced and sold at the Chicago World's

Fair in 1893 boosted a craze for collecting spoons that had developed in the early 1890s.[56] Initially the American mania for spoons was reported with some amusement in British newspapers, but by 1898 spoons produced specifically as souvenirs of places were being sold in England.

A few years later, newspapers reported that Birmingham jewellers were producing coronation spoons to cater for the influx of American visitors.[57] This was a harbinger of things to come: pageant souvenir spoons were created partly with international visitors in mind. Examples that specifically commemorate pageants include Birmingham-manufactured spoons for the Welsh National Pageant in 1909, the Festival of Empire and Pageant of London in 1911, and the Rochester Pageant of 1931. Others, such as those for Bath in 1909, although official souvenirs, had a design less specific to the pageant and therefore enjoyed a longer shelf-life.[58] At Dover in July 1908 the Pageant Committee reported it had received 'a handsome little nickel trinket emblazoned with the arms of Dover, which will prove a very acceptable souvenir of the Pageant', and that

> a Dover Pageant Spoon has been put on the market by Messrs. Hart and Co., 10, Cannon Street, and forms a handsome souvenir of the event. The spoon embodies at the top of the handle the Arms of Dover, surmounted by the Castle, and the Arms of Kent surmounted by the crown. The key underneath the Arms is symbolic of the fact that Dover is Key to England. The bowl of the spoon contains a representation of Episode II. of the Pageant.[59]

This design was a particularly striking illustration of the considerable effort often taken to capture the history, location and significance of a pageant in a souvenir.

Manufactured souvenirs II: ceramic souvenirs

The staging of early twentieth-century historical pageants coincided with a craze for collecting ceramic miniatures decorated with heraldic designs, popularly known as 'crested china' or 'Goss china'. In the early 1880s William Henry Goss, a Stoke-on-Trent manufacturer of decorative ceramics, started to produce small white glazed vases, enamelled with crests of university colleges and public schools. His son Adolphus saw the commercial potential of producing high-quality replicas of local historical artefacts, decorated with local coats of arms, for the expanding middle-class tourist market. These miniatures were modelled on original items from local museums and decorated with the civic coat of arms by permission of the local authority. A transfer of the outline was applied to a miniature glazed porcelain model, and the colours of the crest were then painted in enamels by hand. By appointing a sole agent in each tourist destination, who initially stocked only the local models with the local crests, Goss initiated a collecting craze that proved sufficiently intense to spawn its own club (the 'League of Goss Collectors') and publication (*The Goss Record*, a directory listing agents and models sold).[60] Many firms emulated Goss china, competing in locations where there was a Goss agent and themselves producing crested china for small towns and villages, as well as for commemorative events. These popular collectables with their heraldic decorations had an air of authenticity that aligned neatly with the ideals of historical pageants.

Crested china was produced for most large Edwardian pageants (Fig. 11.4). Foley China produced two substantial models for the 1905 Sherborne Pageant, one a model of a Roman vase found in Sherborne Museum. Both designs were decorated with an image of the statue of St Aldhelm (from Sherborne Abbey's Digby memorial) and the heraldic arms of both the abbey and the school. Very few of these first pageant souvenirs survive, so the extent of their availability is not clear. In 1906 Tuscan China (R. H. & S. L. Plant Ltd) produced crested miniatures, marked underneath as souvenirs of the Warwick Pageant. At St Albans in 1907 the jeweller Ernest Haywood, stockist of official pageant postcards and medals, sold five ceramic models manufactured by Wiltshaw and Robinson Ltd under their Carlton China trademark. These were decorated with a St Albans Pageant design, newly registered specifically

Figure 11.4 Crested china. From left to right: Colchester Pageant 1909 (Swan China), St Albans miniature mug (Carlton China) and National Pageant of Wales 1909 (Swan China). Author's collection.

for the event, and incorporating the arms of the city.[61] The logo for the 1908 Gloucestershire Historical Pageant can be found on a more expansive range of items produced by the same firm. Crested miniatures for the 1909 Bath Pageant were produced under the Arcadian China trademark. Particularly fine porcelain souvenirs marked as 'Swan China' were produced for the Colchester Pageant and the National Pageant of Wales, both staged in 1909; these items were decorated with graphic advertisement designs rather than heraldry. Inferior quality Florentine China souvenirs were produced for the 1909 York Pageant and the 1911 Pageant of London. Surprisingly, W. H. Goss produced relatively few commemorative items for pageants (their short shelf-life was perhaps a disincentive). However, the firm did manufacture pieces for the pageant held in association with the 1907 Romsey millenary which depicted the seal of the abbey. Goss also produced pieces decorated with a King Cole design by local artist Hervey Elwes; these were sold in connection with the Colchester Pageant in 1909.[62]

Goss and his competitors deliberately set out to create ornamental souvenirs. Other potteries, manufacturing domestic ceramics, created pageant souvenirs by designing decorations for their mugs, ashtrays and other crockery. The most extensive range of pageant-related china was produced by Stoke-based Shelley Potteries – notable for their production of items for the 1911 Festival of Empire, such as tobacco jars decorated with the exhibition logo or a view of the Crystal Palace.[63] Alongside these items catering for the traditional souvenir collector, Shelley also produced a range of domestic ware in the contemporary 'art pottery' style. These featured 10 illustrations of scenes from the associated 1911 Pageant of London. Jugs, mugs, teapots, plates and candlestick holders can be found with coloured designs depicting the principal characters in action.[64]

After the First World War ornamental crested china was eschewed in favour of domestic pottery souvenirs with predominantly modern designs. During the 1930s, as shown in chapter 7, civic pageants were staged along with industrial exhibitions and fairs to boost the economies of urban areas.[65] This provided an opportunity for local manufacturers to make and sell pageant souvenirs. In 1931 the Historical Pageant of Newcastle and the North was held alongside an Empire Fair and Exhibition which included displays of local products. For the event local pottery C. T. Maling & Sons produced contemporary-style ceramic souvenirs (Fig. 11.5).

The late 1920s onwards saw a fashion for brightly coloured 'cottage ware' and 'jazz age' style pottery, the latter typified by Clarice Cliff's 'Bizarre' design. The chief designer at Malings, Lucien Boullemier, created a hand-painted plaque featuring a pageanteer standing on a castle turret

Figure 11.5 Maling Pageant Ware, Historical Pageant of Newcastle and the North 1931. Author's collection.

to advertise 'Maling Pageant Ware'. Three pageant designs were produced and featured on a range of domestic pottery, incorporating the firm's zig-zag 'Tango' border.[66] The Maling family were directly involved with the Newcastle pageant: Theo Maling, who had completed her art and design studies in Newcastle the previous year, produced some of the costume designs.[67]

One of the Pageant Ware designs, which bears similarities with Theo's costumes, was also used on advertising stamps, leaflets and on tins of Cremona Toffee (made locally at Wilkin's Garden Toffery, in Heaton; company founder Albert S. Wilkin was chairman of the Empire Fair and Exhibition Committee). Other contemporary examples of functional pageant souvenirs include the Royal Doulton ashtrays made for Lally's 1929 Ashdown Forest Pageant and the ceramic tankard souvenirs of the 1930 Salford Pageant. However, the most extensive range of ceramic souvenirs came relatively late in the lifetime of the pageant movement. This was a complete tea, coffee and dinner service manufactured by William Adams for Langham's China Shop, Bury St Edmunds, for the Pageant of Magna Carta in June 1959.

Local products and disposable souvenirs

Of course many souvenirs associated with commemorative events were strictly local, sold as one-off items by small businesses. One early twentieth-century example is provided by the 'King Alfred Cakes' sold by local bakeries in Winchester, in honour of the Alfred Millenary celebrations of 1901.[68] Anglo-Saxon-themed souvenirs of a different kind were made available to mark the 1907 Romsey Pageant, held in aid of the Romsey Abbey Restoration Fund. Thus the crosses made from 600-year-old wood removed from the roof of the abbey during its restoration, and subsequently sold as 'a memorial of Romsey Pageant', were souvenirs – or perhaps relics – that lent an air of authenticity.[69] Other locally-marketed pageant souvenirs were rather more opportunistic. At Bath in 1909, for example, a range of brassware was promoted by local traders, including tobacco pipe holders and coal buckets depicting 'Bladud and his pigs'; Bath 'Pageant Bouquet' bath soap and perfume was also available from the local firm of Steele & Marsh, chemists and perfumers.[70] Textile souvenirs too were produced for pageants. These included handkerchiefs, as created for the pageants at Sherborne (1905) and Carlisle (1928), and teacloths, created for pageants at Bury St Edmunds (1959) and Wennington (1998). In many cases such souvenirs have been carefully preserved by their original owners, who perhaps saw them as being 'too good to use'.

Most surprisingly of all, perhaps, some seemingly disposable paper items have survived, including commemorative paper napkins of early pageants. Mrs S. Burgess of London was the leading printer of Japanese paper commemorative table napkins; these were imported with a pre-printed coloured border, but with a plain centre that could be overprinted with a specific local message.[71] A cheap and fashionable form of souvenir sold by street vendors, examples of commemorative napkins survive from a wide range of events including royal occasions, sporting events, political movements such as the women's suffrage 1908 demonstration in London's Hyde Park and even disasters such as the sinking of the *Titanic* in 1912. Napkins marketed for the St Albans pageant of 1907 featured centres overprinted with a list of the episodes and a description of the pageant grounds.

Souvenirs and pageant finances

The existence of mass-produced souvenirs demonstrates that large civic historical pageants presented a sufficiently large market for pageant organisers and local businesses to consider commissioning special souvenirs. However, a review of a sample of pageant accounts indicates that the sale of souvenirs, other than official publications such as programmes and books of words, made little contribution to the income received by pageant organisers. By far the biggest source of income was generally from the sale of tickets, which typically amounted to around 80 per cent

Table 11.1 Extracts from selected pageant accounts

Pageant	**Total receipts**	**Ticket sales (% of total receipts)**	**Books of words, programmes and advertising income (% of total receipts)**	**Rights (% of total receipts)**
Oxford 1907	£14,874	£12,643 (85%)	£1,381 (9%)	£504 (3%)
Winchester 1908	£11,127	£10,534 (95%)	£569 (5%) [includes published music]	
York 1909	£14,439	£11,612 (80%)	£407 (9%)	£145 (1%)
Chester 1910	£12,792	£8,467 (66%)	£498 (4%)	£270 (2%)
Scarborough 1912	£4,192	£3,513 (83%)	£314 (7%)	£92 (2%)
Lancaster 1913	£4,095	£3,260 (80%)	£231 (6%)	£88 (2%)
Reading 1921	£6,185	£3,969 (64%)	£653 (10%) [includes badges]	£133 (2%)
Norwich 1926	£2,372	£1,962 (83%)	£200 (8%)	
Spirit of Warwickshire (Warwick Castle) 1930	£6,085	£5,026 (83%)	£196 (3%)	
Birmingham Centenary Pageant 1938	£17,900	£15,700 (88%)	£707 (4%) [includes badges and catering, less costs]	
St Albans Millenary Pageant 1948	£14,986	£12,716 (85%)	£1,844 (12%)	
Three Towns Pageant at Hampton Court Palace 1951	£14,436	£13,740 (95%)	£495 (3%)	
Bury St Edmunds 1959	£11,292	£8,215 (72%)	£2,251 (20%)	
Farnham 1988	£56,916	£35,313 (62%)	£2,033 (4%)	

of generated income (Table 11.1).[72] Sales of official publications and income from advertisements in them usually accounted for between *c.* 5 and 10 per cent of receipts. Other forms of income, such as those derived from catering, photographic, filming and souvenir rights, produced considerably less. Although no two pageants are strictly comparable, and the type and quality of official souvenirs and rights varied considerably, it is nevertheless clear that the likely income to pageant committees from the sale of souvenirs or souvenir rights was insufficient to rescue an unsuccessful pageant. One notable example is Louis Parker's spectacular Dover Pageant of 1908. Despite its splendid souvenirs, which included 'Dover in a nutshell' (36 local views in a real walnut shell with postage tag attached, priced at 3d.), the pageant was not a financial success; final accounts showed a loss of nearly £2,000.[73]

After the show was over: the afterlife of costumes and props

The success of historical pageants was heavily dependent on the performers' costumes successfully creating a representation of the past. Ideally the costumes would be designed and created especially for each scene of the pageant, using colour schemes chosen for the visual effect of the costumes en masse, in the setting of the pageant ground. Local designers could ensure that costumes incorporated the appropriate heraldic symbolism as well as adhering to the requirement of historical authenticity. Mary Kelly and Anthony Parker supported Louis Parker's advice that props and costumes should be made locally, an approach adopted by many pageant committees.[74] However, costumes and props were costly and time-consuming to make, so hiring some or all of them was often the practical solution.

The source of the costumes for a pageant rather dictates whether any surviving costumes are identifiable. The few extant examples have usually been locally made and carefully kept by owners. Some have found their way into museum collections, as in the case of Sherborne and St Albans. Since early pageants were recorded only in black-and-white photographs or on film, surviving costumes or fabric samples can provide evidence to complement the many descriptions of pageant costume-making and performances. Receipts for the hire or purchase of individual costumes in the personal scrapbooks of performers give some insight into the financial commitment of volunteers. And in the absence of original costumes, designers' drawings of the costumes can add considerably to historical understanding of the creation of a pageant, as shown by Swift and Elliott's study of the 1909 Bath Pageant.[75]

The attention to historical and heraldic accuracy often led to the creation of high-quality artefacts whose survival was ensured after the pageant was over. This was certainly the case for the 20 historic craft guild banners created for the 1909 York Pageant. They were included among pageant artefacts displayed, along with archaeological finds and historical paintings, in the 1909 Historical and Pageant Exhibition at Whitechapel Art Gallery. In their long afterlife, the banners have been seen by thousands of people and are still on display to the public in York's Merchant Adventurers' Hall.[76] But while York saw perhaps the most extensive use of heraldry in historical pageants, its use was quite general across the whole lifetime of the movement. In his 1954 manual Anthony Parker recommended the appointment of a Master of Heraldry. He also stipulated that banners should be painted by heraldic experts; even after the Second World War accurate heraldry was still considered to be an essential ingredient of historical pageantry.[77]

After the run of performances had ended, many costumes and props were auctioned to recoup part of the cost spent making them – although pageant committees were frequently disappointed with the meagre financial returns. At Colchester in 1909, following a two-day sale 'of the arms, armour, shields, spears, Roman temple of Claudius, Boadicea's chariot, Roman triumphal car, the equipment of the workshops, office furniture and other properties arising from the Colchester Pageant', it was reported that:

> It had been thought that Pageanteers would have thronged to acquire possession of the arms and armour carried by them 'in the brave days of old'; but it was not so. Roman suits of armour and mediaeval garments were alike knocked down at an alarming sacrifice; all kinds of ancient 'toggery' fell on a flat market, and really beautiful banners went at the price of a comic song.[78]

Items sold at auction may have been kept by performers, and some found a new use – for instance in shop window displays or for fancy dress. But more frequently the items were bought for material that could be re-used.[79] Some costumes and props were sold on to other pageants; the Colchester Pageant Committee minutes, for example, recorded offers of items from Dover and Gorleston, both of which had held pageants the previous year.[80] Indeed it is possible that some of the items used at Colchester had featured in two previous pageants, since the Gorleston Pageant had itself sourced some props and costumes from St Albans (including, for example, the costumes of the narrative chorus emblazoned with the heraldic crest of St Albans).

Scrapbooks and albums

Presentation albums were given as expressions of gratitude to pageant organisers, performers and patrons or distinguished visitors. At Sherborne in 1905 two albums bound in white vellum were presented to Louis Parker, in recognition of the success of his first pageant. One contains an illuminated address signed by the hundreds of pageant performers and workers; the other more than 100 photographs of the pageant itself. The albums preserved at Sherborne School archives, together with the oak lectern designed to hold them, demonstrate the groundswell of enthusiasm that the Sherborne pageant generated, and in recent years have provided a unique source for a study of participation in the pageant.[81] Presentation albums for smaller events are equally valuable, since they can provide evidence of pageants not recorded in souvenir publications or illustrated newspaper coverage. To take just one example, the identical photograph albums of the 1925 Telscombe village pageant, thought to have been gifts to the principal performers, provide an invaluable visual resource for studying this one-day event, about which information is otherwise negligible.[82] This kind of material presents the 'best face' of the pageant as performed, even if it reveals less about the process of pageant-making than scrapbooks and albums compiled by organisers as an official record. So far as this latter category of items goes, these often contain not only comprehensive collections of press cuttings, but also correspondence, receipts, financial records and other details not found in published accounts of the event. Preserved in the archive collections of organising bodies and in local record offices, they contain the private records of those at the heart of conceiving and staging the event, sometimes revealing difficulties, tensions and controversies of various kind (not least those relating to pageant finances).[83]

Personal albums compiled by performers or pageant workers provide evidence for the ways in which individual volunteers contributed to the pageant. In compiling the albums, the creators sought to distil their pageant experience into the form of a personalised memento.[84] Two albums compiled by performers in the 1907 Oxford Historical Pageant survive. The album of Thomas Cook, an 18-year-old bookseller's assistant, is predominantly an extensive collection of press cuttings.[85] It does, however, include the original appeal for volunteers, postcards seeking his attendance at meetings and rehearsals, various items of correspondence and a receipt relating to the fitting and supply of his costume. Cook played minor roles in the pageant and wore the cheapest costume; on one occasion he was invited to a meeting and asked to 'bring other men if possible' – clear evidence of a shortage of male performers (a problem experienced by many pageants throughout the twentieth century). The other album was made by Evelyn Way, a clergyman's daughter who lived with her unmarried aunt in north Oxford. The correspondence in her album includes an invitation to discuss her participation over tea with Oxford University-educated historian K. Dorothea Vernon, Lady Secretary for the thirteenth episode ('Eighteenth century fair').[86] The ephemera in Evelyn Way's album includes receipts, tickets and clippings from published souvenirs, together with studio photographs and a press cutting featuring a photograph of Way herself, which she described as a 'self snap'.[87] In their differing ways these albums preserve the experiences of two of the thousands of individuals attracted by the idea of re-enacting local history in extraordinary spectacles.

Conclusion

The surviving material culture offers a fresh perspective on several themes in the study of historical pageantry. On the one hand, carefully crafted pageant artefacts and the use of heraldry provide evidence of the importance which pageant organisers attached to historical authenticity. At the same time the sheer variety of material – posters, postcards, Cinderella stamps, leaflets and brochures – is evidence of the readiness of organising committees to use the latest methods of advertising, marketing and communication to realise their envisioned pageants.

The technologies of mass production enabled the creation of a range of souvenirs and mementos that facilitated the consumption and commemoration of unique staged performances by a mass audience. These objects helped to make tangible, and lent permanence to, the momentary suspension of disbelief experienced by performers and spectators alike, as the modern world briefly gave way to unfolding historical scenes. That many of these manufactured artefacts – whether teaspoons, china, or postcards – were the subject of contemporary collecting crazes provides further evidence of the place of historical pageantry in mainstream popular culture. Perhaps the most eloquent testimonies to the impact of historical pageants, however, are the scrapbooks that record the pageant-making journeys of their compilers. They memorialise both an individual's personal investment in a pageant and, through their record of participation, a community's engagement in the promotion of a prescribed, localised, imagined past.

Notes

1. See, for example, Deborah Sugg Ryan, 'Spectacle, the Public and the Crowd: Pageants and Exhibitions in 1908', in *The Edwardian Sense: Art, Design and Spectacle in Britain, 1901–1910*, ed. Michael Hatt and Morna O'Neill (New Haven and London: Yale University Press, 2010), 43–71; Ayako Yoshino, *Pageant Fever: Local History and Consumerism in Edwardian England.* (Tokyo: Waseda University Press, 2011), 57–97.
2. Cecil P. Goodden, *The Story of the Sherborne Pageant* (Sherborne: F. Bennett, 1906), 7.
3. *Bournemouth Daily Echo,* 25 November 1905, 4.
4. Newspaper reports reveal such proposals, Sherborne included: *Salisbury and Winchester Journal*, 14 October 1905, 8.
5. For an American example, see Esther Willard Bates, *The Art of Producing Pageants* (Boston: Walter H. Baker, 1925).
6. Louis N. Parker, 'My Reminiscences', *Strand Magazine* 38 (July 1909): 11–18.
7. Louis N. Parker, *Several of My Lives* (London: Chapman & Hall, 1928), 279–94.
8. Parker, *Several of My Lives*, 285–6.
9. *Birmingham Daily Gazette,* 5 April 1907, 4.
10. Mary Kelly, *How to Make a Pageant* (London: Sir I. Pitman & Sons, 1936).
11. Anthony Parker, *Pageants: Their Presentation and Production* (London: Bodley Head, 1954).
12. Kelly, *How to Make a Pageant*, 107; Parker, *Pageants*, 46.
13. C. Wilfred Scott-Giles, *Civic Heraldry of England and Wales* (London: Dent & Sons, 1953), 3–5.
14. Parker, *Pageants*, 48.
15. Alain Weill, *Graphics: A Century of Poster and Advertising Design* (London: Thames & Hudson, 2004), 11–16.
16. *Eastern Daily Press,* 27 May 1907, 8.
17. *Sussex Agricultural Express,* 18 March 1932, 14. Greiffenhagen was a graphic artist known for his commercial poster design.
18. *Thanet Advertiser,* 16 February 1934, 2.
19. *The Pageant of Leicester (City and County) Official Handbook*, ed. F. Shakespeare Herne and R. G. Waddington (Leicester: The Pageant Committee, 1932).
20. *Dover Express,* 5 June 1908, 2.
21. Yoshino, *Pageant Fever*, 76.
22. *Pageant of Leicester*; *Sole Official Souvenir & Programme [of the] Chester Historical Pageant* (Shrewsbury: Wilding & Son, 1937).
23. Kelly, *How to Make a Pageant,* 107.
24. Angela Bartie, Linda Fleming, Mark Freeman, Tom Hulme, Alex Hutton, Paul Readman, 'Bradford Centenary Pageant', *The Redress of the Past,* http://www.historicalpageants.ac.uk/pag eants/1265/ (accessed 28 June 2019).
25. *Dudley Herald* 1951, news-cutting in Dudley Pageant, 1951: Scrapbook of news-cuttings and photographs, Dudley Archives, R 3956. In the event, however, the subsequent poor attendances and large financial loss sustained by this pageant indicate that the hope of attracting an international audience failed to materialise: *Evening Despatch,* 25 June 1951.
26. Cyril Parsons, *100 Years of Slogan Postmarks,* www.postalmuseum.org/blog/100-years-of-slogan-postmarks/ (accessed 28 November 2018).
27. Ellie Reid, 'Pageants and Postcards', *Picture Postcard Monthly* 237 (January 1999): 24–7.
28. A. W. Coysh, *The Dictionary of Picture Postcards in Britain 1894–1939* (Woodbridge: Antique Collectors' Club, 1984), 90; 'Postcard Rates 1860–1978', www.gbps.org.uk/information/rates/inland/postcards.php (accessed 10 November 2018).
29. Anthony Byatt, *Picture Postcards and their Publishers* (Malvern: Golden Age Postcards Books, 1978), 293.

30. Unidentified cutting in the scrapbook of T. C. Cook, Oxford Historical Pageant 1907 (privately held).
31. *Gloucestershire Chronicle*, 4 July 1908.
32. Byatt, *Picture Postcards and their Publishers,* 296.
33. Ryan, 'Spectacle, the Public and the Crowd', 43–71.
34. Yoshino, *Pageant Fever,* 66–9.
35. Kelly, *How to Make a Pageant,* 24.
36. *Historic and Heraldic Guide to the York Pageant 1909*, ed. J. Solloway and Colonel Saltmarshe (York: Ben Johnson & Co., 1909).
37. *Book of the York Pageant 1909* (York: Ben Johnson & Co., 1909); *Yorkshire Post*, 15 May 1909, 8.
38. Kelly, *How to Make a Pageant,* 109.
39. See Table 11.1.
40. Kelly, *How to Make a Pageant,* 109.
41. Parker, *Pageants*, 127.
42. *York Historic Pageant, July 26th to 31st, 1909: The Performances, with Names of Performers, Choruses and Dancers* (York: *Yorkshire Herald,* 1909).
43. *The Pageant Record Containing List of Performers, Press Opinions, Brief Account of Episodes* (Oxford: Fox, Jones & Co. [1907]), 4–5.
44. Richard Wales and Susan Wales, *Souvenirs from the Diamond Jubilee of Queen Victoria* (Bloomington, IA: AuthorHouse, 2012); Kenneth Florey, *Women's Suffrage Memorabilia: An Illustrated History* (Jefferson, NC and London: McFarland & Company, 2013); Julian Richards, *Inspired by Stonehenge: A Celebration of the Weird and Wonderful* (East Knoyle: Hobnob Press, 2009).
45. Yoshino, *Pageant Fever*, 57–97.
46. Jean Debney, *Jewels of Our City: Birmingham's Jewellery Quarter* (Studley: Brewin Books, 2013), 41.
47. Philip Attwood, *Badges* (London: British Museum Press, 2004), 3–5; Paul Martin, *The Trade Union Badge: Material Culture in Action* (Aldershot: Ashgate, 2002), 129–30; Florey, *Women's Suffrage Memorabilia,* 48–56.
48. Attwood, *Badges*, 3–5.
49. Esher Fete Committee, *The Book of the Esher Historical Pageant and Fete* (Esher: Esher Fete Committee, 1932), 5.
50. Robert Withington, *English Pageantry: An Historical Outline* (2 vols, New York and London: Benjamin Blom, 1926), vol.2, 234.
51. *East Anglian Daily Times*, 22 December 1909, 8.
52. J. H. Pinches, *Medals by John Pinches: A Catalogue of Works Struck by the Company from 1840 to 1969* (London: *Heraldry Today*, 1987).
53. *East Anglian Daily Times*, 9 July 1907, 9.
54. 'Mrs Shaw' refers to Mary Jane Shaw, of Welburn Hall, Kirby Moorside.
55. Simon Moore, *Spoons 1650–2000* (Oxford: Shire Publications, 2005), 5–12; http://collections.vam.ac.uk/item/O78098/commemorative-teaspoon-unknown/ (accessed 23 October 2018); Seal-top spoon, https://collections.museumoflondon.org.uk/online/object/109301.html/ (accessed 16 March 2019).
56. 'The Souvenir Spoon Craze', *Collector* [New York], 3 (15 December 1891): 156–7.
57. *Luton Times and Advertiser,* 27 December 1901, 3.
58. Examples of all survive. See also Yoshino, *Pageant Fever*, 78.
59. *Dover Express*, 17 July 1908, 8.
60. Lynda Pine and Nicholas Pine, *William Henry Goss: The Story of the Staffordshire Family of Potters who Invented Heraldic Porcelain* (Horndean: Milestone Publications, 1987), 196–9.
61. Board of trade registered design number: 501230.
62. Nicholas Pine, *The Price Guide to Arms and Decorations on Goss China* (Waterlooville: Milestone Publications, 1991); Louis N. Parker, *Souvenir and Book of Words of the Colchester Pageant* (Norwich: Jarrold & Sons, 1909); Ellie Reid, 'King Coel [*sic*: Cole] and Colchester', *Goss Hawk* 333 (February 1999), 13.
63. John Barter and David Delter, 'The Festival of Empire', *Shelley Group* 86 (March 2008): 12–15.
64. Shelley also produced scenes from Shakespeare in a similar style. See Wileman and Shelley pattern books. Miscellaneous Book Old, Stoke on Trent City Archives, Minton archive, SD 1705/SH/19.

65. Tom Hulme, '"A Nation of Town Criers": Civic Publicity and Historical Pageantry in Inter-War Britain', *Urban History* 44 (2017): 270–92.
66. Steven Moore and Catherine Ross, *Maling: The Trade Mark of Excellence!* (3rd rev. ed., Newcastle upon Tyne: Tyne & Wear Museums, 1989), 61–4.
67. David Johnson, 'History in the Re-making', *Maling Collectors' Society Newsletter* 38 (March 2008): 1, 4; *The Historical Pageant of Newcastle and the North at Newcastle upon Tyne: Official Souvenir and Programme* (Newcastle upon Tyne: J. W. Hindson, 1931).
68. Paul Readman, 'The Place of the Past in English Culture, *c.*1890–1914', *Past and Present* 186 (2005), 154.
69. *Hampshire Chronicle*, 29 June 1907, 10–11.
70. *Souvenir of the Bath Historical Pageant 19th to 24th July 1909* (Bath: Bath Herald Office, 1909).
71. Maurice Rickards, *The Encyclopedia of Ephemera* (London: British Library, 2000), 221.
72. See the *Redress of the Past* pageant database (http://www.historicalpageants.ac.uk/pageants/) and newspaper reports for examples of pageant accounts.
73. *Dover Express*, 27 November 1908, 5.
74. Parker, *Pageants*, 79; Kelly, *How to Make a Pageant*, 96–100.
75. Andrew Swift and Kirsten Elliott, *The Year of the Pageant* (Bath: Akeman Press, 2009), 539–47.
76. Whitechapel Art Gallery, *Historical and Pageant Exhibition 20th October – 5th December 1909* (Whitechapel: Whitechapel Art Gallery, 1909).
77. Parker, *Pageants*, 28, 89.
78. Herbert F. Baskett, *Catalogue of the Arms, Armour, Shields, Spears, Roman Temple of Claudius, Boadicea's Chariot, Roman Triumphal Car, the Equipment of the Workshops, Office Furniture and other Properties Arising from the Colchester Pageant which will be Sold by Auction ... on Friday and Saturday 2nd & 3rd July 1909* (Colchester: Rudkin, 1909); *Evening Star*, 5 July 1909, 4.
79. *Faringdon Advertiser and Vale of White Horse Gazette*, 9 November 1907, 4.
80. *Colchester Pageant Committee Minute Book 1907–10*, Essex Record Office: D/Z 476.
81. Somerset and Dorset Family History Society, www.sdfhs.org/sdfhs-projects/introduction-to-sdfhs-projects/social-records/sherborne-pageant-participants/ (accessed 10 November 2017).
82. Telscombe pageant 1925 photograph album (August 1925), East Sussex Record Office: AMS 7126/7.
83. An example being the bound volumes: *Papers Relating to Oxford Historical Pageant, 1907*, compiled by Falconer Madan, Honorary Secretary, Bodleian Library: G. A. Oxon c. 158–64.
84. Angela Bartie, Linda Fleming, Mark Freeman, Tom Hulme, Alexander Hutton and Paul Readman, '"History Taught in the Pageant Way": Education and Historical Performance in Twentieth-Century Britain', *History of Education* 49 (2019): 175–6. See also Ryan's work on the scrapbook of Miss P. Noel: Deborah Sugg Ryan, 'Staging the Imperial City: The Pageant of London 1911', in *Imperial cities*, ed. Felix Driver and David Gilbert (Manchester: Manchester University Press, 1999), 117–35. Miss Noel consciously restricted her scrapbook entries in the knowledge that her work would become public.
85. Scrapbook of T. C. Cook, Oxford Historical Pageant 1907 (privately held); Ellie Reid, 'Serious Outbreak of Pageantitis', *Oxfordshire Limited Edition* 337 (February 2015), 25–9.
86. 'Oxford Historical Pageant Scrapbook Compiled by Evelyn Way', Oxfordshire History Centre: SF OXFO/394.5.
87. Reid, 'Serious Outbreak of Pageantitis'.

Bibliography

Attwood, Philip. 2004. *Badges*. London: British Museum Press.

Bartie, Angela, Fleming, Linda, Freeman, Mark, Hulme, Tom, Hutton, Alexander and Readman, Paul. 2019. '"History Taught in the Pageant Way": Education and Historical Performance in Twentieth-Century Britain', *History of Education* 48: 156–79.

Byatt, Anthony. 1978. *Picture Postcards and their Publishers*. Malvern: Golden Age Postcards Books.

Coysh, A. W. 1984. *The Dictionary of Picture Postcards in Britain 1894–1939*. Woodbridge: Antique Collectors' Club.

Debney, Jean. 2013. *Jewels of our City: Birmingham's Jewellery Quarter*. Studley: Brewin Books.

Florey, Kenneth. 2013. *Women's Suffrage Memorabilia: An Illustrated History*. Jefferson, NC and London: McFarland & Company.

Hulme, Tom. 2017. '"A Nation of Town Criers": Civic Publicity and Historical Pageantry in Inter-War Britain', *Urban History* 44: 270–92.

Martin, Paul. 2002. *The Trade Union Badge: Material Culture in Action*. Aldershot: Ashgate.

Moore, Simon. 2005. *Spoons 1650–2000*. Oxford: Shire Publications.

Moore, Steven and Ross, Catherine. 1989 (3rd rev. ed.). *Maling: The Trade Mark of Excellence!* Newcastle upon Tyne: Tyne & Wear Museums.

Pinches, J. H. 1987. *Medals by John Pinches: A Catalogue of Works Struck by the Company from 1840 to 1969*. London: *Heraldry Today*.

Pine, Lynda and Pine, Nicholas, 1987. *William Henry Goss: The Story of the Staffordshire Family of Potters who Invented Heraldic Porcelain*. Horndean: Milestone Publications.

Pine, Nicholas. 1991. *The Price Guide to Arms and Decorations on Goss China*. Waterlooville: Milestone Publications.

Readman, Paul. 2005. 'The Place of the Past in English Culture, *c*.1890–1914', *Past and Present* 186: 147–99.

Richards, Julian. 2009. *Inspired by Stonehenge: A Celebration of the Weird and Wonderful*. East Knoyle: Hobnob Press.

Rickards, Maurice. 2000. *The Encyclopedia of Ephemera*. London: British Library.

Ryan, Deborah Sugg. 1999. 'Staging the Imperial City: The Pageant of London, 1911', in *Imperial Cities: Landscape, Display and Identity*, edited by Felix Driver and David Gilbert. Manchester: Manchester University Press, 117–35.

Ryan, Deborah Sugg. 2010. 'Spectacle, the Public and the Crowd: Pageants and Exhibitions in 1908', in *The Edwardian Sense: Art, Design and Spectacle in Britain, 1901–1910*, edited by Michael Hatt and Morna O'Neill. New Haven and London: Yale University Press, 43–71.

Swift, Andrew and Elliott, Kirsten. 2009. *The Year of the Pageant*. Exeter: Akeman Press.

Wales, Richard and Wales, Susan. 2012. *Souvenirs from the Diamond Jubilee of Queen Victoria*. Bloomington, IA: AuthorHouse.

Weill, Alain. 2004. *Graphics: A Century of Poster and Advertising Design*. London: Thames & Hudson.

Withington, Robert. 1926, *English Pageantry: An Historical Outline* (2 vols). New York and London: Benjamin Blom.

Yoshino, Ayako. 2011. *Pageant Fever: Local History and Consumerism in Edwardian England*. Tokyo: Waseda University Press.

12

'The Story of Us'? Kynren and the Uses of the Past

Angela Bartie, Linda Fleming, Mark Freeman, Tom Hulme, Alexander Hutton and Paul Readman

On 15 nights in the summer of 2016 an historical pageant was performed in northeastern England. It was called Kynren – an adaptation of the Anglo-Saxon word for 'generation' or 'family' – and the subtitle was 'an epic tale of England'. It was also billed as 'The Story of Us'. Some shows attracted capacity crowds of 8,000 people to the uncovered grandstand in the outdoor venue, and the organisers claimed a total audience for the year of 100,000.[1] The venue was Flatts Farm near Bishop Auckland, in County Durham, and the show ran again in the summers of 2017, 2018 and 2019. Kynren is part of a larger project, under the auspices of the charity Eleven Arches. It receives substantial funding from the investor and philanthropist Jonathan Ruffer, whose stated aim is to 'transform Bishop Auckland for visitors'[2] by building a large and permanent tourist attraction on the Flatts Farm site. The intention is to incorporate Auckland Castle, the historic home of the prince-bishops and from 1832 to 2012 the seat of the modern bishops of Durham.

Kynren was just one of a number of large-scale historical performances that made the news in 2016. The artist Jeremy Deller, for example, created 'We're Here Because We're Here' on 1 July 2016 – a nationwide project involving amateur actors dressed as First World War soldiers.[3] At the start of September the 350th anniversary of the Great Fire of London was marked with the burning on the River Thames of a massive wooden replica of seventeenth-century London, created by a team of volunteers under the direction of the artist David Best.[4] The following month 2,000 re-enactors converged on Battle in East Sussex to mark the 950th anniversary of the Battle of Hastings; this re-enactment is now a major annual event supported by English Heritage.[5]

Figure 12.1 The 'Pandemonium' scene from the Opening Ceremony of the London 2012 Olympic Games, London, July 2012. Photograph by Matt Lancashire, Flickr; Creative Commons Licence: Attribution 2.0 Generic (CC BY 2.0).

These occasions reflect a seemingly insatiable appetite for anniversaries: recent years have seen various events associated with the octocentenary of Magna Carta, the Thames Pageant celebrating the Queen's Diamond Jubilee in 2012 and a slew of commemorative activities linked to the centenary of the First World War, to name just a few.[6] With its season-long run and the involvement of 1,000 volunteers, not to mention the heavy investment in lighting, sound, special effects, horses, grandstand and spectator facilities, Kynren is arguably the most impressive of all these events. According to press reports, it was 'the biggest live production seen in the UK since the 2012 London Olympic ceremonies' (Fig. 12.1).[7]

Our purpose in this chapter is to evaluate Kynren by situating it in the tradition of popular historical drama in Britain and elsewhere. The most obvious immediate influence is the spectacular *Cinéscénie* show at the Puy du Fou historical theme park in the Vendée, France, which takes place on summer evenings and tells the story of 700 years of local history. Visually Kynren and the *Cinéscénie* are very similar, and many of the same people have been involved in both projects.[8] One of these people, the original project director and later Eleven Arches chief executive officer Anne-Isabelle Daulon, has also acknowledged the influence of the Opening Ceremony of the 2012 Olympic Games; indeed Steve Boyd, the 2012 choreographer, has worked on the Kynren show.[9] Created by Danny Boyle and Frank Cottrell Boyce, the historical elements of the 2012 Opening Ceremony were inspired by Humphrey Jennings's *Pandaemonium*, which told the story of the 'coming of the machine' (Fig. 12.1).[10] These segments of Boyle and Boyce's extravaganza – entitled 'Green and Pleasant Land' and, in honour of Jennings, 'Pandemonium' – are visually echoed in parts of Kynren – but here there is little sense of the 'radical patriotism' widely seen as characterising the Opening Ceremony.[11] Catherine Baker explicitly contrasts 'Pandemonium' – which included depictions of the industrial revolution, suffrage campaigns and the arrival of the *Empire Windrush* – with the 'conservative historical imaginary associated with the revival of H. E. Marshall's *Our Island Story*', the 1905 book that David Cameron named as his childhood favourite in 2010 and whose elite-centred historical narrative was satirised by W. C. Sellar and R. J. Yeatman in *1066 and All That*.[12] In Baker's reading of the 2012 Opening Ceremony, the event was an 'attempt to narrate a multicultural, multivocal nation', a series of overlapping personal and collective histories.[13] By contrast Kynren, while not exactly a reaction against the radical patriotism celebrated in the Olympic Stadium, can certainly be seen as a return – deliberate or otherwise – to older ways of representing shared histories.

Indeed, in terms of its content and organisation, the greatest similarities are undoubtedly with the pageants on which this book focuses. Kynren is a theatrical representation of successive historical episodes; it has a volunteer cast under professional direction; it is ambitious in its use of costumes, props, scenery, music and animals; and it aims to attract both local people and tourists. In many ways Kynren would be recognisable to those who shaped the twentieth-century pageant tradition, even though the similarities have not been widely recognised – and certainly not in the material produced by Eleven Arches itself. Nor does Boyle acknowledge the heritage of historical pageantry in his discussion of the 2012 Olympic Opening Ceremony.[14]

Perhaps this is because pageants have been largely displaced by other forms of historical engagement through performance: the emergence of the community play in the 1960s, often focusing on a single historical episode of working-class rebellion or popular discontent, is one example; another is the remarkable growth of historical re-enactment societies.[15] (Re-enactment is very different from historical pageantry, but it shares a concern for dramatic interpretation of the past and, frequently, a fondness for extravagant costumes. Many of Deller's volunteers for 'We're Here Because We're Here' came from re-enactment societies, and Kynren itself recruited re-enactors to train volunteers in combat techniques.)[16] And yet, while historical pageantry seems to retain little direct influence over contemporary developments in the dramatic representation of the past, Kynren is in total audience terms perhaps the largest pageant since the Second World War.[17] It is also one of the longest-running. In 2019 the fiftieth staging of Kynren took place and very few pageants have reached this landmark. (One exception is the Arbroath Pageant – see chapter 10 – which was performed 106 times across 18 separate years from 1947 to 2005.)[18]

A detailed investigation of Kynren intersects with several areas of scholarship. First, it is partly a study of popular entertainment and the consumption of history, a field that has expanded rapidly in recent years. For scholars such as Jerome de Groot (and before him Raphael Samuel), the enduring appeal of re-enactment is one important example of the 'consumption' of history; although Kynren is definitely *not* an historical re-enactment,[19] it does contain some spectacular battle scenes and its popularity in part reflects the appeal of re-enactment – not least that of the 'living history' at the nearby Beamish folk museum.[20] Second, there is a substantial historiography of theatre and spectacle.[21] A particular kind of dramatic performance of historical episodes can be dated back at least to the late Georgian naval panoramas of Philippe de Loutherbourg,[22] continuing through the spectacular twentieth-century imperial pageants staged at White City and Wembley[23] and on into the post-war period via the enthusiasm for *son et lumière* shows. These last came to Britain from France in the 1950s and in turn find echoes in the popular 'Lumière' festivals of the present day, with notable examples taking place in Durham in 2015 and London in 2016.[24] Third, the story of Kynren – and the historical pageant tradition more widely – is also a chapter in the history of education. In recent decades many historians of education have shifted their focus away from schools and other institutions of formal learning and towards a whole series of informal educational activities and organisations, among them museums, theatres and youth organisations.[25] Participation in historical performance is often seen in explicitly educational terms: de Groot argues that re-enactments serve a 'performative educational function', and that 'living history' – such as that performed at Beamish – demonstrates 'an underlying pedagogical investment in performed reconstruction of historical periods'.[26] Eleven Arches echoes this educational focus: it is a registered charity 'focused on community development, [and] underpinned by a bold, innovative and engaging arts and education programme'.[27] In a period when the school history curriculum has been a matter of sustained debate, the wider popular representation of historical periods and the 'national story' becomes particularly resonant in the context of the history of education.[28]

Kynren: the historical story

Like most major pageants, Kynren is an outdoor show: it is performed against the backdrop of Auckland Castle. More than 1,000 volunteers are involved, mostly as cast but some as crew. This is considerably smaller than some earlier pageants,[29] which might tell us something about the effective ways in which twentieth-century communities were mobilised in the service of pageantry. Nevertheless, the scale of the Kynren spectacle is impressive. The official programme for the 2016 run of performances records that 2,367 costumes were made (and 180 helmets); it also notes the involvement of 34 horses, not to mention the sheep, goats, ducks and geese that feature in some episodes.[30] In form, the spectacle closely follows the Puy du Fou *Cinéscénie*, with similarities in the setting (at Kynren, a lake in front of an historic building; at Puy du Fou, a ruined castle), as well as in the staging, music, choreography and the lavish fireworks of the evening's finale. In content, the historical story dramatised in Kynren is something that contemporary English audiences are largely unused to seeing. The overall effect is an event that administers something of a culture shock – one that, according to Chris Lloyd of the *Northern Echo*, is

> like the opening ceremony of the London Olympics meeting Durham City's Lumiere mixed with Time Team at Horse of the Year Show which has somehow got entangled in the Last Night of the Proms with all the details of a Pieter Bruegel painting and the surreal air, and grassy knolls, of the Teletubbies thrown in for good measure.[31]

Yet although all these elements and influences can certainly be discerned, with even Lloyd's evocation of the Teletubbies not entirely misplaced, the thing that Kynren most resembles is an historical pageant. In this sense it is part of a much longer tradition of historical storytelling through drama.

Kynren tells a version of the national story, though with an intermittent focus on the northeast of England. Although its episodes are less clearly defined and separated than in a normal pageant, 21 are readily identifiable, as well as a prologue and epilogue. The pageant begins in the 1880s with a young boy, Arthur, kicking a football through a window of the Bishop of Durham's palace – an event that, according to the official programme, really did take place.[32] Sometime afterwards Arthur meets Hensley Henson, who was actually bishop from 1920 to 1939.[33] Henson is the narrator of Kynren; he leads Arthur through the 'gatehouse of time', telling him about many episodes in the history of England, or 'The Story of Us', as the souvenir programme has it.[34]

Like many pageants, the early history depicted in Kynren mixes fact and legend. In the first nine scenes Arthur is shown Joseph of Arimathea at Glastonbury, the Knights of the Round Table, the construction of Hadrian's Wall, two scenes featuring St Cuthbert (voiced by the Archbishop of Canterbury, Justin Welby),[35] the battles of Stamford Bridge and Hastings and the coronation of William I at Westminster Abbey. These scenes are a blend of nationally and locally significant events, many of which took place far from the site of Kynren. Pope Gregory (voiced by the Bishop of London, Richard Chartres) is heard making his well-known apocryphal quip 'they are not Angles, but angels', but we also learn of Cuthbert's retirement to the hermitage at nearby Lindisfarne. The depiction of local saints – particularly pre-Conquest ones – was a staple feature of historical pageants for much of the twentieth century; in the Edwardian and inter-war years in particular the Anglo-Saxon period was clearly identified as the origin of the English nation and church.[36] One aspect of this was the Christian struggle against the Vikings, reflected in Kynren's depiction of the battle of Stamford Bridge – a more 'local' event than Hastings, which also appears. Another focus of Christian patriotism prominent at Kynren – although, interestingly enough, one that had rarely featured in earlier pageants – is the story of Joseph of Arimathea, which forms the focus of the first episode.[37] In this way Kynren begins by placing Christianity at the centre of Englishness, using legend as much as history to do so.

The next scene is a medieval festival that took place on the very site of the pageant, following the relocation of the prince-bishops to Auckland in 1283. This 'merrymaking and entertainment' is followed by a spectacular depiction of the battle of Neville's Cross (1346), in which the Scots were defeated by a greatly outnumbered English army. Such episodes were common in pageants in northern England, whereas further south the enemy in medieval scenes was more often the French. King Henry VIII is next, meeting Francis I at Calais in 1520 at the Field of the Cloth of Gold – the scene features an extravagant display of costumes and jousting. Subsequent religious controversies, most notably the dissolution of the monasteries, are absent from the narrative. So – perhaps more surprisingly – are Agincourt and the defeat of the Spanish Armada, both of which would have provided opportunities, which Kynren takes elsewhere, to use well-known snippets of text and verse. After Henry VIII comes William Shakespeare and an imaginary meeting – dreamed by young Arthur – between the

Bard and Elizabeth I at Auckland Castle. In 2016, the year in which the 400th anniversary of Shakespeare's death was marked, some of the most famous lines from the plays were read out and the text projected onto the set. Shakespeare appeared in various pageants in the south and midlands of England in the twentieth century and his plays were often drawn on for scripts, but as a character he was not often seen in the north of England and never in Scotland.[38] Yet here he is set at the heart of the national story, with the dream device being used to place him in Bishop Auckland.

Unlike many Edwardian pageants, Kynren does not end in Elizabethan times. It depicts the Civil War, though not Oliver Cromwell himself, who mainly featured in southern pageants where he appeared at all.[39] The 'Georgian Renaissance' comes next. Perhaps the most remarkable episode in the whole of Kynren, this episode juxtaposes commercial wealth and rural poverty; it involves choreographed peasants sowing corn in a manner that visually echoes Soviet or Maoist propaganda – though of course with a very different message. The subsequent two scenes also feature economic and social history, with a strong local emphasis. The first of these depicts the construction of the Stockton to Darlington railway and includes a fantastic moving replica of George and Robert Stephenson's 'Locomotion No. 1'. This is followed by a mining scene, presented as a tribute to the 69 victims of the Trimdon Grange disaster in 1882, and then by the celebrations of Queen Victoria's Diamond Jubilee in 1897. After this the action moves to the trenches of the First World War and the Christmas truce in 1914. The familiar story is told through a soldier's letter home: 'at noon we might play football together – and, as usual, we *will* beat the Germans'. This is followed by a depiction of the Durham miners' gala in the 1920s, when Henson was bishop (though this fact is not explicitly mentioned). According to the programme the decade 'was a golden age, with a flourishing of prosperity',[40] reflected in another opportunity for lavish costume and choreography.

With these scenes from the nineteenth and twentieth centuries Kynren comes much closer to the present day than was often the case in twentieth-century historical pageants. After the First World War there was a growing tendency to depict later periods: by the 1930s it had become the exception, rather than the rule, to end with Elizabeth I; some pageants indeed incorporated the war itself into their long narratives of local and national history.[41] Yet earlier periods were still heavily represented, with some pageants even in the 1950s focusing heavily on the medieval past.[42] Of Kynren's 21 scenes, excluding the prologue and epilogue, 13 are dated to before 1650, but the action does come right down to the twentieth century.[43] The final substantive scene depicts the Second World War, through Winston Churchill's 'finest hour' speech. The audience hears a slightly longer extract than is often quoted, with 'the long continuity of our institutions and our empire' resounding in the night, as the great statesman's own image is projected onto the walls of Auckland Castle. After this brief but significant appearance of Churchill, Kynren ends with an epilogue featuring 'Land of Hope and Glory' and a firework display, during which many in the audience sing along and wave Union flags.

The 2017 performances of Kynren were similar to those of its first year, with just a few changes. New characters included Boudica, whose revolt – a long way from the site of the pageant – was given a short scene. Mention was also made of the prince-bishop Anthony Bek (d.1311), the first bishop of Durham to reside at Auckland Castle,[44] in connection with the medieval festival episode. A Viking raid on Lindisfarne was also depicted, in a probably unconscious echo of earlier historical pageants, which often included scenes featuring the heathen Danes.[45] There was a change to the mining scene: the 'miners' hymn' *Gresford*, written by Robert Saint to commemorate the Gresford explosion of 1934, was inserted between the depiction of the industry itself and the Diamond Jubilee extravaganza. According to the official programme, the version of *Gresford* used in the Kynren soundtrack was recorded in Durham Cathedral by the Spennymoor and Ferrymoor Colliery brass bands. The narrative device is also amended somewhat: 'Young Arthur' still breaks the bishop's window, but in 2017 Henson's response is to summon 'Old Arthur', the castle 'ground-keeper' – voiced by the well-known Northumbrian actor Kevin Whately – who introduces his young namesake to the Gatehouse of Time.

The most significant addition, however, is a new scene. For reasons that are not made clear this is placed out of chronological sequence, between the Battle of Neville's Cross and the Field of the Cloth of Gold. It features the Knights of the Round Table, and Lancelot is heard explaining to Young Arthur what 'Kynren' means: 'who your people were in the past, who you are in the present and who you choose to become in the future'.[46] The exhortation to enlist a revived knowledge and understanding of the past in the task of shaping the local or national future had been a familiar trope of twentieth-century historical pageantry; it is found again in Kynren.[47] In explaining this ultimate purpose of the pageant narrative, under the heading 'The Story of Us', Eleven Arches are explicitly urging new, creative and potentially controversial 'uses' of history.

History, nation and identity

In purporting to tell 'The Story of Us', the makers of Kynren beg the question: who is meant by 'Us'? Who belongs to 'England' and who can be characters in the 'epic tale'? It is a commonplace in the literature that heritage can disinherit and exclude, even where this is not intended. This point is particularly emphasised in discussion of the heritage institutions of a diverse, multi-faith and multi-ethnic country, which might not always be seen to have kept pace with rapid demographic and cultural change.[48]

Kynren presents a version of national and local identity that certainly has the potential to exclude. It roots the origins of England and the early history of the northeast region in Christianity, giving a prominent role to ecclesiastical history through the narrative presence of Henson, in 2016, and the appearance in 2017 of Bishop Bek. With early scenes featuring Joseph of Arimathea and St Cuthbert, Kynren follows many earlier pageants in foregrounding the early origins of a common Christianity[49] – and in largely avoiding subsequent episodes of religious conflict. Using the voices of Welby and Chartres emphasises the broad affinity of Kynren with the national church. Moreover, although the second half of Kynren presents a largely secularised version of both English and local history, the backdrop of Auckland Castle – the replica castle is huge and the real castle's windows are lit up throughout the performance – ensures that the presence of the Christian past is not forgotten. Young Arthur is inducted into a Christian heritage by Henson and Old Arthur; other religious traditions are not mentioned at any point in the show. There is no sign in Kynren of the religious pluralism that will, apparently, feature in the 'Faith Museum' now under construction at Auckland Castle itself.[50]

Just as there is little evidence in Kynren of religious conflict and difference, so there is minimal acknowledgement of social conflict and industrial politics – despite the declared importance of the region's industrial heritage and the depiction of scenes relating to mining and railways. Like a number of pageants in the years following the Second World War, Kynren acknowledges both poverty and tragedy, with the memorialisation of mining disasters proving the most moving part of the pageant. Yet vast tracts of available social and political history remain unexplored. The 1920s, for example, is represented by the Durham miners' gala, but although this scene does feature some union banners, no acknowledgement is made of the General Strike – surely one of the most significant peacetime political events in this region in the twentieth century.

In this context Henson's role as the narrator is important, though none of his own biography is mentioned in the pageant or the programme. According to Matthew Grimley, Henson had a 'violent, almost obsessional' dislike of trade unions, while Hester Barron explains that 'his stance was virulently anti-socialist and he despised the class consciousness fostered by the labour movement' (although he was undoubtedly sympathetic to the plight of individual miners and their families).[51] It is notable that the miners' gala depicted in Kynren, which is not allotted an exact date, does not feature the infamous assault on Henson's ally, the dean J. E. C. Welldon, in 1925. At this gala Welldon was rescued from a group of miners by police – although he was not actually thrown into the River Wear, as the popular 'retelling' of the story had it.[52]

The conservative version of the national story told at Kynren represents a striking departure from the industrial and political history that formed such a memorable element of the 2012 Olympic Opening Ceremony. Here the 'Pandemonium' section showed top-hatted visionary industrialists, a thrusting factory chimney invading a pastoral scene (Fig. 12.1) – which has been interpreted as a visual echo of the Co-operative and Popular Front pageants of the 1930s and 1940s[53] – half-naked and sweating factory workers in the early industrial age, and political dissent including the suffragettes. Boyle and Boyce's version of the British past (and hi-tech present) neither attempted nor achieved the kind of coherence at which Kynren aims: there was no narrator to unify the disparate sections and only at a few points did the show slip out of its predominantly irreverent tone.[54] Boyle and Boyce focused predominantly on much more recent history than Kynren, and on the varied (and frequently oppositional) identities and postures struck by Britons past and present. Striking workers, campaigners for women's rights, West Indian immigrants, dancing NHS workers and even The Beatles – all these are absent from the very limited treatment of recent history in Kynren. The latter sets itself a more earnest task: to depict a very lengthy history in a way that emphasises the significant individuals, long-standing traditions and shared stories that between them shape Young Arthur's – and 'our' – inheritance. Thus while the figure of Henson provides a safely paternalistic device to remind us of the religious dimensions of this inheritance, so Sir Lancelot and the Knights of the Round Table are the epitome of the Englishness at Kynren's heart. It could, of course, have been done very differently. There is no sign of real or mythical English heroes from a more radical tradition; there is no John Ball, no Robin Hood.

If social conflict is largely missing, then so too is the history of empire: beyond a passing mention in the extract from Churchill's 'finest hour' speech, there are few references to this aspect of the past. Colonial countries are represented in the episode depicting Victoria's Diamond Jubilee, but there is little sense of the empire's role in the 'Georgian Renaissance' or the railway age, where it might conceivably have appeared. It is a moot point as to whether this omission or oversight should be criticised; indeed, there is an ongoing debate about the relative importance of empire in historical pageants, which need not be rehearsed in detail here.[55] Following London 2012 some commentary noted that while Boyle and Boyce's ceremony captured the spirit of the modern multicultural city, it overlooked the imperial dimensions of the industrial revolution that it so memorably portrayed: 'silence as erasure', to use Baker's phrase.[56] Nevertheless, it is certainly true that at Kynren it would have been possible to insert aspects of imperial history into the overall story, perhaps taking inspiration from the multiculturalism and 'radical patriotism' of the Boyle and Boyce ceremony.

There is another important respect in which Kynren differs significantly from the 'radical patriotism' of 2012: the Opening Ceremony, as Baker has noted, was characterised by a 'curious absence of the Second World War and the Blitz'. Although the First World War was memorialised in the Olympic Stadium, and personnel from the armed forces took part, it featured neither 'the unifying "myth of the Blitz", nor the depiction of 1939–1945 as a magical time of national unity under Churchill's guiding hand – even though in contemporary Britain one has come to expect this to be one of the fixed points around which a historical narrative of the nation will be built'.[57] As noted above, Kynren writes this 'myth' back into the national story. And while it is worth emphasising that this is a *national* story, the souvenir programme is careful to give it some local context, at the same time reminding readers of the persistent spirit of the most important local Anglo-Saxon saint:

> Although … [Churchill's] speech in the House of Commons was made to inspire the pilots of the RAF [Royal Air Force] to victory in the Battle of Britain, it has come to reflect the pride felt in all those who gave so much in the conflict overall. As German bombers caused devastation throughout the country, Durham miraculously escaped the bombing, said to have been protected by a thick fog sent by St Cuthbert.[58]

The use of Churchill in the final substantive scene of Kynren emphasises its conservative inspiration and its vigorous flaunting of the main personnel of a traditional, elite-centred version of the English past. By the late twentieth century, Janet Watson argues, Churchill had become a British 'mascot' in commemoration of the Second World War;[59] this was further emphasised in 2016, the year Kynren opened, when the Bank of England issued a new £5 note on which he features, along with one of his most famous lines: 'I have nothing to offer but blood, toil, tears and sweat'.[60] At Kynren, Churchill is the last in a long line of 'great men' and women who feature in the pageant: he epitomises the aim of the pageant to place the Second World War in a longer story of British or English history, as earlier pageants had tried to do with the First World War.[61] The reference in the programme to the RAF and the Blitz reinforces the enlistment of Churchill into a wider social history of modern Britain in wartime – a brief reference to the idea of the 'People's War'[62] – and this in turn leads into the celebratory patriotic extravaganza with which Kynren concludes.

At this end point the issuing of Union flags to the audience is significant, given that Kynren is explicitly presented – most of the time – as an *English* story: 'an epic tale of England', to quote the show's subtitle. The first item in the souvenir programme, after Daulon's foreword, is John of Gaunt's speech from Shakespeare's *Richard II*, which is explicitly about England – but famously used in the 1990s to provide the title for Christopher Lee's BBC Radio series *This Sceptred Isle*. This programme told the history of Britain over 216 episodes, including extracts from Churchill's *History of the English-Speaking Peoples*.

There is some slippage between English and British history in Kynren. Neville's Cross was a battle between the English and Scots – the scene opens with the cry 'The Scots! The Scots are coming!' – but this is about the only moment at which other British nations appear. Moreover, the finale features 'Land of Hope and Glory' and *not* 'God Save the Queen': the programme rather confusingly explains that the closing scene is 'a celebration of *English* history in all its colour and richness. We have chosen "Land of Hope and Glory" as the chorus of our Finale music, a fitting and uplifting anthem to celebrate all that is great about the *British* nation'.[63] This concluding celebration of nationhood was first performed at a particularly significant moment in the history of the British and English nations: Kynren first opened just after the 2016 referendum on British membership of the European Union, in a region that voted predominantly 'Leave', and the timing was not lost on some observers. Charlotte Runcie wrote in the *Daily Telegraph*: '[w]hen the climax came in a rousing chorus of Land of Hope and Glory, there was a moment when I wondered if the evening was some sort of Brexit mirage. In a summer filled with questions of national identity, Kynren feels particularly charged'.[64]

What Kynren tells is the story of England – and, to an extent, Britain – in the tradition of *This Sceptred Isle* and *Our Island Story*: a history populated by William the Conqueror, Henry VIII, Shakespeare and Elizabeth I, Queen Victoria and finally Churchill, but with some elements of local social and economic history, particularly from the eighteenth century onwards. It has a strong undercurrent of patriotic sentiment, an emphasis on social harmony and an intermittent yet clearly discernible sense of a common religious heritage, the origins of which are mainly located in the early medieval period.

There is also a strong local dimension to the history told in Kynren. Daulon describes it as 'a poignant reminder of the tremendous contribution the North East has made to the history of the nation', echoing the sentiments of many pageant-masters, scriptwriters and promoters in the twentieth century, who emphasised the 'local roots of national identity' and the links between local and national history.[65] But if this fits comfortably within the pageant tradition, it also echoes other tellings of history in the northeast of England and elsewhere. Hester Barron has uncovered elementary school history syllabi from the interwar period in the Durham coalfield: here, the inclusion of local social and economic history, especially that of the nineteenth century, created 'a surprising contrast to the expected concentration on kings, queens and battles'.[66] The children who studied history at this time – and many of those who watched pageants in the northeast of England and elsewhere – were inducted into a place-based identity which, as contemporary heritage studies have emphasised, can work in different ways. As G. J. Ashworth, Brian Graham and J. E. Tunbridge have argued, places can 'embody an official public memory'; but place-based identity can also be a 'means of resistance' to 'official' versions of history and heritage.[67] Kynren is neither of these – it is not an 'official' pageant, nor is it 'resistant' – although perhaps the difference between the two is not entirely clear: Boyle and Boyce's Olympic spectacular was, after all, in a sense 'official'. Kynren, by contrast, is a striking counterpoint to the 2012 event in the largely conservative and monocultural version of the national past that it narrates. There is certainly no way that it could be dismissed as 'leftie multicultural crap', as the then Conservative MP Aidan Burley notoriously described the 2012 ceremony on Twitter.[68]

The distinction between the Olympic ceremony and Kynren echoes contemporaneous controversies over the kind of history that should be taught in English schools. In this respect Kynren reflects – or did, at its establishment – the stated aims of the governing Conservative Party in its treatment of history as what Michael Gove, Secretary of State for Education from 2010 to 2014, called a 'connected narrative'.[69] Speaking in the House of Commons in 2013, Gove claimed that his government had re-established in the school history curriculum 'a clear narrative of

British progress with a proper emphasis on heroes and heroines from the past'.[70] Kynren echoes this emphasis very clearly, with even its social and cultural history episodes presented in a fairly conservative way. Yet Kynren is not just about education: it needs to balance education and entertainment, and thus follows earlier pageants in blending faithfulness to the historical record with imagination and outright fiction. Pageants rely on invented dialogue even for episodes that definitely happened; many, of course, have drawn on Shakespeare's plays for this.[71] In addition, it was not uncommon to concoct episodes such as the one in Kynren where Shakespeare meets Queen Elizabeth in a dream.

The educational value of the performance itself is certainly doubtful. There is minimal dialogue and the characters of Henson and Old Arthur provide little context. A small amount of contextual information is given in the souvenir programme, priced at £10, but this is not necessarily sufficient to help spectators navigate their way through a very fast-moving show, lasting little more than 80 minutes in total. Some pageant spectators in the early twentieth century might have felt the same: indeed, without amplified sound it was very possibly even more difficult for them to follow the story. However, the detailed souvenir programmes and full books of words available at many pageants may have helped spectators to understand the history that was being presented to them.[72] Kynren lacks the clear historical contextualisation that might help the audience to make sense of it, despite the narrative devices that it adopts for the sake of drama; and its publicity materials do little – in contrast to some pageant programmes and books of words – to provide the background that might help strengthen Kynren's contribution to 'edutainment'.

Heritage, community and education

Kynren is not the only new heritage-sector development at Bishop Auckland. It will in due course be embedded into a much larger historical theme park – as is the case with the *Cinéscénie* at Puy du Fou. For Jonathan Ruffer, who has a strong sense of personal loyalty to the northeast of England, Kynren is just one part of an ambitious project of regeneration for Bishop Auckland and its surrounding area. In this sense his ambition is rather different from that of the pageant-masters of the twentieth century. The latter were certainly invested in the idea of leaving a permanent mark on the communities that recruited them, and some pageants were memorialised physically, in the form of statues, public buildings and parks, or in street names.[73] However, while these earlier pageants may have played a role in boosting tourism or even initiating some local economic activity, they were not themselves intended to be a long-term feature of the local economy and community. Typically, they were one-off events; Kynren, by contrast, is currently performed every summer. Yet the language of community used at Kynren echoes that heard from pageant-masters and other leaders of the older tradition of community drama; indeed, it is at times strikingly similar. Thus, for example, Anne-Isabelle Daulon commented in 2014 that '[t]he community is at the heart of the project ... What we're trying to achieve is to bring people together behind a very inspiring pursuit, a joint pursuit'.[74]

This compares with Louis Napoleon Parker's description of a pageant as 'a great Festival of Brotherhood, in which all distinctions of any kind are sunk in a common effort',[75] as well as with the approach of the community play pioneer Ann Jellicoe, who argued that 'the fundamental event is not the play itself, but the opportunity the play provides for the continuing evolution of [the] community'.[76] This is not to say that pageants – any more than community plays or Kynren itself – always succeeded in mobilising the undivided loyalty of the communities in which they took place,[77] but the comparability of the aims and rhetoric is striking.

The notion of 'community' that Ruffer is trying to promote at Bishop Auckland is based on a philanthropic impulse inspired by his adherence to Christianity and by acknowledged politically Liberal forebears. His approach to philanthropy echoes that of Samuel Barnett, the founder of Toynbee Hall and the Whitechapel Gallery in the 1880s: Ruffer has declared that '[g]iving people beauty can sometimes change their lives'.[78] He acquired a series of religious paintings as part of the purchase of Auckland Castle and plans to create an art gallery and museum in Bishop Auckland, very much in the tradition of Barnett – although Ruffer claims another Liberal, the philanthropist and MP William Rathbone VI, as his direct inspiration.[79] Rathbone died in 1902, but Barnett lived into the 'new Liberal' age, and adjusted his political stance over time, drawing on his philanthropic experiences. Initially cautious, in the Gladstonian tradition, about state intervention in economic development and welfare provision, Barnett came to embrace more fully the 'new philanthropy' of the Edwardian period, and exerted a strong influence on individuals such as William Temple, William Beveridge and Clement Attlee, who built the mid-twentieth-century welfare state.[80] Ruffer takes a much more conservative attitude to the provision of state welfare than these men did, a perspective reflected in his criticism of the legacy of Christian socialists such as Temple. Here Ruffer argues that, 'from 1940 to 1990' potential philanthropists were deterred by the institutions of the welfare state, and that Temple's *Christianity and Social Order*, seen as one of its founding texts, reads 'pathetically'.[81] Hence, although Ruffer has not publicly acknowledged it, the importance of Henson as the narrator of Kynren: Henson opposed the emergent welfare state and was himself critical of Temple's approach.[82] For Ruffer, people and communities need to be helped to help themselves, a cornerstone of his philanthropic ethos.

One element of this community self-help is the enhancement of human capital. In this respect Kynren performs a function that appears to mark a departure from the pageant tradition, in that participation as a volunteer in the pageant is presented as a training opportunity. Recruiting for 2017, the Eleven Arches website told potential volunteers that 'you will … receive professional training in new skills from some of the world's top-ranking performance experts'.[83] Similar language was used by David Best and his volunteers on the London 1666 project, and many of them did learn carpentry and other skills.[84] Some press and media reports also emphasised this aspect of Kynren: in the *Scotsman* Fiona Laing noted that 'Eleven Arches is focused on community development: the volunteer cast and crew have learnt new skills from world-class professionals – from performing to horse-riding and animal husbandry to customer care – and will take away vast experience from being involved'.[85] One of the volunteers agreed, observing that 'it has given the area a lift and for the young people, in particular, it has given them the feeling that there is something they can do. It'll give them something to put on their CVs'.[86]

At Kynren and elsewhere, pageantry and public art have been co-opted into the service of lifelong learning and skills development. The organisers of Kynren have a stated aim to develop local human capital, in the context of the growing importance of the creative economy and – particularly, perhaps, in the northeast of England – the heritage 'industry'. This seems to resonate with the approach of the Heritage Lottery Fund, which has invested £9m in Eleven Arches and its projects: as Ruffer has explained,

> What the Heritage Lottery Fund feel very strongly is that heritage for its own sake has a sterility about it which is not socially valuable. It chimed absolutely with how I see this place, which is that the key is [to] make it useful for the local community.[87]

Conclusion

In many ways, as one reviewer commented in 2016, Kynren is 'preposterous on so many levels'.[88] It would be easy to decry it as portraying an outdated and monocultural version of British history for which visitors pay an inflated price – at the time of writing in 2019, tickets for adults ranged from £25 to £59. In 1987 Robert Hewison argued that the heritage industry offered a 'shallow' understanding of the past, as a result of which '[w]e have no understanding of history in depth, but instead are offered a contemporary creation, more costume drama and re-enactment than critical discourse'.[89]

This certainly characterises Kynren, in which an emphasis on choreographed spectacle, a very limited use of dialogue and a whistle-stop tour through historical periods all militate against any contribution that it could potentially make to the 'critical culture' that Hewison called for in the heritage industry.[90] Kynren, clearly, is more entertainment than edutainment, although other planned local developments do offer the possibility of a more rounded heritage 'experience' in the future. The show explicitly combines mythical episodes with documented history, prioritising the needs of drama over those of historical veracity and realism. In this respect, however, it is not dissimilar to many historical pageants of the twentieth century, which – as we have shown elsewhere – tried to blend faithfulness to some aspects of the historical record with the portrayal of fictitious and legendary characters and scenes: they featured cavemen fighting dinosaurs, St George and others slaying dragons, and a liberal smattering of characters such as King Arthur and Robin Hood.[91] As one pageant-master, Lawrence du Garde Peach – who wrote for film and television and was also the author of popular *Ladybird* books for children – explained in 1949, a pageant should be 'simply entertainment ... I would sacrifice any historical fact in order to get entertainment value in my script'.[92] His Nottingham pageant of that year was laced with comedy – including a Saxon dispute over tolls and a humorous account of the history of policing – and included various revels and processions; it also featured a colourful Robin Hood scene and included specially composed music. The result was, according to the local press, 'a brilliant spectacle, lavishly staged and blazing with colour'.[93] The musical and pyrotechnic qualities of Kynren far outstrip those of Peach's pageants and others of the twentieth century, although it is important to note that pageants themselves evolved alongside, and under the influence of, amplified sound, recorded music, light and sound shows, radio and television: Peach was by no means the only television scriptwriter who turned his hand to pageants too.[94]

Ultimately Kynren is an attempt to locate a version of local and national history within an identifiable shared landscape – a drama in which, to quote the American pageant-master William Chauncy Langdon, ‘the place is the hero and the development of the community is the plot’.[95] The pageant depicts what Anthony D. Smith has called an ‘evolutionist version’ of the past, emphasising how development took place in ways ‘peculiar to the community’.[96] Such an emphasis brings the links between past and present to the fore, a feature of many pageants in the 1950s, in particular, which sought to explain the importance of the inherited local past in the context of rapid economic and cultural change.[97] There are clear echoes of this in Kynren. Young Arthur, in the 2017 version, is inducted into his inheritance by the Knights of the Round Table, who explain directly what ‘Kynren’ means. This inheritance, though, could be one of blood or place; and the differences of interpretation are important. If blood, then Kynren could be seen to give succour to a racial Anglo-Saxonism – and this was a danger in some pageants of the early twentieth century, encouraged by an emphasis on the ‘Norman yoke’.[98] Alternatively – and this would be much more in line with the pageant tradition – Kynren can be read as an assertion of the viability and strength of a *place*-based identity: the ‘generations’ of the title may be those who successively occupy a place, rather than those of a single national or ethnic ‘family’.

Many twentieth-century pageants addressed this theme, joining together the disparate episodes by employing some kind of narrative figure representing the ‘spirit’ of the place where they were staged.[99] At Kynren the use of a real historical figure, Hensley Henson, in this role is certainly of great political significance. Yet it could also be noted that Henson was himself an incomer to the northeast of England: the inheritance of the local past, it could generously be inferred, is available to anyone and the spirit of place may be shared. This is doubly important given the ambitions that exist to turn Kynren into a major tourist attraction along the lines of Puy du Fou: the show needs to offer thousands of visitors a reason to visit the area. This was also a central aim of many twentieth-century pageants, as Ayako Yoshino has powerfully argued and as chapter 11 in this volume reminds us.[100]

As such, there is no doubt that Kynren echoes many of the aims of the historical pageant tradition that emerged in the twentieth century and declined from the 1950s onwards. Some remnants of this tradition survive today, such as the decennial Axbridge pageant and the occasional small-scale events that happen from time to time elsewhere (see the introduction and afterword to this volume). There are some obvious differences, of course: for one thing, Kynren aims to be a permanent feature of the heritage industry in the northeast of England, whereas pageants were transient events, rarely occurring more than once in a generation in any one particular place.

Differences, then, do exist, but there are also many similarities between what happened at Sherborne in 1905 and the scenes played out at Bishop Auckland every year since 2016. Like the thousands of historical pageants that came before it, Kynren has succeeded in mobilising a large number of volunteers behind a dramatic re-performance of a series of successive episodes from the past, tied to a potentially unifying – though also potentially controversial – local and national narrative, and in the service of both education and entertainment. Like all pageants, it blends history and legend; it prioritises some parts of history over others; it tries – perhaps successfully, perhaps not – both to educate and to entertain. Its broadly conservative account of the English/British past resonates with much of the early twentieth-century pageant tradition. In this respect Kynren is rather out of line with many of the other historical performances in today's heritage settings with which it could be compared. Some of these restagings of the past are considered in the afterword to this book.

Notes

1. 'Kynren in Durham: As the Second Season of Historical Epic Approaches, What Can Visitors Expect?', *Chronicle Live*, 1 July 2017: https://www.chroniclelive.co.uk/whats-on/kynren-what-to-expect-review-13240467 (accessed 5 June 2019).
2. *Kynren: An Epic Tale of England* (Bishop Auckland: Eleven Arches, 2016; official programme; hereafter *Kynren 2016*), 39. Copies of the 2016 and 2017 official programmes are in the authors' possession.
3. *Jeremy Deller: We're Here Because We're Here*, BBC 4 television, broadcast 13 November 2016: http://www.bbc.co.uk/iplayer/episode/b083bk7n/jeremy-deller-were-here-because-were-here?suggid=b083bk7n (accessed 17 November 2016).
4. 'Blaze of Glory: Commemorating Great Fire on the Thames', *BBC Arts*, 5 September 2016: https://www.bbc.co.uk/programmes/articles/19KLTps7SJLrfl0Pqq2QJmN/blaze-of-glory-commemorating-great-fire-on-the-thames (accessed 5 June 2019).
5. '1066: Battle of Hastings Anniversary Marked 950 Years On': https://www.bbc.co.uk/news/uk-england-sussex-37649912 (accessed 5 June 2019).
6. See Magna Carta Trust: https://magnacarta800th.com/ (accessed 5 June 2019); 'Diamond Jubilee Thames Pageant Cheered By Crowds': https://www.bbc.co.uk/news/uk-18312403 (accessed 5 June 2019); 'First World War Centenary': https://www.gov.uk/government/topical-events/first-world-war-centenary (accessed 5 June 2019).
7. Michael Hodges, 'Now That Is Over the Top!', *Daily Mail Event Magazine*, 23 April 2016: http://www.dailymail.co.uk/home/event/article-3551484/Now-Kynren-bring-British-history-Romans-WWII-spectacularly-life-biggest-live-production-Olympic-ceremonies.html (accessed 6 February 2017). See also Stephen Smith, 'Cue the Levitating Longboat: The £35m All-Singing, All-Dancing History of Britain', *Guardian*, 21 June 2016: https://www.theguardian.com/stage/2016/jun/21/kynren-auckland-castle-county-durham-jonathan-ruffer (accessed 6 February 2017); Chris Tighe and Miles Johnson, 'Ruffer Lowers Drawbridge on Ambitious Castle Plan', *Financial Times*, 3 April 2014: https://www.ft.com/content/58cede64-bb4f-11e3-8d4a-00144feabdc0 (accessed 13 February 2017). The claim to be the largest since 2012 may overlook the Commonwealth Games Opening Ceremony in 2014.
8. *Kynren 2016*, 39; http://www.telegraph.co.uk/theatre/what-to-see/kynren-review-a-historical-epic-painted-in-primary-colours/ (accessed 17 November 2016).

9. 'Kynren: Eleven Arches' CEO Anne-Isabelle Daulon on Culture, Collaboration and Community', 13 September 2017: https://blooloop.com/features/kynren-anne-isabelle-daulon/ (accessed 5 June 2019).
10. Frank Cottrell Boyce, 'London 2012: Opening Ceremony Saw All Our Dreams Come True', *Guardian*, 30 July 2012: https://www.theguardian.com/commentisfree/2012/jul/29/frank-cottrell-boyce-olympics-opening-ceremony?CMP=twt_gu (accessed 13 February 2017); Danny Boyle, *Creating Wonder, in Conversation with Amy Raphael* (London: Faber & Faber, 2013 [1st ed. 2010]), 398; Ben Jones and Rebecca Searle, 'Humphrey Jennings, the Left and the Experience of Modernity in Mid-Twentieth-Century Britain', *History Workshop Journal* 75 (2013): 191.
11. Catherine Baker, 'Beyond the Island Story? The Opening Ceremony of the London 2012 Olympic Games as Public History', *Rethinking History* 19 (2015): 414–15. See also Jones and Searle, 'Humphrey Jennings', 192, 196–7.
12. Baker, 'Beyond the Island Story?' 412–13, 421; Andrew Hough, 'Revealed: David Cameron's Favourite Childhood Book is *Our Island Story*', *Telegraph*, 29 October 2010: http://www.telegraph.co.uk/culture/books/booknews/8094333/Revealed-David-Camerons-favourite-childhood-book-is-Our-Island-Story.html (accessed 6 February 2017); W. C. Sellar and R. J. Yeatman, *1066 and All That: A Memorable History of England* (London: Methuen, 1930); Raphael Samuel, *Island Stories: Unravelling Britain, Theatres of Memory, Volume II* (London: Verso, 1998), 209–13.
13. Baker, 'Beyond the Island Story?', 412.
14. Boyle, *Creating Wonder*, 388–440.
15. See Mark Freeman, '"Splendid Display; Pompous Spectacle": Historical Pageants in Twentieth-Century Britain', *Social History* 38 (2013): 452; Baz Kershaw, *The Politics of Performance: Radical Theatre as Cultural Intervention* (London: Routledge, 1992), 185–205; Raphael Samuel, *Theatres of Memory, Volume I: Past and Present in Contemporary Culture* (London: Verso, 1994), 169–202.
16. *Jeremy Deller: We're Here Because We're Here.*
17. So far Kynren is certainly not the most-watched pageant in British history – one million people saw the Empire pageant in 1924 – but few can match it. Figures can be hard to come by for many pageants, but some 120,000 saw the Pageant of Newcastle and the North in 1931 and a similar number saw the Historical Pageant of Bradford in the same year. An estimated 500,000 spectators watched the street procession associated with the Godiva Pageant in Coventry in 1951, but only a small proportion of this number saw the theatrical part of the pageant. For a pageant held since the 1950s, the largest total audience recorded in the *Redress of the Past* database is 24,000 at the one-off 1966 Battle of Hastings nonacentenary pageant (see the *Redress of the Past* database: Angela Bartie, Paul Caton, Linda Fleming, Mark Freeman, Tom Hulme, Alex Hutton and Paul Readman, *The Redress of the Past*, http://www.historicalpageants.ac.uk/pageants/; accessed 5 June 2019). The capacity of the London Olympic Stadium at the time of the games was 80,000, but it has been estimated that the overall television audience was 900 million: Baker, 'Beyond the Island Story?', 412.
18. Calculated from the 18 entries for the Arbroath Pageant in the *Redress of the Past* database. This figure does not include public dress rehearsals.
19. On re-enactment, see Jerome de Groot, *Consuming History: Historians and Heritage in Contemporary Popular Culture* (Abingdon and New York: Routledge, 2008), 105–23; Samuel, *Theatres of Memory*, 169–202.
20. Samuel, *Theatres of Memory*, 146–7, 160; Ryan S. Trimm, 'Taking you Back: Region, Industry and Technologies of Living History at Beamish', *European Journal of Cultural Studies* 15 (2012): 528–46; Robert Hewison, *The Heritage Industry: Britain in a Climate of Decline* (London: Methuen, 1987), 93–7.
21. See, for example, Baz Kershaw, *Theatre Ecology: Environments and Performance Events* (Cambridge: Cambridge University Press, 2007), 214–15, 222–7.
22. Iain McCalman, 'Loutherbourg's Simulations: Reenactment and Realism in Late-Georgian Britain', in *Historical Reenactment: From Realism to the Affective Turn*, ed. Iain McCalman and Paul A. Pickering (Basingstoke: Palgrave Macmillan, 2010), 200–17.
23. See Deborah Sugg Ryan, 'Staging the Imperial City: The Pageant of London, 1911', in *Imperial Cities: Landscape, Display and Identity*, ed. Felix Driver and David Gilbert (Manchester: Manchester University Press, 1999), 117–35.

24. Mark Freeman, 'Lumière London, January 2016', 25 January 2016: http://www.historicalpageants.ac.uk/blog/lumiere-london-january-2016/ (accessed 6 February 2017). On *son et lumière*, see Samuel, *Theatres of Memory*, 179–80.
25. See Gary McCulloch and Tom Woodin, 'Towards a Social History of Learners and Learning', *Oxford Review of Education* 36 (2010): 133–40.
26. de Groot, *Consuming History*, 106, 118.
27. *Kynren 2016*, 48.
28. See Joseph Smith, 'Discursive Dancing: Traditionalism and Social Realism in the 2013 English History Curriculum Wars', *British Journal of Educational Studies* 65 (2017): 307–29.
29. To give one example from a fairly small town, the St Albans pageant of 1907 had a cast of 3,000, not to mention the many non-performing volunteers: Freeman, '"Splendid Display"', 429.
30. *Kynren 2016*, 50–1.
31. Chris Lloyd, 'A Magnificent Riot of Never-Ending History', *Northern Echo*, 19 June 2016: http://www.thenorthernecho.co.uk/news/14566684.A_magnificent_riot_of_never_ending_history__Chris_Lloyd_s_view_on_Kynren/ (accessed 5 June 2019).
32. *Kynren 2016*, fold-out section.
33. Henson's inclusion in the pageant is a contrivance: he was not bishop at the time of the football incident.
34. *Kynren 2016*, 3 and fold-out section (back flap); *Kynren: An Epic Tale of England* (Bishop Auckland: Eleven Arches, 2017; official programme; hereafter *Kynren 2017*), 3 and fold-out section (back flap).
35. For this and the Chartres reference below, see Ruth Sunderland, 'Meet the Philanthropic Fund Guru Who Splashed £30m of His Own Cash on the Most Bonkers Show in Britain', 20 June 2016: http://www.thisismoney.co.uk/money/news/article-3651062/Meet-philanthropic-fund-guru-splashed-30m-cash-bonkers-Britain.html (accessed 13 February 2017).
36. Angela Bartie, Linda Fleming, Mark Freeman, Tom Hulme, Alexander Hutton and Paul Readman, 'Historical Pageants and the Medieval Past in Twentieth-Century England', *English Historical Review* 133 (2018): 880–2.
37. Joseph of Arimathea appeared in only a handful of twentieth-century pageants, usually small ones organised by churches. He is mentioned in five entries in the *Redress of the Past* database: Bartie et al., *Redress of the Past*, http://www.historicalpageants.ac.uk/pageants/ (accessed 5 June 2019).
38. Shakespeare appeared as a character in 17 of the pageants listed in the *Redress of the Past* database, the most northerly being a 1953 coronation pageant in Widnes: Bartie et al., *Redress of the Past*, http://www.historicalpageants.ac.uk/pageants/ (accessed 5 June 2019).
39. Cromwell appeared in two Scottish pageants and three in the north of England, and in more than 20 overall: Bartie et al., *Redress of the Past*, http://www.historicalpageants.ac.uk/pageants/ (accessed 5 June 2019).
40. *Kynren 2016*, fold-out section.
41. See Angela Bartie, Linda Fleming, Mark Freeman, Tom Hulme, Paul Readman and Charlotte Tupman, '"And Those Who Live, How Shall I Tell Their Fame?" Historical Pageants, Collective Remembrance and the First World War, 1919–1939', *Historical Research* 90 (2017): 636–61.
42. Bartie et al., 'Historical Pageants', 894.
43. This is based on the 2016 show, and includes the first episode, 'The Gatehouse of Time', which can be dated to the 1880s or the interwar period.
44. Auckland Castle was the official residence of the bishops from 1832.
45. *Kynren 2017*, fold-out section; Bartie et al., 'Historical Pageants', 875–6.
46. *Kynren 2017*, fold-out section.
47. Bartie et al., 'Historical Pageants', 898–9; Freeman, '"Splendid Display"', 444–5.
48. See G. J. Ashworth, Brian Graham and J. E. Tunbridge, *Pluralising Pasts: Heritage, Identity and Place in Multicultural Societies* (London: Pluto Press, 2007), 37. See also David Lowenthal, *The Heritage Crusade and the Spoils of History* (Cambridge: Cambridge University Press, 1998 [1st ed. 1968]), esp. 192–226.
49. The inclusion of Viking depredations could be seen as further evidence of the centrality of a Christian identity to the story being told in Kynren. In 2019 the show begins with the arrival of 'marauding invaders' in a Viking longship, who burn a fishing village: https://www.kynren.com/ (accessed 5 June 2019).
50. 'Faith Museum: In Development': https://www.aucklandproject.org/venues/faith-museum/ (accessed 5 June 2019).

51. Matthew Grimley, 'Henson, Herbert Hensley (1863–1947)', *Oxford Dictionary of National Biography* (Oxford: Oxford University Press, 2004); Hester Barron, *The 1926 Miners' Lockout: Meanings of Community in the Durham Coalfield* (Oxford: Oxford University Press, 2009), 171, 45–8.
52. Barron, *1926 Miners' Lockout*, 171–2.
53. Baker, 'Beyond the Island Story?', 414, 424 n.1, citing Mick Wallis, 'The Popular Front Pageant: Its Emergence and Decline', *New Theatre Quarterly* 11 (1995): 17–32 and an unpublished paper by Emily Robinson. See Emily Robinson, *The Language of Progressive Politics in Modern Britain* (London: Palgrave Macmillan, 2017), 112–16.
54. The appearance, in quick succession, of Chelsea pensioners and pearly kings and queens is a good example of the irreverence with which Boyle and Boyce approached the task of encapsulating the range of images of modern Britain.
55. See Ayako Yoshino, *Pageant Fever: Local History and Consumerism in Edwardian England* (Tokyo: Waseda University Press, 2011), esp. 124, 133–4, 179; Paul Readman, 'The Place of the Past in English Culture *c*. 1890–1914', *Past and Present* 186 (2005): 185–7; Freeman, '"Splendid Display"', 433, 435.
56. Baker, 'Beyond the Island Story?', 417.
57. Baker, 'Beyond the Island Story?', 417–18. Churchill appeared in the 2012 Closing Ceremony, played by the actor Timothy Spall, but the Second Word War did not feature.
58. *Kynren 2016*, fold-out section.
59. Janet Watson, 'Total War and Total Anniversary: The Material Culture of Second World War Commemoration in Britain', in *British Cultural Memory and the Second World War*, ed. Lucy Noakes and Juliette Pattinson (London: Bloomsbury Academic, 2014), 188.
60. '£5 Note': https://www.bankofengland.co.uk/banknotes/5-pound-note (accessed 22 May 2019).
61. Bartie et al., '"And Those Who Live"'.
62. See Angus Calder, *The People's War: Britain 1939–1945* (London: Random House, 1969).
63. *Kynren 2016*, fold-out section. Emphases added. Note that in the same section of the 2017 programme this was changed to omit any specific mention of Britain or the British.
64. Charlotte Runcie, 'Kynren, Review: A Historical Epic Painted in Primary Colours': *Telegraph*, 30 June 2016: https://www.telegraph.co.uk/theatre/what-to-see/kynren-review-a-historical-epic-painted-in-primary-colours/ (accessed 5 June 2019).
65. Readman, 'Place of the Past', 175–82.
66. Barron, *1926 Miners' Lockout*, 212.
67. Ashworth et al., *Pluralising Pasts*, 54.
68. Quoted in Baker, 'Beyond the Island Story?', 415.
69. Quoted in Smith, 'Discursive Dancing', 313.
70. Quoted in Smith, 'Discursive Dancing', 314.
71. Angela Bartie, Linda Fleming, Mark Freeman, Tom Hulme, Alexander Hutton and Paul Readman, '"History Taught in the Pageant Way": Education and Historical Performance in Twentieth-Century Britain', *History of Education* 48 (2019): 165.
72. See Yoshino, *Pageant Fever*, 77–81; Readman, 'Place of the Past', 174–5; and chapter 11 in this volume.
73. See Bartie et al., '"History Taught in the Pageant Way"', 173–5.
74. 'Benefactor Plans Theme Park for Bishop Auckland', *ITV News*, 3 April 2014: http://www.itv.com/news/tyne-tees/2014-04-03/benefactor-plans-theme-park-for-bishop-auckland/ (accessed 5 June 2019).
75. Louis N. Parker, *Several of My Lives* (London: Chapman & Hall, 1928), 279.
76. Ann Jellicoe, *Community Plays: How to Put Them On* (London: Methuen, 1987), xvii; quoted in Bartie et al., '"History Taught in the Pageant Way"', 173.
77. See, for example, Kershaw, *Politics of Performance*, 190–5.
78. Jonathan Ruffer, 'Beauty, Philanthropy and Auckland Castle', *Spectator*, 30 March 2013: http://www.spectator.co.uk/2013/03/the-art-of-philanthropy/ (accessed 5 June 2019).
79. A. N. Wilson, 'Man on a Mission: Jonathan Ruffer and the Auckland Castle Trust', *Financial Times*, 7 November 2014: https://www.ft.com/content/57d38f48-6421-11e4-8ade-00144feabdc0 (accessed 5 June 2019).
80. See, for example, Standish Meacham, *Toynbee Hall and Social Reform 1880–1914: The Search for Community* (New Haven, CT: Yale University Press, 1987).
81. Quoted in Wilson, 'Man on a Mission'.
82. See Matthew Grimley, *Citizenship, Community and the Church of England: Liberal Anglican Theories of the State between the Wars* (Oxford: Oxford University Press, 2004), esp. chapter 3.
83. 'Kynren: An Epic Tale of England', https://elevenarches.org/ (accessed 31 May 2020).

84. *London 1666*, BBC Four television, broadcast 5 September 2016: http://www.bbc.co.uk/pro grammes/b07v642t (accessed 5 June 2019).
85. Fiona Laing, 'Travel: Kynren Spectacle Ideal Excuse to Explore Durham', *Scotsman*, 28 August 2016: https://www.scotsman.com/lifestyle/travel/travel-kynren-spectacle-ideal-excuse-to-explore-durham-1-4214459 (accessed 5 June 2019).
86. Quoted in David Whetstone, '£30m Kynren History Production in Durham Receives Standing Ovation', *Chronicle Live*, 3 July 2016 : https://www.chroniclelive.co.uk/whats-on/arts-culture-news/30m-kynren-history-production-durham-11559296 (accessed 5 June 2019).
87. Graeme Whitfield, 'Monday Interview: Jonathan Ruffer of Auckland Castle', *Chronicle Live*, 14 June 2015: http://www.chroniclelive.co.uk/business/business-news/monday-interview-jonathan-ruffer-auckland-9444615 (accessed 22 May 2019).
88. Lloyd, 'Magnificant Riot'.
89. Hewison, *Heritage Industry*, 135.
90. Hewison, *Heritage Industry*, 145.
91. Bartie et al., '"History Taught in the Pageant Way"', 166–70.
92. Quoted in Bartie et al., 'Historical Pageants', 897.
93. *Nottingham Evening News*, 28 June 1949, 5.
94. Another example was Arthur Swinson, who wrote for radio and television and who was involved with pageants in St Albans: see Freeman, '"Splendid Display"', 449–52.
95. Quoted in David Glassberg, *American Historical Pageantry: The Uses of Tradition in the Early Twentieth Century* (Chapel Hill, NC: University of North Carolina Press, 1990), 69, 78.
96. Anthony D. Smith, *The Ethnic Origins of Nations* (Oxford: Blackwell, 1988 [1st ed. 1986]), 179.
97. Freeman, '"Splendid Display"', 444–5.
98. Bartie et al., 'Historical Pageants', 876–8.
99. For example, a character called 'Scarborough' narrated the Scarborough pageant of 1912, while the 'spirit of Lynn' provided the chorus in the King's Lynn Charter Pageant of 1954: see the entries in the pageants database. Bartie et al., *Redress of the Past*, http://www.historicalpageants.ac.uk/pageants/ (accessed 5 June 2019).
100. Yoshino, *Pageant Fever*, chapter 2.

Bibliography

Ashworth, G. J., Graham, Brian and Tunbridge, J. E. 2007. *Pluralising Pasts: Heritage, Identity and Place in Multicultural Societies*. London: Pluto Press.

Baker, Catherine. 2015. 'Beyond the Island Story? The Opening Ceremony of the London 2012 Olympic Games as Public History', *Rethinking History* 19: 409–28.

Barron, Hester. 2009. *The 1926 Miners' Lockout: Meanings of Community in the Durham Coalfield*. Oxford: Oxford University Press.

Bartie, Angela, Fleming, Linda, Freeman, Mark, Hulme, Tom, Hutton, Alexander and Readman, Paul. 2018. 'Historical Pageants and the Medieval Past in Twentieth-Century England', *English Historical Review* 133: 866–902.

Bartie, Angela, Fleming, Linda, Freeman, Mark, Hulme, Tom, Hutton, Alexander and Readman, Paul. 2019. '"History Taught in the Pageant Way": Education and Historical Performance in Twentieth-Century Britain', *History of Education* 48: 156–79.

Bartie, Angela, Fleming, Linda, Freeman, Mark, Hulme, Tom, Readman, Paul and Tupman, Charlotte. 2017. '"And Those Who Live, How Shall I Tell their Fame?" Historical Pageants, Collective Remembrance and the First World War, 1919–1939', *Historical Research* 90: 636–61.

Boyle, Danny. 2013 (2nd ed.); 2010 (1st ed.). *Creating Wonder, in Conversation with Amy Raphael*. London: Faber & Faber.

Calder, Angus. 1969. *The People's War: Britain 1939–1945*. London: Random House.

de Groot, Jerome. 2008. *Consuming History: Historians and Heritage in Contemporary Popular Culture*. Abingdon and New York: Routledge.

Freeman, Mark. 2013. '"Splendid Display; Pompous Spectacle": Historical Pageants in Twentieth-Century Britain', *Social History* 38: 423–55.

Glassberg, David. 1990. *American Historical Pageantry: The Uses of Tradition in the Early Twentieth Century*. Chapel Hill, NC: University of North Carolina Press.

Grimley, Matthew. 2004. *Citizenship, Community and the Church of England: Liberal Anglican Theories of the State between the Wars*. Oxford: Oxford University Press.
Hewison, Robert. 1987. *The Heritage Industry: Britain in a Climate of Decline*. London: Methuen.
Jellicoe, Ann. 1987. *Community Plays: How to Put Them On*. London: Methuen.
Jones, Ben and Searle, Rebecca. 2013. 'Humphrey Jennings, the Left and the Experience of Modernity in Mid-Twentieth-Century Britain', *History Workshop Journal* 75: 190–212.
Kershaw, Baz. 1992. *The Politics of Performance: Radical Theatre as Cultural Intervention*. London: Routledge.
Kershaw, Baz. 2007. *Theatre Ecology: Environments and Performance Events*. Cambridge: Cambridge University Press.
Lowenthal, David. 1998 (2nd ed.); 1968 (1st ed.). *The Heritage Crusade and the Spoils of History*. Cambridge: Cambridge University Press.
McCalman, Iain. 2010. 'Loutherbourg's Simulations: Reenactment and Realism in Late-Georgian Britain', in *Historical Reenactment: From Realism to the Affective Turn*, edited by Iain McCalman and Paul A. Pickering. Basingstoke: Palgrave Macmillan, 200–17.
McCulloch, Gary and Woodin, Tom. 2010. 'Towards a Social History of Learners and Learning', *Oxford Review of Education* 36: 133–40.
Meacham, Standish. 1987. *Toynbee Hall and Social Reform 1880–1914: The Search for Community*. New Haven, CT: Yale University Press.
Readman, Paul. 2005. 'The Place of the Past in English Culture *c.*1890–1914', *Past and Present* 186: 147–99.
Robinson, Emily. 2017. *The Language of Progressive Politics in Modern Britain*. London: Palgrave Macmillan.
Ryan, Deborah Sugg. 1999. 'Staging the Imperial City: The Pageant of London, 1911', in *Imperial Cities: Landscape, Display and Identity*, edited by Felix Driver and David Gilbert. Manchester: Manchester University Press, 117–35.
Samuel, Raphael. 1996. *Theatres of Memory: Past and Present in Contemporary Culture*. London: Verso.
Samuel, Raphael. 1998. *Island Stories: Unravelling Britain, Theatres of Memory, Volume II*. London: Verso, 1998.
Smith, Anthony D. 1988 (2nd ed.); 1986 (1st ed.). *The Ethnic Origins of Nations*. Oxford: Blackwell.
Smith, Joseph. 2017. 'Discursive Dancing: Traditionalism and Social Realism in the 2013 English History Curriculum Wars', *British Journal of Educational Studies* 65: 307–29.
Trimm, Ryan S. 2012. 'Taking you Back: Region, Industry and Technologies of Living History at Beamish', *European Journal of Cultural Studies* 15: 528–46.
Wallis, Mick. 1996. 'The Popular Front Pageant: Its Emergence and Decline', *New Theatre Quarterly* 11: 17–32.
Watson, Janet. 2014. 'Total War and Total Anniversary: The Material Culture of Second World War Commemoration in Britain', in *British Cultural Memory and the Second World War*, edited by Lucy Noakes and Juliette Pattinson. London: Bloomsbury Academic, 175–94.
Yoshino, Ayako. 2011. *Pageant Fever: Local History and Consumerism in Edwardian England*. Tokyo: Waseda University Press.

13

Afterword

Angela Bartie, Linda Fleming, Mark Freeman, Alexander Hutton and Paul Readman

As the last chapter has shown, historical pageants have not completely died out: although Kynren has some features that differentiate it from the twentieth-century pageant tradition, it has still more in common with that tradition. Moreover, as noted briefly in the introduction to this volume, historical pageantry continues to rear its head elsewhere. A notable example is to be found in the small town of Axbridge in Somerset, where pageants were staged in 1967, in 1970 and decennially ever since: at the time of writing, the next is due in August 2021 (postponed by a year due to the coronavirus outbreak). The organisers are expecting a cast of more than 400, with over 100 volunteers in supporting roles:[1] this may be small by the standards of many twentieth-century pageants but is impressive given that the population of Axbridge stands at little over 2,000. It is also remarkable that participation in the Axbridge pageant has grown since the 1960s: the cast in 1967 numbered only 175.[2] Performed in the town square (Fig.13.1), the pageant features 12 historical episodes, ranging from the Roman conquest (inspired by the discovery of Romano-British remains in the town) through to the twentieth century; these include scenes depicting a skirmish between Saxons and Danes, the granting of the Elizabethan charter to Axbridge in 1599, an eighteenth-century fair and the coming of the railway to the town.[3] As the organisers claim, the pageant 'is now an institution and has become part of the history of Axbridge itself'.[4]

The success of the Axbridge pageant is unusual; it is an exception to the decline of historical pageantry as a popular vehicle of engagement with the past in the second half of the twentieth century. Pageants flourished in the early 1950s, but the post-war revival of pageant fever abated thereafter, with the 1960s seeing a particularly steep decline. There were

Figure 13.1 A scene from the Axbridge pageant, 2010. Photograph by Chris Loughlin; used with permission.

many reasons for this – some obvious, others perhaps less so. There is no doubt that the appeal of competing forms of entertainment had an important effect. The chief technological enablers of what Raymond Williams called 'mobile privatisation'[5] – the car and the television – had a profound impact on the ways in which individuals and households spent their leisure time and, more specifically, on the ways in which they 'consumed' the past. Historical content was carried, through documentary and drama, onto the small screen; and cars enabled whole families to travel to visit stately homes, castles, museums and other heritage attractions. The revival of the 'country house' was a key aspect of this, both for visitors and television viewers: as Raphael Samuel pointed out in 1995, 'the country house was able to rise, phoenix-like, from the ashes to impose itself as the very quintessence of Englishness … and to provide the leading idiom both for TV costume drama, and for the public museum's "living history" displays'.[6] In these contexts, it became increasingly difficult to enlist participants and audiences in the service of historical pageantry.

This is not to say that the decline of pageants was 'inevitable'. There was, after all, a continuance of the tradition – not least in Arbroath, as chapter 10 in this book has demonstrated, but also in some English towns, with Axbridge providing one such example. But there were others too. In England a key carrier of the tradition was David Clarke (1931–2014). He performed in the Pageant of Farnham Castle in 1950 and was production designer under pageant-master Christopher Ede at Guildford in 1957, before going on to produce pageants in various Surrey locations and in other parts of the country, most notably Carlisle in 1977.[7] Clarke continued to put on historical pageants in the 1980s and 1990s. Many of his later pageants testified to the emphasis on the role of 'ordinary people' in history that featured so prominently in much post-war pageantry (see chapter 9). His last major production was at Cranford in 2000, when there was a modest revival of pageantry to coincide with the Millennium celebrations.[8] Yet by this time even the indefatigable Clarke was somewhat pessimistic about the prospects of his favourite theatrical form, writing that pageantry was now 'a dying art, as the number of pageants dwindle year by year in our towns and villages, the victim of changing lifestyles'.[9]

Changing civic culture also affected the viability of historical pageants. Many of the pageants of the early 1950s can be seen as protests against the etiolation of the power and prestige of local government institutions and the networks on which they relied – and which they in turn sustained. The apparent weakening of local civic identities, especially in small towns, during the period of urban and suburban expansion after the Second World War had a considerable impact. On the one hand, it inspired many individuals and groups to want to stage a pageant; on the other, it made doing so more difficult, especially in the small towns that had been the bulwarks of historical pageantry since the Edwardian period.[10] In St Albans in 1953, for example, pageant-master Cyril Swinson declared that 'it is all to the good to stimulate pride in the city just now, when it is in danger of becoming just a dormitory, or a large disorganized mass'.[11]

Many urban communities, particularly in the southeast of England, were experiencing rapid population change. Jon Lawrence has recently described this phenomenon as 'internal population movements on a scale not seen since the early years of industrialization'.[12] It seems certain that these and other demographic changes – not least in relation to ethnicity – had an effect on inherited understandings of local historical identities, making the long continuities increasingly emphasised in post-war pageant narratives seem less appropriate as means of celebrating community concrescence.[13] Lawrence has observed that the pressures on people to conform to prescribed customs, traditions and standards lessened, both in the family and in wider society, during the post-war period – but that this did not lead to the 'death' of community, rather to changes in how it was lived and understood.[14]

Taken alongside the challenges to traditional historical narratives that arose as 'history from below' took off in the 1950s and 1960s, and opened the doors to feminist and post-colonialist histories in ensuing decades, this flux and rapid change had a major impact on the pageant movement. Specifically, it made it much harder to present a linear version of the past, as so many of the earlier historical pageants had done, that resonated with (and reflected enough of) the community to make for a successful performance. More fragmented and diverse identities – perhaps encouraged further by mobile privatisation – made it harder to imagine and effect the extensive cross-community participation in a common effort that had been a key element of the pageant movement, as least as it was envisaged by pioneers such as Louis Napoleon Parker.[15] It was often less difficult to recruit participants in small towns and villages – places with active churches, schools and volunteer communities – but harder to imagine successfully staging a pageant on the scale of those early twentieth-century spectacles with their hundreds, often thousands, of performers supported by armies of volunteers. The 'People's Pageant' staged in Carlisle in 1977 stands out not only because of its size and its mobilisation of sponsorship and volunteer labour, but also because of its overall success at a time when pageants had largely disappeared from the cultural mainstream. Held to mark Queen Elizabeth II's Silver Jubilee year, this pageant followed two earlier ones in Carlisle, in 1928 and 1951, both of which had been successful and which were a continuing source of pride for many in the city.[16] Oral history interviews with performers and others involved in staging these pageants offer striking insights into the power of dramatic performance in bolstering community pride and bringing to life popular understandings of local history. However, they also point to a variety of reasons for the decline of historical pageants. One interviewee, who had performed in the 1977 pageant as a child, commented that even if a pageant were to be staged where he now lives, he would not get involved. Asked why, he replied:

> We're now in a different world, it was, it was of its time really. It's quite interesting really how … things change like that. And I'm community minded and all that sort of stuff really, but the thought of doing that, I wouldn't do it now.[17]

Other interviewees pointed to the difficulties that would be encountered in raising funds to stage such a large performance, how hard it would be for people to commit the time and energy needed when they had such busy working and social lives, and the risk assessments and applications that would be needed to meet health and safety requirements. As the stage manager for the 1977 Carlisle pageant noted, 'it would just be overwhelmed by bureaucracy [now], whereas [in the past] people just got on with it'.[18]

Gender is another key aspect of the changing circumstances in which pageantry struggled to maintain a presence in post-war British historical culture. From the outset, pageants had reflected and sustained traditional gendered divisions of labour, with – most obviously – women tending to take responsibility for costumes, usually under the overall direction of a male pageant-master. Some significant female pageant-masters did emerge over time (the best known was Gwen Lally, who produced the Birmingham pageant of 1938 and several others), but most pageants retained a clearly gendered organisational hierarchy into the post-war years. For example, at Warwick in 1953 there were 12 named officers of the pageant including the pageant-master (Anthony Parker, grandson of Louis Napoleon Parker); of these all were men except for the 'Mistress of the Robes' and the 'Mistress of the Ballet'. Some women were responsible for the direction of particular episodes, but the 'finance and general purposes committee' included three women out of a total membership of 23, and the 'publicity and printing committee' one out of 11; as for the 'works committee', this comprised 16 men and no women.[19] By contrast, women were at work in large numbers making or altering the costumes: at Warwick there may not have been enough of them, as a substantial sum was spent on costume hire.

The reliance on armies of unpaid women to make costumes (and sometimes props) made the business of putting on a pageant increasingly difficult, as larger numbers of married and unmarried women entered and remained in paid employment outside the home in the post-war period.[20] Further problems were caused by reliance on female participation in other ways too, not least as performers. Across the twentieth century some pageants reported difficulties in recruiting enough men to play key parts, and it was not uncommon for women to dominate the crowd scenes.[21]

* * *

One topic that may deserve more emphasis than this book has given it is the use of historical pageantry as a means of publicity, especially considering the efforts made by many towns to raise their profile nationally and to promote place-based tourism. Chapter 7 makes evident the important role that pageants could play in interwar civic 'boosterism', and it is clear that some urban authorities in the 1950s were keen to use pageants to stimulate investment in their communities.[22] Ayako Yoshino argues that Edwardian pageants were at the forefront of the development of tourism in many of the towns in which they were staged,[23] and other research seems to confirm this: Mark Freeman has shown elsewhere, for example, how the St Albans pageant of 1907 was connected to emergent attempts to promote the city as a tourist destination.[24] To this end, many and various techniques were employed, ranging from the use of boldly modernist imagery in advertising to the arrangement of special excursion trains and the use of associated events to coincide with pageants. The latter included concerts, dances, firework displays, fêtes, hog-roasts and, in the case of some of the larger pageants in the north of England and in Scotland, industrial exhibitions and 'civic weeks'.[25] Moreover, pageants – as chapter 11 in this volume demonstrates – spawned an unusually diverse range of souvenirs and commemorative material culture including programmes, postcards, decorative china and cutlery, commemorative medals and even – in the case of the Carlisle pageant of 1951 – biscuit tins.[26] Many cities and towns enlisted the support of local media and business interests, and invested thousands – even tens of thousands – of pounds in their pageants, these funds being drawn either from wealthy guarantors or local ratepayers. As a result, historical pageants were at the very centre – or, perhaps more accurately, the cutting edge – of twentieth-century efforts to marketise heritage for popular consumption.

Again, it is worth considering the contemporary example of Axbridge. This pageant began in 1967 as a small, free event at which a collection was taken for local hospitals; in 2010 it was funded by the Big Lottery Fund, Bristol Water and other commercial and community organisations, and cost a total of almost £50,000 to stage. Tickets were priced at £15 for adults and £8 for children.[27] All this is very modest in scale compared with the heady ambitions of Jonathan Ruffer for Kynren and Bishop Auckland (see chapter 12), but it nevertheless illustrates the importance of the commercial dimensions of pageantry – which, it should be remembered, were there right from the start.

Pageants were almost always one-off events for the communities that staged them, the frequency of those in Arbroath and the regularity of those in Axbridge being unusual. In this sense pageants differ from the events and rituals that are held up as integral examples of the 'invention of tradition' paradigm.[28] They were never ongoing activities or annual events (Kynren provides a very different model in this respect), and their disappearance and partial replacement by other kinds of historical performance must be seen in this context. Pageants did not support a regular pattern of heritage tourism, nor were they likely to satisfy the demands of those who wanted an ongoing engagement with amateur dramatics; they often (and increasingly) lacked the carefulness and 'authenticity' that has come to be associated with historical performance through re-enactment.[29] Samuel, looking back on the 1960s and early 1970s from the perspective of 1995, identified pageants as one aspect of a revival of 'the taste for historical re-enactment', bracketing them with railway preservation societies, the Sealed Knot, the Ermine Street Guard and the Levellers Day pilgrimage as exemplars of this development.[30] There are, of course, some similarities – much of this heritage activity is costume drama, after all – but pageants did not create an identifiable community of performers, as has been the case with historical re-enactment and other manifestations of performative historical culture.

There is a growing literature on the experience of re-enactment and the meanings associated with it, particularly for those who are actually doing the performing.[31] Performed medievalism includes not only competitive jousting hosted in historical locations – a staple of the events programme of English Heritage, for example[32] – but also medieval fairs with dramatic elements incorporated into them. Like pageants, performed medievalism has an international dimension: the medieval fair at Norman, Oklahoma, for example, has been staged annually since 1977, and now has a large cast of actors playing designated roles including well-known figures from medieval European royal courts.[33] Accessible gatherings such as this allow spectators to mingle with re-enactors in various ways, and in some cases to spend money on 'authentic' food, drink and souvenirs. This kind of activity can also be seen in the heritage sector, where the growth of 'living history' has been a key development in recent years.[34] There is little recognition of the pageant tradition in the academic literature on re-enactment and 'living history', but at some level both meet the same demand for historical engagement through performance.

The contemporary enthusiasm for outdoor theatre and site-specific performance is also animated by many of the same drivers that sustained historical pageantry for such a long period. Outdoor theatre is a feature of the events programme of English Heritage, with various performances having taken place in 2019: two examples were *A Midsummer Night's Dream*, performed by the Lord Chamberlain's Men ('an open air theatre company built on the same principles that William Shakespeare himself followed')[35] at Kenwood House in London, and *Pride and Prejudice*, played by Chapterhouse Theatre, a specialist outdoor company, at Framlingham Castle in Suffolk.[36] These developments have built on the success of the Globe Theatre, a reconstructed Elizabethan playhouse on the South Bank of the Thames in London, which Samuel has contrasted sharply with the modernism of the National Theatre and other post-war developments: 'there were no "historic" performance venues in the 1960s'.[37] The Globe itself has taken Shakespeare's plays around the country for site-specific performances: in 2013, for example, the company performed the series of *Henry VI* plays in locations associated with the Wars of the Roses. Although these are slick professional productions, in contrast to the amateur ethos of historical pageantry, the importance of place in creating a sense of 'authenticity' remains an important feature of these and other site-specific performances.[38]

The same may be said for the community play, another outgrowth of the enthusiasm for history and 'heritage' in the 1960s. Again its proponents and students largely fail to acknowledge the similarities between their activities and the historical pageant.[39] On examination, this oversight is understandable. Most community play pioneers did not consider themselves to be either inheritors or subverters of the Parker pageant tradition. Rather than focusing on the elite-centred history that dominated many earlier pageants, community plays often drew inspiration from the history of popular protest or discontent. One relatively early example was Ann Jellicoe's *The Reckoning* (1978), set and performed in Lyme Regis and depicting the Monmouth Rebellion. Peter Terson's *Under the Fish and Over the Water* (1990) was based on the Bradford on Avon riot of 1791, with members of the local community being involved in historical research to support the production.[40] Community plays have sometimes been criticised for helping to maintain local social inequalities through their organisation – a theme echoed in some of the historiography of pageants – but Jellicoe and others firmly argued the contrary.[41] Whatever the differences and similarities between the two forms may have been, both certainly gave scope for popular participation and were significant vectors of historical engagement through performance.

* * *

Historical pageantry, then, has been largely displaced by other forms of popular engagement with the past, although the process by which this has happened still requires further research. Some pageants staged in the 1960s indicate the ways in which the format was being superseded. In 1966 a one-off 'Grand 1066 Pageant to Commemorate the 900th Anniversary of the Battle of Hastings' was staged at Battle in East Sussex, watched by some 24,000 people. Although styled a 'pageant', it was essentially a re-enactment of the battle, with somewhere between 400 and 500 performers and live commentary by the show-jumping commentator Raymond Brooks-Ward. With various associated heritage performances during the day – including an archery tournament and a jousting display – the 'pageant' was an early example of a medieval fair.[42] The Battle of Hastings has been re-enacted (with a few gaps) every year since this nonacentennial event, thus becoming an important part of the East Sussex events calendar. A large re-enactment was held in October 2016 to commemorate the 950th anniversary.[43] In 1967, the year after the 900th anniversary Battle celebrations, a very different kind of historical pageant was held in Craigmillar, a housing estate on the outskirts of Edinburgh. Anticipating the community play movement in its subject matter, the pageant formed part of the Craigmillar Festival of Drama and Music.[44] It was also, as Lucy Brown notes,

> a knowing inversion of a pageant staged at the same spot in the presence of George V in 1927. Whereas the 1927 pageant had celebrated the Scottish nobility and its ancestral contribution to Scottish history, the 1967 pageant celebrated local miners, suffragettes and trade unionists, played by a cast of over 400 Craigmillar residents.[45]

At both Battle and Craigmillar, the cast was much smaller than for many earlier pageants, the subject matter and style of production was rather different and the number of performances was fewer (two at Craigmillar, just one at Battle). In their different ways these examples show how, to a large extent, historical pageantry was overtaken by other means of re-enacting the past for popular audiences.

This process of eclipse has continued, albeit with the exceptions identified in this afterword. Samuel identified some continuities between the era of pageants and the new waves of popular interest in history that arose in the 1960s,[46] but there has clearly been a shift in the ways in which modern society chooses to celebrate and re-perform its past. This has been accelerated by developments in the broadcast media and, above all, the rise of the internet. Yet it is significant that many aspects of older traditions – notably manifested in 'living history' – retain their purchase in the contemporary heritage 'industry'.[47] Indeed in recent years the appeal of re-enactment and other forms of participatory dramatic representation of the past seems to have increased. In their different ways, the Axbridge pageant and Kynren provide further evidence of the ongoing potential of dramatic engagement with the past.

As chapter 12 has explained, Kynren shows that large numbers of people are willing to spend significant amounts of money, in some cases to travel large distances, and to sit in an uncovered grandstand until late on a weekend evening to watch this kind of entertainment. Axbridge demonstrates the possibilities of mobilising a community – albeit a small one – behind a traditional form of historical pageant. Thus in the southwest and northeast of England at least, historical pageantry can still draw performers and audiences, well over a century after Parker's first production at Sherborne in 1905. The British people may have been mostly cured of pageant fever, but some traces of it remain in their system.

Notes

1. See http://axbridgepageant.com/ (accessed 1 July 2019).
2. Angela Bartie, Linda Fleming, Mark Freeman, Tom Hulme, Alex Hutton, Paul Readman, 'The Axbridge Pageant', *The Redress of the Past*, http://www.historicalpageants.ac.uk/pag eants/973/ (accessed 1 July 2019).
3. Angela Bartie, Linda Fleming, Mark Freeman, Tom Hulme, Alex Hutton, Paul Readman, 'Axbridge Pageant 2010', *The Redress of the Past*, http://www.historicalpageants.ac.uk/pag eants/978/ (accessed 1 July 2019). This pageant expanded on the 11 scenes from 2000, while the original Axbridge pageant had 10. The railway reached Axbridge in 1869 and its station closed in 1963: the A371 bypass, the opening of which the first Axbridge pageant marked, follows the line of the railway.
4. 'Axbridge Tapestry', http://axbridgepageant.com/tapgallery.html (accessed 1 July 2019). For more on the Axbridge pageant and its local community significance, see John Bailey and Harry Mottram, 'Why the Axbridge Pageant Bonds the Whole Community', in *Historical Pageants: Local History Study Guide*, ed. Angela Bartie, Linda Fleming, Mark Freeman, Tom Hulme, Alexander Hutton and Paul Readman (St Albans: Regents Court Press, 2020), 17–20.
5. Raymond Williams, *Television: Technology and Cultural Form* (London: Fontana, 1974).
6. Raphael Samuel, *Theatres of Memory: Past and Present in Contemporary Culture* (London: Verso, 1996), 233. See also Peter Mandler, *The Fall and Rise of the Stately Home* (New Haven, CT: Yale University Press, 1997).
7. Information on these pageants can be found in Angela Bartie, Paul Caton, Linda Fleming, Mark Freeman, Tom Hulme, Alex Hutton, Paul Readman, *The Redress of the Past*, http://www.historicalpageants.ac.uk/pageants/ (accessed 2 July 2019). A film of the 1950 Farnham pageant has recently been made available on the Screen Archive South East website: http://screenarchive.brighton.ac.uk/detail/1639/ (accessed 9 December 2019). For Clarke's career as pageant-master, see the typescripts of his semi-autobiographical histories of the pageant movement, preserved in the David Clarke Collection at King's College London: King's College London Archives, K/PP251/6. Further information on Clarke and his career can also be found elsewhere in the David Clarke Collection and in the Surrey History Centre (SHC Ref. 8147: David Clarke (1931–2014) of Chilworth, theatrical designer, director, film maker and pageant master: records of Surrey productions, 1956–2000).
8. Angela Bartie, Linda Fleming, Mark Freeman, Tom Hulme, Alex Hutton, Paul Readman, 'Cranford Pageant', *The Redress of the Past*, http://www.historicalpageants.ac.uk/pageants/1045/ (accessed 1 July 2019).
9. *Cranford Pageant 2000* (souvenir programme, n.p., n.d. [2000]), unpaginated.
10. See Angela Bartie, Linda Fleming, Mark Freeman, Tom Hulme and Paul Readman, 'Performing the Past: Identity, Civic Culture and Historical Pageants in Twentieth-Century Small Towns', in *Small Towns in Europe in the 20th and 21st Centuries: Heritage and Development Strategies*, ed. Luda Klusakova (Prague: Karolinum Press, Charles University, 2017), 24–51.
11. Quoted in Mark Freeman, '"Splendid Display; Pompous Spectacle": Historical Pageants in Twentieth-Century Britain', *Social History* 38 (2013): 443.
12. Jon Lawrence, *Me, Me, Me? The Search for Community in Post-war England* (Oxford: Oxford University Press, 2019), 71.
13. We borrow the idea of 'concrescent community' from the work of David Monger on patriotism and local/national identities. See David Monger, *Patriotism and Propaganda in First World War Britain: The National War Aims Committee and Civilian Morale* (Liverpool: Liverpool University Press, 2012), 86, 169ff; David Monger, 'Soldiers, Propaganda and Ideas of Home and Community in First World War Britain', *Cultural and Social History* 8 (2011): 331–54.
14. Lawrence, *Me, Me, Me?*, esp. 1, 66.
15. See Louis N. Parker, *Several of My Lives* (London: Chapman & Hall, 1928), 279, 283–4 and the introduction to this volume. It should, however, be pointed out that the example of the 1977 Leicester pageant, which featured an episode depicting the celebration of Diwali by members of the city's immigrant community, does at least suggest that the pageant form itself has the potential to serve the purposes of a multicultural communitarianism; that it has not generally done so in practice is another matter. For this pageant, see Angela Bartie, Linda Fleming, Mark Freeman, Tom Hulme, Alex Hutton, Paul Readman, 'Leicestershire Pageant', *The Redress of the Past*, http://www.historicalpageants.ac.uk/pageants/1120/ (accessed 2 July 2019).

16. See Angela Bartie, Linda Fleming, Mark Freeman, Tom Hulme, Alex Hutton, Paul Readman, 'Carlisle Historical Pageant', *The Redress of the Past*, http://www.historicalpageants.ac.uk/pageants/1025/ (accessed 20 November 2019).
17. Interview with A. Ledger by A. Bartie for *The Redress of the Past*, 17 July 2015.
18. Interview with P. McIntyre by A. Bartie for *The Redress of the Past*, 16 June 2015.
19. Angela Bartie, Linda Fleming, Mark Freeman, Tom Hulme, Alex Hutton, Paul Readman, 'Warwickshire Coronation Pageant', *The Redress of the Past*, http://www.historicalpageants.ac.uk/pageants/1235/ (accessed 1 July 2019).
20. Pat Thane, 'Women since 1945', in *Twentieth-Century Britain: Economic, Social and Cultural Change*, ed. Paul Johnson (London: Longman, 1994), 392–410, esp. 393–5.
21. See, for example, Angela Bartie, Linda Fleming, Mark Freeman, Tom Hulme, Alex Hutton, Paul Readman, 'The St Albans Pageant', *The Redress of the Past*, http://www.historicalpageants.ac.uk/pageants/1207/ (accessed 1 July 2019); Angela Bartie, Linda Fleming, Mark Freeman, Tom Hulme, Alex Hutton, Paul Readman, 'Stoke-on-Trent Historical Pageant', *The Redress of the Past*, http://www.historicalpageants.ac.uk/pageants/1214/ (accessed 1 July 2019).
22. See chapter 7 in this volume, and also Tom Hulme, '"A Nation of Town Criers": Civic Publicity and Historical Pageantry in Inter-War Britain', *Urban History* 44 (2017): 270–92; Freeman, '"Splendid Display"': 443–4.
23. Ayako Yoshino, *Pageant Fever: Local History and Consumerism in Edwardian England* (Tokyo: Waseda University Press, 2011), esp. 57–98.
24. Freeman, '"Splendid Display"': 437. On the St Albans pageants, see also Mark Freeman, *The Pageants of St Albans: An Illustrated History* (St Albans: Regents Court Press, 2020).
25. See Hulme, '"Nation of Town Criers"'; Tom Hulme, *After the Shock City: Urban Culture and the Making of Modern Citizenship* (Woodbridge: Boydell Press, 2019), 77–84, 89–92.
26. There is a Carlisle pageant biscuit tin in the possession of a member of the *Redress of the Past* project team.
27. Bartie et al., 'Axbridge Pageant 2010'.
28. The seminal text is, of course, *The Invention of Tradition*, ed. Eric Hobsbawm and Terence Ranger (Cambridge: Cambridge University Press, 1982).
29. Many early pageant-masters emphasised 'authenticity' in costume, props and staging, but this emphasis was reduced by the 1940s and 1950s: see Bartie et al., '"History Taught in the Pageant Way"'. On authenticity in re-enactment, see Rebecca Schneider, *Performing Remains: Art and War in Times of Theatrical Reenactment* (London: Routledge, 2011).
30. Samuel, *Theatres of Memory*, 191–2.
31. See *Historical Reenactment: From Realism to the Affective Turn*, ed. Ian McCalman and Paul A. Pickering (Basingstoke: Palgrave Macmillan, 2010); Jerome de Groot, *Consuming History: Historians and Heritage in Contemporary Popular Culture* (Abingdon and New York: Routledge, 2008), esp. 105–23.
32. English Heritage, *What's On, July–October 2019* (n.p.: English Heritage, [2019]), e.g. 10, 18: copy in the authors' possession.
33. Medieval Fair of Norman, https://medievalfair.org/ (accessed 1 July 2019).
34. See, for example, *Performing Heritage: Research, Practice and Innovation in Museum Theatre and Live Interpretation*, ed. Anthony Jackson and Jenny Kidd (Manchester: Manchester University Press, 2011).
35. 'About the Lord Chamberlain's Men', http://www.tlcm.co.uk/about/ (accessed 1 July 2019).
36. English Heritage, *What's On, July–October 2019*, 11, 31.
37. Samuel, *Theatres of Memory*, 214.
38. See Bartie et al., '"History Taught in the Pageant Way"': 170; Laurajane Smith, 'The "Doing" of Heritage: Heritage as Performance', in *Performing Heritage*, ed. Jackson and Kidd, 69–81; Mike Pearson, *Site-Specific Performance* (Basingstoke: Palgrave Macmillan, 2010).
39. But see Neil Beddow, *Turning Points: The Impact of Participation in Community Theatre*, ed. Mary Schwartz (Bristol: South West Arts, [2001]).
40. Ann Jellicoe, *Community Plays: How to Put Them On* (London: Methuen, 1987), 3–10; Peter Terson, *Under the Fish and Over the Water: A Community Play for Bradford on Avon* (Bradford on Avon: Ex Libris Press, 1990).
41. See Baz Kershaw, *The Politics of Performance: Radical Theatre as Cultural Intervention* (London: Routledge, 1992), 190–5; Michael Woods, 'Performing Power: Local Politics and the Taunton Pageant of 1928', *Journal of Historical Geography* 25 (1999): 57–74.

42. Angela Bartie, Linda Fleming, Mark Freeman, Tom Hulme, Alex Hutton, Paul Readman, 'Grand 1066 Pageant to Commemorate the 900th Anniversary of the Battle of Hastings', *The Redress of the Past*, http://historicalpageants.ac.uk/pageants/987/ (accessed 8 December 2019).
43. 'Battle of Hastings Re-enactment to be Staged after Absence', *BBC News*, 1 October 2014, https://www.bbc.co.uk/news/uk-england-sussex-29442839 (accessed 8 December 2019).
44. Angela Bartie, Linda Fleming, Mark Freeman, Tom Hulme, Alex Hutton, Paul Readman, 'A Historical Pageant', *The Redress of the Past*, http://www.historicalpageants.ac.uk/pageants/1593/ (accessed 8 December 2019).
45. Lucy Brown, 'The Community Arts Movement in Scotland 1962–1990' (unpublished PhD diss., University of Strathclyde, 2018), 120. For details of the 1927 Scottish Historical Pageant, see Angela Bartie, Linda Fleming, Mark Freeman, Tom Hulme, Alex Hutton, Paul Readman, 'Scottish Historical Pageant', *The Redress of the Past*, http://www.historicalpageants.ac.uk/pageants/1183/ (accessed 20 November 2019).
46. Samuel, *Theatres of Memory*, 169–202.
47. See Robert Hewison, *The Heritage Industry: Britain in a Climate of Decline* (London: Methuen, 1987).

Bibliography

Bailey, John and Mottram, Harry. 2020. 'Why the Axbridge Pageant Bonds the Whole Community', in *Historical Pageants: Local History Study Guide*, edited by Angela Bartie, Linda Fleming, Mark Freeman, Tom Hulme, Alexander Hutton and Paul Readman. St Albans: Regents Court Press, 17–20.

Bartie, Angela, Fleming, Linda, Freeman, Mark, Hulme, Tom, Hutton, Alexander and Readman, Paul. 2019. '"History Taught in the Pageant Way": Education and Historical Performance in Twentieth-Century Britain', *History of Education* 48: 156–79.

Bartie, Angela, Fleming, Linda, Freeman, Mark, Hulme, Tom and Readman, Paul. 2017. 'Performing the Past: Identity, Civic Culture and Historical Pageants in Twentieth-Century Small Towns', in *Small Towns in Europe in the 20th and 21st Centuries: Heritage and Development Strategies*, edited by Luda Klusakova. Prague: Karolinum Press, Charles University, 24–51.

Beddow, Neil. 2001. *Turning Points: The Impact of Participation in Community Theatre*, edited by Mary Schwartz. Bristol: South West Arts.

Brown, Lucy. 2018. 'The Community Arts Movement in Scotland 1962–1990.' Unpublished PhD diss., University of Strathclyde.

de Groot, Jerome. 2008. *Consuming History: Historians and Heritage in Contemporary Popular Culture*. Abingdon and New York: Routledge.

Freeman, Mark. 2013. '"Splendid Display; Pompous Spectacle": Historical Pageants in Twentieth-Century Britain', *Social History* 38: 423–55.

Freeman, Mark. 2020. *The Pageants of St Albans: An Illustrated History*. St Albans: Regents Court Press.

Hewison, Robert. 1987. *The Heritage Industry: Britain in a Climate of Decline*. London: Methuen.

Hobsbawm, Eric and Ranger, Terence, eds. 1983. *The Invention of Tradition*. Cambridge: Cambridge University Press.

Hulme, Tom. 2017. '"A Nation of Town Criers": Civic Publicity and Historical Pageantry in Inter-War Britain', *Urban History* 44: 270–92.

Hulme, Tom. 2019. *After the Shock City: Urban Culture and the Making of Modern Citizenship*. Woodbridge: Royal Historical Society/Boydell & Brewer.

Jackson, Anthony and Kidd, Jenny, eds. 2011. *Performing Heritage: Research, Practice and Innovation in Museum Theatre and Live Interpretation*. Manchester: Manchester University Press.

Jellicoe, Ann. 1987. *Community Plays: How to Put Them On*. London: Methuen.

Kershaw, Baz. 1992. *The Politics of Performance: Radical Theatre as Cultural Intervention*. London: Routledge.

Lawrence, Jon. 2019. *Me, Me, Me? The Search for Community in Post-war England*. Oxford: Oxford University Press.

McCalman, Ian and Pickering, Paul A., eds. 2010. *Historical Reenactment: From Realism to the Affective Turn*. Basingstoke: Palgrave Macmillan.

Mandler, Peter. 1997. *The Fall and Rise of the Stately Home*. New Haven, CT: Yale University Press.

Monger, David. 2011. 'Soldiers, Propaganda and Ideas of Home and Community in First World War Britain', *Cultural and Social History* 8: 331–54.
Monger, David. 2012. *Patriotism and Propaganda in First World War Britain: The National War Aims Committee and Civilian Morale*. Liverpool: Liverpool University Press.
Pearson, Mike. 2010. *Site-Specific Performance*. Basingstoke: Palgrave Macmillan.
Samuel, Raphael. 1996. *Theatres of Memory: Past and Present in Contemporary Culture*. London: Verso.
Schneider, Rebecca. 2011. *Performing Remains: Art and War in Times of Theatrical Reenactment*. London: Routledge.
Smith, Laurajane. 2011. 'The "Doing" of Heritage: Heritage as Performance', in *Performing Heritage: Research, Practice and Innovation in Museum Theatre and Live Interpretation*, edited by Anthony Jackson and Jenny Kidd. Manchester: Manchester University Press, 69–81.
Thane, Pat. 1994. 'Women since 1945', in *Twentieth-Century Britain: Economic, Social and Cultural Change*, edited by Paul Johnson. London: Longman, 392–410.
Williams, Raymond. 1974. *Television: Technology and Cultural Form*. London: Fontana.
Woods, Michael. 1999. 'Performing Power: Local Politics and the Taunton Pageant of 1928', *Journal of Historical Geography* 25: 57–74.
Yoshino, Ayako. 2011. *Pageant Fever: Local History and Consumerism in Edwardian England*. Tokyo: Waseda University Press.

Index

Page numbers in italics refer to illustrations

CPSIA information can be obtained
at www.ICGtesting.com
Printed in the USA
JSHW040021160321
12547JS00001B/1

9 781787 354067